THE LAST CHANCE

The Last Chance

*Nuclear Proliferation
and Arms Control*

William Epstein

THE FREE PRESS
A Division of Macmillan Publishing Co., Inc.
NEW YORK

Collier Macmillan Publishers
LONDON

The Free Press
A Division of Macmillan Publishing Co., Inc.
866 Third Avenue, New York, N.Y.   10022

Collier Macmillan Canada, Ltd.

Library of Congress Catalog Card Number: 75–22765

Printed in the United States of America

printing number

1 2 3 4 5 6 7 8 9 10

Library of Congress Cataloging in Publication Data

Epstein, William
    The last chance.

    Includes index.
    1. Atomic weapons and disarmament. I. Title.
JX1974.7.E55   327'.174   75–22765
ISBN 0-02-909661-8

Text from William Epstein's articles "The Proliferation of Nuclear Weapons" (April) and "Nuclear Free Zones" (November) reprinted with permission. Copyright © 1975 by Scientific American, Inc. All rights reserved.

Text from William Epstein's *Occasional Paper 9*, "Retrospective on the NPT Review Conference: Proposals for the Future" reprinted with permission. Copyright © 1975 by The Stanley Foundation, publishers of the Occasional Paper series.

To Mark and his generation

Contents

Preface

For the first time in a quarter of a century of working with the problems of the arms race and arms control, I am beginning to get scared.

Ever since the invention and use of the atomic bomb in 1945, I have regarded the problem of controlling the nuclear arms race as the most important problem facing the world. True, the problem has been enormously difficult of solution. But ever since the end of World War II, governments, scientists, and thinkers had been grappling with the problem, and slowly, agonizingly slowly, they seemed after all to have found the right road. After eighteen years of deadlock and frustration, the major nuclear powers eventually succeeded in 1963 in agreeing on the Treaty Banning Nuclear Weapon Tests in the Atmosphere, in Outer Space and Under Water (known as the Partial Test Ban Treaty or PTBT). In the following decade, in fairly quick succession, more than a dozen multilateral or bilateral treaties or agreements for arms limitation and control were concluded. These included such important treaties as the Treaty on the Non-Proliferation of Nuclear Weapons (known as the Non-Proliferation Treaty or NPT), the 1972 SALT Treaty on the Limitation of Anti-Ballistic Missile Systems (known as the ABM Treaty), and the Interim Agreement on Certain Measures With Respect to the Limitation of Strategic Offensive Arms (known as the Interim Agreement). It seemed that international sanity would finally triumph over international insanity, and that mankind would succeed in saving itself from nuclear annihilation.

The year 1974 shattered those expectations. That was the year that India exploded a "peaceful" nuclear device that is the equivalent of a nuclear bomb, that Britain resumed nuclear testing for the first time since 1965, and that the United States decided to go beyond MIRVs (multiple independently targetable reentry vehicles) and develop more accurate and less vulnerable MARVs (maneuverable reentry vehicles) and cruise missiles, while the Soviet Union insisted on producing its own MIRVs with bigger warheads than the American. The Nixon–Brezhnev Summit Conference held in that year failed to do anything to halt either the quantitative or the qualitative strategic nuclear arms race and agreed instead on a Treaty on the Limitation of Underground Nuclear Weapon Tests (known as the Threshold Test Ban Treaty or TTBT) that permits unlimited underground tests until March 31, 1976, and, thereafter, bans only those having a yield of more than 150 kilotons while exempting peaceful nuclear explosions—and which is, therefore, regarded as a mockery of the two leaders' commitments to end all nuclear weapons tests. Nineteen seventy-four was also the year in which the energy crisis and the quadrupling of the price of oil created a surge of interest around the world in buying and building nuclear power reactors and a parallel desire on the part of the nuclear supplier countries to sell nuclear reactors, material, equipment, and technology for both foreign exchange and profit. It was the year when the preparatory work for the NPT Review Conference of May 1975 confirmed that the nuclear-weapon powers either did not have a clue as to what they must do to strengthen, or even preserve, the NPT or, if they did know, were incapable of acting or not sufficiently interested to act; their inaction and obduracy foreshadowed the failure of the Review Conference. Finally, China and France continued to conduct nuclear tests in the atmosphere in an attempt to achieve their own minimum nuclear deterrent forces and thus provided a continuing inducement to their neighbors to think in terms of themselves joining the nuclear club—perhaps, following India's lead, under the cloak of exploding peaceful nuclear devices.

With the further development, accumulation, and deployment of nuclear weapons by the nuclear powers* (vertical proliferation) and the increasing likelihood of such weapons being acquired both by non-nuclear countries (horizontal proliferation) and by terrorist and other politically motivated nongovernmental groups (nongovernmental proliferation), there is a clear and present danger of the entire structure of the so-called "non-proliferation regime"—the structure of treaties and agreements which we discuss in the Introduction—crumbling. If this should happen, the nuclear arms race would be out of control and the threat to human survival might become unmanageable.

While I am nervous about the fact that even five great powers possess nuclear weapons, I am positively frightened by the prospect of an additional dozen or two dozen countries having them. The genie would then really be out of the bottle; and the probability of a nuclear holocaust, —if not by design, then by accident, miscalculation, misinterpretation of orders, terrorism, attempted blackmail, or sheer madness—would become almost a certainty.

There is still a last chance to save the NPT and the non-proliferation regime, but only if the nuclear powers live up to their responsibilities and treaty obligations and if they demonstrate real determination to

---

*Throughout this book "nuclear powers" and "non-nuclear powers" are used interchangeably with the more cumbersome expressions "nuclear-weapon powers" and "non-nuclear-weapon powers."

build a saner and better world. All countries have an interest and responsibility in keeping the nuclear arms race from getting out of control. But
the nuclear powers must lead the way. Up to the present, the non-nuclear
powers have lived up to the commitments undertaken by them in the
various treaties that make up the non-proliferation regime. It is only the
nuclear-weapon states that have failed to do so—if not totally, then at
least in substantial part.

I have decided to write this book because of my conviction, which
has become stronger over the years, that, if the international system that
was erected to prevent the proliferation of nuclear weapons fails, human
survival is in doubt. I hope that the book will help to clarify the nature
and components of the problem and provide some ideas and guidelines
for what must be done to take advantage of the last chance to control
the nuclear arms race and ensure the survival of the human race.

Acknowledgments

The writing of this book was made possible by a grant from the Rockefeller Foundation, which awarded me a fellowship in their program in Conflict in International Relations. The grant was administered by the United Nations Institute for Training and Research (UNITAR), which appointed me a Special Fellow and provided a supplementary grant from the Beulah Edge Trust Fund to enable me to complete the project. I am greatly indebted to both the Foundation and the Institute for their support.

I would like in particular to express my appreciation to Mr. Elmore Jackson of the Rockefeller Foundation, to Dr. Davidson Nicol, the Executive Director of UNITAR, and to Mr. Oscar Schachter, the Deputy Executive Director and Director of Studies, for their constant interest in and encouragement of my work. Throughout the project, I had the benefit of numerous discussions with Mr. Schachter on various substantive aspects of the work and of his penetrating criticisms.

Mr. Derek Leebaert admirably performed the services of research assistant before, during, and after his appointment as an interne at UNITAR. His interest in the subject and his deep involvement in the work were a great help to me, particularly during those inevitable periods when I despaired of being able to finish the job.

To Paul Szasz of the United Nations Legal Department and Herbert Scoville, Jr. of both the Arms Control Association and the Federation of American Scientists, I owe a special debt of gratitude. Each read most of the manuscript and was most generous with his time and expertise in making many comments and suggestions for improving it. Ambassador Alfonso Garcia Robles of Mexico, now Foreign Minister, also read parts of the text and made a number of valuable suggestions, as did Warren Donnelly of the Library of Congress.

I must also express my thanks to *Scientific American* for permission to use some of the material in two articles I wrote for the magazine, "The Proliferation of Nuclear Weapons" published in the April 1975 issue, and "Nuclear Free Zones" published in the November 1975 issue. The Stanley Foundation was also kind enough to allow me to reproduce in

Chapter 18 most of the material contained in Occasional Paper 9 which I wrote for the Foundation and which it published in 1975 as "Retrospective on the NPT Review Conference: Proposals for the Future".

The actual writing of the book was divided between my offices at UNITAR, where the typing was done by Mrs. Rosy Thung, and at the University of Victoria in British Columbia, where Mrs. Gloria Orr did most of the typing and retyping. I am grateful to both of these ladies for their help and their patience.

Finally, I must express my profound gratitude to many delegates to the United Nations, to members of the Secretariat, and to many members of the arms control community, too numerous to mention, who, as colleagues and coworkers for many years in the difficult and often frustrating work of arms control and disarmament, taught me by precept and example the importance, indeed the indispensability, of persevering in the noble task of beating swords into plowshares.

William Epstein

New York
December 1975

Introduction

In this study I have attempted to survey and analyze the various problems relating to the non-proliferation of nuclear weapons and the future of the so-called "non-proliferation regime." Although the cornerstone in the structure of the regime is the Treaty on the Non-Proliferation of Nuclear Weapons (known as the Non-Proliferation Treaty or NPT), together with the associated safeguards agreements entered into by the various countries with the International Atomic Energy Agency (IAEA), there are other important building blocks which make up the entire structure. These include the Treaty Banning Nuclear Weapon Tests in the Atmosphere, in Outer Space and Under Water (known as the Partial Test Ban Treaty or PTBT) and the Treaty for the Prohibition of Nuclear Weapons in Latin America (the Treaty of Tlatelolco), together with its control organization (OPANAL). In a sense, the nonproliferation regime also includes the treaties that have been and that may be agreed upon at the Strategic Arms Limitation Talks (SALT). To the extent that these treaties are an attempt to implement those provisions of the NPT calling for a halt to the nuclear arms race and for nuclear disarmament, they can be regarded as part of the system intended to prevent the spread of nuclear weapons.*

The effort to prevent nuclear energy from being exploited for military purposes and to ensure that nuclear energy would be used solely for peaceful purposes goes back to the invention and use of the first atomic bomb. Ever since then, statesmen and scholars have attempted to find a solution to the dilemma posed by nuclear energy, with its potential for enormous good and awesome evil. The United Nations was born in 1945, the same year as was the nuclear age. Since Hiroshima and Nagasaki changed all the old rules, the United Nations gave first priority to lay-

---

*The IAEA itself and the European Atomic Energy Community (Euratom) are not actually integral parts of the non-proliferation system, except insofar as they provide safeguards against the diversion of fissionable material to the manufacture of weapons or nuclear explosive devices. Both agencies were created not to prevent nuclear weapons proliferation but rather to facilitate and promote cooperation in the peaceful uses of nuclear energy.

ing down the principles of disarmament, which had not been spelt out in its Charter. The very first resolution adopted by the General Assembly dealt with the problem of the control of atomic energy. The resolution was based on the Three-Power Declaration on the part of Canada, the United Kingdom, and the United States, which was subsequently confirmed also by the U.S.S.R., on how to deal with atomic energy and atomic weapons. It laid down the following four principles: that scientific information should be exchanged in the interest of the use of atomic energy for peace; that atomic energy should be controlled so as to ensure that it would be used only for peaceful purposes; that atomic weapons should be eliminated from national armaments; and that there should be effective safeguards by way of inspection and other means to make sure that there was no evasion of the required controls. These principles have remained the basis of all subsequent international efforts to deal with the problems of nuclear energy. (After the invention of the hydrogen bomb the word "nuclear," covering both fission and fusion weapons, replaced the word "atomic.")

Ever since the adoption of these principles, the members of the United Nations—nuclear and non-nuclear, large and small, rich and poor—have tried, both inside and outside the organization, to prevent the proliferation of nuclear weapons—both horizontal proliferation (the spread of nuclear weapons to additional countries) and vertical proliferation (the further development, accumulation, and deployment of these weapons). Another, more recent danger is the threat of what we might call nongovernmental proliferation: the acquisition of nuclear weapons and plutonium by nongovernmental terrorist groups, politically motivated disaffected groups, and ordinary criminals. Meanwhile, member states have tried to promote the peaceful uses of nuclear energy—but in doing so they have increased the availability of fissionable plutonium and complicated the problem of ensuring that it would be used only for peaceful purposes.

The nuclear arms race and its repercussions and ramifications—military, political, economic, environmental, and social—are of vital concern to almost every country in the world. Their survival and welfare depend upon the problems being solved or at least kept under control. In the field of nuclear energy what one country does affects all others, in greater or lesser degree. The behavior of the nuclear powers in regard to the nuclear arms race and their success or failure in implementing the provisions of the NPT will have a profound effect on the attitudes and behavior of the non-nuclear-weapon states—particularly in their belief or lack of it in the non-proliferation regime. The attitudes and actions of the non-nuclear-weapon states will equally determine the future of non-proliferation. The emphasis in the past, particularly in the United States, in dealing with the problems of arms control and disarmament has been mainly on the military strategic needs of the United States and the Soviet Union and the competition between them. But the danger of the spread of nuclear weapons is a problem that is not merely or primarily the business and concern of the nuclear powers or even of the other great powers.

It would seem appropriate, therefore, to study the question also from the point of view of the non-nuclear states, and not merely from that of the nuclear powers. The problem has greatest urgency at present for the dozen or so "near-nuclear" countries, that is, those that have the potential to "go nuclear" now or within the next five years or so. But there are many others not far behind.

I have been officially connected with the work of the United Nations in the field of arms control and disarmament for a quarter of a century and have attended almost all of the multilateral official conferences and discussions that have dealt with the subject during that time, often as the representative of the U.N. Secretary-General. Although I have had extremely informative and valuable discussions with representatives of many governments, I have not had access to any secret or confidential information in the possession of national governments. This book, then, is based on my experiences as an international civil servant of the United Nations participating in the various conferences, commissions, subcommittees, etc., which have dealt with the problem over the years, and on published sources.

The problem has been aggravated by the energy crisis. As nuclear power reactors become an increasing source of energy in both the nuclear and non-nuclear states, fissionable materials and nuclear "know-how" will become available to a growing number of people in several dozen countries. It is accordingly of primary importance that the complex of considerations which motivate the non-nuclear countries be understood and fully appreciated, if the non-proliferation regime is to have any chance of succeeding in its task of preventing the spread of nuclear weapons to additional countries.

This study endeavors to analyze the effectiveness and adequacy of the non-proliferation regime and, in particular, of the Non-Proliferation Treaty. To what degree will the regime prevent the spread of nuclear weapons to additional countries? What about those countries that have signed but not ratified the treaty and those that have not even signed it? What are the main concerns and problems of those countries that do not participate in the regime? How adequate are the existing national and international safeguards to prevent the diversion of fissionable material or, indeed, of nuclear weapons themselves? What are the possibilities of nuclear weapons or the ingredients for making them being stolen or hijacked by terrorist and criminal elements and used for blackmail and ransom? What can be done to cope with this danger?

Additionally, to what extent have the nuclear powers carried out their obligations and responsibilities under the PTBT and NPT, and what more must they do? To what extent are security guarantees or assurances to non-nuclear countries necessary and adequate, and how could they be improved? What steps could be taken to strengthen the non-proliferation regime and attract more widespread adherence and support? What are the prospects in this regard?

Finally, in what ways has the energy crisis affected the problems of the non-proliferation regime? To what extent will the regime help to promote the peaceful uses of nuclear energy, and should it include the use of explosions for peaceful purposes?

In my opinion, the question of the success or failure of the non-proliferation regime is the single most important issue facing the governments and peoples of the world. Its outcome might decide not merely the course of human history for generations to come, but the very survival of the human race.

List of Abbreviations

ABM	Anti-ballistic missile
ACDA	United States Arms Control and Disarmament Agency
AEC(UN)	Atomic Energy Commission of the United Nations
AEC(US)	Atomic Energy Commission of the United States
CCD	Conference of the Committee on Disarmament (successor to ENDC)
CNNWS	Conference of Non-Nuclear Weapon States held in Geneva in September 1968
EEC	European Economic Community
ENDC	Conference of the Eighteen-Nation Committee on Disarmament (predecessor of CCD)
ERDA	Energy Research and Development Administration [together with the NRC, the successor bodies to the AEC(US)]
Euratom	European Atomic Energy Community (originally six members —France, West Germany, Italy, Belgium, Netherlands, and Luxembourg—but now nine members with the addition of the U.K., Denmark, and Ireland)
HTGR	High temperature gas-cooled reactor, which uses highly enriched uranium (90%)
HWR	Heavy water reactor, which uses natural uranium
IAEA	International Atomic Energy Agency
IBRD	International Bank for Reconstruction and Development
ICBM	Intercontinental ballistic missile
IRBM	Intermediate-range ballistic missile
Kg	Kilogram (1 kg. equals about 2.2 pounds)
KT	Kiloton (the equivalent of 1,000 tons of high explosives)
LMFBR	Liquid metal fast breeder reactor, which produces more plutonium than it consumes
LWR	Light water reactor, which uses low enriched uranium (2% to 4%)
MARV	Maneuverable reentry vehicle
MIRV	Multiple independently targeted reentry vehicle

MLF	Multilateral Nuclear Force
MRBM	Medium-range ballistic missile
MUF	Material unaccounted for (that is, the fissionable material that disappears or is lost as it goes through the nuclear fuel cycle)
MW	Megawatts (1,000 kilowatts)
MT	Megaton (the equivalent of 1,000,000 tons of high explosives)
NATO	North Atlantic Treaty Organization
NPT	Treaty on the Non-Proliferation of Nuclear Weapons
NRC	Nuclear Regulatory Commission [together with the ERDA, the successor bodies to the AEC(US)]
OAU	Organisation of African Unity
OPANAL	Organismo para la Proscripción de las Armas Nucleares en la America Latina (Agency for the Prohibition of Nuclear Weapons in Latin America)
OPEC	Organization of Petroleum Exporting Countries
PTBT	Partial test ban treaty banning nuclear-weapon tests in the atmosphere, in outer space and under water
Pu	Plutonium
SALT	Strategic arms limitation talks
SIPRI	Stockholm International Peace Research Institute
SLBM	Submarine-launched ballistic missile
TTBT	Threshold test ban treaty
U	Uranium
U_{233}	The fissionable uranium isotope produced from thorium
U_{235}	The fissionable isotope of uranium
U_{238}	The non-fissionable or natural form of uranium that contains 0.7% of U_{235}
UNDP	United Nations Development Program
UNITAR	United Nations Institute for Training and Research

Chapter 1. The Basic Dilemma

The Impact of the Atomic Bomb

The explosion of the atomic bomb at Hiroshima on August 6, 1945, was heard all over the world and stunned nearly all who heard it. Its echoes still reverberate in all parts of the world. The reaction that accompanied it, compounded of fascination, hope, and horror, had no counterpart in modern human experience. The flight of the first airplane at the beginning of the century and of the first orbiting sputnik in 1957 could, in a sense, be said to have ushered in the air age and the space age, respectively. But the first was clearly a peaceful enterprise undertaken by private inventors, and the second, although the result of a carefully planned initiative by the Soviet government, was primarily a scientific venture. Although the military potential of both aircraft and spacecraft was immediately recognized, their peaceful civilian applications were more readily apparent.

The atomic bomb, on the other hand, was conceived in wartime, as the ultimate weapon of war; it was the result of an emergency crash program, during wartime, by the American government to invent one before the German government did. The first atomic bomb, exploded at Alamogordo, New Mexico, on July 16, 1945, was the result of what today would be described as a deliberate and intensive effort of military research and development and testing and evaluation.

Thus the nuclear age was conceived and born during a war, for the specific purpose of war. While the peaceful applications of nuclear energy were also perceived as having tremendous potential, these were regarded at the time of its birth, and unfortunately have been since, as of only secondary importance compared to the military uses.

Nuclear energy was regarded as having potential peaceful, practical uses in industry, medicine, and agriculture. But above all it was considered to provide a new source for the generation of cheap electric power at a time when demands for such power were rapidly increasing and it was becoming clear that resources of fossil fuel were limited and would become

1

increasingly expensive. Nuclear fission reactions could be controlled to take place either explosively in a bomb or slowly in a reactor to produce heat that could be used to generate electricity. Hence nuclear energy could provide either the ultimate weapon or abundant wealth.

It is a commonplace to say that nuclear weapons changed all the rules of conduct of international affairs in both peace and war. Not only was the atomic bomb considered to be the decisive weapon of war; it was also clear that relations between the great powers and between atomic and nonatomic powers would never be the same again and would be profoundly influenced—in undefined, unspoken, and ill-perceived ways—by the shadow cast by the bomb.

Many of the scientists and civilians who played key roles in initiating and developing the A-bomb were soon stricken by a sense of guilt and remorse and were appalled at the destruction inherent in their brainchild. Some of them felt that to ensure the survival of civilization and the human race, is was essential, indeed indispensable, that nuclear energy never again be used as a weapon of war for destructive purposes, but rather be used solely as an instrument of peace for the economic, social, and scientific betterment of mankind. Some argued that the new force was so dangerous that all future devlopment of it should be stopped if possible, while others believed that it would be better to disclose all of its secrets immediately to all the world.

The military and others of similar mind, however, while not actually opposing the idea of the peaceful uses of nuclear energy, were, quite naturally, more interested in the military uses. They simply could not bear the idea of giving up the awesome military superiority that went with the possession of the atomic bomb. They regarded the American monopoly of nuclear power as safe for a decade or more, they saw no reason why that advantage be thrown away or eroded. While it is true that some extremists and crackpots spoke of a preventive war or, more simply, of a preventive strike against the Soviet Union, it must be said in all fairness that the great majority of those who wanted the United States to preserve its monopoly of the bomb did so because they believed in all honesty that it would be safer, not just for the United States but for the whole world, if possession of the bomb was confined to the open, democratic, and peace-loving United States. They feared that its spread to other countries posed a vastly greater threat to national and international peace and security than did its exclusive possession by the United States. So convinced were they of the correctness of this idea that they would not give the bomb or the secrets of its manufacture even to their wartime British ally, which had been a partner of the United States in the research and development effort that produced the bomb. Winston Churchill and the entire British government deeply resented this exclusion from access to the bomb.

As the result of intensive studies initiated by the American government even before the successful bomb test at Alamogordo, in which scientists, statesmen, the military, and representative industrialists participated, some essential ideas were developed which became the basis for the American approach to the problem of the dual nature of atomic energy. Five basic concepts were stated by President Harry S. Truman in an address on October 27, 1945:

1. No nation can long maintain a monopoly of atomic weapons.
2. No nation could long maintain or morally defend a monopoly of the peaceful benefits of atomic energy.
3. For the forseeable future there can be no adequate military defense against atomic weapons.
4. All the initial processes in the production of fissionable materials and certain subsequent processes are identical whether their intended use or purpose is peaceful or military.
5. The nuclear chain reaction required for the release of atomic energy is now based upon uranium or uranium and thorium as the only suitable raw materials occurring in nature. Ores containing these materials are only relatively rare. Although rich deposits are not numerous, the lower concentrations of the ores have a wide geographical distribution.

The Role of the United Nations

Some may regard it as a quirk of history that the United Nations was born in the same year as the A-bomb. The Charter of the Organization was signed at San Francisco on June 26, 1945, just three weeks before the explosion of the first atomic bomb, and entered into force on October 24, 1945, some two and one-half months after the Hiroshima and Nagasaki bombs. The provisions of the Charter were worked out while work on the bomb was proceeding in the greatest secrecy; hence, of course, the document made no reference either to the bomb or to atomic energy.

The United Nations Charter not only makes no reference to atomic weapons, but, unlike the League of Nations Covenant, it makes very little reference to either disarmament or the regulation of armaments. It is a curious fact that Articles 1 and 2 of the United Nations Charter, setting forth the purposes and principles of the Organization, contain not a single reference to disarmament. Article 11 provides that the "principles governing disarmament and the regulation of armaments" are included among "the general principles of co-operation in the maintenance of international peace and security," about which the General Assembly can make recommendations to the members or to the Security Council. Article 26 is more specific: "In order to promote the establishment and maintenance of international peace and security with the least diversion for armaments of the world's human and economic resources, the Security Council shall be responsible for formulating, with the assistance of the Military Staff

Committee referred to in Article 47, plans to be submitted to the Members of the United Nations for the establishment of a system for the regulation of armaments." Article 47, which creates and defines the responsibilities of the Military Staff committee, gives it this task, among others: "to advise and assist the Security Council on all questions relating to . . . the regulation of armaments, and possible disarmament."

One of the reasons for the relatively little attention devoted to arms control and disarmament in the U.N. Charter is that, when the charter was drafted in the spring of 1945, the world had not yet suffered the traumatic shock of the atomic bomb or been awakened to the awful realities of the nuclear age. Moreover, the system of peacekeeping and enforcement measures envisaged by Chapter VII of the charter was predicated upon the continued existence of national armies, navies, and air forces, which would be made available to the Security Council to maintain or restore international peace and security, and which would be used for self-defense, in the case of armed attack against a member of United Nations until the Security Council took the necessary measures.

Nevertheless, the charter provisions have proved to be more than adequate to deal with all aspects of the problem of disarmament, including nuclear weapons and nuclear energy. Multilateral discussions and negotiations on disarmament very largely replaced the traditional channels of diplomacy as soon as the organization came into being. Those who wished to ensure that atomic energy would be used for peace and not for war saw the United Nations as the obvious and natural agency to achieve that goal.

The Three-Power Declaration and the U.N. Atomic Energy Commission

President Harry S. Truman of the United States, Prime Minister Clement Attlee of the United Kingdom, and Prime Minister W.L. Mackenzie King of Canada, whose three countries had all been involved in the work leading to the invention of the atomic bomb, met in Washington in November 1945 for the specific purpose of deciding how to deal with this awesome new product of man's ingenuity. On November 15 they adopted a Three-Power Declaration on the control and use of atomic energy, which set forth the basic principles of dealing with the problems raised by the discovery of atomic energy. It declared that a commission should be set up by the United Nations, and it defined the task of the commission. The Declaration is so fundamental to all subsequent efforts to deal with atomic energy that it is worth quoting in its entirety:

1. We recognize that the application of recent scientific discoveries to the methods and practice of war has placed at the disposal of mankind means of

destruction hitherto unknown, against which there can be no adequate military defence, and in the employment of which no single nation can in fact have a monopoly.

2. We desire to emphasize that the responsibilty for devising means to ensure that the new discoveries shall be used for the benefit of mankind, instead of as a means of destruction, rests not on our nations alone, but upon the whole civilized world. Nevertheless, the progress that we have made in the development and use of atomic energy demands that we take an initiative in the matter, and we have accordingly met together to consider the possibility of international action:

(a) To prevent the use of atomic energy for destructive purposes.
(b) To promote the use of recent and future advances in scientific knowledge, particularly in the utilization of atomic energy, for peaceful and humanitarian ends.

3. We are aware that the only complete protection for the civilized world from the destructive use of scientific knowledge lies in the prevention of war. No system of safeguards that can be devised will of itself provide an effective guarantee against production of atomic weapons by a nation bent on aggression. Nor can we ignore the possibility of the development of other weapons, or of new methods of warfare, which may constitute as great a threat to civilization as the military use of atomic energy.

4. Representing as we do, the three countries which possess the knowledge essential to the use of atomic energy, we declare at the outset our willingness, as a first contribution, to proceed with the exchange of fundamental scientific information and the interchange of scientists and scientific literature for peaceful ends with any nation that will fully reciprocate.

5. We believe that the fruits of scientific research should be made available to all nations, and that freedom of investigation and free interchange of ideas are essential to the progress of knowledge. In pursuance of this policy, the basic scientific information essential to the development of atomic energy for peaceful purposes has already been made available to the world. It is our intention that all further information of this character that may become available from time to time shall be similarly treated. We trust that other nations will adopt the same policy, thereby creating an atmosphere of reciprocal confidence in which political agreement and cooperation will flourish.

6. We have considered the question of the disclosure of detailed information concerning the practical industrial application of atomic energy. The military exploitation of atomic energy depends, in large part, upon the same methods and processes as would be required for industrial uses.

We are not convinced that the spreading of the specialized information regarding the practical application of atomic energy, before it is possible to devise effective, reciprocal, and enforceable safeguards acceptable to all nations, would contribute to a constructive solution of the problem of the atomic bomb. On the contrary, we think it might have the opposite effect. We are, however, prepared to share, on a reciprocal basis with others of the United Nations, detailed information concerning the practical industrial application of atomic energy just as soon as effective enforceable safeguards against its use for destructive purposes can be devised.

7. In order to attain the most effective means of entirely eliminating the

use of atomic energy for destructive purposes and promoting its widest use for industrial and humanitarian purposes, we are of the opinion that at the earliest practicable date a Commission should be set up under the United Nations Organization to prepare recommendations for submission to the Organization.

The Commission should be instructed to proceed with the utmost dispatch and should be authorized to submit recommendations from time to time dealing with separate phases of its work.

In particular the Commission should make specific proposals:

(a) For extending between all nations the exchange of basic scientific information for peaceful ends,

(b) For control of atomic energy to the extent necessary to ensure its use only for peaceful purposes,

(c) For the elimination from national armaments of atomic weapons and of all other weapons adaptable to mass destruction,

(d) For effective safeguards by way of inspection and other means to protect complying states against the hazards of violations and evasions.

8. The work of the Commission should proceed by separate stages, the successful completion of each one of which will develop the necessary confidence of the world before the next stage is undertaken. Specifically it is considered that the Commission might well devote its attention first to the wide exchange of scientists and scientific information, and as a second stage to the development of full knowledge concerning natural resources of raw materials.

9. Faced with the terrible realities of the application of science to destruction, every nation will realize more urgently than before the overwhelming need to maintain the rule of law among nations and to banish the scourge of war from the earth. This can only be brought about by giving wholehearted support to the United Nations Organization, and by consolidating and extending its authority, thus creating conditions of mutual trust in which all peoples will be free to devote themselves to the arts of peace. It is our firm resolve to work without reservation to achieve these ends.

The following month, a meeting in Moscow of the foreign ministers of the Soviet Union, the United Kingdom, and the United States approved the establishment of a U.N. commission as proposed in paragraph 7 of the Declaration, and agreed on the text of a draft resolution to be presented to the forthcoming first meeting of the General Assembly. At the insistence of the U.S.S.R., it was agreed that the commission would work under the authority of the Security Council, where each of the five permanent members had a veto.

Canada, China, and France also cosponsored the draft resolution. On January 24, 1946, it was adopted unanimously by the General Assembly, in the first substantive decision of the new world body. It was appropriately designated Resolution 1 (I), signifying that it was resolution number 1 of the first session of the General Assembly.

Atoms for War or Peace

Thus it was clear from the very beginning of the atomic age that the United States, all the great powers, and indeed all the members of the United Nations recognized the dichotomy between the military and the peaceful uses of atomic energy. Their desire to promote the latter, however, was subordinated to their fear of the former. The Three-Power Declaration warned in paragraph 6 against "the spreading of the specialized information regarding the practical application of atomic energy", before "effective, reciprocal and enforceable safeguards acceptable to all nations" were devised. This created a most formidable precondition to the dissemination of practical industrial information, as distinct from basic scientific information.

The subsequent history of the postwar world reflects the dilemma posed by the dual nature of atomic energy. If its peaceful uses were promoted, and knowledge of what later came to be known as nuclear technology was widely disseminated, this held out high promise of bringing great benefits to mankind in science, in industry, in agriculture, and in medicine. But the same knowledge could also be used for making atomic bombs that could bring about unimaginable destruction and might indeed destroy all civilization and the human race. It was recognized that the science and technology of the utilization of atomic energy could not be kept secret for very long and that it was not possible either to confine atomic energy to solely military purposes or to preserve the American monopoly. Hence the struggle to control atomic energy fluctuated between efforts to eliminate nuclear weapons and in the meantime prevent their use and their spread, and attempts to promote and facilitate the wider use of this new source of energy for peaceful civilian purposes. As was clear from paragraph 3 of the Three-Power Declaration, the authors wanted the best of both possibilities—"to prevent the use of atomic energy for destructive purposes" and "to promote . . . the utilization of atomic energy for peaceful and humanitarian ends." They wanted to disseminate knowledge about atomic energy without at the same time disseminating the technology of the atomic bomb. In other words, they favored the proliferation of the peaceful uses of nuclear energy but not the proliferation of nuclear weapons.

Whether these are mutually exclusive goals has not yet been clarified up to the present day. The dilemma calls to mind the Biblical warning, "For in much wisdom is much grief; and he who increaseth knowledge increaseth sorrow" (Ecclesiastes 1:18). The matter was further complicated when the United States launched its "Plowshare" program in the latter part of the 1950s, which was designed to use nuclear explosions for peaceful purposes. We shall come to that problem later; at this point it is only necessary to stress that from the very outset the United States was determined to prevent the spread of nuclear weapons to other countries; it was prepared to share its scientific knowledge about nuclear energy but not detailed information about its practical applications (i.e., technology for weapons) until effective enforceable safeguards to prevent the use of nuclear energy for destructive purposes were agreed upon.

The McMahon Act

On September 6, 1945, Senator Brian McMahon introduced in the United States Congress "a bill to conserve and restrict the use of atomic energy for the national defense, to prohibit its private exploitation, and to preserve the secret and confidential character of information concerning the use and application of atomic energy." The Congress finally on August 1, 1946, passed and the President signed the Atomic Energy Act of 1946, which came to be known as the "McMahon Act." Like much American legislation, this act was a compromise between those who favored sole governmental control and those who wished to open up the development of nuclear energy to private industry. But in the case of this new and fearsome discovery, additional compromises were necessary between those who insisted on civilian control and those who supported military control, those who wanted to ban the bomb and those who wanted to keep it, those who wished to prevent its possible proliferation and those who wished to promote its peaceful uses, and those who wished to "internationalize" its control and those who wished to preserve the American monopoly.

The act declared it to be "the policy of the people of the United States that, subject at all times to the paramount objective of assuring the common defense and security, the development and utilization of atomic energy shall, so far as practicable, be directed toward improving the public welfare, increasing the standard of living, strengthening free competition in private enterprise, and promoting world peace." It designated the United States Atomic Energy Commission as the exclusive owner, on behalf of the United States, of all fissionable materials and of all facilities for their production, except those used for research purposes and those using less material than was needed to produce an atomic bomb, and it prohibited the distribution of any fissionable material to any unauthorized person or to any foreign government. It also provided that the dissemination of restricted data should be controlled to assure the common defense and security. The dissemination of scientific and technical information was to be encouraged, but "until Congress declares by joint resolution that effective and enforceable international safeguards against the use of atomic energy for destructive purposes have been established, there shall be no exchange of information with other nations with respect to the use of atomic energy for industrial purposes."

The passage of the act was considered to be a great victory for the principle of civilian, as distinct from military, control of atomic energy. It was received with something less than enthusiasm in Great Britain, where it was felt that, despite British participation in the work leading to the development of the atomic bomb, Britain was being excluded from both the military and industrial applications of atomic energy. Criticism by Britain and Canada was somewhat muted, however, by recognition of the dangers of the dissemination of information and material that could lead to the spreading of atomic weapons.

The act put the final seal on the American policy to give first priority to preventing the spread of nuclear weapons and to relegate the peaceful uses of nuclear energy to a very secondary position. The United States intended, in the long run, to beat its swords into plowshares, but until it was satisfied that it was safe and timely to do so, it intended not merely to keep its swords but to sharpen and multiply them. In those early days, however, there were real hopes that the United Nations might at an early date establish an international system for the control of atomic energy which would prevent its use for military purposes and promote its use for civilian purposes.

The Baruch Plan

In the meantime, a group of high officials from the United States government, together with a number of scientists and industrialists, had been meeting under the leadership of Dean Acheson, then Under-Secretary of State, and David Lilienthal, chairman of the Tennessee Valley Authority, to work out a plan for dealing with atomic energy. They prepared what came to be known as the "Acheson–Lilienthal Report," which was designed to carry out the Three-Power Declaration. It was a bold and ingenious plan to ensure that atomic energy would be used solely for peaceful purposes by placing all the nuclear resources of the world under the ownership and control of an independent international authority. Its essential features were incorporated in what came to be known as the "Baruch Plan."

President Truman had appointed Bernard Baruch as his representative to the United Nations Atomic Energy Commission. At the first meeting of the commission, on June 14, 1946, Mr. Baruch outlined the proposals of the United States for the international control of atomic energy. In a dramatic speech, he stated that "we are here to make a choice between the quick and the dead. . . . We must elect World Peace or World Destruction . . ." He continued:

> The United States proposes the creation of an International Atomic Development Authority, to which should be entrusted all phases of the development and use of atomic energy, starting with the raw material and including—

1. Managerial control or ownership of all atomic-energy activities potentially dangerous to world security.

2. Power to control, inspect, and license all other atomic activities.

3. The duty of fostering the beneficial uses of atomic energy.

4. Research and development responsibilities of an affirmative character intended to put the Authority in the forefront of atomic knowledge and thus to enable it to comprehend, and therefore to detect, misuse of atomic energy. To be effective, the Authority must itself be the world's leader in the field of atomic knowledge and development and thus supplement its legal authority with the great power inherent in possession of leadership in knowledge. . . .

When an adequate system for control of atomic energy, including the renunciation of the bomb as a weapon, has been agreed upon and put into effective operation and condign punishments set up for violations of the rules of control which are to be stigmatized as international crimes, we propose that—

1. Manufacture of atomic bombs shall stop;

2. Existing bombs shall be disposed of pursuant to the terms of the treaty; and

3. The Authority shall be in possession of full information as to the know-how of the production of atomic energy.

He went on to stress that the punishments for violations were not to be subject to veto in the Security Council.

Baruch was responsible for adding enforcement measures, punishments, and the abolition of the veto in this context to the American proposals. As could have been foreseen, any tampering with the right of veto, particularly at a time when the United States could command a voting majority in all organs of the United Nations, touched a peculiarly sensitive Soviet nerve and made the task of the American negotiators far more difficult, if not actually impossible. But even without this provision, the fundamental differences between the United States and the Soviet Union in their attitudes toward the control of nuclear energy, which both regarded as of vital importance, were such as to preclude any possibility of agreement at this time.

The Soviet Response: Ban the Bomb

At the second meeting of the commission, on June 19, 1946, Andrei Gromyko, the representative of the U.S.S.R., made no mention of the Baruch proposals, but himself proposed a counter-plan. The Soviet approach was set forth in a draft convention which provided for the prohibition of the production, storing, and use of atomic weapons and for the destruction of all such weapons within three months of the entry into force of the convention. It also provided that the parties would, within six months after the convention entered into force, pass legislation providing severe penalties for violators.

Although Gromyko did not mention the American approach in his first statement, it was clear that he was rejecting it completely, since the Soviet approach was, in a sense, the exact opposite. The American plan was based on the idea of first controlling all atomic energy with a view to eventually eliminating all atomic weapons, whereas the Soviet approach provided first for a ban on production, storage, and use of nuclear weapons and for their destruction, and only thereafter for the introduction of a control system. This basic difference between the two approaches continued to plague all of the discussions and negotiations over the ensuing years. The Americans wanted first control and then disarmament, and they insisted on very strict control; the Soviet Union wanted first disarmament and then control, and its concept of control was much less strict—it was based on national means of control, with inspections to be allowed in case of suspicion of violations. The American position called for abolition of the veto power in the control apparatus, which the Soviet Union could not countenance. Thus the efforts to control atomic energy became deadlocked from the very outset.

Failure of the Baruch Plan

The discussions continued for several years in various committees and subcommittees which hammered out a comprehensive plan based on the Baruch proposals. This plan was finally approved by the General Assembly, in November 1948 by an overwhelming majority, and became known as the "United Nations Plan." This plan continued to be the basic reference or starting point for all further discussions with regard to the control of atomic energy, but in the absence of any reconciliation of the opposing points of view, no practical progress was possible.

In the field of armaments or atomic energy, effective decisions and progress can come about only as the result of some general consensus on the part of all the main parties. Solutions cannot be imposed on any party, and certainly not on a Great Power. Thus the initial ideas and plans to control atomic energy and prevent its spread or use for military purposes foundered on the basic deadlock between the United States and the Soviet Union.

The Soviet Union, which, like the United States, had been working (in secrecy) on the development of an atomic bomb since the middle of World War II, succeeded in September 1949 in exploding an atomic bomb, thus becoming the second nuclear power. Although this changed the entire nuclear picture much sooner than had been expected, the U.S. and the U.S.S.R. continued to maintain their respective positions and the deadlock continued. The United States continued to insist that, unless a more or equally effective system was devised, the United Nations Plan for the control of atomic energy and the prohibition of atomic weapons should continue to serve as the basis for the international control of atomic energy so as to ensure the prohibition of atomic weapons and the use of atomic energy for peaceful purposes only. The Soviet Union continued to maintain that the United Nations Plan, which it regarded as merely an adaptation of the Baruch Plan, constituted an unwarranted infringement on national sovereignty and was thus unacceptable in that, on the pretext of establishing international control, it would enable states to interfere in the internal economic life of other states. Soviet representatives continued to object to the vast international machinery required to carry out the American plan and stated that "the Soviet Union does not intend to make the fate of its national economy dependent on the U.S. financiers, industrialists, and their underlings who seek to bind other countries and in particular the Soviet Union hand and foot."

Years later, in 1962, Nikita Khrushchev, in discussing the Baruch Plan with American journalists, put the Soviet concern bluntly. He said that the United States "wanted to prevent the development of the atomic industry in other countries, leaving the monopoly of nuclear arms to the United States. We, of course, could not agree to this." Putting the development of atomic energy under U.N. control "would have meant to put it under control of the U.S."

In retrospect, it seems inevitable that the Soviet Union would have rejected the American plan, which would, in effect, have confirmed and preserved the American monopoly over both atomic weapons and atomic energy until an international authority was set up and was fully operative. Indeed, in those early days of the United Nations, it seemed that the U.S. would be able to command a voting majority in the U.N., if not forever, then for many years to come. And the authority would have such extensive powers that it would, to some extent, constitute a form of limited world government. Nevertheless, the Baruch Plan was an imaginative, idealistic proposal that, if implemented, would have succeded in solving the dilemma posed by the discovery of atomic energy. It would have enabled the proposed international authority to promote and facilitate the peaceful uses of nuclear energy and at the same time effectively prevent the military uses and the spread of atomic weapons and eventually eliminate those weapons. One can only regret that the political situation and the juxtaposition of forces and ideology in the world at the time made it inevitable that this far-reaching plan was doomed to be stillborn.

Faced with the almost overwhelming difficulty of preventing the proliferation of nuclear weapons in the world today because of the widespread proliferation of nuclear material and technology, some persons and governments are harking back to the old Baruch Plan and suggesting that only such an international authority, with very broad powers of management and control (if not ownership) over all forms of nuclear energy and all nuclear facilities, could effectively halt the further proliferation of nuclear weapons and ensure that nuclear energy in the future would be used only for peaceful purposes. But it is clearly too late. What might conceivably have been effective in 1946, when there was only one nuclear power in the world, or even in 1949 and 1950, when there were two nuclear powers, could have no practical relevance in the present world, where there are six nuclear powers and more than two dozen potential ones and vast quantities of nuclear materials are spread far and wide throughout the globe.

"Atoms for Peace"

After the failure of the Baruch Plan, there was no significant new initiative in the field of atomic energy control for several years. In the meantime, Great Britain exploded its first atomic bomb in Otober 1952, the United States exploded its first hydrogen bomb in November of the same year, and in August 1953 the Soviet Union also exploded its first hydrogen bomb. While weapons were proliferating, work was also proceeding on the peaceful uses of atomic energy, particularly the use of nuclear reactors to generate electric power. American industry became interested in the commercial possibilities of building and exporting nuclear reactors. The promotion of peaceful commercial uses came to be regarded not merely as an end in itself but also as a possible means of shifting interest from the military to the peaceful uses of nuclear energy and of exploiting the good rather than the evil that was inherent in the atom.

Accordingly on December 8, 1953, President Dwight D. Eisenhower delivered to the United Nations General Assembly a dramatic speech which came to be known as the "Atoms for Peace" proposal. He outlined the terrible dangers of atomic weapons which were shared by all and he acknowledged that the secrets of atomic power were already possessed by several nations and that they would eventually be shared by others. He went on to propose an international program to develop the peaceful uses of the atom which would help the world "shake off the inertia imposed by fear and . . . make positive progress toward peace." He declared:

> The United States would seek more than the mere reduction or elimination of atomic materials for military purposes.

> It is not enough to take this weapon out of the hands of the soldiers. It must be put into the hands of those who will know how to strip its military casing and adapt it to the arts of peace.

> The United States knows that if the fearful trend of atomic military buildup can be reversed, this greatest of destructive forces can be developed into a great boon, for the benefit of all mankind.

> The United States knows that peaceful power from atomic energy is no dream of the future. That capability, already proved, is here—now—today. Who can doubt, if the entire body of the world's scientists and engineers had adequate amounts of fissionable material with which to test and develop their ideas, that this capability would rapidly be transformed into universal, efficient, and economic usage.

The President proposed that the governments principally involved should begin to make joint contributions from the stockpiles of normal uranium and fissionable materials to an international atomic energy agency to be set up under the aegis of the United Nations. He went on:

> Undoubtedly initial and early contributions to this plan would be small in quantity. However, the proposal has the great virtue that it can be undertaken without the irritations and mutual suspicions incident to any attempt to set up a completely acceptable system of worldwide inspection and control.
>
> The Atomic Energy Agency could be made responsible for the impounding, storage, and protection of the contributed fissionable and other materials. The ingenuity of our scientists will provide special safe conditions under which such a bank of fissionable material can be made essentially immune to surprise seizure.
>
> The more important responsibility of this Atomic Energy Agency would be to devise methods whereby this fissionable material would be allocated to serve the peaceful pursuits of mankind. Experts would be mobilized to apply atomic energy to the needs of agriculture, medicine, and other peaceful activities. A special purpose would be to provide abundant electrical energy in the power-starved areas of the world. Thus the contributing powers would be dedicating some of their strength to serve the needs rather than the fears of mankind.

The "Atoms for Peace" proposal had a profound impact and attracted the interest and attention of all countries. After the death of Stalin and the ending of the Korean War, the Soviet Union had developed a softer international attitude. It agreed to enter into the negotiations that resulted in the elaboration of the Statute of the International Atomic Energy Agency (IAEA), which entered into force on July 29, 1957.

Thus the United States had initiated the setting up of an organization that would permit and facilitate the international distribution of fissionable material before the system visualized for the control of atomic energy was in operation. Furthermore, the safeguards envisaged and eventually agreed upon for the IAEA to ensure that nuclear materials, equipment, and assistance would not be diverted from peaceful to military purposes were a far cry from those that had been advocated by the United States in the Baruch Plan and very much less strict than those it was proposing in the disarmament negotiations that were proceeding at that time.

In order to implement this new development in United States policy the 1946 Atomic Energy Act had to be changed, and a new act, known as the Atomic Energy Act of 1954, was approved by Congress. This act authorized a program "to encourage widespread participation in the development and utilization of atomic energy for peaceful purposes to the maximum extent conistent with the common defense and security and with the health and safety of the public." The act also empowered the U.S. Atomic Energy Commission to negotiate cooperation agreements without Senate approval, but these agreements were required to contain a guarantee by the cooperating nation that no equipment or material transferred under the agreement would be used for nuclear weapons or for any other military purpose. And it authorized, for the first time, the private ownership of major nuclear facilities and the possession under license of special fissionable material by private industry. The act opened the door to a large number of bilateral agreements under which the United States provided nuclear assistance to other countries under U.S. safeguards. The safeguarding functions were eventually taken over by the IAEA or by Euratom (see below).

In 1955, the first of a series of world conferences on the Peaceful Use of Atomic Energy was held in Geneva. The conference helped to further fire the imaginations of both the rich and the poor countries of the world and to nourish their hopes that the peaceful applications of atomic energy, in particular in the generation of power, would lead to a second industrial revolution.

At about the same time, in 1955, the member states of the European Coal and Steel Community decided that, as part of the concept of a European Common Market, they should create a European organization for atomic energy which would promote the peaceful uses of atomic energy. This resulted in the creation by the Treaty of Rome on March 25, 1957, of the European Atomic Energy Community (Euratom) at the same time as the establishment of the European Economic Community and with the same six members — France, West Germany, Italy, the Netherlands, Belgium, and Luxembourg. The main purpose of Euratom was to facilitate the development and integration of nuclear industry in the six countries under a system of control and safeguards to ensure that nuclear materials and facilities were used exclusively for peaceful purposes. Unlike the IAEA, however, Euratom has the exclusive right of ownership of special fissionable materials for peaceful uses, and has regulatory and administrative powers (not restricted to safeguards) over the peaceful nuclear activities of its members. Because they had their own nuclear organization and control system and had developed their own sources of supply, the member states of Euratom did not place any of their nuclear material or plants under IAEA safeguards, although all of them became members of the IAEA, which was established at about the same time. And since the United States considered the Euratom safeguards adequate, it was prepared to supply nuclear materials and equipment to the Euratom countries, which were subject only to Euratom safeguards. A somewhat unusual situation developed whereby Euratom itself and all of its member states are required to ratify certain international agreements. This led to some problems in connection with the Non-Proliferation Treaty some years later.

The "Atoms for Peace" proposal led to a considerable erosion of the line between the peaceful and the military exploitation of atomic energy. On the one hand, it facilitated the spread of nuclear technology and nuclear materials which, although intended solely for peaceful purposes, were also a prerequisite for making nuclear weapons. On the other hand, it reduced the safeguards previously envisaged to prevent the diversion of nuclear fuel to making bombs. The Baruch Plan, based on the concept of the international ownership, management, and control of nuclear energy and nuclear facilities, was replaced by a much less effective concept of international safeguards and inspections. The IAEA safeguards prior to the NPT were applied not universally, nor to all of a country's nuclear facilities and activities, but only to a limited number of specific facilities and a small fraction of the fissionable material available in the world; and the safeguards applied only to projects in which the agency itself assisted countries in the development of peaceful uses, or to cases where the agency was requested by states to apply its safeguards system to already existing projects. Agency inspectors would periodically inspect or check nuclear facilities to verify that there had been no diversion. But the agency had no police powers, and it could only denounce diversions uncovered by its inspections. Hence, agency safeguards could *detect* but not *prevent* diversions. But once a state had tasted of the hitherto forbidden fruit of nuclear technology in an assisted and safeguarded project, there was nothing to prevent it from applying that "know-how" in any way it saw fit to its own, otherwise acquired materials and facilities.

The danger of the spread of nuclear weapons was greatly enhanced by the dissemination of nuclear technology and the proliferation of nuclear power reactors among the non-nuclear states pursuant to the "Atoms for Peace" program. The inevitable link between atoms for peace and atoms for war was described in detail by William B. Bader in his book *The United States and the Spread of Nuclear Weapons* (New York; Pegasus, 1968). The peaceful atom can beget a military one. Plowshares can be beaten into swords.

It is only fair to say that up to the present time there have been no charges of any diversion, either open or clandestine, from peaceful to military purposes of any nuclear materials or assistance subject to agency safeguards. Perhaps one of the reasons for this is that there has been no need or reason for a state to undertake any diversion, since it could do what it wished, relying on its own, otherwise acquired technology and resources. That, at least, has been the case with France and India, members of the IAEA who exploded their first nuclear devices after the agency was created.

In any case, as the authors of the Three-Power Declaration of November 15, 1945, recognized in that remarkably prescient document, "No system of safeguards that can be devised will of itself provide an effective guarantee against production of atomic weapons by a nation bent on aggression." They might well have added, "or by any nation determined to produce them."

In the United States, the Soviet Union, Great Britain, and China, military programs for the use of the atom preceded civilian ones; atoms for peace were a by-product or offshoot of atoms for war. In the case of France and India the reverse was true, and the development of nuclear explosives followed and was made possible by the development of rather advanced peaceful nuclear programs. It is quite likely that the latter experience will become the pattern of the future. If other countries decide to "go nuclear" in a military sense, they will do so as a result of having first traveled the road of developing the peaceful uses of nuclear energy.

In the space of a few years, then, attempts to control the development and spread of nuclear weapons seemed to have failed, and efforts were switched to promoting the development and spread of nuclear energy for peaceful purposes with only very limited and vague ideas as to how to prevent these peaceful uses from leading to the further spread of nuclear weapons.

As a result of the growing danger of theft or diversion of fissionable material and the need to ensure that there were no leakages of radioactivity by accident, defective equipment, or otherwise, the United States Congress decided in 1974 to replace the Atomic Energy Commission with two new, separate agencies. One of these new agencies, the Energy Research and Development Administration (ERDA), was given responsibility for nuclear weapons development as well as for research and development programs in all areas (not only nuclear) of energy production. The other agency, the Nuclear Regulatory Commission (NRC), was charged with the licensing and regulation of all aspects of commercial nuclear programs. From the time that the Atomic Energy Commission was abolished and replaced by the two new bodies in January 1975, atoms for war and atoms for peace have been dealt with in the United States by two separate agencies.

Thus, during a period of thirty years after the explosion of the first atomic bomb, the basic dilemma—whether nuclear energy and technology would be used for military or for peaceful purposes, and whether they were so interlinked that they could not be used for the one without fostering the other—remained unsolved. At the present time, the use of nuclear energy for both purposes seems to be growing, and at an accelerated rate. As the technology of nuclear energy and the availability of fissionable material proliferate throughout the world, the potential for human destruction may outstrip the potential for human betterment. The problems posed by the discovery of nuclear energy, then, still constitute the greatest threat and the gravest challenge facing mankind.

Chapter 2.   Atoms for War: The Proliferation
of Nuclear Weapons

During the years immediately following the end of World War II, the grand alliance of the great powers that had led to the great victory in the war rapidly eroded and crumbled. Whether the Soviet Union or the United States was responsibe for initiating the Cold War is irrelevant for the purposes of this volume. What is important is that both parties seemed prepared to maintain and wage the Cold War with vigor. The meteorology of the Cold War included the establishment of Communist regimes in the countries of Eastern Europe and the threats to Greece and Turkey; the American policy of containment and the enunciation of the Truman Doctrine; the takeover of Czechoslovakia and the Berlin Blockade; the Marshall Plan and the creation of NATO; and the victory of the Communists in China and the Korean War. Action and reaction followed with bewildering speed, more by improvisation than by plan, and each new event helped to turn the chilling atmosphere into a blinding blizzard.

The Baruch Plan was undoubtedly doomed to failure with or without the Cold War, but its failure can be regarded as another nail in the coffin of great-power cooperation, as was the failure to agree on setting up an international military force under the Security Council as required by the United Nations Charter.

Under these circumstances, it is hardly surprising that the thoughts of Governments and people turned more to arming and rearmament than to arms control and disarmament. In 1953, however, the blizzard abated and there seemed to be a pause in the Cold War. That was the year in which Eisenhower took over as president in Washington while Stalin died and a new and more cautious government took over in Moscow; the Korean War ended; and the Soviet Union exploded its first H-bomb in August, only nine months after the first American H-bomb.

The Decade of the 1950s

In those days, the United States, which had quickly dismantled its huge conventional military machine after the end of the war, regarded its original monopoly and subsequent superiority in nuclear weapons as offsetting Soviet superiority in armed forces and conventional armaments and as the chief deterrent that kept the Soviet Union, which had maintained its forces in Eastern Europe at almost wartime strength, from overrunning all of Western Europe. The U.S. concentrated on developing a family of nuclear weapons—strategic ones to be delivered by long-range bombers capable of striking targets in the Soviet Union, and tactical ones for battlefield use on land and sea and in the air in the region of Central Europe. Nuclear weapons appeared to give much greater power at less cost than did conventional arms and forces; in the vernacular of the 1950s, they gave "a bigger bang for a buck."

President Eisenhower, in his "Atoms for Peace" address to the United Nations on December 8, 1953, outlined the fearful potential of nuclear weapons:

> Atomic bombs today are more than 25 times as powerful as the weapons with which the atomic age dawned, while hydrogen weapons are in the ranges of millions of tons of TNT equivalent.
>
> Today, the United States' stockpile of atomic weapons, which, of course, increases daily, exceeds by many times the explosive equivalent of the total of all bombs and all shells that came from every plane and every gun in every theatre of war in all of the years of World War II.
>
> A single air group, whether afloat or land-based, can now deliver to any reachable target a destructive cargo exceeding in power all the bombs that fell on Britain in all of World War II.
>
> In size and variety, the development of atomic weapons has been no less remarkable. The development has been such that atomic weapons have virtually achieved conventional status within our armed services. In the United States, the Army, the Navy, the Air Force, and the Marine Corps are all capable of putting this weapon to military use.
>
> But the dread secret, and the fearful engines of atomic might, are not ours alone.

President Richard Nixon, in his first report (Feb. 18, 1970) to Congress on American foreign policy in the 1970s, stated: "From 1945 to 1949, we were the only nation in the world possessing an arsenal of atomic weapons. From 1950 to 1966, we possessed an overwhelming superiority in strategic weapons."

Nevertheless, during the early 1950s, the American military were obsessed by a "bomber gap" that they claimed gave the Soviet Union an advantage; toward the end of the 1950s they forgot about the so-called "bomber gap" and shifted their attention to a "missile gap" that they again claimed would leave them inferior to the Soviet Union in nuclear missiles.

Information about the Soviet buildup of nuclear weapons and bombers was rather sketchy in the early 1950s, but it was obvious that they were moving ahead as fast as possible in an attempt to catch up with the Americans. In the summer of 1952, a study group of American scientists from the Massachusetts Institute of Technology surveyed the Soviet threat and concluded (wrongly, as it turned out) that within two or three years the Soviet Union would have sufficient long-range strategic air power to cripple the United States in a surprise attack—a view that accorded with those of the Defense and State Departments. At that time the Soviet Union was preparing to replace its obsolescent World War II–type bombers with long-range turboprop bombers, which the Americans designated "Bear"; heavy jet bombers, designated "Bison"; and medium jet bombers, designated "Badger," which were in fact introduced in 1954 and 1955. But the United States B-36 heavy bombers and B-47 medium jet bombers, which were introduced before the Korean War, and the B-52 all jet heavy bomber, which was flight tested in April 1952 and introduced in 1955, were superior in both numbers and performance and had the overwhelming advantage of being able to operate from a network of bases in Western Europe, Morocco, and Japan and to be refueled in flight. There never was a bomber gap. The United States at all times had a massive nuclear superiority.

In October 1953 the Eisenhower administration decided that the military services could plan on using both strategic and tactical nuclear weapons wherever militarily desirable in future large-scale wars. Conventional weapons would be limited only to "brushfire" wars or "border skirmishes." In January 1954, Secretary of State John Foster Dulles enunciated the doctrine of "massive retaliation" to any attack, consisting in response by the U.S. with its rapidly expanding arsenal of nuclear weapons and growing number of bombers.

In 1955, the year of the Geneva Summit Conference, there were indications—which were confirmed later that year when Premier Bulganin said that the Soviet Union was developing rocket missiles, and in early 1956 when Marshall Zhukov spoke of mighty guided missiles—that the Soviet Union was undertaking a missile test program. Late in 1955, the U.S. also began intensive development of strategic missiles, and in 1956 funds were first allocated to the Polaris submarine, capable of firing nuclear missiles while submerged, which was actually deployed in November 1960. At about the same time, the U.S. began to launch surveillance satellites which enabled it to monitor Soviet missiles.

Exploitation of the so-called missile gap in the 1960 electoral campaign helped to win the election for President John F. Kennedy, although by February 1961 his Secretary of Defense, Robert McNamara, said that there never had been any missile gap.

The Soviet Union at that time was clearly inferior in strategic nuclear capabilities. In 1961, Khrushchev acknowledged that the "brandishing" of thermonuclear bombs by Dulles was "barefaced atomic blackmail, but it had to be reckoned with at the time because we did not possess sufficient means of retaliation, and, if we did, they were not as many and not of the same power as our opponents'."

Despite this inferiority, the Soviet Union was not adverse to using nuclear blackmail itself—when it alluded to the possibility of rocket attacks against Great Britain and France on November 4, 1956, during the Suez crisis. Nor did it refrain from sending its troops into Hungary at the same time.

When the Soviet Union announced the successful testing of an intercontinental ballistic missile on August 26, 1957, and launched the first sputnik on October 4, 1957, American strategists and the military promptly discovered the "missile gap" and forecast a three-to-one Soviet superiority by 1963. The Soviet Union cleverly and successfully exploited its rocket and sputnik feats to produce an image of rapidly growing strategic power that did not, in fact, exist. As early as December 1957, the United States had successfully tested its first Atlas ICBM missile, with an operational target date in 1959. One can only speculate about the motives for the Soviet deception strategy, but the results were clear. The American strategists and military began to operate on the "worst case hypothesis," that is, a hypothetical or imagined situation which might give the Soviet Union some technological or numerical advantage. They overreacted in an intensive effort for a massive buildup of strategic nuclear missiles that quickly overcame any imagined missile gap and put them far ahead of the Soviet Union. While the strategists debated the possibilities and usefulness of a "first strike" or "preemptive strike" and a "second strike" or "invulnerable retaliatory capacity" to deter a nuclear attack, the American strategic arsenal was taking shape and was ready for an explosive expansion that would demonstrate to all the world the extent of Soviet strategic nuclear inferiority.

During the latter part of the 1950s, the U.S. also produced a large and varied arsenal of tactical nuclear weapons, so that in January 1957, Secretary of Defense Charles E. Wilson told Congress that these smaller weapons had in a real sense become conventional weapons. Henry Kissinger, in his *Nuclear Weapons and Foreign Policy* (New York: Harper, 1957), published in the same year, argued in favor of the use of tactical nuclear weapons in Europe as a feasible and credible military doctrine, a view he was later to retract.

Thus, during the decade of the 1950s the political action–reaction pattern of the Cold War was repeated in the nuclear sphere. The nuclear arms race was launched in earnest and took on the shape it was to have until the late 1960s. The United States, in its desire to maintain its overwhelming superiority, and the Soviet Union, in its efforts to catch up with the United States or at least ensure its own deterrent capability, went all out in the nuclear arms race that embraced a wide range of tactical and strategic nuclear weapons. This arms race was in fact a race of scientific and military technology. Because of the range and complexity of nuclear weapons, the American government had to seek the assistance of industry and scientists. Many were brought into the Department of Defense and the Atomic Energy Commission. Both inside and outside of government, their influence became so great that President Eisenhower, in his farewell address, felt constrained to warn against the power of the "military–industrial complex" and against the emergence and influence of a "scientific–technological elite." While less is known about the specifics and details of the decision-making process in the Soviet Union, sufficient is known to appreciate that they too have a "Pentagon problem" and a "military–bureaucratic" complex which carries very great and perhaps decisive weight in all decisions affecting the military posture of the Soviet Union.

The Decade of the 1960s

In his final State of the Union message in January 1961, President Eisenhower declared that "the 'bomber gap' of several years ago was always a fiction and the 'missile gap' shows every sign of being the same." Nevertheless, both had served to fuel the nuclear arms race and to ensure that the U.S. would embark on the programs that gave it a tremendous superiority in strategic nuclear arms in the early 1960s. The nuclear arms race, begun in the 1950s, continued in the 1960s and 70s at an accelerated rate that soon resulted in the possession of a massive "overkill" capability by both sides.

During the time of President Kennedy's administration, the missile gap was quickly and officially buried. On October 21, 1961, the Deputy Secretary of Defense stated: "The President was determined that our strategic power must be sufficient to deter any deliberate nuclear attack on this country or its allies by being able to survive a first strike by the enemy with sufficient arms to penetrate his defenses and inflict unacceptable losses upon him." He added:

> The U.S. has today hundreds of manned intercontinental bombers capable of reaching the Soviet Union, including 600 heavy bombers and many more medium bombers equally capable of intercontinental operations because of our highly developed in-flight refueling techniques and worldwide base structure. The U.S. also has 6 Polaris submarines at sea carrying a total of 96 missiles, and dozens of intercontinental ballistics missiles. Our carrier strike force and land-based theater forces could deliver additional hundreds of megatons. The total number of our delivery vehicles, tactical as well as strategic, is in the tens of thousands; and, of course, we have more than one warhead for each vehicle.
>
> . . . In short, we have a second-strike capability which is at least as extensive as what the Soviets can deliver by striking first. Therefore, we are confident that the Soviets will not provoke a major nuclear conflict.

It was also during the Kennedy administration that the doctrine of nuclear "massive retaliation" against any attack was discarded; the doctrine had lost its credibility when both the Soviet Union and the United States had acquired the capability of inflicting "unacceptable damage" or "assured destruction" on the other. The counter-city strategy, which was a key element of the massive retaliation doctrine, was also recognized as encouraging mutual suicide and as lacking credibility and morality, and the idea of a counterforce strategy, aimed at an opponent's military forces and bases and not his civilian population, was adopted but soon abandoned. Finally a new strategy was developed based on controlled and flexible response graduated to meet a variety of levels and forms of aggression. It envisaged more options and more flexibility in choice of weapons, and hence required a panoply of offensive and defensive weapons and warning systems.

During this period, the strategic weapons that had been the subject of research and development in the 1950s—the Atlas and Minuteman ICBMs and the Polaris submarine-launched ballistic missiles (SLBMs)—were deployed in great numbers, so that when they were considered together with the megaton bombs that could be delivered by bombers, it was estimated that the American and Soviet strategic nuclear forces together had a nuclear weapons capability equal to 15 kilotons (i.e., 15,000 tons) of high explosive for every inhabitant on earth, or the equivalent of 60 kilotons for every man, woman, and child in the NATO and Warsaw Pact member states.*

It was also during the Kennedy presidency that the Cuban missile crisis occurred, in October 1962. In the aftermath of the return from the brink of war, the Soviet Union and the United States entered into the "Hot Line" agreement in June and the Partial Test Ban Treaty (PTBT) in August 1963. But these efforts to control the nuclear arms race failed even to slow down that race.

When the Partial Test Ban Treaty was being considered for ratification by the U.S. Senate in 1963, the Joint Chiefs of Staff put forward a document which they called "Safeguards . . . with regard to the Limited Nuclear Test Ban Treaty," containing a number of measures which they regarded as essential. President Kennedy accepted these measures in order to gain Senate approval of the treaty. The first "safeguard" specified:

> The conduct of comprehensive, aggressive and continuing underground nuclear test programs designed to add to our knowledge and improve our weapons in all areas of significance to our military posture for the future.

At that time, the U.S. was far ahead of the Soviet Union in the number and variety of nuclear weapons tests that it had conducted, as well as in the number and sophistication of both its strategic and tactical nuclear weapons. One might well have thought that it would have been in the American interest, as well as that of the entire world, to seek to ban all nuclear tests including underground ones, pursuant to the treaty provisions

* The Hiroshima bomb had a yield of about 15 kilotons.

obligating the parties to do so. But the Joint Chiefs of Staff insisted on the continuation of underground testing and thus aborted the intention of the treaty and helped the Soviet Union to overcome its inferiority in nuclear weaponry and make rapid progress toward achieving parity with the U.S. by the early 1970s.

Secretary of Defense McNamara, in testifying to the Senate Foreign Relations Committee about the PTBT on August 13, 1963, compared American and Soviet nuclear capabilities as follows:

> The U.S. force today now contains more than 500 missiles—Atlas, Titan, Minuteman, Polaris—and is planned to increase to over 1,700 by 1966. In addition, the United States has SAC bombers on quick reaction alert.
>
> By comparison, the consensus is that today the Soviets could place less than half as many bombers over North America on a first-strike mission; the Soviets are estimated to have today only a fraction as many ICBM missiles, and their sub-launched ballistic missiles are short range, require surface launch, and generally are not comparable to our Polaris force. Between now and 1966, it is estimated that our ballistic missile numerical superiority will increase both absolutely and relatively.
>
> Further, the United States at present has in stockpile or planned for stockpile a large number of nuclear explosives for tactical purposes. These weapons are planned for employment on the battlefield, in anti-submarine warfare, and against aircraft; they consist of warheads for artillery, battlefield missiles, demolition munitions, bombs, depth charges, air-to-air missiles, and surface-to-air missiles. The yield spectrum associated with these weapons extends from the subkiloton range to hundreds of kilotons.

He added that, with or without a test ban, the U.S. already had the capability to develop an antiballistic missile (ABM) system and to be able to penetrate any Soviet ABM system. Most significantly, McNamara pointed out that the indefinite continuation of unrestrained testing would likely result ultimately in parity between the U.S. and U.S.S.R., except for weapons of very high yield, which the Soviet Union was developing but in which the U.S. had no particular interest. Limiting the Soviet Union to underground testing would retard Soviet progress and prolong the duration of American superiority.

In fact, the PTBT did not impose any practical restraints on testing. In the eighteen years between 1945 and 1963, the U.S.S.R. conducted some 164 nuclear tests (of which 3 were underground) and the United States some 282 tests (of which 89 were underground); in the period August 1963–June 1973, the U.S.S.R. conducted 121 tests and the U.S. 259 tests, all of them underground. This indicates a considerable increase in the *rate* of testing—33% by the U.S.S.R. and 65% by the U.S.

On February 13, 1960, France exploded its first atomic bomb. On October 16, 1964, China also exploded its first atomic bomb. Neither event appeared to have any effect on either the American or Soviet weapons programs.

During the 1960s there was a continuing effort both in the U.S. and in the U.S.S.R. to upgrade the quality of their missile systems. Several types of tactical and strategic weapons systems were developed and phased out when they became obsolete. For example, in the strategic missile field, the U.S. Minuteman I was followed by the II and III, and the Polaris A-1 by the A-2 and A-3 and finally the Poseidon missile. In the U.S.S.R., newer and better models of their ICBMs were introduced, but with some time lag behind the U.S.

While efforts at improving strategic systems continued, the United States, which had an overwhelming nuclear superiority, unilaterally decided to place a limit on its strategic systems. In deciding the question of "How much is enough?" the United States concluded that it was neither necessary nor desirable to maintain strength beyond what was sufficient for deterrence of a deliberate nuclear attack on the U.S. or its allies. In 1964, it was decided to limit the number of Polaris submarines (each carrying 16 missiles) to 41, with a total of 656 missiles. In 1965, it was decided to limit the number of Minuteman missiles to 1,000. The Soviet Union, meanwhile, with far fewer land- and sea-based missiles, continued in its efforts to catch up with the United States.

During this period the U.S.S.R. also began to build an ABM system around Moscow, which is known as the "Galosh" system, as a defense against the American lead in missiles. For several years, Secretary McNamara had opposed the construction of such a system by the United States. In 1963, McNamara said that the U.S. had spent $4.85 billion on ABM research and development but that he did not think that the U.S.S.R. had an operational ABM system, and he opposed the deployment of ABMs by the U.S. In 1965 he stated that no matter what improvements were made in an ABM system, an enemy could develop penetration tactics to overcome it; a defense system could destroy a percentage of incoming warheads but not all.

In January 1967, in presenting the U.S. military posture statement to Congress McNamara gave estimated figures of expected fatalities in the event of an all-out strategic nuclear exchange between the U.S. and the U.S.S.R. He stated that, on the basis of the approved U.S. nuclear programs at that time, in an all-out exchange U.S. fatalities would amount to from 100 to 120 million and Soviet fatalities from 70 to more than 120 million, depending on which side struck first. These figures represented deaths from blast and fallout only, and did not include the many additional deaths that would result from firestorms, disease, and the general disruption of life. He further estimated that, even after a Soviet first strike, more than one-half of U.S. strategic missiles would survive and one-fifth of the surviving missiles (i.e., about 200) would be sufficient to kill some 73 million of the Soviet population and destroy about one-half of its industrial capacity. In truth, then, nuclear war is not only unthinkable, it is unsurvivable.

On June 17, 1967, the first Chinese hydrogen bomb was exploded, which was followed on August 24, 1968, by the first French hydrogen bomb. So great was the superiority of both American and Soviet nuclear arsenals in number, variety, and sophistication of weapons systems that the world, which had in any case accepted these developments as inevitable, hardly took notice.

On September 18, 1967, McNamara, in a rather strange speech, warned about the "mad momentum of the arms race" and argued that the action–reaction phenomenon made it foolish and futile.

With respect to the American and Soviet nuclear forces, he said:

> We both have strategic nuclear arsenals greatly in excess of a credible assured destruction capability. These arsenals have reached that point of excess in each case for precisely the same reason: we each have reacted to the other's build-up with very conservative calculations. We have, that is, each built a greater arsenal than either of us needed for a second-strike capability, simply because we each wanted to be able to cope with the "worst possible case."
>
> But since we now each possess a deterrent in excess of our individual needs, both of our nations would benefit from a properly safeguarded agreement, first to limit, and later to reduce, both our offensive and defensive strategic nuclear forces.

Even so, in the same speech he announced President Lyndon Johnson's decision to proceed with the deployment of a limited ABM system known as "Sentinel."

Earlier the decision had been taken by the United States to develop a multiple independently targetable reentry vehicle (MIRV) which could be used to penetrate ABM systems. In 1967 it was decided to produce and deploy such MIRVs. Three warheads were to be fitted onto the Minuteman III land-based missile and up to fourteen, with an average of ten, onto the Poseidon sea-based missile. In his final defense posture statement in 1968, McNamara warned that strategic "superiority" was of little significance in terms of national security. Nevertheless, the decision was made to proceed with the deployment of MIRVs. The first flight tests took place in August 1968.

When the United States decided to proceed to develop MIRVs, it also concluded that smaller nuclear warheads were much more efficient than larger warheads and that gross megatonnage was not a reliable indication of the destructive power of an offensive force. According to a table prepared by the Pentagon at that time, ten 50-kiloton warheads totaling one-half a megaton could inflict much more damage than one 10-megaton warhead. The table was as shown on the next page.

The Soviet Union, on the other hand, has always been partial to large-size weapons, even in the area of testing. In the fall of 1961 the Soviet Union announced that it would conduct a nuclear test equivalent to about 50 megatons. (The largest American test to date has been the explosion

T A B L E 2 – 1. Comparative Effectiveness of Two Hypothetical Missile Payloads

	Number of Targets Destroyed	
Type of Target Destroyed	TEN 50-KT. WARHEADS	ONE 10-MEGATON WARHEAD
Airfields	10	1
Hard missile silos	1.2–1.7	1
Cities of 100,000 population	3.5	1
Cities of 500,000 population	0.7	1
Cities of 2,000,000 population	0.5	0.6

in the Marshall Islands in 1954 of a hydrogen bomb estimated at about 14 megatons.) The Soviet test, conducted at Novaya Zemlya, was reported to be of 57 megatons, although some experts say that its actual capacity was over 90 megatons. In warheads, too, the Soviet Union's medium-range ballistic missiles (MRBMs), with a range of 1,000 to 1,500 miles, have 1-megaton warheads, and their ICBMs can deliver up to 20 to 25 megaton warheads.

After lengthy negotiations (outlined in Chapter 5), agreement was reached in 1968 on the Treaty on the Non-Proliferation of Nuclear Weapons (NPT), which was signed on July 1. Among other provisions, the treaty called for a ban on underground nuclear tests, for the cessation of the nuclear arms race, and for nuclear disarmament. At the time of signature, it was announced that the U.S. and the U.S.S.R. would begin discussions in the near future on the "limitation and reduction of both offensive and defensive strategic nuclear weapon delivery systems." Agreement on the beginning of the Strategic Arms Limitation Talks (SALT) was reached on August 19, but the agreement was aborted on the following day by the Soviet invasion of Czechoslovakia, and the talks did not get under way until November of 1969.

In the meantime, Richard Nixon was elected president of the United States. In January 1969, he announced that he favored "sufficiency" in nuclear weapons rather than superiority or parity, but it is clear that the word was a cloak for the basic concept of a rough balance or parity between the U.S. and U.S.S.R. On March 14, he announced his decision to proceed with the deployment of a larger-scale ABM system (for the purpose of missile defense) than was originally foreseen for the Sentinel program (intended for defense against a Chinese attack), and its name was changed to "Safeguard." He also decided to continue deploying MIRVs, but he promised, as a reassurance to the Soviet Union and to domestic critics, that the U.S. would refrain from improving the accuracy of the MIRVs, which might be regarded as giving them a counterforce or first-strike capability, since MIRVs were theoretically capable of extreme accuracy. He also continued to rely on the "triad" of strategic forces—land-based missiles (ICBMs), sea-based missiles (SLBMs), and bombers—although the Polaris submarine was virtually invulnerable and itself contained far more nuclear second-strike capability than was required for deterrence of any nuclear attack.

Thus, the decade of the 1960s saw the greatest accumulation in killing power in all human history. The amount of overkill that was generated is beyond the capability of the human mind to grasp. Whenever a new weapon was devised, a counter-weapon was developed to neutralize it and then a counter-counter-weapon. Scientists do not wait for a potential enemy to react, but, operating on the "worst case" theory, themselves react against their own brainchildren. During the decade, manned bombers were replaced as the main strategic weapon by missiles, beginning with liquid-fueled intermediate-range rockets and proceeding to intercontinental ones. They were replaced in the U.S. by solid-fuel missiles, although the U.S.S.R. continued to rely on liquid-fueled ones, but in both countries the missiles were placed in underground concrete silos for protection against attack. At the same time, submarine-launched ballistic missiles were developed and deployed in submarines. To defend against attacking missiles, ABM systems were developed, although it was recognized that they had only limited usefulness. At the same time, MIRVs were developed, capable of hitting a number of targets from a single missile launch and thus of overwhelming or circumventing any possible missile defense; these multiplied the already appalling overkill capacity by a factor of 3 to 10.

At the beginning of the decade there were only some 50 ICBMs in existence and only 2 Polaris submarines with 32 SLBM missiles. By the end of the decade there were well over 2,000 ICBMs and nearly 1,000 SLBMs, as well as tens of thousands of tactical nuclear weapons.

The 1970s and Salt

In May 1972, the U.S. and the U.S.S.R., at a summit meeting in Moscow, signed a Treaty on the Limitation of Anti-Ballistic Missile Systems and also an Interim Agreement on Certain Measures with Respect to the Limitation of Strategic Offensive Arms and a Protocol thereto. Under the ABM treaty, each of the parties agreed to deploy no more than 100 ABM launchers and missiles at each of two launch sites in their respective countries. They also agreed to certain qualitative limitations on their ABM radars, but modernization and replacement of ABM systems was permitted. Under the Interim Agreement and Protocol thereto, which has a duration of five years, the United States is entitled to increase the number of its nuclear submarines from 41 to 44 with 710 nuclear missiles, and the Soviet Union is entitled to build up to 62 submarines carrying 950 nuclear missiles; the U.S. can also retain 1,000 and the Soviet Union 1,410 land-based ICBMs. No limitation was placed on MIRVing either sea-based or land-based missiles. Thus the agreement established quantitative limitations—at a higher level—but made no provision for any qualitative limitation or reductions.

The U.S. had previously announced that it would equip 31 of its submarines with Poseidon missiles, each having 10 to 14 separately targeted warheads, and that it would MIRV 550 of its land-based missiles. The Soviet Union, which only in 1973 had successfully tested MIRV missiles for ICBMs but not for SLBMs, did not announce how many of its submarine-launched or land-based missiles it proposed to MIRV. Thus it was envisaged under programs permitted by the Interim Agreement that by 1977 the American nuclear arsenal would contain more than 7,000 strategic nuclear warheads mounted on 1,710 missiles, while that of the Soviet would comprise whatever number of strategic nuclear warheads it decided to MIRV on 2,360 missiles. In additon, both countries would retain their strategic bombers, which carried heavier bomb loads than either ICBMs or SLBMs and which were not dealt with in the Interim Agreement.

At the Washington Summit Conference in June 1973, another agreement was signed, entitled Basic Principles of Negotiations on the Further Limitation of Strategic Offensive Arms. By this agreement, the U.S. and the U.S.S.R. agreed to "continue active negotiations in order to work out a permanent agreement on more complete measures on the *limitation* of strategic offensive arms as well as their *subsequent reduction*" (emphasis added). The agreement specifically permitted the modernizing and replacement of strategic offensive arms, but added that "the limitations placed on strategic offensive weapons can apply both to their quantitative aspects as well as their qualitative improvement."

The two parties also entered into an Agreement on Prevention of Nuclear War, which contained rather far-reaching provisions for consultation in order to avoid the risk of nuclear war between the parties or between either party and other countries.

In 1974, it was estimated by American government officials that the total U.S. strategic nuclear arsenal was sufficient to drop 36 bombs on each of the 218 Soviet cities with a population of 100,000 or more. The U.S.S.R. had 11 nuclear weapons for each comparably sized American city.

The Summit III meeting in Moscow from June 27 to July 3, 1974, was something of a shambles as regards restraining the nuclear arms race. The two parties agreed to restrict their ABMs to only one site each instead of the two permitted under the 1972 agreement. (The new agreement was practically without significance, as neither party intended to build a second site.) They also signed a threshold Test Ban Treaty which may have been worse than no agreement at all. The new treaty does not go into effect until March 31, 1976, and thereafter it permits underground tests up to a threshold of 150 kilotons, which is high enough for almost any conceivable weapons purpose. It placed no restriction at all on underground peaceful nuclear explosions. Most important, there was complete failure to reach any agreement to limit or restrict offensive strategic nuclear weapons. As Henry Kissinger stated in his press conference on July 3, 1974, in order to avoid "the hell of an arms race" it was necessary to reach agreement "well before 1977," or there would be an "explosion of technology and an explosion of numbers." We have, Kissinger noted, "about eigheeen months to gain control of the multiple warheads, control not in the sense of eliminating it [sic], but by introducing some stability into the rate and nature of their deployment." "Both sides," he warned, in an historic statement, "have to convince their military establishments of the benefits of restraint, and that is not a thought that comes naturally to military people on either side."

The table opposite sets forth the growth in the comparative strength of the U.S. and the U.S.S.R. in strategic nuclear arms up to 1975. It does not take into account the number or size of warheads or of nuclear bombs carried aboard bombers; nor does it indicate the types or numbers of intermediate-, medium-, and short-range ballistic missiles or tactical nuclear weapons.

The Vladivostok agreement in November 1974 was hailed as a "breakthrough" that put a "cap" on the strategic arms race. It incorporated the previous Interim Agreement and fixed a ceiling on the number of all strategic nuclear weapons that the two superpowers can possess until December 31, 1985, on the basis of equality between them. Each side is permitted to have 2,400 strategic delivery vehicles, including land-based intercontinental ballistic missiles (ICBMs), submarine-launched ballistic missiles (SLBMs), and heavy bombers. Of that number, 1,320 can be armed with mulitple warheads (MIRVs).

The agreement was said to establish ceilings well below the levels that otherwise could be expected to be operative in ten years. But the ceilings established are substantially *above* the levels that each side had at the time, and are even higher than those envisaged for 1977 under the Interim Agreement. There are always discrepancies in estimates of relative strength depending on who makes the estimates and what items are included. In 1975, the official Pentagon estimate was that the United States had 2,208 strategic delivery vehicles and the Soviet Union 2,450.

As regards the number of MIRVs permitted, the figure of 1,320 represents a considerable increase for both countries. The United States had previously announced that it would MIRV 550 land-based Minutemen and 496 SLBM Poseidon missiles, for a total of 1,046 MIRVed missiles. By 1975 it had MIRVed about 800 of its missiles. Thus the ceiling of 1,320 represents a considerably higher level than the United States had or planned to have.

T A B L E 2 – 2. Growth in Comparative Strength of the U.S.A. and U.S.S.R. in Strategic Nuclear Arms

		1959	1960	1961	1962	1963	1964	1965	1966	1967	1968	1969	1970	1971	1972	1973	1974	1975
U.S.A.	ICBMs	None	18	63	294	424	834	854	904	1054	1054	1054	1054	1054	1054	1054	1054	1054
	SLBMs	Some	32	96	144	224	416	496	592	656	656	656	656	656	656	656	656	656
	Long-range bombers				600	630	630	630	630	600	545	560	550	505	455	442	437	432
U.S.S.R.	ICBMs	None	35	50	75	100	200	270	300	460	800	1050	1300	1510	1527	1527	1575	1618
	SLBMs	None	None	Some	Some	100	120	120	125	130	130	160	280	440	560	628	720	784
	Long-range bombers				190	190	190	190	200	210	150	150	150	140	140	140	140	135

SOURCE: Various annual issues of *The Military Balance*, published by the International Institute of Strategic Studies.

The Soviet Union has just begun to deploy MIRVs. It is developing several new MIRVed missiles, including the SS-17, the SS-18 (a replacement for the SS-9), and the SS-19 (a replacement for the SS-11), each with 4 to 8 heavy warheads. It has not announced how many if its land- or sea-based missiles it intended to MIRV, but 1,320 obviously represents a very high and costly ceiling that will take it several years to reach.

The Vladivostok agreement put no limit on either the number of warheads that can be placed on each missile or the size or "throw-weight" of the warheads. Since it is generally believed that the Soviet Union has much heavier warheads with greater missile "throw-weight" than the American ones, there will be pressures on the United States to increase the size or number of its warheads, although it had earlier decided that smaller warheads were more effective than larger ones. The agreement also puts no limitation on improvements or "modernization" of missiles by increasing their accuracy and maneuverability.

At his press conference on December 2, 1974, President Ford stated that the United States had an "obligation" to keep its strategic forces up to the ceiling level. He also said: "It is recognized that the Soviet Union has a heavier throw-weight, but the agreement does not preclude the United States from increasing its throw-weight capability."

On December 6, 1974, the then Secretary of Defense James Schlesinger said that he foresaw a need for larger, restructured strategic forces for the United States as a result of the agreement, including 12 instead of 10 of the monster Trident submarines (each having 24 missiles with 14 to 20 warheads, for a total of about 5,000 nuclear warheads), larger, MIRVed ICBMs, and a new bomber. This program, he said, would require "some upward adjustment" in the strategic arms budget.

It is clear that the "limitation" envisaged by the Vladivostok agreement, while it will put an eventual cap or ceiling on the number of strategic nuclear weapons, permits an expansion in both the quantitative and qualitative nuclear arms race. Since no limit is fixed on the number or size of warheads on the 1,320 MIRVed missiles or of nuclear arms carried in bombers, each of the two superpowers can build 20,000 or more strategic nuclear warheads under the agreement. For all practical purposes, both the U.S. and the U.S.S.R. have acquired a nuclear destructive capability approaching infinity.

In a press conference on July 3, 1974, Henry Kissinger posed the right questions in a *cri de coeur* that went to the very heart of the matter: "One of the questions we have to ask ourselves as a country is: What in the name of God is strategic superiority? What is the significance of it? What do you do with it?"

Despite the weird calculations of many nuclear-war strategists, there are not really a hundred targets for nuclear attack in either the Soviet Union or the United States, and only sick minds could think of destroying that many cities in either country. Each of the several thousand nuclear warheads on either side could obliterate a city much more thoroughly than Hiroshima and Nagasaki were destroyed. What purpose then, can these weapons conceivably serve? If the purpose is to ensure mutual deterrence, this could equally well be achieved with no more than 50 to 100 submarine-launched ballistic missiles on each side. Yet the mad race goes on. And continuing vertical proliferation will of necessity breed further horizontal proliferation.

One of the reasons given for maintaining such an unconscionably high level of overkill capacity is the "counterforce" argument. According to the counterforce theory, strategic nuclear arms should be used not for the hideous task of knocking out cities and their populations but rather against military targets such as missile silos, ammunition dumps, and nuclear bases, and for this purpose two or more warheads are needed for each target; in addition, sufficient arms must be kept in reserve for a second-strike capability against the enemy's cities if he launches a first strike against your strategic nuclear sites. What this argument conventiently overlooks is that a nuclear exchange of such magnitude would poison most of the inhabitants of the Northern Hemisphere with radioactive fallout and perhaps destroy the ozone layer of the earth's atmosphere, with all the unknown dangers that might entail. In either case, whether the arms were used against cities or against nuclear targets, such an exchange would constitute a form of international insanity and suicide.

Apart from the MIRVs discussed, the United States is presently developing a new, more accurate maneuverable missile called MARV, and there is talk of the U.S. and the Soviet Union building mobile ICBMs, although the U.S. announced at the time of the SALT I agreements that it would regard the building of these as contrary to the spirit of the SALT I agreements.

In addition, the U.S. is proceeding to develop a highly accurate long-range (up to 2,000 miles) nuclear cruise missile that could be launched from aircraft, submarines, or surface vessels and land within about 10 meters of its target. It has become a subject of disagreement and requires further international negotiation to determine whether or not these will be considered strategic weapons.

At the other end of the nuclear spectrum, the U.S. is continuing to develop and improve its tactical and battlefield nuclear weapons. While less is known about the Soviet Union's intentions and program, one can expect that it, too, is developing new generations of tactical nuclear weapons or "mini-nukes," which tend to blur the line of distinction between nuclear and conventional weapons.

The SALT agreements may have been a diplomatic success. They do tend to stabilize mutual deterrence between the two superpowers, at least for the present, on the basis of each side retaining a second-strike capability. They have also helped to promote the spirit of détente. But they have not served to achieve a cessation or any real limitation of the nuclear arms race, far less nuclear disarmament. In fact, many critics of SALT say that these negotiations have served only to replace the quantitative nuclear arms race with a more dangerous qualitative one, and that the action–reaction process that formerly fueled the nuclear arms race has now been transformed into an internal domestic technological competition for the improvement (if that is the right word) of the accuracy, variety, and lethality of weapons that proceeds by a dynamic of its own. It seems that the agreements already concluded, and indeed those now being ne-gotiated, are designed not to halt or reverse the arms race but rather to institutionalize it and regulate it so that it may continue within each country on its own momentum and under conditions of relatively less instability and insecurity for the two great powers—in other words, a blueprint for the continuation of the arms race under agreed-upon terms and conditions.

The depressing picture that emerges from these agreements is hardly likely to reassure the other nations of the world, nuclear as well as non-nuclear, that the nuclear arms race is being brought under control or that their security is being enhanced.

The Secondary Nuclear Powers

Up to this point we have been dealing with the nuclear arms race of the two superpowers. The United Kingdom, France, and China, however, are also continuing to develop arsenals of nuclear weapons. None of them, of course, is anywhere near a situation of comparability with the two superpowers, in fact, the nuclear forces of all three of these nuclear powers, taken together, would represent only a tiny fraction—a very small percentage—of the awesome nuclear weapon force possessed by the Soviet Union, and an even smaller fraction of that of the United States.

Nevertheless, each of the three secondary nuclear powers possesses a devastating arsenal of nuclear killing power of tremendous magnitude. They appear to be small, even insignificant forces only when compared to those of the superpowers. For example, the United Kingdom in 1975 had 4 Polaris submarines with 64 Polaris A-3 SLBMs carrying three 200-kiloton warheads each, and 50 medium-range Vulcan bombers each capable of carrying a bomb load of 10 tons. France had 3 Polaris-type submarines with 48 SLBMs carrying single 500-kiloton warheads, and was building 2 more nuclear missile submarines, in addition to about 2 dozen IRBMs and short-range nuclear land-based missiles and 52 Mirage strike aircraft and short-range bombers. China had several hundred nuclear weapons and about 100 IRBMs and MRBMs, some of which are reported to be in caves and to be mobile. It is developing a long-range ICBM and a nuclear missile–firing submarine. It also has some 100 medium-range bombers.

All three countries are regarded as great powers, though not in the superpower class, and each is a permanent member of the United Nations Security Council. Their reasons for going nuclear differed, but it can be assumed that they shared some common motivations, such as wanting to be able to deter an attack from either or both of the superpowers, national prestige, and the desire for a greater voice and influence in international affairs. As regards their desire for independent deterrent forces, it is obvious that the economic, industrial, and technological gap between them and the superpowers is so great that none of them (except perhaps China in the long-range future) can hope to acquire a nuclear capability that could in any way be comparable to that of the superpowers. Nevertheless, so great is the destructive power of nuclear weapons, and particularly of thermonuclear weapons, that each of the three powers must be regarded as having a credible deterrent force. Each of them has weapons several tens of times as powerful as those that destroyed Hiroshima and Nagasaki. And some of those in submarines or caves could survive a preemptive first strike and be capable of retaliating against the large cities of an attacker. How can anyone measure deterrence with precision? Would the risk of knocking out one or two or more large Soviet or American cities be a sufficient deterrent? No one knows, but I think that the risk of the destruction of Moscow or Leningrad, or of New York or Washington, would have a very powerful deterrent effect on the Soviet Union or the United States. It seems clear, at least to me, that even the secondary nuclear powers can justifiably claim to have a very credible deterrent capability. A nuclear exchange with either superpower would be suicidal for such secondary nuclear powers, as indeed it would be for the superpowers themselves. But in de Gaulle's phrase, their ability at least to "tear off the arm" of an attacker might very well deter an attack.

The irony, or rather the tragedy, of the "awful arithmetic" of nuclear weaponry is that the same reasons or arguments that led to the emergence of five nuclear powers can be used, whether rightly or wrongly is largely irrelevant, by the Nth nuclear power. The sixth, seventh, and eighth nuclear powers might be third-class nuclear powers who would have no effective deterrent capacity against either the superpowers or the secondary nuclear powers for many years or decades. But a third-class nuclear power would certainly have an overwhelming military advantage in its own local area or region if it were the sole nuclear power there; it would have a deterrent capability against any local attack even if it lost its monopoly and one or more countries in the region acquired nuclear weapons.

But there are a number of near-nuclear powers that would definitely not be third-class. Japan and West Germany, if they ever decided to go nuclear, would certainly be capable of becoming at least secondary nuclear powers and might eventually enter the superpower class. Countries such as Canada, Sweden, Italy, and Australia could certainly become secondary nuclear powers, along with perhaps, India, East Germany, the Netherlands, Belgium, and Switzerland. Somewhat further behind in terms of present resources and industrial developments would be South Africa, Spain, Taiwan, Argentina, Brazil, Norway, Denmark, Israel, Iran, and Czechoslovakia. The list could be extended or altered depending on the vagaries of economic and technological development and the effects of the energy crisis. All of the developed countries, as well as Mexico, Poland, Romania, South Korea, Egypt, and Yugoslavia, can also be considered potential nuclear powers, though not of secondary rank and not for some years to come.

This list is rather arbitrary and it not intended to suggest that any of the countries named will necessarly acquire nuclear weapons or in what order. It is merely an indication of the existing potentialities of various countries, more or less advanced in the field of nuclear technology and industrialization, to become nuclear powers if they decide to do so.

Chapter 3.   Atoms for Peace: The Proliferation of Nuclear Power Reactors and Plutonium

As we have seen, ever since the "Atoms for Peace" proposal of 1953 the United States has favored the promotion of the technology of peaceful uses of nuclear energy while insisting on controls, or "safeguards," in order to prevent diversion of that technology to military uses.

By 1963, the United States had entered into bilateral agreements for cooperation in the peaceful uses of atomic energy, with respect to either research or power reactors, with 28 non-nuclear countries as well as with Euratom and the IAEA. It had also agreed to provide nuclear assistance for peaceful purposes to 45 non-nuclear countries. All of the agreements with individual countries made provision for safeguards, including the right of the U.S. to send inspectors to verify that the nuclear materials were being used solely for peaceful purposes. Almost all of the safeguards were subsequently transferred to the IAEA by trilateral agreements. Agreements with Euratom and its member countries were implemented through Euratom, which had its own safeguards system.

The development and spread of nuclear power plants, which use nuclear reactors to generate electricity, at first proceeded at a slower pace than was originally expected. Recently, however, spurred on by a growing demand for electrical power, by the escalating price of oil, and by fears of a shortage of easily accessible fossil fuels, a widespread proliferation of nuclear power reactors is under way. Many reactors are just beginning to become operational or are under construction in both nuclear-weapon and non-nuclear-weapon states. These nuclear reactors, both research and power reactors, produce plutonium.

Types of Reactors

There are a number of different types of reactors. The most common one in use throughout the world utilizes low-enriched uranium (containing about 2 to 4% U235) as fuel and ordinary water as moderator. It is by far the most common type, since it was first developed by the nuclear-weapon states, who had large uranium enrichment facilities originally built to produce nuclear weapons. It is the most popular kind in the United States, where it is known as the light water reactor (LWR), and more than 70% of existing and planned reactors in all countries are of this type.

Another type of reactor is one that uses natural uranium (U238), with heavy water as moderator. It produces plutonium at a rate 50 to 100% greater than the LWR. This type was pioneered by Canada, which had abundant uranium resources but no enrichment facilities. It is known as the heavy water reactor (HWR). The United Kingdom and France at first developed gas-cooled natural uranium reactors (GCR), but have since switched to gas-cooled low-enriched uranium reactors.

Two other types of reactors are now under development and are likely to be in use in the 1980s. One is the high-temperature gas-cooled reactor (HTGR), which uses highly enriched uranium (90%) that is the equivalent of weapons grade. It is based on the thorium–uranium 233 fuel cycle, which is expected to operate with greater efficiency than either the LWR or HWR power plants. The other new type of reactor is known as the "breeder reactor" or "fast breeder reactor"; it uses plutonium and natural uranium and produces more fissionable plutonium than it consumes as it generates electric power, by converting the uranium 238 into plutonium 239. Several types of fast breeder reactors are now under development in the United States, West Germany, India, Italy, and Japan; France, the United Kingdom, and the Soviet Union already have such experimental reactors in operation. The liquid metal fast breeder reactor (LMFBR) is currently receiving a great deal of attention in research and development programs in the United States. Breeder reactors may prove to be more economical to operate than the other types because of the extra plutonium they produce. If they become popular they will result in the production and accumulation of vast quantities of plutonium.

The Nuclear Fuel Cycle

The typical nuclear fuel cycle for uranium–plutonium types of reactors involves six or seven stages as follows:

1. The uranium ore is mined.
2. The uranium contained in the ore is concentrated and purified as natural uranium, which consists of 99.3% uranium 238 and .7% uranium 235, which is the fissionable isotope.
3. The proportion of the fissionable uranium 235 isotope, which is increased in an enrichment plant from .7% to a range of about 3%,

for LWRs and about 90% for weapons purposes and for HTGRs. This step is by far the most complex and costly in the nuclear fuel cycle. It can be bypassed for the HWRs, which use natural uranium.

4. The next step is fuel fabrication, in which either natural or enriched uranium (or reprocessed plutonium) is put into the form desired as fuel rods for the reactor.

5. The fuel is put into the reactor, where relatively slow nuclear fission reactions take place to produce a continuous source of heat which is converted to electric power. After a period of operation lasting as much as a year or more, the irradiated or spent fuel is removed and is replaced by fresh fuel rods. In the LWRs, but not the HWRs, the reactor must be shut down to replace the fuel rods.

6. The spent fuel from the LWRs, which contains plutonium and other highly radioactive elements, is reprocessed in a chemical separation plant which separates out the plutonium and uranium from the other elements. Because the HWR uses natural uranium, which costs only $25 to $35 a pound, it is not economical to reprocess the spent fuel for reuse. At present, the spent fuel is stored and not reprocessed. It might be economical to reprocess the spent fuel if the price of natural uranium rises to $100 per pound.

7. The reprocessed plutonium and uranium can be recycled and used again, while the other radioactive elements are stored as radioactive wastes or for special uses.

As we indicated above, the enrichment step is omitted for HWRs, but it is necessary to obtain heavy water, either by manufacturing it or by purchase. For HTGRs, the fuel cycle is known as the thorium–uranium 233 cycle, since the reactor also uses thorium, which is converted into fissionable uranium 233, which can also be recycled as fuel.

Uranium ore exists in most parts of the world, and most countries can mine and mill uranium if they are willing to pay the price. For commercial power reactors, countries are interested in obtaining uranium supplies at low cost. But if a country is interested in obtaining uranium for weapons purposes, the additional cost of mining low-grade ore is not very significant.

Most of the world's low-cost (under $25 per pound) uranium comes from a few countries—the United States, the Soviet Union, Canada, South Africa, France, Australia, Spain, Gabon, and Niger. China, Czechoslovakia, and East Germany also produce uranium, while Argentina, Brazil, India, and Iran, have substantial resources. Sweden has large reserves of shale containing higher-cost (up to $50 or more per pound) uranium. On the other hand, a number of highly advanced industrial countries with large nuclear power programs, such as the United Kingdom, West Germany, Italy, and Japan, have very little uranium resources and must import their uranium fuel. But almost all countries have some uranium. Brazil and India both have large resources of thorium, which can be converted into fissionable U233; but until the development of the HTGR, thorium was not used as a nuclear fuel.

As regards uranium enrichment, there are gaseous diffusion plants in each of the five nuclear-weapon powers—that is, the United States, the Soviet Union, the United Kingdom, France, and China—but in no other countries. These were originally built to produce highly enriched uranium for nuclear weapons. However, the United Kingdom, West Germany, and the Netherlands have entered into a tripartite agreement to develop and produce enriched uranium by an alternative process known as the gas-centrifuge process, and Japan is also developing a gas-centrifuge process. A third technology, developed in West Germany, is the jet-nozzle (or Becker-nozzle) process. West Germany has agreed to sell an enrichment plant based on this process to Brazil. South Africa has announced that it is developing its own secret enrichment process, which a number of experts believe is related to the jet-nozzle process. Finally, laser techniques to separate uranium isotopes are under scientific investigation in several countries, including Australia, West Germany, Israel, and the United States. Many experts believe that the laser technique may prove to be cheaper than the others and very effective. Other technologies for the enrichment of uranium are being studied, but at the present time they appear to be more expensive and less advanced than the generally known methods. Iran has entered into agreements with the United States and France for enrichment of Iranian uranium in the two countries.

Large commercial fuel fabrication plants exist in each of the five nuclear-weapon states and are also in operation or are planned in a few other countries—Argentina, Austria, Belgium, Brazil, Canada, India, Italy, Japan, the Netherlands, Spain, Sweden, and West Germany. Chemical reprocessing plants, also known as chemical separation plants exist in the nuclear countries (although none is at present operating in the United States) and in Belgium and India. Construction has begun or is planned in Canada, West Germany, Italy, Japan, and Sweden. The technology for both fuel fabrication and chemical separation is rather complicated, and large-scale plants are necessary for economical operation. Pilot separation plants exist in several countries, however, including Argentina, Japan, Spain, and Taiwan. It has been estimated that a separation plant capable of producing 15 to 20 kilograms of plutonium 239 a year (enough for 2 or 3 explosive devices) could be built in a year or two by any reasonably advanced country at a cost of 1 to 3 million dollars. Even if the cost has been grossly underestimated, it is clear that the amount of money involved is not large.

Fissionable materials are extremely valuable. For example, at 1974 prices, highly enriched uranium (90%) was worth about $15,000 per kilogram and low-enriched uranium (3%) about $330 per kilogram. Plutonium was worth about $10,000 per kilogram, or about double the value of gold.

Growth of Nuclear Power Production

Most of the world's nuclear reactors are at present concentrated in the industrially advanced countries, where, until recently, only large reactors of a size of 1,000 or more megawatts were considered economically efficient for power production (although many are smaller than this size). At the beginning of 1975 there were about 180 operable power reactors in 19 countries. Of these, the United States had 55, the United Kingdom 29, the U.S.S.R. 16, France 10, West Germany 8, and Canada and Japan 7 each. But such is the recent burgeoning in the production of nuclear reactors that as of 1975 the U.S. had commitments for 180 additional reactors, France for 39, West Germany for 29, Japan for 22, Canada for 15, Iran for 10 or 12, and Brazil for 8. By 1985, the number of operating power reactors throughout the world is expected to have quadrupled.

There are some 400 nuclear reactors of various kinds in operation today in 49 countries, and it is estimated that about 250 research and 100 power reactors are operating in the non-nuclear-weapon states.

While reactors for power production are large and expensive undertakings that take five or more years for construction and start-up, research reactors of a few megawatts in size are relatively simple and easy to build. In fact, once any country has been given a research reactor, it is not difficult for it to build one or more by itself. And many such reactors can be utilized or "programmed" to produce the maximum amount of plutonium 239 if their operation for generating power at the lowest possible cost is not the object. A small research experimental reactor using natural uranium as a fuel, which produces more plutonium than one using enriched uranium, can be built at relatively low cost. And since low-grade uranium resources are present in many countries, these reactors can be used to produce plutonium in sufficient quantities to make one or two bombs a year. As we mentioned above, a small chemical separation plant can also be built at relatively low cost. As far back as 1966, Dr. Glenn Seaborg, the chairman of the U.S. Atomic Energy Commission, stated with regard to the process of separating weapons-grade plutonium from the plutonium produced in civil power reactors, "It is perfectly feasible to build a clandestine chemical processing plant using readily available technology and equipment." Now, ten years later, it is even more feasible to do so.

The development of small-scale research or pilot plants gives a country a dual technology and capability, both for peaceful power production and for nuclear weapons production. The proliferation of reactors to non-nuclear countries provides them with the equipment, the know-how, and the fissionable material that will eventually enable them to build their own bombs or nuclear explosive devices.

In 1971, the Fourth United Nations Conference on the Peaceful Uses of Atomic Energy estimated that nuclear power would account for about one-fourth of the total installed electrical generating capacity in the world by 1985 and about one-half by the year 2000. In the United States alone, President Ford, in his State of the Union address on January 15, 1975, called for the construction of 200 additional power reactors by the year 1985.

There was a great proliferation of nuclear power reactors even before the energy crisis became acute in October 1973. Pre–energy crisis estimates and forecasts of future nuclear power capacity varied widely, but all anticipated a very rapid increase.

Current information concerning the future production of electricity from nuclear power reactors, compiled from forecasts of the U.S. Atomic Energy Commission in 1974 and of ERDA in 1975 is as follows:

Estimated Output for the United States

1975—37,000 megawatts (55 nuclear power reactors)
1980—85,000 to 112,000 megawatts
1990—410,000 to 575,000 megawatts
2000—850,000 to 1,400,000 megawatts (about 1,000 nuclear power reactors)

Estimated Output for the Rest of the World

1975—35,000 megawatts (100 nuclear power reactors)
1980—113,000 to 157,000 megawatts
1990—640,000 to 900,000 megawatts
2000—1,600,000 to 2,550,000 megawatts (about 1,500 nuclear power reactors)

Forecasts of both U.S. and world output of electricity from nuclear power reactors vary quite markedly, particularly for the longer-range future. Estimates of the IAEA are considerably higher than those set out here. (See, for example, E. Goodman and R. Krymm, "Nuclear Power Growth and Fuel Requirements 1975–2000," *IAEA Bulletin* [June 1975].) The 1974 forecasts have been scaled down by later ones, but the growth trend seems to be clearly established.

At the present time, most of the world's energy is obtained from fossil fuels and only about 6% from nuclear power plants. Some energy is also obtained from hydroelectric power, and an even smaller amount is derived from wind and from tidal, geothermal, and solar power. In the more distant future, fusion or thermonuclear power may become an important source of energy; but for the foreseeable future, the fossil fuels and nuclear energy will by far continue to be the main sources of power, with an accelerating advantage going to nuclear fuels over fossil fuels, despite the dangers from pollution and radiation hazards. The Atomic Energy Commission has predicted that by the year 2000, about 55% of all the electricity generated in the United States and in the non-Communist world will be produced by nuclear power.

Impact of the Energy Crisis

The energy shortage that became critical in October 1973 initiated many dramatic changes in the area of nuclear power development. While it is not possible to forecast all of the consequences with any precision, they are undoubtedly likely to be immense, as is apparent from the estimates quoted above.

Until the sudden great increase in the price of oil in 1973, it was considered by the IAEA that nuclear power plants of 600 megawatts or larger were necessary for nuclear power to be competitive with oil in the developing countries. After the quadrupling of the price of oil, however, it is considered that nuclear power plants in the 200- to 400-megawatt range, or even smaller, may be competitive in those countries.

According to the U.S. Atomic Industrial Forum, a non-profit organization formed to promote the peaceful use of nuclear energy, in 1974 nuclear power plants in the United States were producing electricity at about 40% less cost than fossil fuel power plants. One kilowatt-hour of electricity produced by nuclear power cost an average of 10.52 mills, as compared to 17.03 mills for fossil fuels. (A mill is one-tenth of a cent.)

Euratom regards the promotion of nuclear energy as more important than ever because of the oil crisis. In February 1974, it estimated that, after 1980, nuclear energy could supply all future increases in electricity production in its member countries and could first limit and then reduce the role of petroleum products in electricity generation.

Whatever the differences in the various projections for the future, it it clear that there is likely to be a very marked proliferation of nuclear power reactors in both the industrial and the developing countries. The huge increase in the availability of plutonium and other fissionable materials will greatly multiply the problems of preventing the diversion of such materials from peaceful to military uses.

Growth of Plutonium Production

The U.S. Atomic Energy Commission has proposed that the nuclear power industry be authorized to use plutonium together with low-enriched uranium as fuel in commercial reactors, and that the plutonium be recycled. Plutonium recycling would mean that much more plutonium would be used in power reactors and would be available in the U.S. and throughout the world.

It is worth recalling that the Alamogordo and Nagasaki bombs were plutonium bombs while the one at Hiroshima was a uranium 235 (U235) bomb. It is generally considered that 5 to 7 kilograms of Pu are needed for a small bomb of the Nagasaki size and 10 to 15 kilograms of U235 for a small bomb of the Hiroshima size. The yield of each of these two bombs was in the 15-to 20–kiloton range, i.e., the equivalent of 15,000 to 20,000 tons of high explosive.

It has been estimated that the United States has produced, since 1945, about 500,000 kilograms of fissionable plutonium, mainly for military purposes. Since only about 2% of this has been used, the balance is stored.

A large nuclear reactor of 600 to 1,000 megawatts can produce from 150 to 300 kilograms of plutonium annually, depending on how it is operated and whether it uses enriched or natural uranium. Forecasts of future production of plutonium have varied widely. According to the 1974 estimate of the United States Atomic Energy Commission, the amount of Pu that will be produced from power reactors in the world over the next twenty-five years is as follows:

T A B L E 3 – 1. Production of Fissionable Plutonium, in Kilograms

	United States		Foreign		Total	
YEAR	ANNUAL	CUMU-LATIVE	ANNUAL	CUMU-LATIVE	ANNUAL	CUMU-LATIVE
1975	230	230	3,600	9,600	3,830	9,830
1980	10,300	36,900	16,500	62,600	26,800	99,500
1985	30,400	143,200	46,400	223,500	76,800	366,700
1990	63,200	388,000	96,700	595,500	159,900	983,500
2000	229,000	1,767,300	454,300	3,117,700	683,300	4,885,000

According to this estimate, sufficient plutonium will be produced by 1980 to make 15,000 to 20,000 small Nagasaki-size bombs a year. Since plutonium has a half-life of about 24,400 years, it can last for well over 200,000 years, and the cumulative total in existence will keep growing to enormous quantities. By 1985, there will be enough Pu in the world to make more than 60,000 Nagasaki-size bombs, and by the year 2000, enough for more than 750,000 such bombs. Since Pu is one of the most poisonous substances known, the mere task of safe storage and inventory of such huge quantities will be staggering, as will be the problem of disposing of radioactive wastes.

How much plutonium will be produced depends, of course, on the amount of power produced by nuclear reactors. This in turn will depend on whether plutonium recycling and fast breeder reactors come into general use and on whether the public will permit the uncontrolled proliferation of nuclear power plants, or whether fears concerning their safety, radiation and pollution hazards, and the dangers of nuclear weapon proliferation will result in their limitation. There appear to be increasing doubts on the part of members of the public and governmental officials about the further spread of nuclear plants as a source of power, and a growing debate can be expected about the relative costs and advantages and disadvantages of nuclear energy as compared with fossil fuels and other sources of energy such as solar or geothermal power, wind and tides, and eventual fusion or thermonuclear processes.

Thus, any long-term estimates of the production of nuclear energy and of plutonium should be regarded with extreme caution. It is certain, however, that for the next decade at least the use of nuclear energy as a source of power will increase greatly, and with it the risks of nuclear weapon proliferation.

There are already charges of quantities of nuclear material amounting to more than a thousand kilograms lost or unaccounted for in the United States. Even if such losses or material unaccounted for were to occur at the extraordinary and almost impossibly low rate of one-tenth of one percent, the amount involved, in view of the huge quantity of nuclear material in existence, would be sufficient to make dozens of bombs.

As more and more power is produced from nuclear energy, there will be a widespread proliferation not only of research and power reactors but of all nuclear facilities and activities involved in the fuel cycle, including enrichment plants, fuel fabrication plants, and chemical separation plants. There will also be an increasing traffic in and transport of nuclear material from one plant and locality to another. This will provide the widespread dissemination of knowledge of nuclear technology and increasing opportunities and temptations for national governments and agencies, as well as for subnational nongovernmental groups, to acquire fissionable material and nuclear explosives.

Chapter 4.   Steps Leading to the Non-Proliferation Regime

It is widely assumed that international action to prevent the spread of nuclear weapons was formalized in and codified by the Treaty on the Non-Proliferation of Nuclear Weapons. While it is true that the NPT (Non-Proliferation Treaty) is the cornerstone of the international structure created to prevent nuclear proliferation, there has developed over the years a complex of treaties and agreements constituting an international system or regime for coping with the problem.

In addition to the NPT, other treaties that deal with the problem, in a direct though partial way, are the Treaty Banning Nuclear Weapon Tests in the Atmosphere, in Outer Space and Under Water (commonly known as the Partial Test Ban Treaty or PTBT) and the Treaty for the Prohibition of Nuclear Weapons in Latin America (the Treaty of Tlatelolco), together with its control organization (OPANAL). In a sense, the non-proliferation regime also includes the treaties that have been and may be agreed upon at the Strategic Arms Limitation Talks (SALT), insofar as such treaties attempt to implement the provisions of the NPT calling for an underground test ban, for the cessation of the nuclear arms race, and for nuclear disarmament. Treaties or agreements that may be entered into in the future to promote the peaceful uses of nuclear energy, as provided for in the NPT, would also be part of the non-proliferation regime.

The IAEA and the European Atomic Energy Community (Euratom) are not, strictly speaking, integral parts of the non-proliferation regime, since they were created not to prevent weapons proliferation but rather to promote cooperation in the peaceful uses of nuclear energy. Nevertheless, to the extent that the IAEA provides safeguards against the diversion of fissionable material to the manufacture of nuclear weapons or explosive devices, as provided for in the NPT, it can also be regarded as constituting a part of the regime.

The Antarctic Treaty of 1959 provided for the demilitarization and denuclearization of Antarctica and specifically prohibited any nuclear testing or disposal of radioactive waste material there. The Outer Space Treaty of 1967 provided for the denuclearization of outer space and the demilitarization of the moon and other celestial bodies. The Seabed Treaty of 1971 provided for the denuclearization of the seabed, the ocean floor, and the subsoil thereof. These treaties can, in a sense, be regarded as limiting or preventing the proliferation of nuclear weapons to the areas concerned, but since those areas are not inhabited regions and no governments are located there, they may be left aside for our purposes when considering the structure of the non-proliferation regime.

All the discussions on nuclear arms control and disarmament since the end of World War II have been concerned with two basic goals: first, limiting and eventually eliminating atoms for war; and second, promoting and exploiting atoms for peace. The basic dilemma has been that the development of nuclear energy for either purpose necessarily served to enhance its usefulness for the other. It may not be possible to make an exact statistical computation of the correlation between the two types of uses, but there is no doubt that there is a direct interrelationship between the two potential uses and that they have a reinforcing and symbiotic effect on each other. This has resulted in two widely held competitive beliefs. One is that the development of military uses of nuclear energy provides "spin-off" benefits for the development of peaceful uses. The other holds that the development of peacful applications, and in particular the proliferation of nuclear power plants, leads to the development of military uses and the proliferation of nuclear weapons.

In essence, all of the efforts toward and negotiations for nuclear arms control and disarmament have had two aims: First, limiting, with a view to eventually eliminating, all nuclear weapons; and second, preventing their spread to other countries. In a word, the primary objective was to prevent the further proliferation of nuclear weapons, both "vertically" and "horizontally," and the ultimate objective was to eliminate them entirely.

With the failure of the Baruch Plan, little hope remained for achieving the elimination of nuclear weapons. Nevertheless, efforts continued in this direction. In 1955, at the meetings of the Sub-Committee of the Disarmament Commission in London, the four Western members (Canada, France, the United Kingdom, and the U.S.), acting jointly, and the Soviet Union put forward alternative programs for comprehensive disarmament that provided, among other things, for a ban on the production, testing, and use of nuclear weapons in stages and for their elimination at the end of the program. These plans were aborted at the Geneva Summit Conference in July 1955 when the Western powers abandoned negotiations for comprehensive disarmament and proposed instead partial measures that left aside all provisions for nuclear arms control or disarmament. President Eisenhower submitted a proposal for aerial inspections to prevent surprise attack, Prime Minister Eden proposed the joint inspection of forces on either side of the line dividing Eastern and Western Europe, and Prime Minister Faure proposed plans for the financial supervision of disarmament, with part of the funds resulting from the reduction of military budgets to be used for domestic peaceful purposes and for the developing countries.

In 1962, at the meetings of the Eighteen-Nation Disarmament Committee (ENDC) in Geneva, the Soviet Union and the United States again each proposed a plan for general and complete disarmament in three stages—including provisions banning the testing, production, and use of nuclear weapons and providing for their phased reduction and elimination at the end of the third stage. For the first time, both plans contained express provisions, operative during the first stage, prohibiting nuclear states from transferring control over nuclear weapons or information about their production to non-nuclear states and also prohibiting non-nuclear states from manufacturing or acquiring nuclear weapons. Negotiations on the respective plans became deadlocked, however, over questions of priority for the various measures, questions of control and verification, and matters relating to peacekeeping. In 1963, serious negotiations on general and complete disarmament were abandoned, and thereafter negotiations in the Eighteen-Nation Committee and elsewhere concentrated on partial or limited measures of arms control and disarmament. Since then there have been no negotiations aimed at eliminating nuclear weapons.

Efforts To Ban Nuclear Weapons Tests

Suggestions to ban nuclear weapons tests, or experimental explosions, as they are sometimes called, as a means of limiting or controlling the development or spread of nuclear weapons were first made in 1954. The United States exploded the world's first hydrogen or thermonuclear bomb in October 1952, and the Soviet Union conducted a similar experiment in August 1953. On March 1, 1954, the U.S. exploded a thermonuclear device on the Bikini Atoll which had a yield of 14 megatons, the largest nuclear test up to that time. That test produced more radioactive fallout than had been expected and over a larger than anticipated area. It affected not only some Marshall Islanders about 100 miles away, but also the crew of a Japanese fishing boat, the *Fukurya Maru* (*Lucky Dragon*) that was outside the test area. Worldwide concern about radioactive fallout from nuclear testing led to protests by the Japanese Diet and the Bandung Conference of nonaligned nations and to suggestions to restrict or suspend such tests.

On April 2, 1954, Prime Minister Nehru proposed "some sort of . . .

stand-still agreement in respect, at least, of these actual explosions, even if arrangements about the discontinuance of production and stockpiling must await more substantial agreements among those principally concerned." Later that year, in the General Assembly, Burma called for an agreement on the "cessation of all further experiments designed to produce greater and better thermonuclear and atomic weapons." The idea of a test ban was first taken up by a nuclear power in 1955, when the Soviet Union proposed (on May 10), as part of a larger disarmament plan, that "as one of the first measures for the execution of the program for the reduction of armaments and the prohibition of atomic weapons, States possessing atomic and hydrogen weapons shall undertake to discontinue tests of these weapons." The question of banning nuclear tests was actively discussed during the ensuing year. At the 1955 General Assembly, the Soviet Union and India called for an early and separate agreement on the banning of all nuclear tests without supervision, holding that no significant testing could go undetected. The United States, Great Britain, and France, however, regarded the limitation and eventual banning of nuclear testing, with adequate supervision, as part of a comprehensive disarmament program. India and Sweden also suggested a moratorium on nuclear tests and various other proposals were made, but all came to naught.

At the meeting of the Five-power Sub-Committee of the Disarmament Commission in London in 1957, the Soviet Union proposed that, independently of other measures, there should be an agreement on "the immediate cessation of all atomic and hydrogen tests if only for a period of two or three years" as well as "the establishment of an international commission" to supervise the agreement and "the establishment on a basis of reciprocity of control posts on the territory of the Soviet Union, the United States of America, and the United Kingdom and in the Pacific Ocean area." The four Western powers, insisted, however, that the suspension of nuclear tests be linked to the cessation of the production of fissionable material for weapons purposes and also to other disarmament measures. In April 1958, Premier Khrushchev wrote to President Eisenhower that the Soviet Union had decided to end nuclear testing and called on the Western powers to do likewise, while reserving the right to resume testing if the Western powers continued to do so. No agreement was reached with respect to the suspension of nuclear testing, and all three powers—the United States, the United Kingdom, and the Soviet Union—resumed testing and continued doing so until October of that year.

In the meantime, however, the United States and the Soviet Union agreed to convene a conference of experts to study the possibility of detecting violations of a possible agreement on the suspension of nuclear tests. The conference of experts met in July and August and unanimously concluded that the various methods for detecting nuclear explosions made it possible, within limits, to detect and identify nuclear explosions down to 1 to 5 kilotons. The experts, hence, considered it technically feasible to establish a workable and effective control system. They noted that some 20 to 100 earthquakes each year would be indistinguishable from underground tests of 5 kilotons and would require on-site inspection.

The Soviet Union, the United Kingdom, and the United States subsequently agreed to begin negotiations in Geneva on October 31, 1958, to reach agreement on a treaty for the discontinuance of nuclear weapons tests on the basis of the experts' report. The U.S. and the United Kingdom also proposed that, subject to reciprocity, nuclear testing be suspended for one year from the beginning of the negotiations. This voluntary suspension or moratorium actually went into effect on November 3, 1958, and remained in effect until the Soviet Union resumed testing on September 1, 1961. In the meantime, France, which had announced that it was proceeding with plans to conduct its own nuclear tests, stated that it would not sign a test ban treaty unless it were accompanied by other measures of nuclear disarmament. France subsequently exploded its first atomic bomb on February 13, 1960.

The Conference on the Discontinuance of Nuclear Weapon Tests, composed of the Soviet Union, the United Kingdom, and the United States, began on schedule on October 31, 1958, and continued until January 9, 1962, when its work was transferred in March of that year to the Eighteen-Nation Disarmament Committee. At first the conference appeared to be making considerable progress, and it had actually reached provisional agreement on a number of articles of a draft treaty on the discontinuance of nuclear testing. But the U-2 aircraft incident in May 1960, when an American spy plane was shot down over the Soviet Union, along with the growing dissatisfaction of the Soviet Union with the way things were developing in the Congo, hardened the Soviet position and all progress was blocked. The Soviet Union also reverted to the position that the test ban issue must be considered within the context of the question of general and complete disarmament.

On August 30, 1961, the Soviet government announced that it was going to resume carrying out nuclear weapons tests, and it did so on September 1. On September 3, the United Kingdom and the United States proposed an end to all atmospheric tests without international control. On September 15, the United States resumed underground testing. In October, the Soviet Union announced that it would test a 50-megaton bomb. On October 27, the General Assembly adopted a resolution solemnly appealing to the government of the Soviet Union to refrain from carrying out its intention to explode in the atmosphere a 50-megaton bomb. The test explosion was carried out, however, on October 30. Its actual yield was over 50 megatons, and estimates of the size of the monster explosion, the largest ever undertaken, varied from 57 megatons to almost 100 megatons.

In November, the General Assembly adopted two resolutions. The first, proposed by a group of nonaligned nations, urged the nuclear powers to refrain from further test explosions pending the conclusion of internationally binding agreements. The second, proposed by the United Kingdom and the United States, reaffirmed the urgent need for reaching an agreement prohibiting all nuclear weapons tests under effective control, which "would be a first step towards reversing the dangerous and burdensome arms race, would inhibit the spread of nuclear weapons to other countries, would contribute to the reduction of international tension and would eliminate any health hazards associated with nuclear testing."

In March 1962, the Eighteen-Nation Disarmament Committee convened in Geneva to consider proposals for general and complete disarmament and also partial measures of disarmament, which came to be known as "collateral measures." Among the latter was the question of the cessation of nuclear weapons tests. On April 16, a joint memorandum was submitted by the eight nonaligned members of the ENDC: Brazil, Burma, Ethiopia, India, Mexico, Nigeria, Sweden, and the United Arab Republic (Egypt). The joint memorandum stated that there were possibilities for establishing, by agreement, a system of continuous observation and effective control on a purely scientific and nonpolitical basis. The system could be built upon already existing national networks of observation posts and institutions together with new posts as agreed. The memorandum also raised the possibility of setting up an international commission consisting of highly qualified scientists, possibly from nonaligned countries, which would process all data received from the agreed system of observation posts and report on any nuclear explosion or "suspicious event." All parties to the treaty would be obliged to furnish the proposed commission with the facts necessary to establish the nature of any suspicious and significant event, and the parties to the treaty "could invite" the commission to visit their territories or the site of the event that was in doubt. The Soviet Union accepted the proposals in the joint memorandum as the basis for further negotiations, while the United Kingdom and the United States would only go as far as accepting the document as *one* of the bases for negotiation, but in fact they disapproved of it. They differed with the Soviet Union on the interpretation of the joint memorandum—in particular, on whether it set forth obligatory or optional provisions for on-site inspection. Only provisions for obligatory on-site inspection were acceptable to them.

In August, the United States and the United Kingdom submitted two alternative draft treaties. One was for a comprehensive test ban with an unspecified quota of on-site inspections in the case of suspicious underground events. The other was for a partial test ban limited to the three noncontroversial environments—that is, to tests in the atmosphere, in outer space, and under water—and without any international verification. The Soviet Union rejected both draft treaties, but on September 10 proposed the use of automatic seismic stations ("black boxes") in addition to existing national means of detection—i.e., without international verification. Two or three such stations could be established on the territory of each of the nuclear powers, along with some in neighboring countries. The United States agreed that the "black boxes" might be a useful adjunct to manned detection stations, but it would not relax the requirement for manned stations or on-site inspections.

When the Eighteen-Nation Disarmament Committee reconvened in February 1963, it concentrated on a comprehensive test ban treaty in all environments. The Soviet Union proposed 2 or 3 on-site inspections a year, such as had been proposed by Premier Khrushchev to President Eisenhower in correspondence. The United States, which had originally proposed 12 to 20 on-site inspections, now insisted on 8 to 10, which it later reduced to 7. Similarly, the Soviet Union proposed the establishment of three automatic seismic stations, while the United States proposed seven "black boxes." The three African nonaligned members of the committee submitted a joint memorandum suggesting a compromise of "three, four or so" on-site inspections a year or an adequately proportionate figure spread over more years.

The Partial Test Ban Treaty, 1963

On June 10, it was announced that the Soviet Union, the United States, and the United Kingdom had agreed to hold talks in Moscow in mid-July on the cessation of nuclear tests. On July 2, Premier Khrushchev said that the insistence by the United States and the United Kingdom on on-site inspections made an underground test ban treaty impossible, but the Soviet Union was now prepared to sign a limited treaty banning tests in the three noncontroversial environments.

The Treaty Banning Nuclear Weapon Tests in the Atmosphere, in Outer Space and Under Water was signed in Moscow on August 5, 1963. (The text of the treaty is set out in Appendix II.) By 1975, 106 countries had become parties to the treaty. France and the People's Republic of China have not signed or become parties to the treaty, and 14 countries, including Algeria, Argentina and Pakistan have signed but not ratified it. The Preamble of the treaty states that the government of the United States, the United Kingdom, and the Soviet Union, "seeking to achieve the discontinuance of all test explosions of nuclear weapons for all time, determined to continue negotiations to this end, . . . have agreed as follows." The treaty prohibits not only nuclear weapons test explosions but also "any other nuclear explosion" in the three environments. Underground explosions are not banned unless they cause radioactive debris to be present outside the territory of the state where the explosion is conducted, but the treaty explicitly states that this provision is "without prejudice to the conclusion of a treaty resulting in the permanent banning of all nuclear test explosions, including all such explosions underground, the conclusion of which, as the Parties have stated in the preamble to this Treaty, they seek to achieve."

The treaty also contains an article known as the "withdrawal clause" whereby each party can withdraw from the treaty on giving three months' notice of such withdrawal, if it decides that extraordinary events, related to the subject matter of the treaty, have jeopardized its supreme interests. This was the first time that a withdrawal clause had been included in any arms control treaty; it established a sort of precedent and it has now become standard practice to include a similar clause in every arms control treaty, multilateral or bilateral. Some scholars have tended to regret this as reflecting an overly permissive approach that enables a party to a treaty to escape too easily from the commitments undertaken. The practice is defended, however, on the ground that it accords with present-day realities. It is highly unlikely that any sovereign state would continue to abide by any treaty or international obligation that it regarded as jeopardizing its supreme interests.

The Partial Test Ban Treaty (PTBT) entered into force on October 10, 1963. The treaty was hailed at the time as the first significant breakthrough in efforts to control and limit the nuclear arms race. It was considered that the treaty would put an effective brake on the development of new and more sophisticated nuclear weapons as well as limit the possibilities for the spread of such weapons. Although underground tests were excluded from the ban, nobody foresaw at that time that the rate of underground testing would exceed that of previous tests in the atmosphere and the other environments. Rather, it was thought that since underground tests were somewhat more complicated to conduct than tests in the atmosphere, the development of new and more sophisticated nuclear weapons would be effectively restricted. These expectations, however, have not been borne out in fact. Underground testing has provided a loophole for the development of an entire range of new weapons, from "mininukes" to weapons in the multimegaton range. Nor has the Partial Test Ban Treaty prevented the emergence of new nuclear powers. China and France, who are not parties to the treaty, conduct nuclear weapons tests in the atmosphere, and India, which is a party, has conducted a nuclear test underground.

But in November 1963, in the somewhat euphoric atmosphere that prevailed at that time, the General Assembly welcomed the treaty, noting with satisfaction that the Preamble stated that the parties were seeking to achieve the discontinuance of all test explosions of nuclear weapons for all time and were determined to continue negotiations to this end. The Assembly called on all states to become parties to the treaty and requested the Eighteen-Nation Disarmament Committee to continue with a sense of urgency its negotiations to achieve the objectives set forth in the Preamble.

Such, in brief, was the long and tortuous history of nine years of efforts to achieve a test ban, which resulted in the Partial Test Ban Treaty of 1963. During that period the various parties kept changing their position from time to time as to whether a test ban should be linked to a cutoff of production or to general and complete disarmament or other disarmament measures; whether on-site inspection was needed and, if so, how much; and whether a test ban should be partial or comprehensive. It seemed that the parties were struggling to avoid halting nuclear tests. In fact, when it looked as though the parties might be forced to agree to stop weapons tests, some American scientists dreamed up the false notion of "clean" bombs with practically no radioactive fallout and the perhaps equally dubious idea of explosions for peaceful purposes—seeking almost any pretext to be able to continue nuclear testing. Finally, compelled by public opinion and by fears of radioactive fallout entering the food chain and causing leukemia, bone cancer, genetic damage, and other health hazards, and despite soothing but incorrect reports by government agencies that the tests were relatively innocuous, the parties were forced to agree to stop the tests that were most dangerous to health.

In January 1958, a deputation of scientists led by Nobel laureate Dr. Linus Pauling had presented to Secretary-General Dag Hammarskjöld a petition signed by nine thousand scientists from forty-three countries, including some dozens of other Nobelists, pointing to the grave dangers arising from nuclear testing and urging that "an international agreement to stop the testing of nuclear bombs be made now." Some observers credit this petition with playing an important role in leading to the moratorium on testing that began in 1958. In any case, the Partial Test Ban Treaty is one of the few instances in the history of the efforts for arms control and disarmament wherein public opinion had a direct and observable effect on military policies and actions. Even Khrushchev acknowledges, in his *Khrushchev Remembers,* that public concern in the Soviet Union was a factor that helped prod the Soviee Union to agree to halt nuclear tests in the atmosphere.

This period is replete with lost opportunities. On several occasions it seemed that the Conference on the Disarmament of Nuclear Weapons Tests was approaching agreement on a comprehensive test ban, but something always occurred to thwart agreement. And when the Soviet Union in 1962 and 1963 offered two or three on-site inspections a year to verify a ban on underground tests, a comprehensive test ban was within easy reach. Moreover, since the United States was far ahead of the Soviet Union in nuclear weapons technology, it would have been clearly in its interest to freeze the situation on the existing basis. The only rational explanation of why the United States rejected this offer is that, because of the policies of the atomic energy and defense establishments, it wished to continue to make technological and qualitative improvements in its nuclear weapons systems. Had a comprehensive test ban been agreed upon at that time—

when, under the pressure of public opinion, almost every country in the world, with the exception of China and France, appeared committed to end all nuclear tests—the problem of preventing the spread of nuclear weapons might have become easily manageable.

Unfortunately, that was not to be. And the history of the twelve years of efforts since the entry into force of the PTB has, if anything, been even more tortuous and frustrating than the period prior to the treaty. One pretext after another was raised by both sides as a reason or excuse for not agreeing to an underground test ban, despite the repeated calls and pleas of the overwhelming majority of members and successive Secretaries-General of the United Nations. The failure of the nuclear parties to the NPT to live up to their commitments regarding nuclear disarmament is set out in Chapter 14.

Treaty for the Prohibition of Nuclear Weapons in Latin America (The Treaty of Tlatelolco)

In the latter half of the 1950s, two different approaches to the problem of preventing the spread of nuclear weapons were explored: first, the creation of nuclear-free zones from which all nuclear weapons would be prohibited; and second, negotiation of a treaty that would specifically ban the dissemination of nuclear weapons by the nuclear powers and the acquisition of such weapons by states not possessing them. These two approaches were in addition to the ban on nuclear weapons tests, which it was recognized, was not only important in itself, but would also help to prevent the proliferation of nuclear weapons.

In 1958, the so-called "Rapacki Plan" was proposed by the foreign minister of Poland for the denuclearization of Central Europe (Poland, Czechoslovakia, and East and West Germany). Since that time, various proposals have been put forward for the denuclearization of other geographical areas, including the Balkans, the Mediterranean, the Middle East, the Nordic Countries, and Asia and the Pacific Region. Formal and specific plans, however, have dealt mainly with Central Europe, Africa, and Latin America. All of these proposals except those concerning Latin America and Africa have failed to make progress because of the complex political and strategic questions involved. In 1974, the proposal for a nuclear-free zone in the Middle East was revived and a new proposal for a nuclear-free zone in South Asia was put forward; these two proposals are dealt with in Chapter 15, dealing with nuclear-free zones.

In general, all these proposals for nuclear-free zones were supported by the Communist states, but those affecting Europe, the Mediterranean, and Asia were opposed by the Western powers as they would involve the withdrawal of Western nuclear bases and would thus give some military and political advantages to the Communist states. The Western powers argued that any arrangements for nuclear-free zones should be initiated by the major countries in the area, should not upset the existing military balance, and should be subject to verification.

In 1961, on the initiative of a number of African states, the General Assembly adopted a resolution aimed at making Africa a "denuclearized zone." It called on all member states to refrain from carrying out nuclear tests in Africa and from testing, storing, or transporting nuclear weapons in the territory, waters, or air space of Africa; it also called on all member states to respect the continent of Africa as a denuclearized zone. In 1965, and again in 1974, the General Assembly adopted resolutions which endorsed the denuclearization of Africa and called upon all states to refrain from using or threatening to use nuclear weapons on the African continent; it also called upon all states to take action to prevent the spread of nuclear weapons to Africa. Despite the adoption of these resolutions, no active steps were taken to create an African nuclear-free zone.

The Cuban crisis of October 1962, precipitated by the transfer of Soviet nuclear missiles to Cuba, suddenly and dramatically confronted the states of Latin America with the fact that their area had become involved in the strategic plans and rivalries of the nuclear powers. Ideas were formulated in order to prevent the recurrence of the Cuban crisis in some other country of Latin America and also to preclude the possibility of a nuclear arms race developing among the countries of that area. On April 29, 1963, the heads of state of five Latin American republics (Bolivia, Brazil, Chile, Ecuador, and Mexico) issued a joint declaration supporting a Latin American multilateral agreement whereby all countries of Latin America would undertake not "to manufacture, store, or test nuclear weapons or devices for launching nuclear weapons." Later that year, the General Assembly of the United Nations adopted a resolution giving its support and encouragement to the idea. On the initiative of Mexico, a Preparatory Commission for the Denuclearization of Latin America was established in November 1964, in Mexico City.

Intensive negotiations took place over the ensuing two and one-half years on the elaboration of a treaty to create a nuclear-free zone in Latin America. While the nuclear powers all gave their blessing in public to these efforts, they expressed much skepticism and many doubts in private. The author had been appointed technical advisor to the Preparatory Commission by the Secretary–General of the United Nations and took part in the work of elaboration of the treaty. On several occasions, different officials of the four nuclear powers indicated to me that I was wasting my time, that the idea of a Latin American nuclear-free zone was premature and unlikely to succeed; it was too difficult to get agreement among all of the Latin American states and some of them were not really serious about the project; furthermore, it was unlikely that all of the nuclear powers would give their support to it. These officials apparently underrated the enthusiastic support for the concept that had been generated in the countries of the area. They had also obviously underrated the capabilities of Ambassador (now Foreign Minister) Alfonso Garcia Robles, then Under-Secretary for Foreign Affairs of Mexico and chairman of the Preparatory Commission. Ambassador Garcia Robles, one of the ablest of diplomats and for many years dedicated to the cause of disarmament, was the main moving spirit in promoting the concept, and his ingenious and fertile mind produced solutions to the most difficult problems.

There were a number of difficult and complex questions to be solved. Would it be necessary for all of the states of Latin America to become parties to the treaty before its entry into force, or could a treaty limited to only part of the zone be effective, even if all areas in this part were not contiguous? Would it be necessary for all foreign countries having responsibility for territories in the zone (France, the Netherlands, the United Kingdom, and the United States) to agree that their territories should be included? Would it be necessary for all five nuclear powers to undertake to respect the zone? These problems were solved in an ingenious manner. It was decided that the treaty would enter into force when ratified by all the Latin American countries, when all of the countries mentioned above having responsibility for territories in the zone ratified a protocol (Protocol I) undertaking to apply the treaty to those territories, when all five nuclear powers ratified a protocol undertaking to respect the nuclear-free status of the zone (Protocol II), and when each of the parties to the treaty concluded agreements with the IAEA for the application of the IAEA's safeguards system to its nuclear activities. These requirements were very far-reaching and a long time would elapse before all of them would be met; it was therefore also provided that signatory states could waive those requirements in whole or in part so that the treaty would enter into force for such states immediately upon their depositing their instruments of ratification and their declaration of waiver.

As regards the control provisions of the treaty, a comprehensive system of verification was provided, which included the application of the IAEA safeguards system, periodic reports of the parties to the agency established to implement the treaty (OPANAL), special reports when requested by the General Secretary of OPANAL, and special inspections in addition to the IAEA's safeguards system in the case of suspicion of violation.

It was also agreed that nuclear materials and facilities would be used for exclusively peaceful purposes, and that nuclear explosions for peaceful purposes could be carried out, including explosions involving a device similar to that used in nuclear weapons so long as such a device did not constitute a nuclear weapon. The Treaty of Tlatelolco, unlike the PTBT and the NPT, did provide a definition of nuclear weapons: Article 5 of the treaty provided that "a nuclear weapon is any device which is capable of releasing nuclear energy in an uncontrolled manner and which has a group of characteristics that are appropriate for use for warlike purposes."

The main obligations of the parties are defined in Article 1 of the treaty, which reads as follows:

1. The Contracting Parties hereby undertake to use exclusively for peaceful purposes the nuclear material and facilities which are under their jurisdiction, and to prohibit and prevent in their respective territories:

(a) The testing, use, manufacture, production or acquisition by any means whatsoever of any nuclear weapons, by the Parties themselves, directly or indirectly, on behalf of anyone else or in any other way, and

(b) The receipt, storage, installation, deployment and any form of possession of any nuclear weapons, directly or indirectly, by the Parties themselves, by anyone on their behalf or in any other way.

2. The Contracting Parties also undertake to refrain from engaging in, encouraging or authorizing, directly or indirectly, or in any way participating in the testing, use, manufacture, production, possession or control of any nuclear weapon.

Article 18 sets out the provisions regarding explosions for peaceful purposes:

1. The Contracting Parties may carry out explosions of nuclear devices for peaceful purposes—including explosions which involve devices similar to those used in nuclear weapons—or collaborate with third parties for the same purpose, provided that they do so in accordance with the provisions of this article and the other articles of the Treaty, particularly articles 1 and 5.

2. Contracting Parties intending to carry out, or to co-operate in carrying out, such an explosion shall notify the Agency and the International Atomic Energy Agency, as far in advance as the circumstances require, of the date of the explosion and shall at the same time provide the following information:

(a) The nature of the nuclear device and the source from which it was obtained,

(b) The place and purpose of the planned explosion,

(c) The procedures which will be followed in order to comply with paragraph 3 of this article,

(d) The expected force of the device, and

(e) The fullest possible information on any possible radioactive fall-out that may result from the explosion or explosions, and measures which will be taken to avoid danger to the population, flora, fauna and territories of any other Party or Parties.

3. The General Secretary and the technical personnel designated by the Council and the International Atomic Energy Agency may observe all the preparations, including the explosion of the device, and shall have unrestricted access to any area in the vicinity of the site of the explosion in order to ascertain whether the device and the procedures followed during the

explosion are in conformity with the information supplied under paragraph 2 of this article and the other provisions of this Treaty.

4. The Contracting Parties may accept the collaboration of third parties for the purpose set forth in paragraph 1 of the present article, in accordance with paragraphs 2 and 3 thereof.

The treaty was signed in the borough of Tlatelolco in Mexico City on February 14, 1967. The complete text of the treaty is set forth in Appendix III.

Twenty-three states of Latin America and the Carribean Sea have have signed the treaty, and 22 of them have ratified it. Of the 22 states that have ratified, the treaty is in force for 20, each of which has deposited a declaration of waiver of the requirements for entry into force. Although Brazil and Chile have ratified the treaty, they have not deposited a declaration of waiver and the treaty is therefore not in force for them, nor has it entered into force for Argentina, which has signed but not ratified the treaty. The fact that Argentina, Brazil, and Chile (none of which is a party to the NPT) are not bound by its provisions certainly reduces the treaty's effectiveness. It is important, however, from the point of view of non-proliferation that not only Mexico, which is a potential nuclear power, but also such countries as Colombia and Venezuela, which have not ratified the NPT but will soon become potential nuclear powers, should be parties to the Treaty of Tlatelolco and bound by its provisions.

The Netherlands and the United Kingdom have signed and ratified Protocol I to the treaty, so that it applies to the territories in the zone for which they have responsibility, but neither France nor the United States has yet signed or ratified Protocol I, although the General Assembly has specifically called on them to do so. Protocol II has been signed and ratified by China, France, the United Kingdom, and the United States, so that they are bound to respect the zone and not to use or threaten to use nuclear weapons against it.

Despite a number of resolutions of the General Assembly calling on it to sign and ratify Protocol II, the Soviet Union has not yet done so. Among the reasons it gives for not signing the protocol is that the treaty permits peaceful nuclear explosions. Among other reasons given is that the treaty does not apply to the Panama Canal Zone or prohibit the transit of nuclear weapons, and that the area of the zone takes in a large part of the Atlantic and Pacific oceans. It is noteworthy in this connection that the area of the Latin America Free Zone is substantially the same as that of the "security zone" established by the Latin American states in World War II, on the initiative of the United States, which was accepted by all the Allied Powers including the U.S.S.R. The Soviet Union has, however, said that it will respect the nuclear-free status of each state in the area that remains nuclear-free. Many observers feel that the Soviet Union may adhere to Protocol II if the boycott against Cuba is lifted by the Organization of American States and if Cuba itself signs and ratifies the treaty.

As regards peaceful nuclear explosions, Ambassador Garcia Robles, who was responsible for the final drafting of the texts of Articles 5 and 18, has explained that by virtue of the wording of Article 1 and the definition of a nuclear weapon in Article 5, no peaceful nuclear explosion may be carried out if the device has "a group of characteristics that are appropriate for use for warlike purposes," as that would make it a nuclear weapon. This interpretation was expressly supported by the United States when it signed Protocol II. When Argentina signed and Brazil ratified the treaty, however, they stated their understanding that the treaty permitted the explosion of nuclear devices for peaceful purposes.

After the conclusion and signing of the treaty in 1967, it was welcomed by the United Nations General Assembly "with special satisfaction" as "an event of historic significance in the efforts to prevent the proliferation of nuclear weapons . . ." In creating a nuclear-free zone in a large inhabited portion of the earth, the treaty was, in fact, the first multilateral agreement that had as one of its specific and stated aims the prevention of the proliferation of nuclear weapons. As such, it is a notable constituent part of the non-proliferation regime. In fact, its provisions were copied in part in Article III of the NPT concerning IAEA safeguards, and the existence of the treaty was responsible for the inclusion in the NPT of Article VII concerning nuclear-free zones. The treaty was also hailed at the Conference of Non-Nuclear-Weapon States in September 1968, which recommended that other non-nuclear-weapon states study the possibility and desirability of establishing such zones in their areas. The treaty has also been described as a model for proposals for the establishment of other nuclear-free zones.

Chapter 5.   The Making of the Non-Proliferation Treaty (NPT)

As was indicated previously, all of the efforts and negotiations for the control of atomic energy had as one of their main objectives the prevention of the proliferation of nuclear weapons. Two different approaches to this problem were dealt with in the previous chapter—a ban on nuclear weapons tests, which would put a brake on the proliferation of nuclear weapons by both the nuclear and non-nuclear powers; and the creation of nuclear free-zones, which would prevent the dissemination of nuclear weapons within a given zone by the nuclear powers and prevent the acquisition of such weapons by the countries in that zone. The third and most important approach to the problem of proliferation is by direct action to ban the acquisition of all such weapons by all non-nuclear states and the dissemination of such weapons to them—a comprehensive and universal approach.

This approach was first brought up by Ireland at the General Assembly in the fall of 1958 when it submitted a draft resolution specifically aimed at preventing the spread of nuclear weapons. It did not press its resolution to a vote but contented itself with having brought the question to the attention of the members of the United Nations as a separate problem distinct from other questions of arms control and disarmament. At that time, there were only three nuclear powers in the world, the United States, the Soviet Union, and the United Kingdom, all of which had tested hydrogen as well as atomic bombs. In those days, it was common to speak of the "Nth-country problem." Governments and peoples throughout the world feared not only radioactive fallout from existing nuclear testing but also that additional countries would become nuclear powers and engage in acquiring and testing nuclear weapons and that the process of the dissemination, acquisition, and testing of these dreaded weapons would go on without end or at least without limit.

Initiatives by Ireland and Other
Non-Nuclear Countries

In 1959, at the next session of the General Assembly, Ireland inscribed the question of prevention of the wider dissemination of nuclear weapons as a separate item in the Assembly's agenda. Ireland stressed that even a universal test ban would not check the actual dissemination of nuclear weapons, and that the nuclear powers should, in their own enlightened self-interest, see to it that these weapons were not spread throughout the world. The Assembly approved the Irish proposal, suggesting that the Disarmament Committee consider means whereby the danger of an increase in the number of nuclear states might be averted by an international agreement whereby the nuclear powers would refrain from handing over control of nuclear weapons to any nation not possessing them and the non-nuclear powers would refrain from manufacturing them. The United States and the United Kingdom supported the Irish proposal but the Soviet Union did not, because the proposal did not deal with cases in which nuclear weapons were transferred by a nuclear power to the territory of an ally. France also did not support the Irish proposal, since it believed that the only effective way of dealing with the matter was by discontinuing the manufacture of fissionable material for weapons purposes, discontinuing the production of nuclear weapons, reconverting stockpiles to peaceful uses, and controlling the manufacture of nuclear delivery vehicles. This amounted to the well-known tactic of "all or nothing."

In 1960, France became the world's fourth nuclear power. At the General Assembly that fall, Ireland again raised the problem of nuclear weapons dissemination. This time its proposal went further. It called on all governments to make every effort to achieve permanent agreement on the prevention of the wider dissemination of nuclear weapons; pending the negotiation of such a permanent agreement; it called upon the nuclear powers, as a temporary and voluntary measure, to refrain from relinquishing control of such weapons to any nation not possessing them and from transmitting the information necessary for their manufacture; and upon the non-nuclear powers, on a similar temporary and voluntary basis, to refrain from manufacturing these weapons and from otherwise attempting to acquire them. This time the Soviet Union supported the Irish proposal, stressing in particular the dangers that would ensue from giving nuclear weapons to West Germany. The United States, however, withheld its support, among other reasons because the proposal failed to recognize that other nations would not indefinitely deny nuclear weapons to themselves if the nuclear powers themselves did not halt the stockpiling of nuclear weapons. The U.S. also took exception to the fact that the Irish proposal called for an unverified commitment of indefinite duration. The General Assembly, however, approved the Irish proposal.

Ireland again raised the question of nondissemination in 1961, expressing the conviction that nuclear war was inevitable if the nonnuclear states became, one by one, possessors of nuclear weapons. This time the General Assembly unanimously adopted the Irish proposal, which called upon all states, particularly the nuclear states, to conclude an international agreement containing: (a) provisions under which the nuclear states would refrain from relinquishing control of nuclear weapons and from transmitting the information necessary for their manufacture to states not possessing them, (b) provisions under which states not possessing nuclear weapons would undertake not to manufacture or otherwise acquire control of them. Since this resolution called only for an international agreement without any temporary and voluntary unverified commitment, the U.S. was able to vote for it.

Sweden also submitted a proposal, requesting the Secretary-General to make an inquiry as to the conditions under which countries not possessing nuclear weapons might be willing to enter into specific undertakings to refrain from manufacturing or otherwise acquiring such weapons and to refuse to receive, in the future, nuclear weapons on their territories on behalf of any other country. The Soviet Union supported the Swedish proposal but the United States opposed it, on the ground that it sought to shift the emphasis entirely to non-nuclear powers receiving nuclear weapons on their territory on behalf of another country and thus to prejudice existing defensive arrangements. The results of the inquiry were inconclusive. Reciprocity was the most frequent condition cited; some countries insisted on the reciprocal adherence of specific states and others demanded universal adherence, including that of nonmembers of the United Nations (obviously meaning such countries as the People's Republic of China and West Germany). Some countries also called for the implementation of disarmament measures by the nuclear powers, and others viewed the objective of establishing a "non-nuclear club" as being part of general and complete disarmament, which was the line taken by the three Western nuclear powers.

During the period from roughly 1960 to 1963, the nuclear powers were mainly preoccupied with the idea of general and complete disarmament (GCD) which had been launched in the United Nations by Premier Khrushchev in 1959 and unanimously supported by that body. The United States was at first reluctant to consider GCD seriously but finally agreed to do so during the Zorin–McCloy negotiations, which produced a Joint Statement of Agreed Principles for Disarmament Negotiations in September 1961. One week later, President Kennedy submitted to the United Nations an American "Program for General and Complete Disarmament in a Peaceful World."

The draft treaties for general and complete disarmament introduced by the Soviet Union and the United States in the ENDC in 1962 both contained provisions during the first stage to prevent the dissemination or acquisition of nuclear weapons. Both countries also agreed, however, that this issue could be discussed as a separate or collateral measure, but no serious examination of the matter was undertaken at that time.

At a summit conference of the Organization of African Unity held in Cairo in July 1964, the assembled heads of state agreed to declare Africa a nuclear-free zone and to undertake in an international treaty not to manufacture or acquire control of atomic weapons. At a summit conference of nonaligned states held later that year, a declaration was adopted urging all states to "conclude nondissemination agreements" and to agree to "the gradual liquidation of the existing stockpiles of nuclear weapons." They also declared their own readiness "not to produce, acquire or test any nuclear weapons."

It is somewhat surprising that in the late 1950s and early 1960s, initiatives for preventing the spread of nuclear weapons came mainly from the smaller and "third-world" countries, who feared the increasing testing and proliferation of these weapons and wanted to curb the nuclear arms race. While preventing the spread of nuclear weapons to additional countries was obviously in the interest of the existing nuclear powers, they were at first reluctant to take any initiatives in this direction. The Soviet Union's main concern was evidenced by a series of proposals intended to keep or get American nuclear weapons out of Central Europe in general and West Germany in particular. In 1957, Poland proposed the "Rapacki Plan" for a nuclear-free zone covering East and West Germany, Poland, and Czechoslovakia, but it was rejected by the Western powers. The main concern of the U.S. and its allies was to be able to station nuclear weapons in Europe as an offset and deterrent to the superior Soviet conventional forces. Although West Germany had signed a treaty in 1954 with its Western European allies not to produce atomic weapons *on its territory*, the Soviet Union professed an abiding fear of the possibility that Germany might acquire such weapons.

At the 1963 session of the General Assembly, the Soviet Union for the first time criticized a Western plan for establishing a NATO multilateral nuclear force (MLF), deeming such a force contrary to the principle of nondissemination. The United States maintained that the projected MLF would not violate the principle of nondissemination of nuclear weapons as it did not envisage a transfer of *control* over such weapons. For the next few years, controversy over the compatibility of the proposed NATO nuclear force with the principle of nondissemination remained an obstacle to progress. The Soviet Union was adamant in opposing any action which might give what it called the "revanchist" elements in Germany, its wartime enemy, any "access" whatsoever to nuclear weapons.

At the same session, the Soviet Union and the United States both opposed an attempt by nonaligned countries to call on the ENDC to take measures to prevent the proliferation of nuclear weapons. They obviously had not yet decided to give priority to this objective.

In those days, India, together with Ireland and Sweden, was in the forefront of those non-nuclear countries urging the nondissemination and nonacquisition of nuclear weapons. But after China exploded an atom bomb in October 1964, the Indian position underwent a change. Thereafter it put more emphasis on the question of security and on linking nuclear disarmament by the nuclear powers to an undertaking by non-nuclear powers not to acquire or manufacture nuclear weapons. At a meeting of the U.N. Disarmament Commission in June 1965, the Indian representative suggested an "integrated solution" consisting of the following:

1. An undertaking by the nuclear Powers not to transfer nuclear weapons or nuclear weapons technology to others;
2. An undertaking not to use nuclear weapons against countries which do not possess them;
3. An undertaking through the United Nations to safeguard the security of countries which may be threatened by Powers having a nuclear weapons capability or about to have a nuclear weapons capability;
4. Tangible progress towards disarmament, including a comprehensive test ban treaty, a complete freeze on production of nuclear weapons and means of delivery as well as a substantial reduction in the existing stocks; and,
5. An undertaking by non-nuclear Powers not to acquire or manufacture nuclear weapons.

It was at about this same time that the term "non-proliferation of nuclear weapons" came into general usage; it was considered to be a broader term that included the concepts of "dissemination" (meaning the spreading of nuclear weapons by the nuclear powers) and "acquisition" (meaning the manufacture or otherwise obtaining of nuclear weapons by non-nuclear powers), and, in due course, it also was taken to include the concept of the further development, accumulation, and deployment of nuclear weapons by the nuclear powers.

Opposing American and Soviet Draft Treaties of 1965

In June 1965, the Disarmament Commission of the United Nations adopted a resolution calling upon the ENDC to meet as soon as possible and to "accord special priority to the consideration of the question of a treaty or convention to prevent the proliferation of nuclear weapons, giving close attention to the various suggestions that agreement could be facilitated by adopting a programme of certain related measures." Both the United States and the Soviet Union made it clear that the program of related measures did not, in their view, constitute a package or a condition for a non-proliferation treaty.

On August 17, 1965, the United States submitted at the ENDC a draft treaty to prevent the spread of nuclear weapons. The draft treaty would:

1. Prohibit nuclear powers from transferring nuclear weapons into the "national control" of any non-nuclear state, either directly or indirectly through a military alliance;
2. Prohibit nuclear powers from taking any other action which would cause an increase in the total number of states and other organizations having independent power to use nuclear weapons;
3. Prohibit nuclear powers from assisting any non-nuclear state in the manufacture of nuclear weapons.

The draft treaty also contained provisions whereby the non-nuclear states would undertake corresponding obligations on their part. The United States stated that the proposed NATO nuclear arrangements that were being discussed were not disseminatory and would comply with the provisions of the Non-Proliferation Treaty. The Soviet Union objected to any non-proliferation treaty which would not ban all direct and indirect forms of *access* to nuclear weapons, whether by the NATO multilateral nuclear force (MLF); by an Atlantic nuclear force, as suggested by the United Kingdom; or by a NATO nuclear planning committee, as suggested by U.S. Secretary of Defense McNamara. It declared that any NATO nuclear-sharing arrangement would give West Germany either direct or indirect access to nuclear weapons and was, therefore, incompatible with a non-proliferation treaty.

Before the explosion of the first Chinese atomic bomb in October 1964, India had been among the most active and vocal of the non-nuclear states in calling for the non-proliferation of nuclear weapons In 1965, India began insisting that the renunciation of non-nuclear powers of the production, acquisition, and control of and access to nuclear weapons must be simultaneous with the renunciation by nuclear powers of further production of these weapons and with agreement on the reduction of existing nuclear stockpiles. Sweden took the position that a comprehensive test ban would be the most practical measure to prevent an increase in the number of nuclear powers, and it called for a solution of the non-proliferation problem within a package of measures that would include a comprehensive test ban and a cutoff of production of fissionable material for weapons purposes. Nigeria also called for a ban on the use of nuclear weapons or a renunciation of their first use and for freezing the production of nuclear weapons and nuclear delivery vehicles; however, Nigeria was willing to proceed with the negotiation of a non-proliferation agreement as a separate first step The eight nonaligned members of the ENDC—Brazil, Burma, Ethiopia, India, Mexico, Nigeria, Sweden, and the United Arab Republic (Egypt)—submitted a memorandum setting out their joint views on the non-proliferation question. It stated that they were convinced that measures to prohibit the spread of nuclear weapons should be "coupled with or followed by tangible steps to halt the nuclear arms race and to limit, reduce and eliminate the stocks of nuclear weapons and the means of their delivery."

On September 24, 1965, the Soviet Union submitted its draft for a non-proliferation treaty to the General Assembly. The Soviet draft would:

1. Prohibit nuclear powers from transferring nuclear weapons in any form, or assistance and information about their manufacture or use, directly or indirectly through third states or groups of states, into the ownership or control of states or groups of states not possessing nuclear weapons, and from according to such states or groups of states "the right to participate in the ownership, control or use of nuclear weapons";
2. Prohibit nuclear powers from transferring nuclear weapons or control over them or over their emplacement and use, to units of the armed forces or military personnel of the armed forces of states not possessing nuclear weapons, "even if such units or personnel are under the command of a military alliance";
3. Require powers not possessing nuclear weapons to undertake corresponding obligations on their part.

The Soviet Union stressed that the greatest danger of proliferation came from the plans for the creation of a NATO multilateral or Atlantic nuclear force, which, it alleged, was intended to give access to nuclear weapons to West Germany.

The eight nonaligned members of the ENDC proposed a resolution in the General Assembly for the early conclusion of a treaty to prevent the proliferation of nuclear weapons. The resolution, which was adopted, called on the ENDC to negotiate an international treaty based on the following main principles:

(a) The treaty should be void of any loop-holes which might permit nuclear or non-nuclear Powers to proliferate, directly or indirectly, nuclear weapons in any form;
(b) The treaty should embody an acceptable balance of mutual responsibilities and obligations of the nuclear and non-nuclear Powers;
(c) The treaty should be a step towards the achievement of general and complete disarmament and, more particuarly, nuclear disarmament;
(d) There should be acceptable and workable provisions to ensure the effectiveness of the treaty;
(e) Nothing in the treaty should adversely affect the right of any group of States to conclude regional treaties in order to ensure the total absence of nuclear weapons in their respective territories.

This resolution, which became famous as "Resolution 2028," thereafter became the basis of the positions of the nonaligned countries in the ENDC, who put primary emphasis on the necessity for any non-proliferation treaty to provide for an acceptable balance of mutual responsibilities and obligations on the part of the nuclear and non-nuclear powers.

Throughout all of 1966, agreement was impossible because of the basic differences between the Soviet and American attitudes toward their respective interpretations of the word "proliferation," in relation, particularly, to the question of nuclear defense arrangements within the NATO alliance. The Soviet Union continued to insist that the United States' draft treaty contained a loophole which would enable the use of nuclear weapons by the NATO allies of the United States, including West Germany. The U.S., on the other hand, held that the language of the Soviet Union's draft treaty was so sweeping that it would bar existing arrangements for the deployment of United States nuclear weapons under American control on the territory of its NATO allies and would even preclude consultations on nuclear strategy between the NATO allies. The Soviet treaty, argued the U.S., was aimed not at non-proliferation but at weakening the Western alliance and giving an advantage to the U.S.S.R.

In March 1966, the U.S. submitted amendments to its draft treaty of August 17, 1965, to clarify that the control of nuclear weapons would not be given to any ally or to NATO as a whole in the sense that an allied state would have the right or ability to fire nuclear weapons without the decision of the United States. There would, therefore, be no increase in the number of states or associations of states having control of nuclear weapons. The United States stressed the right of military allies to consult each other with regard to the nuclear defense of the alliance and argued, in effect, that the sharing arrangements discussed would not put an additional finger on the trigger of a nuclear weapon but rather would put additional fingers on the safety catch. The Soviet Union maintained its objections, however, and said that it would not sign a non-proliferation treaty which did not rule out all forms of participation by West Germany and the other NATO non-nuclear powers in the control of a NATO nuclear deterrent.

On the other hand, however, the Soviet Union, the United States, and the United Kingdom were united in agreeing that it would be harmful to the cause of non-proliferation if the nonaligned members of the ENDC insisted on making the Non-Proliferation Treaty dependent on the implementation of other disarmament measures.

During the 1966 discussions, two new questions came to the fore: that of guaranteeing the security of non-nuclear states and that of peaceful nuclear explosions. Both of these questions are discussed in detail in later chapters, and they are mentioned here only to indicate the overall range of the debate. It became increasingly evident that many of the non-nuclear nations were worried about their security and were interested in obtaining adequate security assurances. The United States recalled the declaration of President Johnson after the First Communist Chinese nuclear test in 1964, when he declared that nations that did not seek nuclear weapons could be sure that, "if they need our strong support against some threat of nuclear blackmail, then they will have it." Premier Kosygin, in his 1966 message to the ENDC, offered to include in the Non-Proliferation Treaty a provision banning the use of nuclear weapons against non-nuclear treaty parties that had no nuclear weapons on their territory. The Western powers rejected the so-called Kosygin Formula (or Kosygin Proposal) because it would be impossible to verify and would discriminate against non-nuclear members of NATO that participated in allied defense arrangements involving the deployment of United States–controlled nuclear weapons on their territory. The nonaligned members of the ENDC, on the whole, favored the multilateral approach to the question of security assurances or guarantees and opposed any formulae that implied a degree of alignment on their part or that appeared to put them under the protection of any one nuclear power. Most of them favored a blanket undertaking by the nuclear powers never to use or threaten to use nuclear weapons against non-nuclear countries, but the Kosygin Formula did gain support among the non-nuclear countries. The question of security assurances continued to be a major preoccupation of the non-nuclear powers throughout all the negotiations.

As regards the question of nuclear explosions for peaceful purposes, which was raised by several nonaligned members of the ENDC, the United States stressed that the restrictions on the proliferation of nuclear weapons should apply equally to nuclear explosions for peaceful purposes, because the technology of the two were essentially indistinguishable. It suggested, however, that nuclear-weapon states should make available services to other states for peaceful nuclear explosions if and when such explosions proved technically and economically feasible. This question, too, became a major matter of controversy between the nuclear and the non-nuclear powers; although a generally acceptable formula was finally agreed on for inclusion in the NPT, it has not been fully resolved to the present time.

At the 1966 session of the General Assembly, secret conversations were entered into between Soviet Foreign Minister Andrei Gromyko and U.S. Secretary of State Dean Rusk in an effort to overcome the impasse surrounding a non-proliferation treaty. As a result of their discussions, a compromise formula was arrived at whereby the United States would abandon proposals for any multilateral NATO nuclear force and the Soviet Union would, in the context of a non-proliferation treaty, abandon its objections to the presence of American nuclear weapons on the territory of NATO countries and to consultations within NATO regarding the use of nuclear weapons, as had been suggested by Secretary of Defense McNamara in proposing a special NATO committee to study nuclear planning. This compromise made it possible for the U.S. and the Soviet Union to work out common language that would ban the transfer of nuclear weapons or control over them "to any recipient whatsoever."

The United States then agreed to cosponsor a Soviet draft resolution which appealed to all states to "refrain from any actions which might hamper the conclusion of an agreement" and to "take all necessary steps for the earliest possible conclusion" of a non-proliferation treaty. Both the Soviet Union and the United States stressed the importance of a non-proliferation treaty for the security of all states, non-nuclear as well as nuclear. They also urged that a non-proliferation treaty should not be linked to additional disarmament measures. India reaffirmed its views that a balanced treaty should require that both nuclear-weapon and non-nuclear-weapon states refrain from manufacturing nuclear weapons and that other measures to reduce and eliminate nuclear weapons and delivery vehicles could be coupled with or follow a non-proliferation treaty. India also maintained that controls should apply not only to peaceful nuclear industry but even more so to nuclear weapons production. It also opposed a ban on the development of peaceful nuclear explosives by non-nuclear-weapon states, saying that this would be tantamount to the non-proliferation of science and technology. The resolution by the Soviet Union and the United States was adopted by an overwhelming majority, as was a second resolution sponsored by the nonaligned countries reaffirming Resolution 2028 and calling on the ENDC to consider urgently the Kosygin Proposal for nonuse of nuclear weapons.

Identical American and Soviet Draft Treaties of 1967

As a result of the basic agreement reached by the United States and the Soviet Union at the 1966 General Assembly, the two powers continued their bilateral negotiations in 1967 and at the same time were consulting with their respective allies concerning the provisions that ought to be included in a non-proliferation treaty. The non-nuclear powers who were not allied to the two superpowers were concerned mainly about questions of security assurances, the balance of mutual obligations and responsibilities between the nuclear and non-nuclear powers, and questions of nuclear disarmament and an underground test ban. The allies of the United States, however, were chiefly concerned about the peaceful uses of nuclear energy and about whether the treaty might in any way circumscribe their development of such peaceful uses, including the use of peaceful nuclear explosions; they wanted the spin-off benefits resulting from the development of nuclear energy for military purposes which could promote peaceful uses. They were also, of course, very much interested in safeguards. The European allies of the United States who were members of Euratom wanted Euratom safeguards for their peaceful reactors and other nuclear facilities, rather than having to submit them to IAEA safeguards. On the other hand, the Soviet Union regarded the Euratom safeguards as a form of self-inspection by the Euratom countries and insisted that IAEA safeguards should apply to all the non-nuclear powers.

While less is known about the concerns and problems of the allies of the Soviet Union and none of those concerns or problems (except those of Romania) was put officially on the record or made public, nevertheless it is known from private contacts that Czechoslovakia and Poland also had considerable reservations concerning various aspects of the treaty which were not very different from those of the allies of the United States. They, too, were worried about the peaceful uses of nuclear energy and the availability of peaceful nuclear explosions for their civilian engineering programs, and they, too, were not happy about some of the discriminatory features in connection with safeguards. Romania was the sole Warsaw Pact country to submit a number of proposals and suggestions for improving the treaty, some of them in writing, which were circulated as official documents.

That the concerns of the allies of the United States were serious and important is evidenced by the intensive debates in the West German Parliament concerning the entire matter. The German Foreign Ministry submitted a list of more than fifty questions to the United States concerning various aspects of the proposed treaty. Japan, which was also very much concerned about the peaceful uses of nuclear energy and the possible restrictions or limitations that might be placed on the development of these peaceful uses as a result of a non-proliferation treaty, seemed to be willing to allow West Germany and Italy to lead the way in the negotiations with the United States and to be satisfied to coordinate its efforts with those two countries and to accept whatever compromise understandings they arrived at with the United States.

The consultations between the Soviet Union and the United States, and between them and their respective allies, proceeded parallel to the negotiations that were going on in the ENDC among all of the member states. Finally, on August 24, 1967, the United States and the Soviet Union submitted to the ENDC identical but separate and still incomplete drafts of a non-proliferation treaty. These identical drafts superseded the earlier separate and different Soviet and United States drafts. One article—Article III—was left in blank because no agreement had yet been reached between the two parties and between the United States and its allies concerning the provisions of an international safeguards system.

It was never publicly explained why the two countries submitted separate, identical draft treaties. Privately, the Americans let it be known that this curious procedure was insisted on by the Soviet Union because of some domestic reason. Apparently the Soviet Union felt that until agreement between it and the United States was fully achieved on the entire text and on the tactics for having it approved by the ENDC, it would be wiser to leave the door open for some unilateral last-minute changes. The same peculiar procedure was followed not only in the case of the NPT but also in the case of the Seabed Treaty and the Biological Convention, when separate but identical drafts were submitted and a joint draft treaty text was submitted only when the two countries were prepared to recommend the acceptance of an agreed-upon draft to all the members of the United Nations.

The draft treaty did not define what was a nuclear weapon, but it did define a nuclear-weapon state as one which had manufactured and exploded a nuclear weapon or other nuclear explosive device prior to January 1, 1967. The treaty followed the practice initiated by the United States in the amendments it had submitted on March 21, 1966, to the original draft of its treaty, in which, instead of using the expression "nuclear state" and "non-nuclear state" it began to use the expression nuclear-weapon state" and non-nuclear-weapon state." This was done in order to make clear that other countries that were advanced in the field of nuclear technology for peaceful purposes, such as, for example, India, had refrained from developing nuclear weapons.

The basic provisions of the treaty setting out the fundamental obligations of the parties are contained in Articles I and II of the draft treaty. They read as follows:

Article I

Each nuclear-weapon State party to this Treaty undertakes not to transfer to any recipient whatsoever nuclear weapons or other nuclear explosive devices or control over such weapons or explosive devices directly, or indirectly; and not in any way to assist, encourage, or induce any non-nuclear-weapon State to manufacture or otherwise acquire nuclear weapons or other nuclear explosive devices, or control over such weapons or explosive devices.

Article II

Each non-nuclear-weapon State party to this Treaty undertakes not to receive the transfer from any transferor whatsoever of nuclear weapons or other nuclear explosive devices or of control over such weapons or explosive devices directly, or indirectly; not to manufacture or otherwise acquire nuclear weapons or other nuclear explosive devices; and not to seek or receive any assistance in the manufacture of nuclear explosive devices.

The provisions of these two articles, which remained unchanged during the various drafts of the treaty and appear in the same form in the final text, contain the agreement which was originally arrived at between the United States and the Soviet Union in the fall of 1966 under which each nuclear party undertook not to transfer "to any recipient whatsoever nuclear weapons or other nuclear explosive devices or control over such weapons or explosive devices directly or indirectly." This provision effectively ended any further talk or action toward the creation of an MLF or ANF. It did nothing, however, to bar consultations or planning for the use of nuclear weapons by a NATO committee, as had been suggested by Secretary of Defense McNamara. Hence the NATO Nuclear Planning Committee was established in due course.

These two articles, also, for the first time, equated nuclear explosive devices with nuclear weapons and barred their transfer to or acquisition by non-nuclear states. The preamble of the draft treaty affirmed the principle that the potential benefits from any peaceful applications of nuclear technology, including nuclear explosions, would be available to non-nuclear states on a nondiscriminatory basis. Article IV of the draft treaty stated that nothing in the treaty would be interpreted as affecting the right of all parties to develop research, production, and use of nuclear energy for peaceful purposes. It stated that all parties had the right to participate in the fullest possible exchange of information for, and to contribute to, the further development of the applications of nuclear energy for peaceful purposes. It did not, however, contain any positive commitment by the nuclear powers to facilitate or promote the peaceful uses of nuclear energy or to make such uses of nuclear energy available to other countries. Nor was there any article in the treaty providing for the carrying out of peaceful nuclear explosions.

The preamble also contained a paragraph whereby the parties declared their intention to achieve at the earliest possible date a cessation of the nuclear arms race, but there was no positive commitment to this effect in the body or the operative part of the treaty. The remaining four articles of the treaty dealt with formal or procedural matters.

The basic provisions of the treaty in Articles I and II were generally acceptable to most of the members of the ENDC. The representative of the United Arab Republic, however, thought that there were loopholes in these articles. He submitted amendments to ensure that there could be no dissemination by private organizations and individuals nor assistance by one non-nuclear-weapon state to another. The Soviet Union and the United States and other members of the ENDC, however, felt that these problems were adequately covered by the existing language of the treaty and that it was not necessary to reopen this matter, which had been so carefully negotiated. Brazil and India, as is discussed later, objected to the ban on peaceful nuclear explosive devices by non-nuclear nations.

As regards the question of safeguards, although negotiations were proceeding outside of the ENDC with respect to the application of safeguards to the Euratom countries, a number of suggestions were made for IAEA safeguards to apply on a nondiscriminatory basis to both nuclear and non-nuclear parties to the treaty, and Sweden submitted a text to this effect for a draft Article III. Brazil and India proposed making safeguards compulsory for all parties and not merely non-nuclear states, on a nondiscriminatory and universal basis. This view was also supported by several other nations, including Ethiopia, Burma, Nigeria, and Switzerland. (Although Switzerland was not a member of the ENDC, it submitted its views in writing to the committee.) In order to meet these objections, the United States and the United Kingdom announced in December 1967, that they would voluntarily accept IAEA safeguards over all their peaceful nuclear activities, excluding only those with direct national-security significance. While these pledges served to reassure West Germany, Italy, and the other Euratom countries as well as Japan that they would be placed on an equal footing with the United States and United Kingdom, they did not entirely satisfy all the non-nuclear states, and particularly the nonaligned countries, who noted that these pledges were unilateral and voluntary and hence not legal commitments and that they did not apply to the Soviet Union, thus continuing the discriminatory nature of the application of safeguards.

As regards the peaceful uses of nuclear energy, Mexico led the way in arguing that the treaty should impose a positive obligation on the nuclear states to aid the non-nuclear parties in developing the peaceful applications of nuclear energy. It said that it was only fair for the non-nuclear parties to receive as a right the scientific and technological benefits derived from activities they would renounce under the treaty. Mexico's views were supported by the United Arab Republic, Sweden, and Nigeria and also by Romania, which submitted an amendment having a similar aim. Italy suggested the conclusion of an agreement which could either be incorporated in the treaty or be made independently, whereby the nuclear powers would tranfer to the non-nuclear parties an agreed quantity of fissionable material. This would indirectly restrict production of nuclear weapons by the nuclear powers. The non-nuclear nations would buy the materials below market price, with part of the payments going to the supplying countries and part to a United Nations fund for the developing countries.

With regard to peaceful nuclear explosions, Brazil and India firmly maintained that the non-nuclear countries should have the right to develop and use their own peaceful explosive devices. India was willing, however, to accept nondiscriminatory and universal safeguards to ensure that no country produced nuclear weapons while developing peaceful nuclear explosives. Mexico proposed a middle course whereby the nuclear parties would be obligated to make available to non-nuclear parties to the treaty the potential benefits from any applications of nuclear explosions. Under the Mexican amendment, assistance would be provided on a nondiscriminatory basis at low cost and would be made available through appropriate international bodies subject to procedures laid down in a special agreement. Canada, Sweden, Nigeria, and Switzerland supported the Mexican proposal of writing a formal treaty obligation into the operative part of the treaty. Sweden wanted an explicit assurance that the arrangements would be truly nondiscriminatory—that is, that they would apply equally to the nuclear and to the non-nuclear countries. The ideal solution of the problem, according to Sweden, would be to link it with a comprehensive test ban treaty barring all underground explosions except those that were specifically permitted according to agreed-upon procedures; this would put all countries on an equal footing, or as near thereto as the circumstances permitted.

With respect to nuclear disarmament, Brazil and India again took the lead in criticizing the draft treaty as one-sided and discriminatory and as failing to provide the balance of mutual responsibilities and obligations which the General Assembly had called for in 1965. Brazil wanted a legal commitment to definite disarmament measures, including the conversion to peaceful uses of some military stocks of fissionable material and the channeling to developing countries of part of the resources freed by disarmament. It also wanted the nuclear powers to negotiate a nuclear disarmament treaty at the earliest possible date and wished the draft NPT treaty to specify that the Review Conference envisaged by the draft treaty would consider the extent of progress toward disarmament. India wanted the treaty to prohibit the manufacture of nuclear weapons by all states. It wanted a treaty article to affirm the solemn resolve of the nuclear powers to undertake meaningful measures of nuclear disarmament and wanted this provision linked to the Review Conference.

Mexico again proposed a compromise, suggesting that an article be included in the treaty whereby the nuclear parties would undertake to "pursue negotiations in good faith" to arrive at agreements on a comprehensive test ban, the cessation of the manufacture of nuclear weapons, the liquidation of existing stockpiles, and the elimination of nuclear weapons and delivery vehicles as well as an agreement on general and complete disarmament. The U.A.R., Ethiopia, Canada, and Sweden favored the Mexican proposal. Sweden also urged that a new preambuar paragraph be added to reaffirm the pledge made in the Partial Test Ban Treaty to continue efforts toward a comprehensive test ban. Burma wanted an article obligating the nuclear powers to take tangible steps toward nuclear disarmament including a comprehensive test ban, a cutoff of fissionable materials production, a halt to nuclear weapons production, a freeze on production of nuclear delivery vehicles, and the progressive reduction and final destruction of stockpiles. Romania wanted specific mention of the prohibition of the use of nuclear weapons and a new treaty article to be added whereby the nuclear parties would undertake specific measures to bring about the cessation of nuclear weapons production and the reduction and destruction of nuclear weapons and delivery vehicles; if such measures were not adopted within five years, the parties would consider the situation and decide on the measures to be taken. The United Kingdom, supported by Italy, proposed that the provisions respecting the Review Conference be enlarged so as to ensure that the purposes of the preamble as well as the provisions of the treaty were being realized.

With respect to nuclear-free zones, Mexico proposed that the provision in this regard be transferred from the preamble to the operative part of the Treaty. The United States and the Soviet Union agreed to this.

Proposals were also made for amending and improving other provisions of the draft treaty. Italy and Switzerland opposed a treaty of unlimited duration and wanted a definite, fixed period. Switzerland noted that the non-nuclear states could not tie their hands indefinitely if the nuclear states failed to arrive at positive results on specific disarmament measures. Romania and Brazil wished to delete from the withdrawal clause of the treaty the requirement that a withdrawing state submit an explanatory statement of its reasons. With respect to amendments, Romania wanted amendments to come into effect only for those who approved them rather than for all parties; it also criticized the draft treaty for giving a privileged veto position to states belonging to the IAEA Board of Governors. Nigeria and Canada favored the Romanian amendments.

The question of a non-proliferation treaty raised important security problems for the non-nuclear nations, and some of them were interested in obtaining security assurances or guarantees from the nuclear powers. The draft treaty said nothing about any security assurances or guarantees, and a number of proposals were made in this regard by the non-nuclear nations. The problem of assuring the security of non-nuclear countries is dealt with later in chapter 10.

In the meantime, a group of international experts had, at the request of the General Assembly, prepared a study on "The Effects of the Possible Use of Nuclear Weapons and the Security and Economic Implications for States of the Acquisition and Further Development of those Weapons." The Secretary-General submitted the report of the experts to the General Assembly on October 10, 1967. The study showed that the cost of acquiring nuclear weapons varied depending on the scope of the program. A small program to produce 10 20-kiloton devices in ten years would cost $104 million, while a moderate program for 100 such devices would cost $188 million. To these costs there would, of course, have to be added the cost of delivery systems, which would vary depending on whether these systems consisted of jet bombers, missiles, or submarines. For example, a larger force consisting of 30 to 50 jet bombers, 20 to 30 thermonuclear weapons, 100 intermediate-range ballistic missiles, and 2 nuclear submarines would cost $560 million annually for ten years. The experts estimated that French nuclear expenditures up to 1969 would be $8.4 billion and that British nuclear expenditures were similar. They found that only six countries other than the five existing nuclear-weapon powers

—West Germany, Japan, Italy, Canada, Sweden, and Australia—could divert sums of this order to acquiring such a force. The experts warned that by 1980 the production of nuclear power in the world would result in the production of plutonium sufficient for thousands of bombs each year. The experts also believed that the advent of new nuclear states or the "further elaboration of existing nuclear arsenals" would lead to greater tension and instability, and would increase the danger of nuclear war by accident or miscalculation. They concluded that the solution to the problem of ensuring security was not to be found in the further proliferation of nuclear weapons or in their retention by the present nuclear powers.

Revised Identical American and Soviet Draft Treaties, 1968

On January 18, 1968, the United States and the Soviet Union submitted identical texts of a revised draft treaty to the ENDC. These drafts contained an Article III on safeguards, which had been left blank in the previous draft. Article IV, on the peaceful uses of nuclear energy, had been revised. A new Article V included an obligation on the part of nuclear-weapon states to make potential benefits from peaceful nuclear explosions available to non-nuclear-weapon parties. A new Article VI was added, containing a provision to negotiate further measures of disarmament. And a new Article VII was added, providing for nuclear-free zones. The duration of the treaty was fixed at twenty-five years, and other amendments of a minor nature were incorporated. The revised draft text was welcomed by most countries as an improvement on the previous text, but a number of members of the ENDC remained dissatisfied with the text as revised. Some of the previous objections were restated, and suggestions were made for further improvements.

The new article on safeguards was criticized by a number of countries on the grounds that it was discriminatory, because the safeguards applied only to non-nuclear parties and not to the nuclear parties to the treaty. Criticisms were made by Romania, Brazil, India, West Germany, and Spain. Sweden also criticized the article, regretting that it did not cover the peaceful activities of the nuclear powers and that it did not require safeguards on transfers between the nuclear powers. Canada also agreed that the safeguards provisions were discriminatory but feared that any attempt to renegotiate the article might jeopardize the treaty itself.

With respect to the peaceful uses of nuclear energy, while most ENDC members welcomed the new wording of the article on peaceful uses, Italy, Mexico, Nigeria, and Spain all considered that the provisions did not go far enough and made suggestions for their improvement.

With respect to the new Article V on peaceful nuclear explosions,

Brazil and India continued to maintain their objections to any ban on the development and use of these explosions for peaceful purposes by non-nuclear countries. They considered that it would be harmful for most of the world to have to be dependent on the few nuclear states for the knowledge and application of this technology. Canada and Sweden considered that bilateral arrangements for explosive services should be placed under international supervision, as did the U.A.R. Sweden proposed that nuclear explosions in nuclear countries should be placed under international supervision and that an international authority should license each projected explosion; special treatment for the nuclear powers or special bilateral arrangements for some non-nuclear powers, it argued, should not be permitted.

Article VI of the revised draft treaty, which obliged the parties to negotiate on disarmament measures and on general and complete disarmament, did not list any specific disarmament measures, as had been provided in the Mexican amendment. This new article led to more discussion and controversy than any other article of the revised draft treaty. Romania, Brazil, and India criticized the draft for failing to halt vertical proliferation by the nuclear-weapon powers. In addition, Brazil wanted the article to contain a specific obligation on the part of the nuclear parties to set aside for the benefit of developing countries a substantial part of the resources freed by measures of nuclear disarmament. India reaffirmed its view that the article should set a time limit for halting vertical proliferation and should also provide for a cutoff of production for military purposes, a comprehensive test ban, and a freeze on the production of nuclear delivery vehicles. It stated that, after the Chinese explosion of a thermonuclear bomb in June 1967, not only India but other countries were concerned about the growing nuclear capacity of China. This made it necessary to prevent the further proliferation of nuclear weapons by all nuclear powers, including China, and to link non-proliferation with disarmament measures. Unless this were done, India warned, no matter how many countries signed the treaty, it would not be effective and would not last. The United States and the Soviet Union were opposed to listing specific measures of nuclear disarmament in the article and thought that an attempt to do so might endanger the treaty. They argued that a non-proliferation treaty would enhance the security of all parties, especially the non-nuclear countries, and would help to create a favorable atmosphere for progress in achieving limitations on nuclear arsenals; the treaty draft represented the maximum agreement that was now obtainable and a heavy burden of responsibility would rest on any states that withheld their support of the treaty only because it did not go as far as they wished. Sweden proposed to include in Article VI the words "at an early date" and to add the word "nuclear" before "disarmament," and that reference to a comprehensive test ban be made in the Preamble of the treaty. The Swedish amendments were supported by the United Kingdom,

Mexico, the United Arab Republic, Nigeria, Bulgaria, and Canada and they were accepted by the two sponsors of the treaty draft and included in the final joint draft treaty of March 11. Spain suggested strengthening the article by including a provision for the destruction of nuclear weapons and delivery vehicles. West Germany thought that the obligations in Article VI should be expressed more concretely and that the preambular declaration of intention should list partial nuclear disarmament measures separately and in addition to general and complete disarmament.

With respect to the review conference, the United Kingdom restated its proposal whereby the conference would consider whether the purposes of the Preamble as well as the provisions of the treaty were being realized. The British amendment was supported by the United Arab Republic, Sweden, and Canada, and the United States and the Soviet Union accepted it and included it in the joint draft treaty of March 11. Italy, Romania, Spain, and West Germany wanted Review Conferences to be held automatically every five years, and Nigeria proposed that the Review Conference should adopt its findings by a majority of the signatory states present. The U.S. and the U.S.S.R., however, did not accept these proposals. Sweden proposed to amend Article VIII so that a majority of the parties could call a Review Conference every five years. The U.S. and U.S.S.R. accepted this amendment, and it was incorporated in the joint draft treaty of March 11.

As regards the provision that the treaty should last initially for twenty-five years, some countries felt that this was rather long and others thought that this indicated that the nuclear powers did not really expect that there would be any nuclear disarmament for that period of time.

As regards the withdrawal clause, some delegations, including Nigeria and Sweden, considered that the language was rather unclear, and Romania and Brazil thought that it constituted a limitation on the exclusive sovereign competence of every state.

Joint American–Soviet Draft Treaty, 1968

On March 11, 1968, the United States and the Soviet Union introduced a joint draft treaty in place of the previous identical treaty texts, which incorporated some of the suggestions made by Sweden and the United Kingdom. A reference was added to the Preamble recalling the pledge in the Partial Test Ban Treaty to seek a comprehensive test ban. Article VI was revised to the form in which it appeared in the final text of the treaty. The Review Conference would judge whether the purposes of the Preamble as well as the provisions of the treaty had been realized, and, at the request of a majority of the parties, further Review Conferences could be held at five-year intervals.

The Approval of the NPT

The joint draft treaty of March 11, 1968, was submitted by the ENDC to the General Assembly, which reconvened on April 24 to consider it. An extensive and detailed debate on its relative merits and shortcomings then took place. The Soviet Union, the United States, and the United Kingdom led those nations that supported the treaty. They stressed that it would increase the security of both the nuclear and non-nuclear states, that it would enable all nations, particularly the developing nations, to share in the benefits of the peaceful applications of nuclear energy, and that it would facilitate the cessation of the nuclear arms race.

The United States believed that the treaty would check the spread of nuclear weapons among nations and would thus enhance the security of all nations and especially that of the non-nuclear states. For its part, the U.S. would carry out its pledge to contribute to the peaceful applications of nuclear energy and would share the benefits of peaceful nuclear explosions with other countries. The treaty contained a new and solemn treaty obligation to continue efforts for nuclear disarmament, which was the strongest and most meaningful undertaking that could be agreed upon concerning disarmament, and the U.S. believed that the "permanent viability" of the treaty would depend on the success of such further disarmament negotiations.

The Soviet Union made similar points. It felt that the treaty blocked all possible forms of access to nuclear weapons by non-nuclear nations and closed all loopholes. The Soviet Union favored complete nuclear disarmament, but attempts to tie the questions of non-proliferation to other measures restricting the nuclear arms race could only result in an impasse in which neither the question of non-proliferation nor that of disarmament could be solved. The Non-Proliferation Treaty also was a treaty on the proliferation of benefits from the peaceful application of nuclear energy, including peaceful nuclear explosions, to all non-nuclear parties. The benefits obtained by non-nuclear states from the treaty would outweigh whatever disadvantages could result from their foreswearing nuclear weapons.

The proposed treaty received broad general support, but a number of members expressed reservations and some rejected the treaty altogether.

France stated that the only solution to the threat resulting from the existence of nuclear weapons was the cessation of their manufacture and the complete destruction of existing stockpiles. France stated, however, that while it would not sign the treaty, it would "behave in the future in this field exactly as the States adhering to the Treaty." In addition, France asserted that no nuclear state "will ever envisage sharing" nuclear weapons with anyone.

A number of members of the ENDC, such as Ethiopia, Nigeria, and

Sweden, while criticizing some aspects of the treaty, stated that they would support the treaty in the hopes that further measures would be taken in the direction of improving the operation of the treaty and in achieving further measures of disarmament.

Brazil and India strongly criticized the treaty, and India stated that it would not sign it. Brazil opposed the ban on peaceful nuclear explosive devices by non-nuclear nations. It saw no real and tangible commitment on the part of the nuclear countries to nuclear disarmament. The nuclear powers would enjoy a "privileged status," since they would not have to submit to IAEA safeguards. The tripartite security assurances were insufficient, and a formal obligation not to use nuclear weapons against signatories, such as had been agreed upon by the U.S. and the U.K. in signing Protocol II of the Tlatelolco Treaty, was necessary. India again insisted that the treaty should provide for a fissionable materials production cutoff which would require the nuclear powers to accept international safeguards. The provisions of Article VI of the draft treaty were insufficient and did not place sufficient pressure on the nuclear powers to achieve nuclear disarmament. The threat of the Chinese Communist nuclear weapons program showed the need both for nuclear disarmament and for a treaty that would prevent proliferation by all nuclear powers, including China. India also was opposed to a ban on peaceful nuclear explosions and criticized the provision permitting bilateral arrangements for such peaceful explosive services. It also considered that the safeguards provisions were discriminatory.

Japan stated that the draft treaty did not yet provide an "acceptable balance of mutual responsibilities" between the nuclear and nonnuclear states. It considered that the treaty would "lose its moral basis" unless the nuclear states made progress in disarmament. The treaty was defective in failing to prohibit transfers between nuclear states and in not providing that IAEA safeguards should apply to the peaceful nuclear activities of the nuclear powers. Japan asked that the international flow of nuclear materials should be further liberalized in order to promote peaceful nuclear activities. It considered that the ban on peaceful nuclear explosive devices should not apply to explosions that did not amount to a nuclear weapon, as, for example, those by thermonuclear fusion reactors.

Pakistan also felt that the treaty failed to provide an "acceptable balance." The non-nuclear nations should be provided with adequate security guarantees against the threat or use of nuclear weapons from any quarter. The nuclear powers should assure a supply of nuclear fuel to non-nuclear nations. Pakistan hoped that the nuclear powers would be able to make progress on nuclear disarmament before the non-nuclear conference met at the end of August.

Australia said that it would support the draft treaty but expressed concern about the security assurances. It urged the Soviet Union to follow the American and British example and accept IAEA safeguards over its peaceful nuclear activities. And it asked for clarification to ensure that the safeguards would not apply to the mining and early processing stages of uranium.

South Africa felt that the draft treaty did not take into account the legitimate interests of nonnuclear countries. Article VI did not establish any compelling obligation to end the nuclear arms race. There was no control on dissemination by the nuclear powers and no guarantee against discrimination in peaceful nuclear explosive services. As a uranium producer, South Africa opposed the application of IAEA safeguards to uranium ores or unrefined materials.

Israel stated that it would support the resolution commending the draft treaty but hoped that the treaty would be revised to include a commitment by nuclear powers not to use their nuclear weapons against non-nuclear countries. It also wanted an operative paragraph added to reaffirm the principles of the U.N. Charter. It felt that the provisions on peaceful nuclear uses should be clarified, and it regretted the lack of universality of participation by the nuclear powers in the treaty and in the security assurances.

Canada stated that Canadian peaceful nuclear development had not been handicapped by lack of information on nuclear weapons and that Canada was able to compete with the nuclear powers in the production and marketing of reactors. Canada, like South Africa, was also a uranium producer, but it was satisfied that IAEA safeguards would not be applied to uranium ores or unrefined ore concentrates. The United States also confirmed that IAEA safeguards would not apply to uranium mines or ore-processing plants.

Romania again maintained that the treaty should incorporate a commitment to stop the production of nuclear weapons, reduce stockpiles, and eliminate nuclear weapons and delivery vehicles The nuclear states should also pledge not to use nuclear weapons against non-nuclear states that did not possess them and had undertaken not to produce them.

Mexico urged that the resolution endorsing the treaty should receive as large a majority as possible. It accordingly urged the authors of the treaty to make a final revision of the draft in the light of the debate. It proposed adding to the draft treaty a preambular paragraph based on the U.N. Charter provision on the nonuse of force. It also wished to strengthen Article IV by adding language whereby the parties would "undertake to facilitate" the exchange not only of scientific and technological information but also of equipment and material. This should be done with "due consideration for the needs of the developing areas of the world." It also proposed amendments to Article V to provide a positive commitment whereby each party would undertake "to take appropriate measures to ensure that in accordance with the Treaty, under appropriate international observation and through appropriate international procedures," the potential benefits from any peaceful nuclear explosion would be made available to non-nuclear states. The new language also provided that "non-nuclear-weapon States party to the Treaty shall be able to obtain such benefits, pursuant to a special international agreement or agreements, through an appropriate international body with adequate representation of non-nuclear-weapon States. . . . Negotiations on this subject shall commence as soon as possible after the Treaty enters into force. Non-nuclear-weapon States party to the Treaty so desiring may also obtain such benefits pursuant to bilateral agreements."

Most of the other participants in the General Assembly debate also urged that the treaty text be improved. After five weeks of detailed examination of the text, and taking into account the comments made during the discussion, the American and Soviet delegations submitted a revised draft treaty on May 31, 1968. This revised draft accepted the various proposals made by Mexico. The two countries hoped that the treaty would now be able to obtain broad support.

On June 12, the General Assembly, by vote of 95 to 4 with 21 abstentions, adopted the revised resolution which commended the treaty. The text of the General Assembly resolution read as follows:

The General Assembly,

Recalling its resolution 2346 A (XXII) of 19 December 1967, 2153 A (XXI) of 17 November 1966, 2149 (XXI) of 4 November 1966, 2028 (XX) of 19 November 1965 and 1665 (XVI) of 4 December 1961,

Convinced of the urgency and great importance of preventing the spread of nuclear weapons and of intensifying international co-operation in the development of peaceful applications of atomic energy,

Having considered the report of the Conference of the Eighteen-Nation Committee on Disarmament, dated 14 March 1968, and appreciative of the work of the Committee on the elaboration of the draft non-proliferation treaty, which is attached to that report,

Convinced that, pursuant to the provisions of the treaty, all signatories have the right to engage in research, production and use of nuclear energy for peaceful purposes and will be able to acquire source and special fissionable materials, as well as equipment for the processing, use and production of nuclear material for peaceful purposes,

Convinced further that an agreement to prevent the further proliferation of nuclear weapons must be followed as soon as possible by effective measures on the cessation of the nuclear arms race and on nuclear disarmament, and that the non-proliferation treaty will contribute to this aim,

Affirming that in the interest of international peace and security both nuclear-weapon and non-nuclear-weapon States carry the responsibility of acting in accordance with the principles of the Charter of the United Nations that the sovereign equality of all States shall be respected, that the threat or use of force in international relations shall be refrained from and that international disputes shall be settled by peaceful means,

1. Commends the Treaty on the Non-Proliferation of Nuclear Weapons, the text of which is annexed to the present resolution;

2. Requests the Depositary Governments to open the Treaty for signature and ratification at the earliest possible date;

3. Expresses the hope for the widest possible adherence to the Treaty by both nuclear-weapon and non-nuclear-weapon States:

4. Requests the Conference of the Eighteen-Nation Committee on Disarmament and the nuclear-weapon States urgently to pursue negotiations on effective measures relating to the cessation of the nuclear arms race at an early date and to nuclear disarmament, and on a treaty on general and complete disarmament under strict and effective international control;

5. Requests the Conference of the Eighteen-Nation Committee on Disarmament to report on the progress of its work to the General Assembly at its twenty-third session.

The vote on the resolution was as follows:

For—Afghanistan, Australia, Austria, Barbados, Belgium, Bolivia, Botswana, Bulgaria, Byelorussian S.S.R., Cameroon, Canada, Ceylon, Chad, Chile, China, Colombia, Democratic Republic of the Congo, Costa Rica, Cyprus, Czechoslovakia, Dahomey, Denmark, Ecuador, El Salvador, Ethiopia, Finland, Ghana, Greece, Guatemala, Guyana, Honduras, Hungary, Iceland, Indonesia, Iran, Iraq, Ireland, Israel, Italy, Ivory Coast, Jamaica, Japan, Jordan, Kenya, Kuwait, Laos, Lebanon, Lesotho, Liberia, Libya, Luxembourg, Madagascar, Malaysia, Maldive Islands, Malta, Mauritius, Mexico, Mongolia, Morocco, Nepal, Netherlands, New Zealand, Nicaragua, Nigeria, Norway, Pakistan, Panama, Paraguay, Peru, Philippines, Poland, Romania, Senegal, Singapore, Somalia, South Africa, Southern Yemen, Sudan, Sweden, Syria, Thailand, Togo, Trinidad and Tobago, Tunisia, Turkey, Ukrainian S.S.R., U.S.S.R., U.A.R., U.K., U.S., Upper Volta, Uruguay, Venezuela, Yemen, Yugoslavia.

Against—Albania, Cuba, Tanzania, Zambia.

Abstaining—Algeria, Argentina, Brazil, Burma, Burundi, Central African Republic, Congo (Brazzaville), France, Gabon, Guinea, India, Malawi, Mali, Mauritania, Niger, Portugal, Rwanda, Saudi Arabia, Sierra Leone, Spain, Uganda.

An analysis of the vote shows that the three nuclear powers and all the Warsaw Pact and NATO allies with the exception of Portugal voted in favor of the treaty. The members of the ENDC with the exception of Brazil, Burma, and India also voted in favor of the treaty. Other important abstentions among the non-nuclear powers were Argentina and Spain. France also abstained. The only four countries which voted against the draft resolution were countries which had ties of one sort or another with the People's Rebublic of China. Among the countries that voted in favor of the resolution commending the NPT but did not sign the treaty were Israel, Pakistan, and South Africa.

The Non-Proliferation Treaty was widely hailed as a remarkable and important achievement that could prove to be a turning point in human history. Immediately after the vote, President Johnson addressed the General Assembly and called the treaty "the most important international agreement in the field of disarmament since the Nuclear Age began." He also pledged American determination "to make this but a first step toward ending the peril of nuclear war." In an address to the Supreme Soviet of the U.S.S.R. on June 27, Foreign Minister Gromyko said that "the conclusion of the treaty will be one of the most important steps ever undertaken to restrain the nuclear arms race in the name of the lasting interests of peace."

The People's Republic of China at that time had not yet occupied the seat of China in the United Nations and hence had not participated in any of the discussions there concerning the NPT. On several occasions in the past, however, the Chinese Communists had denounced the NPT as a demonstration of the attempts of the United States and the Soviet Union to establish nuclear hegemony over the entire world. For example, when the Soviet Union and the United States presented their identical draft treaty texts to the ENDC in August 1967, the Chinese government issued a statement criticizing the treaty in strong terms. Among other things, it said:

> The U.S.–Soviet treaty is an outright hoax. They want to use this scrap of paper to lull the people's vigilance so that under cover of this treaty they can have a free hand to vigorously carry out their nuclear blackmail and nuclear threat, control and bully other countries, sabotage the revolutionary movements of the people of the world and realize their fond hope of being overlords of the world.

When the joint Soviet–American draft treaty had been submitted to the ENDC on January 18, 1968, the Chinese Communists denounced it as a "landmark of the stepped-up counter-revolutionary global collusion between U.S. imperialism and the Soviet revisionist clique." They also claimed that the United States and the Soviet Union wished "to deprive the non-nuclear nations under U.S.–Soviet nuclear threat of their right to develop nuclear weapons" and wanted to place some of them under their nuclear umbrella so that they could maintain their status as "nuclear overlords." On the day after the approval of the NPT by the General Assembly, the People's Republic of China again attacked the treaty as "something imposed on the non-nuclear states to bind them hand and foot." The treaty was "a big plot and a big fraud of the U.S. imperialists and Soviet revisionists," while the non-nuclear powers were "totally deprived of their right to develop nuclear weapons for self-defense and are even restricted in their use of atomic energy for peaceful purposes."

The treaty was opened for signature on July 1, 1968, simultaneously in London, Moscow, and Washington, the capitals of the three depositary governments. It was signed on that day by the three nuclear powers and by more than fifty other countries. At the signing ceremony in Washington, President Johnson called it a "reassuring and hopeful moment." He said that the treaty had three simple purposes: (1) to prevent proliferation, (2) to assure that non-nuclear nations could have the full peaceful benefits of the atom, and (3) to commit the nuclear powers to move forward toward effective measures of arms control and disarmament. In this connection, he announced that the United States and the Soviet Union had agreed to hold early discussions on the limitation and reduction of offensive and defensive strategic nuclear delivery systems. In this way, on the day of the signing of the NPT the world was apprised of the intention of the two superpowers to undertake the strategic arms limitation talks, known by the acronym "SALT."

Thus, after years of lengthy and complicated negotiations, the NPT was completed and opened for signature. The non-nuclear powers had succeeded in wringing a number of concessions from the nuclear powers which improved the treaty sufficiently so as to make it possible for the overwhelming majority to go along with it, but they did so without great enthusiasm, as many of them sympathized with the criticisms of those that refused to sign. Nevertheless, they held high hopes that, if the nuclear powers lived up to their commitments and promises, the treaty would mark the beginning of the end of the atoms for war and a real beginning toward atoms for peace.

The treaty entered into force on March 5, 1970, when it had been ratified by the three nuclear depositary states and forty other states. The text of the treaty and a list of states that had signed and ratified it by January 1, 1976, appear in Appendices IV and V.

Chapter 6.   Analysis of the Non-Proliferation Treaty

The Non-Proliferation Treaty, like any political document or instrument, represents a compromise among a number of differing points of view and positions. As such, its provisions are not always clear, nor are their limits always precisely defined. The negotiation of the treaty took so long, however, and it was subjected to such a careful examination in the ENDC and at the United Nations General Assembly, that the meaning of most of its provisions is clearly understood, although the precise language of the treaty leaves something to be desired from a drafting viewpoint.

Nuclear-Weapon and Non-Nuclear Weapon States

The basic and fundamental distinction made in the treaty is between the nuclear-weapon states and the non-nuclear-weapon states. A nuclear-weapon state is defined in paragraph 3 of Article IX—hereinafter referred to as Article IX(3)—as one which has "manufactured and exploded a nuclear weapon or other nuclear explosive device prior to January 1, 1967." Hence there are only five nuclear-weapon states in the world insofar as the NPT is concerned, namely, China, France, the United States, the Soviet Union, and the United Kingdom. All other states are non-nuclear-weapon states. This means that India would be regarded as a non-nuclear-weapon state, even if she should now or later adhere to the NPT, and the same would be true of any other country which exploded a nuclear weapon or other nuclear explosive device, whether or not it was a party to the NPT.

A question may arise over what is known as the "European option." If the countries of the European Common Market should create a federation by 1980, as they have stated is their objective, or at some later date, such a Western European federation would be the successor state of the members constituting the federation and would inherit the nuclear capabilities of France and the United Kingdom. The question would then be raised as to whether this federation would be regarded as a nuclear-weapon state, since, on the one hand, it would have been established after January 1, 1967, but, on the other hand, it would be inheriting the nuclear status of those of its constituents that were nuclear-weapon states prior to January 1, 1967. The question is far from clear, although the United States has notified its allies that the treaty does not deal with the problem of European unity and would not bar succession by a new federated European state to the nuclear status of one of its former components.

The matter is not without importance, because if the new federation were regarded as a non-nuclear-weapon state it would be subject to all the restrictions applying to such a state under the treaty. This would seem to be most unrealistic and highly unlikely. If the new federation were regarded as a nuclear-weapon state, however, it would be possible for the U.S. to render whatever technological assistance it wished to it, as this is not barred by Article I.

It will be noted that Nationalist China (Taiwan), which is a party to the NPT, has been excluded from all United Nations bodies including the IAEA, which casts some doubt on the validity of its participation in the NPT. The People's Republic of China is neither a party to the treaty, nor has it taken its seat in the IAEA. Byelorussia and the Ukrainian S.S.R., which are members of the United Nations and the IAEA, did not sign the NPT, although they did sign and ratify the PTBT in 1963. While there has been no official statement to that effect, for purposes of the treaty they are presumably regarded as constituent parts of the U.S.S.R. Nevertheless, if they are regarded as separate states, as is logical to assume from their separate membership in the U.N., a problem might arise some day. As they are non-nuclear-weapon states and non-parties to the NPT, there would be no legal bar to their helping other nuclear-weapon states that were not parties, or any other recipients, to acquire nuclear weapons. While the problem seems hypothetical and remote, it is there.

It will also be noted that, unlike the Treaty of Tlatelolco, the NPT does not define a nuclear weapon, nor does it define a nuclear explosive device.

Article I

Article I of the Non-Proliferation Treaty bans the transfer to "any recipient whatsoever" of a nuclear weapon or explosive device. This would mean that such a transfer to any country or alliance or group of countries or private organizations or corporations, whether national or multinational, would be barred. Thus any possible MLF or any other form of nuclear sharing is banned by this article. Likewise, transfers to any nuclear-weapon state or to any international or supranational organization, including the United Nations, is banned.

As was agreed by the United States and the Soviet Union in the fall of 1966, the article does not ban the establishment or operation of a Nuclear Planning Committee within NATO; such a committee would involve joint planning but not joint control over the weapons or their use.

The second part of Article I bans assistance only to non-nuclear-weapon states and does not specifically mention private organizations or corporations, either national or multinational. Thus it is arguable, at least in theory, that a nuclear-weapon state is not barred from rendering assistance to such private organizations. The Article does not apply to the rendering of assistance by one nuclear-weapon state to another nuclear-weapon state, nor does it specifically ban assistance by a non-nuclear-weapon state to another non-nuclear-weapon state or to a private corporation or association. In fact, these very points were made by the United Arab Republic (Egypt) at every stage of the negotiation and revision of the NPT, when it submitted amendments designed to close these "loopholes." Both the Soviet Union and the United States considered that no such amendments were necessary. They considered that Articles I and II and the Preamble to the treaty make it clear that all loopholes are closed from any realistic or practical point of view. Canada thought that the U.A.R. might have detected a "theoretical loophole" but doubted that any such situation would arise in practice and questioned the desirability of reopening debate over the text of Articles I and II, which had been so carefully negotiated by the two authors. It is true that at the present time there seems to be little prospect of anyone taking advantage of the loopholes foreseen by the U.A.R. It is not at all clear, however, given all the fissionable material that will be available in the world in the future and the possibility of political or criminal terrorists, that this possibility might not at some point become a real danger.

There is, of course, no ban or restriction whatsoever on non-parties to the treaty. China, France, and India, therefore, are not prevented by the treaty from transferring nuclear explosive devices or nuclear weapons to any recipient they wish. As noted earlier, however, France has in fact stated that she would not do so and that although she would not become a party to the treaty she would behave exactly as if she were one.

Article II

Article II forbids non-nuclear-weapon parties to the treaty from manufacturing or otherwise acquiring nuclear weapons or nuclear explosive devices. It does not forbid research and development of any nature in the nuclear field. Since neither a nuclear weapon nor a nuclear explosive device is defined in the treaty, it could be argued that a nuclear device is not a nuclear weapon or a nuclear explosive until it has been fully assembled, that is, until the last screw has been turned. It can also be argued that a device cannot be considered a nuclear weapon or nuclear explosive device unless it has been successfully tested, on the theory that a device that does not work cannot be either a weapon or an explosive device. Thus it is possible for any non-nuclear party to the treaty to conduct all of the preparations for manufacture of a nuclear weapon, including research, development, and fabrication of the nuclear material and containers, right up until the very last stage. Since there is no prohibition whatsoever on the manufacture of nuclear-weapon delivery vehicles, these can of course be manufactured freely by any party.

As indicated above under Article I, there is no ban on a non-nuclear party helping another non-nuclear country that is not a party to the treaty. This was, as we mentioned, one of the concerns of the U.A.R., which wished to add to Article I a ban on nuclear proliferation by or to private individuals or organizations and to Article II a prohibition on assistance by one non-nuclear state to another.

Article III

This article, dealing with controls and inspection or "safeguards," was the most difficult one to negotiate and has been the basis of numerous charges of discrimination. Safeguards are to be accepted only by non-nuclear-weapon states; there are no provisions for verification of the fulfillment by nuclear-weapon states of their obligations regarding nuclear weapons or peaceful nuclear explosive devices. It would, of course, be extremely difficult to devise such a verification system in respect of the transfer of nuclear weapons and explosive devices from one country to another since the nuclear-weapon states are very concerned to preserve the secrecy of their weapons systems.

The only nuclear activities subject to safeguards are peaceful ones, and the safeguards are intended to prevent diversion of nuclear energy from peaceful uses to nuclear weapons or explosive devices. There is, however, no prohibition on nonexplosive miltary applications, such as nuclear propulsion of submarines or warships. Such uses, although they are proscribed by the IAEA Statute, are not banned by Article II. Accordingly, fissionable material for permitted military purposes is not subject to safeguards. There are also no safeguards over material intended for nonpeaceful purposes which is exported or transferred to nuclear-weapon countries by non-nuclear countries. Thus transfers for military uses, which are uninspected, are not banned or safeguarded. It will be noted that the Treaty of Tlatelolco applies safeguards to all nuclear activities, with no limitation whatsoever.

Article III (2) provides an obligation on the part of each party to the treaty not to provide source or special fissionable material or equipment or material therefor to any non-nuclear state, whether a party to the treaty or not, unless the source or special fissionable material is subject to the safeguards "required by this article." In other words, even non-parties to the treaty must agree to accept IAEA safeguards if they wish to obtain fissionable materials or equipment from any party. It is not clear whether a non-nuclear country that is not a party to the treaty must agree to accept IAEA safeguards over "all source or special fissionable material in all peaceful nuclear activities" in its territory, as is the case with non-nuclear parties under the provisions of paragraph 1 of Article III, or only over current supplies. It would certainly be unusual, indeed absurd, if states that are not parties to the treaty should be in a more favorable position in this regard than those that are. A clarifying policy declaraion by supplier states might be in order.

Actually, the provisions of Article III (2) were violated for a number of years. Starting on August 22, 1974, however, a number of important supplier states, 13 in all, joined in public undertakings (in letters to the IAEA) stating that they would not provide source or special fissionable material or equipment and material therefor to any non-nuclear-weapon state unless such material and equipment were subject to IAEA safeguards. But these undertakings applied only to future supplies and not to past supplies or existing or indigenous stocks. In any case, some supplier and potential supplier states, such as France, South Africa, China, and India, have not given similar undertakings, and so the possibility remains that material can be supplied to countries that do not put such material under IAEA safeguards.

Article III (3) was included in the treaty at the request of such advanced nuclear countries as West Germany, Japan, Italy, and Switzerland, who feared that the safeguards provided for might hinder their development of peaceful atomic power and who also were concerned about the risks of industrial espionage. Accordingly, Article III (3) and the sixth preambular paragraph of the treaty were designed to reasssure such countries that the safeguards would neither be too intrusive nor in any way hamper their peaceful development of nuclear energy. Such a nonintrusive system of safeguards was worked out by an IAEA committee in which a large number of states participated, and in 1971 the IAEA/NPT safeguards system was adopted by the IAEA. There is a theoretical possibility of future conflict here, in that the IAEA/NPT system of safeguards is specifically stated to be intended merely to deter any diversion of nuclear material to military uses, whereas Article III (1) of the treaty states that safeguards are accepted with a view toward "preventing" diversion of nuclear energy. It is unlikely, however, that this difference would lead to any significant problems in practice. Some other problems, may arise, however, from the fact that according to its statute, IAEA safeguards are required to prevent all military activities and not merely explosions, but are not intended to prevent any peaceful activities such as peaceful nuclear explosions.

Article III (4) was included in the treaty because of the problems raised in connection with Euratom, which had its own safeguards system and which included both nuclear states (originally France, but now also the United Kingdom) and non-nuclear states. As a result of detailed negotiations by the United States with the Euratom countries and with the Soviet Union, it was finally agreed that the Euratom countries would accept IAEA safeguards but that they could do so "either individually or together with other states." After further negotiations, an agreement was arrived at between the non-nuclear members of Euratom and the Euratom community on the one hand, and the IAEA, on the other, for the acceptance of the IAEA system of safeguards. The agreement was signed in all the members of the Euratom community itself. The agreement is April 1973 and entered into force upon its ratification in April 1975 by accompanied by a Protocol which takes account of the existence of the Euratom safeguards system and specifies conditions and means of cooperation between the two organizations in the application of safeguards. The entry into force of this agreement had been held up because of a delay by Italy in completing the ratification procedures. Italy, which was not very enthusiastic about the NPT and its basic discriminatory features from the beginning, was reluctant to foreclose its nuclear option. It was concerned about the fact that a number of other Mediterranean Powers—in particular, Israel, Egypt, Spain, and Algeria—have not become parties to the NPT. It finally completed the process of ratification, however, on the eve of the convening of the NPT Review Conference in May 1975.

The fact that the treaty's safeguards do not apply to the nuclear-weapon states was regarded as adding another discriminatory element to the inherent discrimination resulting from the fact that there are nuclear-weapon states and non-nuclear-weapon states and that the latter must continue to remain non-nuclear. In addition, as indicated above, there were fears on the part of some of the non-nuclear powers of the possibility of commercial discrimination. In order to meet these criticisms, the United States and the United Kingdom, in December 1967, unilaterally and voluntarily agreed to accept IAEA safeguards in respect of their peaceful nuclear activities. Although the Soviet Union has not made any such offer, the willingness of the United States and the United Kingdom to do so has served to reassure the concerned non-nuclear states. By August 1975, negotiations had not been completed between the U. S. or the U. K. and the IAEA regarding application of the latter's safeguards to the peaceful nuclear activities of the two nuclear states.

Article IV

This article was included in the treaty at the insistence of the non-nuclear states as part of the *quid pro quo* for their agreeing not to develop nuclear weapons or nuclear explosive devices. The nuclear powers maintained that there were little or no "spin-off" benefits to be derived from their military nuclear programs, but as a result of pressure from the non-nuclear states, they agreed that the benefits which they enjoyed from their advanced nuclear technology should be shared with the non-nuclear powers who renounced military programs. In its original form, the article merely referred to the inalienable right of all parties to produce and use nuclear energy for peaceful purposes and to participate in the fullest possible exchange of information; this was changed to provide for a positive commitment to promote the peaceful uses of nuclear energy, especially in the territories of non-nuclear parties and with due consideration for the needs of the developing areas of the world. The non-nuclear parties feel that the nuclear states have done little to fulfill their commitment under this article.

Article V

This article, too, was included in the treaty as part of the bargain between the nuclear states and the non-nuclear states. Since the treaty prohibited the transfer or acquisition of nuclear explosive devices for peaceful purposes, the non-nuclear states insisted that the benefits of such explosions should be made available to them. Like Article IV, this article, underwent several revisions in order to strengthen the obligations of the nuclear powers to make available to the non-nuclear powers the benefits of peaceful nuclear explosions. In order to remove any economic incentive for non-nuclear states to develop their own peaceful nuclear explosives, it was specified that they would be able to obtain the explosive services at as low a cost as possible; since research and development charges would be excluded, this would be lower than any country could provide for itself.

In order to make sure that the non-nuclear countries would not be at any disadvantage in negotiating bilaterally with any of the nuclear powers for peaceful explosive services, it was also provided that these could be obtained pursuant to a special international agreement and through an appropriate international body with adequate representation of non-nuclear states. Negotiations to create the necessary international machinery and procedures were to commence "as soon as possible after the treaty enters into force." As of the end of 1975, no negotiations on this subject had commenced, although the IAEA had taken certain steps in order to be able to discharge the responsibilities that might be placed upon it under this article.

In view of the prohibition in Article I against the transfer of a nuclear explosive device to "any recipient whatsoever," a nuclear-weapon state would be barred from transferring a device to the IAEA or any other international body and would have to conduct any explosion itself.

Article VI

This article, which contains a commitment on the part of the nuclear powers to seek further measures of disarmament, in particular nuclear disarmament, must be read in conjunction with paragraphs 9, 11, and 12 of the Preamble of the treaty. Although Articles I and II of the treaty are regarded by the nuclear powers as containing the basic provisions, Article VI and the three preambular paragraphs mentioned are unquestionably regarded by the non-nuclear powers as at least equally important. The non-nuclear states insisted that if they were to forego nuclear weapons, the nuclear powers must stop the nuclear arms race and begin to disarm. In other words, the stopping of the horizontal proliferation of nuclear weapons should be matched by action to stop their vertical proliferation. The question of the meaning and implementation of Article VI is discussed at length in Chapter 14.

The nuclear powers firmly rejected all propsals which would commit them to any specific measures of disarmament or to any time limits; it is possible that, had the non-nuclear powers insisted on such provisions, there never would have been a non-proliferation treaty. The most that the nuclear powers would agree to was to undertake "to pursue negotiations in good faith" for the cessation of the nuclear arms race at an early date and for eventual nuclear disarmament and the conclusion of a treaty on general and complete disarmament. They did agree, however, to include references to specific measures of disarmament in the Preamble of treaty. In preambular paragraph 11, they recalled their commitment to seek to achieve a comprehensive test ban. Preambular paragraph 12 implied that an easing of international tensions and the strengthening of trust between nation-states would be necessary in order to facilitate the cessation of the manufacure of nuclear weapons and the liquidation of all existing stockpiles, and also implied that the elimination of nuclear weapons and means of delivery could take place only pursuant to a treaty on general and complete disarmament.

The General Assembly resolution of June 12, 1968, which commended the NPT, refers to the promotion of the peaceful uses of nuclear energy and the need for effective measures for the cessation of the nuclear arms race and eventual nuclear disarmament only in its preamble. It is noteworthy that the only commitment contained in the treaty that is also referred to in the operative part of the resolution (paragraph 4) is that concerning the undertakings made in Article VI. (See text of the resolution in the preceding chapter, pages 83–84 above.)

Article VII

There were no difficulties concerning this article, which merely preserved the right of any group of states to enter into agreements for the establishment of nuclear-free zones.

Article VIII

Procedures for amendment of the treaty, which are outlined in this article, are so complicated and cumbersome as to make any amendments very unlikely in practice. It is necessary for one-third or more of the parties to the treaty to request a conference of the parties to consider any amendment. In order for any amendment to succeed it must be approved by a majority of the parties to the treaty (not merely of those voting at a conference), and a veto right is given to all the nuclear-weapon parties as well as to all the parties which are members of the Board of Governors of the IAEA on the date the amendment is circulated. This will ensure that there will rarely, if ever, be any amendments. As was urged by Romania, amendments do not apply to countries that do not ratify them even after they have entered into force for other parties. Thus, every party has a veto as regards the application of any amendment to itself.

Since the NPT entered into force on March 5, 1970, the review conference provided for in paragraph 3 of this article would ordinarily have begun by March 5, 1975. By agreement of the Preparatory Committee, however, the review conference took place in Geneva in May 1975.

As was indicated in the preceding chapter, as a result of pressure from the non-nuclear states and also from the United Kingdom, it was decided that the review conference would work to assure that the purposes of the Preamble as well as the provisions of the treaty were being realized. The two nuclear superpowers would not agree to periodic review conferences every five years, but did agree to such conferences being held at intervals of five years if a majority of the parties to the treaty so request. The review conference did, in fact, decide that a second conference would be held in 1980.

While the IAEA safeguards system is to apply in order to ensure that the non-nuclear parties to the treaty live up to their commitments not to manufacure nuclear weapons or nuclear explosive devices, the review conference is the only means for ensuring that the nuclear parties live up to their obligations under the treaty. No committee or other organ has been established for purposes of consultation or to hear complaints in this regard, as has been done under subsequent arms limitation treaties.

Article IX

This article specifies that the U.S.S.R., the U.K., and the U.S. are designated as depositary governments. Originally, paragraph 3 of this article provided that the treaty would enter into force after its ratification by the "nuclear-weapon States signatory to the Treaty" and forty other states, but this was changed in the final draft to require ratification by the depositary governments and forty other states, since it was pointed out that Communist China might decide to sign the treaty and not ratify it and thus prevent the treaty from entering into force.

Article X

This article contains the withdrawal clause that permits any party in the exercise of its national sovereignty to withdraw from the treaty if it decides that extraordinary events, related to the subject matter of the treaty, have jeopardized its supreme interests. Unlike the simple withdrawal clause in the Partial Test Ban Treaty, the NPT requires that three months' notice be given not only to other parties to the treaty but also to the United Nations Security Council. It also provides that such notice shall include a statement of the extraordinary events which the withdrawing country regards as having jeopardized its supreme interests. Several countries argued during the negotiation of the treaty that it was a derogation of national sovereignty to require that notice be given to the Security Council as well as to other parties to the treaty and to require that it should be accompanied by a statement of the extraordinary events prompting the withdrawal. However, the nuclear powers argued that the requirements of giving notice to the Security Council and submitting an accompanying statement would act as a restraining influence on any country that might wish to withdraw from the treaty and would allow time for international efforts to endeavor to persuade the country not to proceed with its intention of withdrawing. If a country is intent on withdrawing, however, the restraint provided by this requirement would not seem to be very formidable.

Article XI

The only matter of interest in this article is that it provides that the English, Russian, French, Spanish, and Chinese texts are all equally authentic. These were the five official languages of the United Nations at the time the treaty was approved. Chinese was included in the NPT text not merely to follow the practice of the United Nations but also because it was expected that Nationalist China (Taiwan) would become a party to the treaty (as it did); it was also hoped that, by making Chinese an official text, some slight encouragement might be held out to the People's Republic of China to do so as well. This hope, of course, has turned out to be completely illusory.

Chapter 7. The Politics of Nuclear Non-Proliferation

The concept of the non-proliferation of nuclear weapons has had a rather curious history. The Americans, who invented nuclear weapons and were the only people ever to use them in war, were from the outset anxious to prevent the further spread of these weapons. They proposed the Baruch Plan and passed the McMahon Act. As we have seen, after the failure of the Baruch Plan, the United States began promoting the idea of atoms for peace, which was bound to facilitate the possibility that nuclear weapons would spread to other nations. During the 1950s the United States was so absorbed in developing atoms for war and in promoting atoms for peace that it paid little, if any, attention to the possibilities and dangers of nuclear proliferation. It was only after some of the non-aligned nations directed world attention to the danger of the spread of nuclear weapons that the American officials began, somewhat reluctantly, to apply their minds to the problem. The Soviet Union, for its part, was so obsessed with developing its own nuclear arsenal in an attempt to catch up with the United States, and with its fears of Germany—particularly a Germany that might acquire nuclear weapons—that it also gave little or no attention to the overall problem.

The United States was the first of the two superpowers to recognize the problem. In 1963, President Kennedy publicly spoke of the nightmare world that would exist in the 1970s if not just four but possibly ten or fifteen countries possessed nuclear weapons; he feared that the genie would then really be out of the bottle and could not be put back in.

The nuclear superpowers lost a splendid opportunity in 1962 and 1963 to ban all nuclear weapon tests in all environments, including underground. This would have put a real brake on the spread as well as the development of nuclear weapons and might perhaps, except for France and Communist China, have halted it entirely. The security of the Soviet Union would not have been in any way endangered if it had agreed to permit on-site inspection of its territory to monitor or verify a comprehensive test ban, nor would that of the United States have been endangered if it had agreed to such a comprehensive ban without any on-site inspection whatsoever. As it happened, the Soviet Union did offer 2 to 3 on-site inspections and agreed to the placing of 3 "black boxes" on its territory in order to supervise an underground test ban. For reasons that are still not wholly comprehensible, the United States rejected these offers, and thus ensured that its security would be worsened by the continuation of the nuclear arms race, with all the risks and dangers of nuclear proliferation. One can only conclude, and this conclusion is bolstered by an examination of the efforts since that time to achieve an underground test ban, that the military and the scientists in the United States were themselves obsessed with a compulsive desire to go on testing and to research and develop new generations of nuclear weapons. This is all the more inexplicable in that from 1945 to the present day, there has never been a moment when the United States was not far superior to the Soviet Union and all other plausible combinations of hostile powers in the field of nuclear weapons. One would have thought that it would have been in the clear interest of the United States to obtain Soviet agreement to halt all nuclear testing, and thus practically ensure that the American margin of superiority would be maintained for a long and indefinite period of time. It has been a cliché of political leaders for a number of years to say that the risks of continuing testing, with the resulting continuation of the nuclear arms race, far exceed the risks of halting it.

It is also somewhat strange that the Soviet Union lagged behind the United States in putting the problem of non-proliferation of nuclear weapons at the top of its disarmament agenda. The potential nuclear powers are nearly all allied with or at least friendly to the United States and form a sort of ring around the Soviet Union. Apart from Great Britain, France, and Communist China, which had already become nuclear powers, the potential capabilities of West Germany, Italy, and Sweden to the west, Israel, India, and Pakistan to the south, Japan to the east, and and Canada to the north must surely have given Soviet strategists much food for thought. The geopolitics of nuclear proliferation were so heavily weighted on the side of the United States that not only some military leaders but also some leading scientists and scholars in the United States, while not quite going so far as to urge that "proliferation is good for you," did seem to hold the view that "proliferation isn't all that bad." George Ball, the then Deputy Secretary of State, argued forcibly that the United States should proceed with all speed to create an MLF and that its efforts to arrive at a treaty with the Soviet Union on nuclear non-proliferation endangered the entire Western alliance (*The Discipline of Power* [Boston: Little, Brown, 1968]). James Schlesinger, the former Secretary of Defense, maintained when he was a fellow of the Rand Corporation, that while there were some risks in nuclear proliferation, these risks were neither very great nor unmanageable ("The Strategic Consequences of

Nuclear Proliferation" in *The Reporter*, October 20, 1966; and "Nuclear Spread: The Setting of the Problem," in *Nuclear Nonproliferation*, American Assembly Paper, University of Notre Dame Press, 1967).

Over the years, some experts have argued that, just as the development of nuclear weapons by the United States and the Soviet Union led to a situation of mutual deterrence which has made war less likely, so too would the development of nuclear capability, particularly if it were in a balanced way by two or more regional adversary powers, lead to a situation of mutual deterrence and avoidance of conflict.

Among the major powers, only China has officially supported the idea of the proliferation of nuclear weapons, but even China has been careful to point out that she would not, herself, be a source of supply of nuclear material or technology. Up to the present time, China still maintains the view that third-world countries have the right to develop, by their own independent means, nuclear weapons to defend themselves against nuclear attack, threats, and blackmail from the nuclear superpowers. There are some indications, though, that China, as it proceeds to develop its own nuclear arsenal and to approach a state of nuclear deterrence, may be having some second thoughts about the desirability of seeing nuclear weapons spread to additional countries. Although its public statements still seem to imply that it favors the proliferation of nuclear weapons to third-world countries, the language is never clear or categorical in this regard. It is a fact, however, that China has never, at any time, uttered a word of condemnation of or opposition to the further spread of nuclear weapons to other countries. It had no unfavorable reaction even to the Indian nuclear explosion, and its attitude seemed to be more one of unconcern than anything else.

The Soviet Union and the United States, however, did, although rather late, come to realize how much in their interest it would be to prevent the further spread of nuclear weapons to other countries. And once they started to promote the idea of non-proliferation in earnest, a remarkable change came over the atmosphere of the disarmament sessions. Prior to 1963, at the various conferences and committees where disarmament was being discussed, there was a distinct chill, if not actually a continuation of the Cold War by other means, between the Soviet and Western delegations. Before and after meetings and at official luncheons, receptions, and cocktail parties, members of the Western delegations would usually tend to congregate together for the exchange of views or for socializing. Members of the United Nations Secretariat who serviced these conferences often made it a point to go over to speak to members of the Soviet and East European delegations, not only to show their impartiality but also to help ease a rather awkward situation. In fact, in the 1950s and early 1960s the head of the Soviet delegation would frequently ask the Secretariat to arrange a reception or cocktail party for all delegations in order to make it possible for the Soviet negotiators to meet other delegations on an informal basis and establish contact with them. In 1963, there was a noticeable change in this regard. That was the year of the Hot Line agreement, the Partial Test Ban Treaty, and the American–Soviet agreement not to station or orbit nuclear weapons in outer space. Beginning in that year, contacts between the Soviet delegation and other delegations, most particularly that of the United States, became less formal and more regular and casual.

When Harold Stassen, the chief American negotiator on disarmament from 1955 to 1958, tried in 1957 to establish direct bilateral contacts and meetings with the Soviet delegation at the Sub-Committee meetings in London, the difficulties and irritations that developed among the Western powers almost became an international incident. Even in 1962, after the establishment of the ENDC under American and Soviet cochairmen, exchanges between the two delegations were still rather formal and correct. Although they began to warm up in 1963, they were far from what could be described as friendly. As late as 1966, one of the senior members of the Soviet delegation told me that nothing of any importance was discussed by the American and Soviet delegations when they met privately as cochairmen of the ENDC. The meetings dealt almost exclusively with procedural questions relating to the work of the ENDC, and substantive questions were rarely, if ever, touched on.

The role of social functions in diplomacy should not be belittled. The perpetual round of cocktail parties, receptions, luncheons, and dinners provides occasions for informal and less official contacts at which ideas may be launched, positions probed and explored, and views exchanged, tested, revised, and brought up to date, in an easy and casual manner. Such social contacts provide the opportunity for polite conversation or pleasant banter during which one may seek information, drop hints, and float trial balloons without one's delegation being committed in any way. They are not only very useful; they are the very stuff of diplomacy and are well-nigh indispensable.

I remember one fascinating evening in February 1966, just after the ENDC resumed its 1966 session. Ambassador Cavaletti of Italy had arranged a dinner party at one of Geneva's best restaurants, and after the dinner he invited his guests to his apartment for champagne. Among those present were Ambassador Tsarapkin of the Soviet Union, Ambassador Timberlake of the United States, Lord Chalfont of Great Britain, Madame Myrdal of Sweden, General Burns of Canada, Ambassador Blusztajn of Poland, and myself as the representative of the Secretary–General. In the friendly atmosphere that existed after a good meal and with lots of champagne, the conversation turned to the usual discussion of the deadlock between the American and Soviet positions over the question of the MLF. Both Tsarapkin and Blusztajn kept repeating the familiar Soviet argument that any nuclear sharing arrangement whatsoever in NATO would be bound to give Germany access to nuclear weapons, meaning some form of physical control, and that this was totally unacceptable. After a while somebody asked, "Well, what about the McNamara suggestion for a committee for nuclear planning in NATO?" Blusztajn observed that this involved only consultations between allies and did not involve the actual sharing of physical control over nuclear weapons. He added, "How could we prevent consultation?" Someone then asked, "Then you would not object to the nuclear planning committee?" Blusztajn again replied, "How could we stop your consulting with your allies or object to your talking to them?" At this, a hush descended on the gathering and all eyes turned to Tsarapkin as someone asked him if he agreed. He shrugged but did not answer. But his failure to denounce the idea of the McNamara committee as he had in the past, or to deny the validity of Blusztajn's remarks, was itself sufficient. When the party broke up shortly thereafter, I went to my rooms and wrote a letter home to my wife saying that I thought that I was in at the birth of a non-proliferation treaty that night or, at least, at its successful conception. It is almost unheard-of for Communist negotiators to be other than serious about matters of business, and I was convinced that Blusztajn's remarks, if not actually planned, had been considered and weighed by him in advance. Since Tsarapkin had previously attacked the McNamara committee and it was barred by the terms of the Soviet draft treaty of September 1965, his silence on this occasion gave Blusztajn's remarks added importance. They certainly pointed the way toward a compromise solution of the deadlock. As it turned out, this was, in fact, the solution that was accepted by Secretary Rusk and Foreign Secretary Gromyko at the General Assembly in the fall of that year and that made agreement on a non-proliferation treaty possible. It is, of course, quite likely that, if the Soviet Union was intent on proposing such a compromise, it could and would have found other occasions and means for doing so. Nevertheless, this social function provided an ideal occasion for throwing out this particular idea, which, when followed up, helped to break the deadlock in the negotiations.

Concerns of the Nuclear Powers

The basic concern of the nuclear powers, as expressed by President Kennedy in 1963, was that once nuclear weapons proliferated the genie would be out of the bottle, and everybody would be living in a nightmare world. The nuclear powers were more involved and had more to lose than any other states. The tremendous power they wielded and their worldwide interests and commitments could be challenged and endangered if additional and smaller powers acquired nuclear-weapon capability. International diplomacy and the exercise of political influence would become much less manageable. The smaller powers could use their newly acquired nuclear prowess—or even the threat of exercising the option to go nuclear —to enhance their negotiating stance and bargaining power vis-à-vis the nuclear superpowers. They might even exploit their nuclear status, or potential nuclear status, as a means of "blackmail" to extract concessions from one or the other superpower, or to play the superpowers off against each other, not by threatening them directly but by threatening to launch a nuclear war or issue an ultimatum against a neighbor, which might involve or affect one or both of the superpowers.

The political and strategic relations among a few nuclear powers, even if they are involved in a great worldwide competition and struggle, encompass situations where they have parallel if not common interests which, once understood, can serve as a brake and control on conflict. But the whole nature and structure of relations between the nuclear powers would be altered in profound, ill-defined, and ill-perceived ways as nuclear weapons spread from one power to another. The risk of the outbreak of nuclear war as a result of deliberate action in an acute but minor regional conflict would be greatly magnified. And the risk of such a war as a result of miscalculation, accident, blackmail, or madness would also multiply, probably in an exponential manner, with every increase in the number of nuclear powers.

When President Johnson sent the Non-Proliferation Treaty to the Senate for ratification, he summed up the American interest in the treaty as follows:

> I consider this treaty to be the most important international agreement limiting nuclear arms since the nuclear age began. It is a triumph of sanity and of man's will to survive.
>
> The Treaty takes a major step toward a goal the United States has been seeking for the past twenty-two years. Beginning with the McMahon Act in 1946, our statutes have forbidden the transfer of our nuclear weapons to others.
>
> In the Executive branch, efforts to prevent the spread of nuclear weapons have complemented those of the Congress. Ever since the Baruch Plan of 1946, we have sought to achieve an international consensus on this subject.
>
> In making the first United States test ban proposal, President Eisenhower noted that his purpose was to curtail the uncontrolled spread of nuclear weapons.
>
> When President Kennedy announced the successful negotiation of the Nuclear Test Ban Treaty in 1963, he expressed the hope that it would be the opening wedge in a campaign to prevent the spread of nuclear weapons. He pointed out that a number of other nations could soon have the capacity to produce such weapons, and urged that we use whatever time remained to persuade such countries not to follow that course. . . .
>
> By 1985 the world's peaceful nuclear power stations will probably be turning out enough by-product plutonium for the production of tens of nuclear bombs every day. This capability must not be allowed to result in the further spread of nuclear weapons. The consequences would be nuclear

anarchy, and the energy designed to light the world could plunge it into
darkness.

   But the treaty has a significance that goes beyond its furtherance of these
important aspects of United States nuclear policy. In the great tradition of
the Nuclear Test Ban Treaty, it represents another step on the journey
toward world peace. I believe that its very achievement, as well as its provisions, enhances the prospects of progress toward disarmament.

It was plain that the Soviet Union had similar considerations in mind.
One of the top Soviet negotiators told me at the General Assembly in the
fall of 1966 that a non-proliferation treaty would be the most important
treaty since Yalta. Not only would it remove the danger of the spread of
nuclear weapons, but it would also define and improve relations between
the nuclear powers and between them and the non-nuclear powers for
decades to come.

The position of the United Kingdom is almost identical to that of the
United States. It regards the proliferation of nuclear weapons to additional
countries as a potential threat to its own security and to that of the world
at large.

The position of France as regards nuclear proliferation is basically
similar; its position is more complicated, however, because of the decision
of President de Gaulle to remain outside of the arms control and disarmament negotiations and to steer France onto an independent path while it
was building its own nuclear arsenal. France maintained that the only
solution to the threat resulting from the existence of nuclear weapons was
the cessation of their manufacture and the complete destruction of stockpiles—a position not far removed from that of China and India. However,
France asserted at the General Assembly session at which the NPT was
approved that no nuclear-weapon state "will ever envisage sharing" nuclear weapons with anyone. While it would not sign the NPT, France
would "behave in the future in this field exactly as the States adhering to
the Treaty."

Only China among the nuclear powers seems to regard the spread of
nuclear weapons to additional countries with equanimity, if not with favor.

Concerns of the Non-Nuclear Powers

   The concerns of the non-nuclear and smaller powers with respect to
nuclear proliferation are just as real and important to them as those of the
nuclear powers are to them. First and foremost, of course, is their overriding concern about their security. All powers, both nuclear and non-
nuclear, feel less secure in a nuclear-armed world, but the nuclear powers,
at least, have nuclear weapons to deter attacks upon them. The smaller
non-nuclear powers, on the other hand, are, in a sense, at the mercy of

nuclear great powers. Hence, those non-nuclear powers that have little, if any, prospect of going nuclear for a very long time to come have no interest in seeing any near-nuclear country or any potential nuclear neighbor go nuclear. Consequently, all non-nuclear countries would much prefer to live in a world free of nuclear weapons. But if nuclear weapons are to be an accepted fact of national and international life, many non-nuclear countries, particularly those who are near-nuclear or potential nuclear powers, can discern certain strategic and political advantages that might accrue to them by going nuclear. Just as in the days of the Wild West, possession of a six-shooter was a great equalizer among men, so some of the smaller powers could visualize scenarios wherein possession of nuclear weapons might have a great equalizing effect among nations. There are, of course, heavy economic costs involved in going nuclear as well as military and political risks, but there are also risks, albeit of a different kind, for nations who decide not to go nuclear.

Accordingly, the non-nuclear nations, if they were to foreswear the option of going nuclear, wanted firm and credible assurances guaranteeing their security. If they remained non-nuclear their security could be enhanced in several ways: first, by positive guarantees on the part of the nuclear powers to protect and defend them if they are threatened or attacked with nuclear weapons, and second, by negative assurances whereby the nuclear powers undertake not to attack or threaten them with nuclear weapons. A third way that indirectly helps to enhance their security is for the nuclear powers to undertake to halt the nuclear arms race and to take concrete measures of nuclear disarmament leading eventually to the elimination of nuclear weapons, thus improving the security of the whole world.

The first way, by positive security guarantees, is the most direct and credible means of providing assurances. It is the standard and traditional form of assurance, and it constitutes the basis of most defense agreements and collective security pacts, but it raises complicated and difficult political and strategic problems for the nuclear powers. It can also create problems for some neutral advanced states, such as Sweden and Switzerland, which might feel that their position would be compromised if they accepted protection from the nuclear powers. They therefore prefer negative assurances whereby the nuclear powers undertake not to use or threaten to use nuclear weapons against them. Nearly all other non-nuclear powers, however, are interested in positive as well as negative security assurances. But it is difficult to visualize any of the nuclear powers giving blanket open-ended guarantees of this kind to non-nuclear powers. The United States was not prepared even to give negative guarantees of a direct nature.

After the explosion of the first Chinese atomic bomb, India sought for years to obtain effective and credible guarantees of its security from the nuclear powers, but all its efforts were in vain. Having failed to obtain any adequate direct security guarantees, India shifted to the indirect approach and demanded that all nuclear powers stop manufacturing nuclear weapons and start reducing their nuclear arsenals. When this approach also seemed likely to fail, India began stressing its right to conduct nuclear explosions for peaceful purposes. One can speculate as to whether India would have gone ahead so soon, or at all, with the explosion of its own nuclear device if it had been offered adequate guarantees of its security, perhaps by means of a joint American–Soviet nuclear umbrella (as Japan had accepted an American one). Unfortunately, that possibility was never put to the test.

The United States at first spoke in terms of positive assurances by "giving strong support" to those non-nuclear states who might be threatened by nuclear attacks or by threats. But these promises were never followed up or implemented. The Soviet Union, on the other hand, put forward the so-called Kosygin Proposal for negative security assurances by offering to write into the NPT a pledge by the nuclear powers never to use or threaten to use nuclear weapons against non-nuclear powers that did not have nuclear weapons in their territory. The U.S. opposed the Kosygin Formula, as it believed that it could undermine the treaty commitments it had with its allies, and it refused to agree to such negative assurances. Thus the non-nuclear powers, despite their repeated insistence on the need for clear, adequate, and credible security guarantees, were left with only the flimsy formula of the Tripartite Declarations and Security Council Resolution 255.

No other question in the long consideration of the non-proliferation problem received as much attention as that of security assurances. Because of the political sensitivity of the question it was discussed more in private than in public, and much of the public discussion was in general terms. At first, non-nuclear countries spoke of "security guarantees," but over the months this phraseology was changed to the less specific term "security assurances." In the end, the non-nuclear states received neither positive nor negative security assurances. It was, at the time, and still is a matter of some surprise to me that the non-nuclear nations were content to accept the rather vague promises of the three nuclear parties to the NPT of immediate action in the Security Council in accordance with the provisions of the United Nations Charter.

The non-nuclear powers were at least a little more successful with regard to indirect security assurances by the way of nuclear disarmament. While the direct security guarantees were steadily eroded during the years of negotiation, the indirect assurances in the form of disarmament were steadily augmented in language and scope.

The language finally agreed to for Article VI and preambular paragraphs 9, 11, and 12 did not provide for any specific commitment to any concrete measure of disarmament, but it did provide a legal commitment on the part of the nuclear powers to pursue negotiations in good faith on effective measures relating to the cessation of the nuclear arms race at an early date and to nuclear disarmament. Thus, the non-nuclear powers succeeded to some extent in achieving a positive assurance that the nuclear powers would work toward disarmament. They have had little if any success in having this assurance implemented, however, as is shown in Chapter 14 below.

Next to these two crucial areas, concerning direct security assurances and indirect ones by way of disarmament, the third major area of concern to the non-nuclear powers was that of obtaining the benefits of the development of peaceful uses of nuclear energy, including peaceful nuclear explosions. The non-nuclear powers were convinced that the development of a nuclear-weapon capability by the nuclear powers gave the latter great economic advantages in the exploitation of the peaceful applications of nuclear energy. If they were to forego these benefits and advantages by refraining from developing a nuclear-weapons capability themselves, the non-nuclear nations wished to be sure that they would not also forego the benefits of the peaceful applications of nuclear energy. This area was the major concern of the industrial allies of the United States in NATO and of Japan, who did not have to worry about their security as they were under the American nuclear umbrella. These allies carried on a lengthy negotiation with the United States to make sure that they would not suffer any disadvantage by giving up the option to acquire nuclear weapons and other nuclear devices. The other non-nuclear states, in particular the non-aligned states, maintained their pressure for concessions by the nuclear powers right up until the last days of the General Assembly that approved the draft non-proliferation treaty. They were successful in obtaining positive commitments from the nuclear powers in Article IV of the NPT as regards the general peaceful uses of nuclear energy and in Article V as regards peaceful nuclear explosions. But in this area, too, there is a noticeable gap between the promises and the performance of the nuclear powers.

Another area of major concern to non-nuclear powers was the question of the discriminatory nature and provisions of the NPT. Their efforts to ensure that the discriminatory aspects of the treaty would be eliminated, or at least reduced to the lowest possible level, were given formal and polite expression in General Assembly Resolution 2028 of November 1965, which stipulated that the treaty should "embody an acceptable balance of mutual responsibilities and obligations of the nuclear and non-nuclear powers." Throughout the negotiations, the non-nuclear powers felt that they were being made to accept an entire series of discriminatory provisions. Apart from the basic fact of discrimination inherent in the very nature of the treaty, which perpetuated a distinction between nuclear and non-nuclear states that nearly all of the non-nuclear powers were prepared to acknowledge and accept, there were a number of additional features of a discriminatory nature which many of the non-nuclear powers were most reluctant to accept and unhappy about accepting. One of these, of course, was the provision barring them from conducting peaceful nuclear explosions. Another one was that they were accepting an immediate and important restriction on their sovereignty by agreeing not to go nuclear, while the nuclear powers were committed only to a promise to attempt to divest themselves of their nuclear weapon capability at some indefinite future time.

Perhaps that area of discrimination that was most difficult for the non-nuclear powers to accept was that concerning safeguards. A number of them felt that the safeguards provision of the treaty added a form of insult to the discriminatory injury which they suffered. They were being subjected to IAEA safeguards to ensure that they would abide by their promises not to go nuclear, while the nuclear powers were subjected to no safeguards whatsoever and remained free to continue to develop nuclear weapons and explosive devices. In addition, many of the non-nuclear powers—in particular, the members of Euratom, Japan, and Switzerland—felt that they would not only be at a commercial disadvantage in giving up the possible "spin-off" benefits derived from the acquisition of nuclear technology and the expertise gained from weapons production, but might also suffer a loss of secrets because of industrial espionage by IAEA inspectors. These concerns were dealt with, in large part, in three ways. As regards the Euratom countries, a deal was worked out between them and the United States and also the Soviet Union, as explained in the discussion of Article III in the previous chapter, for a cooperative arrangement between Euratom and IAEA. As regards the countries with advanced nuclear technology for peaceful purposes, a new, nonintrusive safeguards system was worked out for NPT safeguards, which is explained in Chapter 11 on International Safeguards. Finally, the element of discrimination was removed in part by the United States and the United Kingdom agreeing voluntarily to accept IAEA safeguards on their peaceful nuclear activities. Although the non-nuclear powers were not as concerned about suffering a disadvantage from the Soviet Union's refusal to accept voluntary safeguards over its peaceful nuclear activities, nevertheless the maintenance by the Soviet Union of this discriminatory position, and the delays of the United States and the United Kingdom in implementing their acceptance of safeguards, gave rise to some degree of resentment among the non-nuclear powers.

There are other, less important, areas, mainly in the procedural provisions, where discriminatory features appear in the treaty, such as in the veto right over amendments and in the lack of any machinery for supervising the implementation of the treaty other than the Review Conference, but these are of a marginal nature.

Another area of concern on the part of the non-nuclear powers is that the treaty should be universal in its application and should cover all nuclear powers as well as all non-nuclear ones. Some non-nuclear powers feel that it not only creates an additional element of discrimination but can actually be a serious threat to their security if two or more nuclear powers and several near-nuclear powers remain outside of the treaty and are not bound by its provisions. The fact that one more country has exploded a nuclear device and thus acquired a nuclear-weapon capability since the entry into force of the treaty cannot fail to have an important impact upon the non-nuclear powers.

Non-Nuclear Powers with Special Concerns

The concerns of a number of the non-nuclear powers were indicated in some detail in Chapter 5, describing the making of the Non-Proliferation Treaty. The countries that are of main interest to us here are those that have not signed the Non-Proliferation Treaty or have signed it but announced that they will ratify it only under certain conditions. The near-nuclear powers that failed to sign the treaty after it was opened for signature in 1968 were India and Pakistan, Israel and Egypt (which has signed but announced that it would ratify only if Israel did), South Africa and Spain, and Argentina and Brazil. It is not necessary to go into any detailed explanations or analyses of the positions and concerns of these eight countries. They have been discussed at length in many books and articles, such as *The Politics of Nuclear Proliferation* by Professor George Quester, (Johns Hopkins University Press, 1973), and *The Near-Nuclear Countries and the NPT* published by the Stockholm International Peace Research Institute (SIPRI) in 1972. Suffice it to say at this point that India is concerned about China, and Pakistan about India; Israel is concerned about the Arab states, and Egypt about Israel; South Africa is concerned about black Africa and the fact that it is an important producer of natural uranium; Spain is concerned that it is outside the NATO alliance and other Western European arrangements such as the Common Market; Brazil has visions of becoming a great power in the not very distant future, and Argentina is, of course, concerned about Brazil.

In practically all of these cases, security considerations are of paramount and decisive importance, but questions concerning the development of peaceful nuclear technology and matters of prestige and status also play an important role. Some combination of all these considerations has motivated the decision on the part of each of the above states to remain outside of the Non-Proliferation Treaty and the non-proliferation regime and keep open its option to go nuclear if it finds it necessary to do so. Each of them has had to weigh very carefully the advantages and disadvantages of whatever course of action it decided on. Only a basic change in the circumstances affecting each of these states and its position in the world, as it sees it, is likely to change its decision.

The Different Sets of Negotiations

Although the negotiations that went on in the United States and in the ENDC were the only ones that took place in public and that received public attention, there were, in fact, not one but five sets of negotiations proceeding all at the same time. Two sets of negotiations went on in the Western world, and no doubt there were similar ones going on at the same time within the Soviet Union and the Warsaw Pact nations, but little is known about these. Accordingly, this discussion deals only with the following five sets of negotiations:

1. Those within the U.S. government.
2. Those between the U.S. government and its allies.
3. Those between the United States and the Soviet Union.
4. Those among the nonaligned, non-nuclear powers.
5. Those between the nuclear powers, on the one hand, and the non-nuclear powers, on the other.

Within the U.S. Government

The negotiations within the United States government were between those who supported the idea of an MLF and those who gave priority to the achievement of a non-proliferation treaty. The proponents of some form of nuclear sharing within NATO gave priority to this over the NPT; they regarded the prevention of the proliferation of nuclear weapons as of secondary importance. At first, a fierce battle was fought by those who regarded NATO as the cornerstone of American security and wished to complete the structure by working out some plan for nuclear sharing. Later, the line was taken within the American government that it was not a question of priority for one or the other, that there was no real conflict between the MLF and a treaty on non-proliferation, and that both concepts were compatible one with the other. At that time it was thought that all that was necessary was to find appropriate language that would define the precise nature of the MLF in such a way as to make it clear that it did not amount to the proliferation of nuclear weapons. This effort continued all during 1965 and '66, but the Soviet Union remained adamant in insisting that no form of nuclear sharing within NATO was acceptable to it. As was indicated in Chapter 5, a compromise was finally worked out between the United States and the Soviet Union on the basis of the U.S. abandoning all plans for an MLF and the Soviet Union abandoning its opposition to the McNamara proposal for the creation of a nuclear planning committee within NATO.

Between the U.S. and Its Allies

The second of negotiations was between the United States and its allies in and outside NATO. This was one of the most difficult sets of negotiations; in fact, in the very midst of the negotiations in the ENDC in 1967, at the insistence of its allies (in particular, West Germany), the United States had to ask for a recess of the ENDC from March 23 to May 18 so that it could provide explanations and clarifications to its allies and consult further with them.

In November 1965, Chancellor Erhard of West Germany recalled the German government's pledge of 1954 to renounce the production of atomic, biological, and chemical weapons in its territory and stated that Germany did not desire "national control of nuclear weapons" but felt that all NATO allies should be given a "share in the nuclear defense" through some "joint nuclear organization." The following month Chancellor Erhard visited Washington, and President Johnson and the Chancellor issued a communiqué containing the following: "The President and the Chancellor were in agreement in upholding the principle of non-proliferation of nuclear weapons into the national control of States. They were of the view that alliance nuclear arrangements would not constitute proliferation of nuclear weapons and, in fact, should contribute to the goal of preventing the spread of nuclear weapons."

After the lengthy controversy about the MLF had been settled and it was agreed that there could be NATO nuclear planning but not NATO nuclear sharing, the concerns of America's allies turned to the question of the peaceful uses of atomic energy. On February 3, 1967, Foreign Minister Brandt of West Germany said that in the long run a ban on nuclear explosions would impair the civilian nuclear industry of the non-nuclear countries and that he feared that the non-proliferation treaty might unduly restrain research and industrial activities. There was also the problem of the spin-off benefits that accrued to civilian nuclear activities from military nuclear programs. Brandt stated that it was a "decisive question how negative repercussions of the Non-Proliferation Treaty on the civilian sphere of nuclear research can be prevented." He thought that the "non-nuclear countries might insist on the inclusion of provisions enabling them, under appropriate conditions, to participate in the experience and know-how gained by the nuclear powers" from military nuclear programs. West German Chancellor Kiesinger stated that Germany not only wanted to be among the leading nations in peaceful nuclear industry but wanted as well to prevent a "drastic retrogression in our technical, scientific and economic development." On April 7, 1967, the West German government circulated a comprehensive memorandum which, among other things, stated that the NPT should explicitly guarantee "the free use of nuclear energy for peaceful purposes" and that nuclear explosives for peaceful purposes should be made available to the non-nuclear States as soon as technical developments allow. The memorandum also said that the nuclear states should undertake to share spin-off from military programs with the non-nuclear countries. Later that month, Foreign Minister Brandt stated that his government would support everything that prevented the military misuse of nuclear energy but would not accept anything that hindered peaceful nuclearization.

Another area of difficulty between the United States and its allies was the question of safeguards. Foreign Minister Brandt stated that his government considered Euratom "a very effective system" and was interested in what relationship there would be between it and any new system that might be introduced. On February 10, Secretary of State Rusk stated that "I have no doubt at all that the safeguards in Euratom ensure that the activities of Euratom will not be abused. I have no problem about that myself. The problem is, how do you persuade 120 other nations that that is the case? We have not found an answer to this question yet." Foreign Minister Brandt said later that month that West Germany would meet its obligations to Euratom but that it might be possible to link the Euratom and IAEA safeguards systems in some way. He declared that "discrimination against any other disadvantage pertaining to the non-nuclear powers in the non-military sphere must be prevented." West Germany also wished to be sure that controls did not lead to industrial espionage. In its memorandum of April 7, it stated in connection with safeguards, "The controls should fulfill their purposes as effective checks on the non-proliferation agreement but should not have an obstructive or discriminatory influence. The efficiency of reliable control systems already in existence should not be impaired. Equal treatment for all parties to the treaty would considerably facilitate the world wide negotiations."

West Germany was also interested in the question of nuclear disarmament. Its memorandum of April 7 noted that the NPT would impose restrictions only on the non-nuclear-weapon states. West Germany felt that the world could not stop at a "limited non-proliferation treaty" but needed more comprehensive solutions. It said, "It is incumbent on the nuclear-weapon powers to stop the further development of increasingly more dangerous weapons, not to increase existing stocks, including the means of their delivery, to begin reducing them, to stop the production of fissionable material for military purposes, and to aim at a comprehensive test ban." An explicit announcement by the nuclear powers of their willingness to disarm would make the treaty a beginning of international cooperation toward a genuine guarantee of peace in the nuclear age. In his speech in the Bundestag on April 27, Brandt stated that the world could not stand still with a non-proliferation treaty and that it was incumbent on the nuclear powers to take the steps mentioned in the German memorandum.

Italy, which was a member of Euratom, and Switzerland, which was and is neutral and not allied to any country, also felt that there should be no double control under two safeguards systems and no commercial discrimination favoring states not under control. Switzerland also favored the extension of control to the civilian nuclear installations of the nuclear states. West Germany and Spain also stated that safeguards would be discriminatory if they did not apply to the nuclear-weapon parties.

During this time, Japan also had reservations concerning the problem of the peaceful uses of nuclear energy, the question of safeguards, and progress toward nuclear disarmament. At the General Assembly session in the spring of 1968 at which the draft non-proliferation treaty was approved, Japan stated that the draft treaty would not provide an acceptable balance of mutual responsibilities between nuclear and non-nuclear states, as was laid down in Resolution 2028 of the General Assembly. The Tripartite Proposal on security assurances would not completely eliminate the security fears of nonnuclear nations. Moreover, the treaty would "lose its moral basis" unless the nuclear-weapon states kept "their part of the bargain" and made progress in disarmament as called for by Article VI of the treaty, in the first place by a ban on underground testing. The treaty should also have provided for prohibition of transfers between nuclear-weapon states, and the nuclear powers should accept IAEA safeguards on their peaceful nuclear activities. The IAEA safeguards should be simplified and mechanized as much as possible, and the international flow of nuclear materials should be liberalized in order to promote peaceful nuclear activities. Japan also made it clear in private that it would not accept any discrimination in the application of IAEA safeguards to Japanese installations and nuclear facilities and would insist on the same treatment that was given to other countries, in particular to members of Euratom.

Throughout this period, negotiations continued between the United States and its Euratom allies and Japan in connection with the safeguards article. When the U.S. worked out the provisions of Article III of the treaty with its allies and also with the Soviet Union, it agreed at the same time with its allies on a statement of principles concerning the application of Article III. These principles were read into the record by the United States both at the ENDC and at the General Assembly. They are as follows:

1. There should be safeguards for all non-nuclear-weapon parties of such a nature that all parties can have confidence in their effectiveness. Therefore safeguards established by an agreement negotiated and concluded with the IAEA in accordance with the Statute of the IAEA and the Agency's safeguards system must enable the IAEA to carry out its responsibility of providing assurance that no diversion is taking place.
2. In discharging their obligations under Article III, non-nuclear-weapon parties may negotiate safeguards agreements with the IAEA individually or together with other parties; and, specifically, an agreement covering

such obligations may be entered into between the IAEA and another international organization the work of which is related to the IAEA and the membership of which includes the parties concerned.

3. In order to avoid unnecessary duplication, the IAEA should make appropriate use of existing records and safeguards provided that under such mutually agreed arrangements the IAEA can satisfy itself that nuclear material is not diverted to nuclear weapons or other nuclear explosive devices.

In addition to problems regarding safeguards, there were a number of other questions that were discussed between the United States and its allies concerning the meaning of different provisions of the treaty and the scope of application of the treaty. Included in the list of over fifty questions that West Germany submitted to the United States in connection with various aspects of the NPT were questions concerning the precise nature of what could be transferred under the treaty and what was prohibited, whether or not consultations and planning on nuclear defense would be prohibited, whether or not the United States could itself deploy nuclear weapons under its control on the territory of non-nuclear NATO members, and whether or not the treaty would prohibit the unification of Europe if a nuclear state was one of the constituent states. These matters were of such importance to the NATO allies of the United States that the questions and answers were committed to writing and made public. They are as follows:

1. Q. What may and what may not be transferred under the draft treaty?
   A. The treaty deals only with what is prohibited, not with what is permitted.

   It prohibits transfer to any recipient whatsoever of "nuclear weapons" or control over them, meaning bombs and warheads. It also prohibits the transfer of other nuclear explosive devices because a nuclear explosive device intended for peaceful purposes can be used as a weapon or can be easily adapted for such use.

   It does not deal with, and therefore does not prohibit, transfer of nuclear delivery vehicles or delivery systems, or control over them to any recipient, so long as such transfer does not involve bombs or warheads.

2. Q. Does the draft treaty prohibit consultations and planning on nuclear defense among NATO members?
   A. It does not deal with allied consultations and planning on nuclear defense so long as no transfer of nuclear weapons or control over them results.

3. Q. Does the draft treaty prohibit arrangements for the deployment of nuclear weapons owned and controlled by the United States within the territory of non-nuclear NATO members?
   A. It does not deal with arrangements for deployment of nuclear weapons within allied territory as these do not involve any transfer of nuclear weapons or control over them unless and until a decision were made to go to war, at which time the treaty would no longer be controlling.

4.   Q. Would the draft prohibit the unification of Europe if a nuclear-weapon state was one of the constituent states?

A. It does not deal with the problem of European unity and would not bar succession by a new federated European state to the nuclear status of its former components. A new federated European state would have to control all of its external security functions including defense and all foreign policy matters relating to external security, but would not have to be so centralized as to assume all governmental functions. While not dealing with succession by such a federated state, the treaty would bar transfer of nuclear weapons (including ownership) or control over them to any recipient, including a multilateral entity.

It may safely be said that, even after the question of the MLF had been solved, the negotiations between the United States and its allies were more difficult and complicated than those between the U.S. and the Soviet Union.

It is an interesting exercise at the present time to speculate on whether the Soviet Union might have been persuaded to accept IAEA safeguards over its peaceful nuclear activities on the same voluntary basis as did the United States and the United Kingdom. It had become very plain during the negotiations that the Soviet Union had become extremely interested in having the Non-Proliferation Treaty adopted. It had become a major element of Soviet policy to prevent the proliferation of nuclear weapons, and the Soviet Union was particularly anxious to ensure that West Germany did not have any access to such weapons. The U.S. was also very concerned to complete the work on the Non-Proliferation Treaty and have it approved and opened for signature. Some observers feel that, had the United States negotiated the matter a little longer and without such urgency, it might have been possible to persuade the Soviet Union to accept IAEA safeguards on a voluntary basis. In view of the overriding importance attached to the treaty by the Soviet Union, the acceptance of such voluntary safeguards would have been a very small price to pay. Certainly if the Soviet Union thought that it would have to accept such safeguards in order to obtain the treaty, it is quite likely that it would have been willing to pay that price. When the Soviet Union is really anxious to obtain an agreement it has been known to make many concessions that had previously seemed unlikely, as was the case with the agreement concerning Berlin. Some observers believe that the same thing would have happened in the case of the IAEA safeguards. While the matter seems academic now, it is not entirely so, because it can and probably will be raised again.

Another interesting speculation is whether the United States, which in 1968 insisted that it would not accept the Kosygin Formula for the nonuse of nuclear weapons against non-nuclear-weapon states that did not have nuclear weapons on their territory, might have considered accepting or working out some alternative sort of formula that would provide greater assurances of security in this regard to the non-nuclear-weapon states. The question is discussed further in Chapter 10. At this point it is worth noting that the NATO allies of the United States were all opposed to any American commitment not to use or not to be the first to use nuclear weapons. They regarded the threat of American use of nuclear weapons as the chief deterrent against any Soviet attack, whether with nuclear or conventional weapons. They and the United States also regarded the Kosygin Formula as dangerous for NATO, as it could provide some inducement to elements within their respective countries to call for the removal of all nuclear weapons from their territories as a means of avoiding the risk of nuclear attack. This they considered a clever means of removing or weakening the nuclear deterrent. While they recognized the attractiveness of the formula for the nonaligned, non-nuclear countries, they were in agreement with the United States in resisting it.

Between the U.S. and the U.S.S.R.

The third set of negotiations was between the United States and the Soviet Union as the coauthors of the draft of the Non-Proliferation Treaty. Once the problem of the MLF had been removed, however, these negotiations became fairly straightforward. Some problems arose in connection with the negotiation of the terms of the safeguards article, but, after the Euratom countries had agreed to try to reach some accommodation with the IAEA on the application of its safeguards system, this matter, too, became negotiable without much difficulty. There were few other matters of major difficulty between the two superpowers. The U.S. apparently did not press the Soviet Union very hard to accept IAEA safeguards, nor did the Soviet Union press the Americans to accept the Kosygin Formula for security assurances.

Among the Nonaligned, Non-Nuclear Powers

The fourth set of negotiations was the one that took place among the nonaligned, non-nuclear powers. These took place mainly within the nonaligned group of eight in the ENDC, but also at the General Assembly. While the nonaligned group generally gave the impression of being a united group with a solid front, they actually represented a whole spectrum of points of view depending on their respective national interests and attitudes.

At one end of the spectrum were Mexico and Sweden, who were strongly in favor of the NPT and were willing to settle for what they regarded as feasible in the way of improving and strengthening its provisions. While they recognized the discriminatory nature of the treaty and were fully conscious of its shortcomings, they felt that a less than perfect treaty was better than none at all. Accordingly, they often were the authors of compromise proposals which the two superpowers accepted in whole or in part in order to defuse the arguments of the treaty's critics and, by pointing to their own flexibility and reasonableness, obtain maximum support for the treaty.

At the other end of the spectrum were Brazil and India, who were far from enthusiastic about the basic approach of the superpowers to the NPT. They were willing to go along with the idea of non-proliferation and the NPT, but only if there was a true "balance of mutual responsibilities and obligations of the nuclear and non-nuclear powers," without any discrimination against the latter. Hence they demanded much more from the nuclear powers in terms of security assurances, commitments to specific measures of disarmament, equality in the research, development, and application of the peaceful uses of nuclear energy, including peaceful nuclear explosions, and equality as regards the application of safeguards. They led the opposition to the U.S.–U.S.S.R. draft treaty and appeared to regard no treaty at all as preferable to an inadequate one.

Between these two extremes were Egypt (the U.A.R.), Ethiopia, Nigeria, and Burma. These countries supported the idea of the NPT, but, in varying degrees, leaned to one side or the other depending on their national points of view on specific issues.

The nonaligned nations did nevertheless succeed in presenting a solid front. When Brazil and India called for the treaty to include provisions for specific measures of nuclear disarmament, while Mexico and Sweden were content to accept the promise of the nuclear powers to pursue negotiations in good faith for a halt to the nuclear arms race and for measures of nuclear disarmament, the nonaligned nations agreed on a joint memorandum which stated that the treaty should be "accompanied with or followed by" concrete measures of nuclear disarmament. The eight nonaligned members of the ENDC understood that they could exert maximum leverage on the nuclear powers by maintaining a united front and by using their expertise and leadership to influence the large number of third-world countries in the General Assembly. Because the questions of disarmament and non-proliferation had become extremely complex and tangled, the smaller delegations in the United Nations often lacked expertise and self-confidence in these matters and tended to rely on the experts from the nonaligned members of the ENDC.

In the end, the majority of nonaligned members of the ENDC came to accept the views of Mexico and Sweden, and they played a major role in obtaining the support of the majority of the third-world countries in the United Nations. Of the eight nonaligned members of the ENDC, only Brazil, Burma, and India failed to sign the NPT, and, because they were in a distinct minority in the General Assembly, they did not actively attempt to block approval of the treaty but contented themselves with stating their opposition for the record.

Between the Nuclear and the Non-Nuclear Powers

The final and most important set of negotiations took place publicly in the ENDC and at the United Nations. These very quickly developed into negotiations between the two nuclear superpowers, on the one hand, and the non-nuclear powers, on the other, and they were long and difficult. For the first time in international affairs in the postwar world, there seemed to be a close, tacit understanding between the United States and Soviet Union. In the past, the nonaligned states and, to a much lesser extent, sometimes also the allies of the two superpowers were engaged in trying to find compromise formulas between the Soviet Union and the United States in order to be able to make progress. This picture was entirely changed during the negotiation of the Non-Proliferation Treaty. In the context of this treaty the negotiations took on the appearance of a two-sided dialogue, with the nuclear powers on one side and all the non-nuclear powers on the other. There were, of course, variations of substance and degree in the different views of the non-nuclear powers, but the essential and surprising aspect of these negotiations was the sustained efforts of the non-nuclear powers to extract concessions from the nuclear powers. In this, they succeeded only to a limited extent.

Actually, in my opinion the nuclear powers realized that they were doing very well in the negotiations. At one point, one of the American negotiators conceded privately that the NPT was one of the "greatest con games of modern times." While Soviet negotiators would never permit themselves to even think in those terms, let alone give expression to such thoughts, they displayed great nervousness at the General Assembly as to whether the treaty would be approved. The anxiety they demonstrated at that time is some evidence not only of the importance which they attached to the treaty but also of their recognition of the fact that there were many grounds for countries not to go along with the treaty. In fact, the Soviet head of the Political Department of the United Nations Secretariat would ask me every day or two for a report on the prospects for approval of the treaty—something never heard of before or since in the Department. On every occasion I reported that the treaty would be carried by an overwhelming majority because of the tacit alliance that had developed between the nuclear powers and those non-nuclear powers who had no hope whatsoever of going nuclear for the foreseeable future. In other words, there was a common interest on the part of the nuclear powers and those small and less advanced nuclear powers who had no significant nuclear programs in preventing any near-nuclear powers from going nuclear. Furthermore, it seemed that while many nations had serious reservations about the provisions of the treaty, very few, if any, would vote against it; most would confine themselves to abstaining.

In addition, I kept urging the Soviet and American negotiators to make some additional final concessions both in the text of the treaty and in the draft resolution for its approval. Ambassador Garcia Robles of Mexico had, in fact, proposed amendments to Articles IV and V and to the Preamble of the treaty that required only small concessions from the nuclear powers. The nuclear powers attempted but failed to get the government of Mexico to drop these amendments, and eventually they reluctantly agreed to accept them and incorporate their substance in the treaty text. The successful outcome of the lengthy and complicated efforts to negotiate a non-proliferation treaty was then assured.

Chapter 8. Why the Non-Proliferation Treaty Was Approved

Some may wonder, in view of all of the criticisms made of the treaty by the non-nuclear-weapon states and their many serious reservations about its effectiveness and discriminatory nature, why it was approved. There are, of course, a complex of reasons, but perhaps the overriding one was that the time had come for capping the efforts that had been made for non-proliferation with a treaty. All of the five permanent members of the Security Council of the United Nations, each of which had a veto over any action in the Security Council, had become nuclear-weapon powers. The Partial Test Ban Treaty had been signed in 1963, and while the three countries participating in the arms control negotiations—the United States, the Soviet Union, and the United Kingdom—were continuing to test nuclear weapons underground, it was hoped that they might be persuaded to stop these underground tests and that China and France, who were testing in the atmosphere and had mastered the technology of both atomic and hydrogen bombs, might be persuaded to stop their tests in the atmosphere and to join in the efforts to prevent the further spread of nuclear weapons. Additional impetus was given to the idea of nuclear non-proliferation by the approval in January 1967, of the Outer Space Treaty, which provided for the denuclearization of outer space, and the approval in February 1967 of the Treaty of Tlatelolco, which created a nuclear-free zone in Latin America. These treaties, as well as a report by an international group of experts, appointed by the U.N. Secretary-General, on the effects of nuclear weapons, all helped to create both a climate and a momentum in favor of non-proliferation. The time was ripe for some further progress in the field of nuclear arms control, and a non-proliferation treaty seemed to be the logical and necessary next step.

Moreover, once the Soviet Union and the United States had reached agreement between themselves on the abandonment by the U.S. of NATO nuclear sharing in exchange for Soviet abandonment of opposition to

NATO nuclear planning, the main obstacles to agreement by the super-powers on a non-proliferation treaty were removed. After the two super-powers had agreed on joint action and on the draft of a non-proliferation treaty, it was not easy either for their allies or for the nonaligned states to withold their support for the idea. For years the nonaligned states had urged the two superpowers to end the Cold War and to come to grips with arms control and disarmament in order to enhance their own and the world's security. It was the smaller and nonaligned states that had first aroused the world in the late 1950s to the dangers of the further spread of nuclear weapons and alerted the nuclear powers to the threat posed to them. For some ten years, there had been a swelling tide of propaganda by government spokesmen as well as by experts and scholars in favor of halt-ing the spread of nuclear weapons and containing the increasing dangers of the nuclear arms race. Once the two superpowers had decided that non-proliferation was a priority matter of top policy, and began to exercise the many modalities available to them to influence the policies of other states, there was a convergence of objectives on the part of the nuclear and non-nuclear powers. It became an almost universally accepted axiom by both groups that the further spread of nuclear weapons was bad for them.

With the tide running so strongly in favor of non-proliferation, many of the near-nuclear and potential nuclear powers began to examine the implications of their committing themselves by a binding international treaty never to go nuclear and to remain forever "second-class" powers as regards nuclear weapons. But once again, the juxtaposition of forces in the world militated in favor of non-proliferation. Of all the great powers in the world, only Germany and Japan had not gone nuclear, but these two countries still bore the stigma of aggressor powers and the scars of having been defeated in World War II. Not only international opinion but also domestic opinion in the two countries—particularly in Japan, which had borne the brunt of a nuclear attack—was decisively against their going nuclear. Both countries were engaged in promoting the economic recovery that had raised them from prostration to the level of great powers once again, and they neither thought nor sought to upset their economic and social progress, or reawaken the fears of their own and other peoples, by even contemplating the possibility of going nuclear. The Japanese had traumatic memories of the holocausts of Hiroshima and Nagasaki, and had adopted a constitution abjuring armed forces, and West Germany had agreed by treaty in 1954 never to manufacture nuclear weapons in its ter-ritory. Consequently, these two great powers were definitely committed to the idea of nuclear non-proliferation, and during the negotiation of the treaty they confined their activities to attempting to obtain a good treaty that would not, in any way, detract from the benefits that they could ob-tain from the exploitation and application of the peaceful uses of nuclear energy. With these two great powers committed to supporting an appropriate non-proliferation treaty, it followed that West Germany's non-nuclear partners in Euratom—Italy, the Netherlands, Belgium, and Luxembourg—would go along.

Canada, which had participated in the production of the first atomic bomb, was a special case. Not only was it under the nuclear umbrella of the United States and the United Kingdom in NATO, but it was also a partner with the United States in the North American defense agreement, NORAD. With or without the NATO and NORAD ties, however, it is inconceivable that any country could launch an armed attack against Canada without the United States becoming immediately involved. As some scholars have remarked, Canada is the only country that need never acquire its own nuclear weapons for its defense.

Sweden was another country with advanced nuclear technology which had no intention of going nuclear. While some military elements in Sweden (as in Switzerland) argued that the very fact of Sweden's neutrality required it to go nuclear in order to be able to defend its independence and nonaligned position, others argued that a country possessing nuclear weapons automatically became a potential nuclear target and that going nuclear would hence not reduce but rather increase the dangers for Sweden. The strong current of nonalignment and progressivism in Sweden prevailed and overwhelmingly inclined Sweden toward supporting the idea of non-proliferation.

Like Germany and Japan, therefore, Canada and Sweden, confined their activities to trying to obtain the best non-proliferation treaty possible. Actually, both would have preferred a better treaty than that actually agreed upon, but they preferred a "second-best" treaty to none at all. They did not want to encourage or support any possible "holdouts," and the philosophy of half a loaf or even a quarter of a loaf being better than none seemed irrefutable to them.

As we indicated earlier, the nonaligned, non-nuclear countries were not a solid bloc with a single point of view, but rather were divided among themselves and constituted a whole spectrum of opinion. Countries such as Ireland, Mexico, and Sweden were strongly in favor of non-proliferation and convinced that a non-proliferation treaty would greatly enhance their own and the world's security, while countries such as Argentina, Brazil, and India believed that a non-proliferation treaty would enhance their own and the world's security only if the nuclear powers embarked on a definite program of arms control and disarmament so that the world would move toward containing and reducing the nuclear arms race while at the same time encouraging and promoting the peaceful uses of nuclear energy in order to raise the standard of living of the developing countries. Despite these differences of opinion, there was sufficient common ground among the nonaligned, non-nuclear countries that they were all interested in achieving four basic objectives:

1. improving to the maximum extent possible, their own security positions;
2. bringing pressure on the nuclear-weapon states to begin disarmament;
3. obtaining assistance from the nuclear-weapon states in developing their own peaceful uses of nuclear energy; and
4. ensuring that all this was brought about in as equitable and non-discriminatory a fashion as possible.

In working toward these common goals, the nonaligned, non-nuclear powers found that they had a great deal in common with the non-nuclear allies of the nuclear powers, and their independent but parallel efforts led to similar efforts and demands in a common attempt to improve and strengthen the provisions of the Non-Proliferation Treaty. Thus a sort of momentum in favor of the treaty developed.

While the two superpowers were working out compromise positions with their respective allies, they also found that they could achieve something in the nature of a consensus among the nonaligned countries by accepting compromise positions put forward by Mexico and Sweden at the Eighteen-Nation Disarmament Committee and at the General Assembly. Thus, while not fully satisfying or meeting the views or hopes of either the enthusiastic or reluctant supporters of the Non-Proliferation Treaty, they managed to achieve substantial agreement on provisions that at least held out the hope of progress to the great majority of countries of the world. For example, an outstanding Japanese opinion leader said that since the treaty would freeze the number of nuclear-weapon states at five and there would be no further increase beyond this number, Japan could accept a position of perceived inferiority in nuclear weapons. A leading Nigerian official, whose words carried weight among the African countries, also said at the time that approval of the treaty was under consideration by the General Assembly that, while the treaty had a number of shortcomings and defects, it nevertheless represented the best chance of getting the nuclear powers to begin disarming and facilitate their diverting their huge military expenditures to peaceful purposes, including the granting of more aid to the developing countries.

The views of the nonaligned, non-nuclear countries, such as Mexico and Sweden, that had participated actively in the negotiation of the draft of the Non-Proliferation Treaty in the ENDC also played an important role in persuading nonaligned powers who were not participants in the negotiations to give their approval to the treaty. There was one additional element which ensured that the treaty would obtain overwhelming approval. This was the role of the non-nuclear countries that had acquired no significant knowledge or capability in the field of nuclear energy and that could not have gone nuclear for many years or decades, if ever. These "never-nuclear" countries obviously had a direct interest in ensuring that nuclear weapons did not spread to the near-nuclear or potential nuclear countries. Since nearly all of them were developing countries, mainly in Africa, Asia, and Latin America, they recognized that if any countries in their respective regions of the world were to go nuclear, it would put them at a double disadvantage: not only would they continue to be poor and weak developing countries as compared with the rich, developed ones of the Northern Hemisphere, but they would also be in an inferior position in their own regions as compared to those relatively poor and developing countries who succeeded in going nuclear. Accordingly, these "never-nuclear" powers joined forces with the nuclear powers in pressing for the approval of the Non-Proliferation Treaty as a means of restraining their near-nuclear and potential nuclear neighbors from going nuclear.

Actually, when one looks at the complicated and protracted negotiations for the treaty in the light of hindsight it seems almost a miracle that the NPT, with its evident shortcomings and with the many and serious reservations about it held by the non-nuclear powers, was approved by the overwhelming majority of the members of the United Nations. The same would not happen again today. I remember when the Japanese advisor, who had been in Geneva following the work of the ENDC on the NPT, arrived in New York to attend the debate on the NPT, he was startled and almost shocked to learn that the treaty was likely to be approved in the form it had been submitted or with only minor amendments. He had felt sure that the treaty would be sent back for further consideration and improvement.

The time was ripe, however, for the NPT. The non-nuclear powers were on the whole really convinced that there was a genuine opportunity for them to make progress toward a better and more peaceful world. They hoped and even believed that the nuclear powers would seriously endeavor to negotiate and achieve significant measures of disarmament and that the promotion of the peaceful uses of nuclear energy would help produce a better world for all. Others felt that the only hope of progress on nuclear disarmament was by first approving the Non-Proliferation Treaty. Many of them agreed with Secretary-General U Thant, who stated, "I regard the successful conclusion of the Treaty for the Non-Proliferation of nuclear weapons as an indispensable first step towards further progress in disarmament. In fact, it is difficult to conceive of any agreement in the foreseeable future on any measure of disarmament if it is not possible to reach agreement on the treaty to prevent the spread of nuclear weapons."

It is extremely doubtful whether the treaty could, at the present time, receive anywhere near the support it received in 1968. Although there are today more than 100 signatories to the treaty and 96 parties (see Appendix V), the treaty seems weaker and in greater peril today than at any time since its approval. The disillusionment of many of the near-nuclear powers with what they regard as the failure of the nuclear powers, in particular the two superpowers, to live up to their commitments under the treaty has eroded a great deal of the original support for it. In addition, the explosion of a nuclear device by India, although repeatedly stated to be intended solely for peaceful purposes, has meant that there are now six members of the "nuclear club" instead of five and has changed the entire nuclear picture.

Chapter 9. The "Forgotten Conference" of the Non-Nuclear States

The Conference of Non-Nuclear-Weapon States (CNNWS) was unique in United Nations history. It was initiated and organized by the non-nuclear states themselves without the full participation of the nuclear states and, indeed, against their wishes. Ninety-six countries participated in the conference, including the four nuclear powers that were members of the United Nations—France, the Soviet Union, the United Kingdom, and the United States. The four nuclear powers had the right of full participation in the conference but not the right to vote. They did not, however, avail themselves of their right to speak, although they were busy in the lobbies and behind the scenes pressing their points of view.

This was the first conference dealing with any aspect of disarmament attended by France since the Ten-Nation Disarmament Conference collapsed in 1960; it was also the first United Nations conference dealing with *any* political matter attended by the Federal Republic of Germany. West Germany was represented by its foreign mininster, Willy Brandt, who made a statesmanlike speech that was widely acclaimed. Many participants and observers were curious to see how West Germany would perform at the conference and what role it would play. In fact, its delegation participated actively in all of the work of the conference, and it was the general feeling that it had made a useful contribution.

Why the Conference Was Held

The idea of the Non-Nuclear-Weapon-States Conference originated with Pakistan. In July of 1966, it addressed a letter to the U.N. Secretary-General warning that India was preparing to go nuclear and requesting that the matter be aired. The two cochairmen of the Geneva Disarmament Conference, the U.S. and the U.S.S.R., decided against circulating the letter to the members of the Eighteen-Nation Disarmament because of India's opposition. This was the only occasion on which a communication from a member of the United Nations was not circulated as a document of the ENDC and was contrary to the normal practice. Understandably, Pakistan was far from pleased.

At the General Assembly session that fall, Pakistan proposed that the Assembly convene a Conference of Non-Nuclear-Weapon States in order to consider:

1. how the security of the non-nuclear-weapon states could best be assured;
2. how non-nuclear-weapon states might cooperate among themselves in preventing the proliferation of nuclear weapons; and
3. how nuclear devices might be used for exclusively peaceful purposes.

Pakistan also proposed that the Assembly create a Preparatory Committee to arrange for the holding of the conference and to report on how the nuclear-weapon states would be associated with its work. Pakistan stressed that the aim of the proposed conference would be to evolve a common viewpoint on the part of the non-nuclear-weapon countries which would enable them to enter into a fruitful dialogue with the nuclear powers. The General Assembly approved the proposal, with only India voting against it and with the Soviet Union and the United States abstaining. India considered that the resolution was mainly directed against it; and it may, indeed, have been Pakistan's original intention to use the conference as a restraining influence on India's going nuclear. The nuclear powers, on the other hand, feared that the conference might be harmful to the negotiation of a non-proliferation treaty. They thought that it might provide an opportunity for the non-nuclear states to work out a common position on a number of demands that might be unacceptable to the nuclear powers.

The Preparatory Committee recommended that the conference be held in March and April 1968, and that the nuclear states be invited to participate but without the right to vote. The Soviet Union and the United States, concerned about what the conference might do but reconciled to the fact that it would be held, then directed their efforts to attempting to have the conference postponed until after the Non-Proliferation Treaty was approved by the United Nations General Assembly. The Assembly had called on the ENDC to report by March 15, 1968, on its work on the draft treaty. The nuclear powers felt that if the CNNWS met before the Assembly had considered and approved the draft treaty, the demands of the non-nuclear states worked out at their conference might overturn, or at the very least require reconsideration of, the carefully worked out provisions of the NPT. The non-nuclear states, on the other hand, realized that their leverage would be greatest before, rather than after, the General Assembly passed on the draft treaty. A considerable struggle proceeded behind the scenes, with much lobbying and arm-twisting. Finally, the nuclear powers had their way, and Pakistan and the main sponsors of the conference agreed to its postponement from March–April 1968 to August–September of the same year. In return, the nuclear states agreed to support the resolution for the convening of the conference, which was therefore adopted by an overwhelming majority and without any significant opposition. This time, India, too, did not oppose the resolution, seeing in the conference possibilities for explaining and justifying its opposition to the NPT. However, once the non-nuclear states agreed to the postponement of the conference, and particularly once the Assembly approved the draft NPT, which was opened for signature on July 1, 1968, and was signed by a large number of countries, the CNNWS had lost whatever real political clout it might have had.

In pressing for the resolution convening the conference, Pakistan made it clear that it was primarily interested in obtaining adequate security guarantees. It wanted the draft Non-Proliferation Treaty to be supplemented by additional security guarantees on the part of the nuclear powers toward non-nuclear states that were outside the context of alliances.

The Decisions of the Conference

Since the Non-Proliferation Treaty in its final form had been approved and signed, the conference's work was directed mainly to obtaining the best possible implementation of the provisions of the treaty. It attempted to put some flesh on the skeleton of the treaty and to persuade the nuclear powers not only to fulfill all of the obligations they had undertaken in the treaty, but to improve their security assurances.

The work of the Non-Nuclear-Weapons-States Conference proceeded in four specific areas:

1. security assurances for the non-nuclear states;
2. measures of nuclear disarmament;
3. prevention of the further proliferation of nuclear weapons by way of safeguards and other measures; and
4. programs for cooperation in the field of peaceful uses of nuclear energy, including peaceful nuclear explosions.

The conference adopted a declaration and fourteen resolutions dealing with these matters.

The declaration of the conference was adopted unanimously. It declared that:

—The future of mankind cannot be secure without the complete elimination of the use or threat of use of force, in the spirit of the United Nations Charter.

—An early solution of the question of security assurances in the nuclear era, through a multilateral instrument, is necessary.

—Immediate cessation of the arms race and acceleration of the process of nuclear and general disarmament under effective international control are indispensable for world peace and economic progress.

—Pending achievement of general and complete disarmament, steps should be undertaken to reach agreements on collateral measures.

—The Treaty on the Non-Proliferation of Nuclear Weapons should be followed up by disarmament measures.

—Nuclear-weapon-free zones, established under appropriate conditions, constitute an effective contribution to non-proliferation and disarmament.

—It is imperative to ensure conditions to promote the peaceful uses of nuclear energy and ensure an unhampered flow of nuclear materials under appropriate safeguards, as well as of scientific knowledge and advanced nuclear technology for peaceful purposes, on a nondiscriminatory basis.

—The use of nuclear explosive devices for peaceful purposes, within appropriate international arrangements and under strict international control, should be promoted.

—International assistance, including financing, is needed for the greater application of the peaceful uses of nuclear energy. All nations, particularly the nuclear powers, should facilitate international cooperation in this field.

—The United Nations General Assembly is urged to continue efforts to deal with these problems, taking into consideration the best ways and means of implementing the conference's decisions, including the convening of another conference at an appropriate time.

On the problem of security assurances, the only decision taken by the conference was the adoption of a proposal submitted by West Germany. The West German resolution was adopted by a large majority with only five votes against it, all of which were cast by Soviet allies. It reaffirmed the principle of the nonuse of force and the prohibition of the threat of force in relations between states, employing nuclear or non-nuclear weapons; it reaffirmed the right of every state to equality, sovereignty, territorial integrity, and nonintervention in its internal affairs; it reaffirmed the inherent right under Article 51 of the U.N. Charter of individual or collective self-defense, "which, apart from measures taken or authorized by the Security Council of the United Nations, is the only legitimate exception to the overriding principle of the nonuse of force in relations between states." The conference requested that the nuclear states reaffirm these principles.

The conference failed by one vote to obtain the necessary two-thirds majority for another resolution on security assurances proposed by fourteen Latin American states. This resolution would have had the General Assembly convene a conference of all its members and all nuclear states for the purpose of "concluding a multi-lateral instrument whereby the nuclear-weapon states undertake to adopt the appropriate measures to assure the security of all non-nuclear-weapon states."

The conference adopted four resolutions in the field of arms control and disarmament. The first one favored the establishment of nuclear-free (or what the resolution called "nuclear-weapon-free") zones as an effective measure for halting nuclear proliferation and stated that the necessary cooperation of the nuclear-weapon states should take the form of commitments undertaken in a legally binding international instrument. It recommended that non-nuclear states study the possibility of establishing nuclear-free zones in their area by treaty. It regretted that not all the nuclear powers had signed the Protocol to the Treaty of Tlatelolco obligating them to respect the nuclear-free status of Latin America and not to use nuclear weapons against parties to that treaty.

As regards the cessation of the nuclear arms race and nuclear disarmament, the conference noted that the achievement of the goal of nuclear non-proliferation requires the adoption of measures to prevent both horizontal and vertical proliferation, and it requested the United Nations to recommend that the ENDC should begin, not later than March 1969, negotiations for: (a) the prevention of the further development and improvement of nuclear weapons and their delivery vehicles; (b) the conclusion of a comprehensive test ban treaty; (c) immediate cessation of the production of fissionable materials for weapons purposes and of the manufacture of nuclear weapons; and (d) the reduction and subsequent elimination of all stockpiles of nuclear weapons and their delivery systems.

Concerning the bilateral Soviet–American discussions on strategic arms limitation, the conference urged the two governments to enter at an early date into discussions on the limitation of offensive strategic nuclear-weapons delivery systems and systems of defense against ballistic missiles. It also expressed deep concern at "the imminent danger of a renewal of the strategic nuclear arms race and its escalation to new levels which would become uncontrollable."

On matters relating to the prevention of nuclear proliferation and the question of safeguards, the conference adopted two resolutions. The first stated that the proliferation of nuclear weapons would endanger the security of all states and that it was therefore of great importance to prevent their proliferation. It recommended that all non-nuclear-weapon states accept the safeguards system of the IAEA, to be set forth in agreements which would specifically provide against diversion of all source or fissionable material from peaceful applications to nuclear weapons or peaceful explosive uses.

In the second resolution dealing with safeguards, the conference recommended the establishment within the IAEA of institutional machinery on safeguards, with the participation both of countries supplying nuclear materials and of countries not possessing such materials. It recommended that existing safeguards procedures should be simplified by the use of instruments and other technical devices at certain strategic points in order to restrict the procedures to the necessary minimum, and that rules be adopted against industrial risks, including industrial espionage. It also urged the nuclear-weapon powers to accept IAEA safeguards and stressed the need for drawing up rules to avoid duplication of safeguards procedures and consequent commercial discrimination.

The conference adopted seven resolutions on the subject of cooperation in the field of peaceful uses of nuclear energy. It requested the U.N. Secretary-General to appoint a group of experts to prepare a full report on all possible contributions of nuclear technology to the economic and scientific advancement of the developing countries. It called on the IAEA to undertake studies on arrangements to facilitate the exchange of scientific and technical information, on ways to increase the funds available for technical assistance, on effective means to ensure access to special fissionable materials, and on the agency's possible role in regard to nuclear explosions for peaceful purposes. It invited the nuclear-weapon states to declassify scientific and technical information when possible and urged them to facilitate the availability of fissionable material for the peaceful nuclear programs of the non-nuclear-weapon states. Since nuclear projects are capital-intensive, it recommended that the IAEA should endeavor to make arrangements to secure finances from international sources for the creation of a "Special Nuclear Fund," to be disbursed in the form of grants and low-interest loans for financing nuclear projects in the territories of non-nuclear-weapon states, particularly developing ones. It requested the General Assembly to consider establishing within the United Nations Development Program (UNDP) a "Nuclear Technology Research and Development Program" for the benefit of the developing countries and requested the International Bank for Reconstruction and Development (IBRD) to consider establishing for the benefit of developing countries a "Program for the Use of Nuclear Energy in Economic Development Projects," and invited the nuclear-weapon states to give firm undertakings for the supply of materials and money. It recommended that the IAEA broaden the representation on its Board of Governors so as to reflect equitable geographical distribution and the views of a broad spectrum of developing countries. It requested all nuclear-weapon states and non-nuclear-weapon states in a position to do so, to provide access for students and scientists to training and acquisition of knowledge of nuclear technology on a nondiscriminatory basis. As regards peaceful nuclear explosions, the conference stated that there was an urgent need both to obtain a comprehensive test ban treaty, and, at the same time, to create in a separate international instrument a regime to regulate and internationally control all explosions for peaceful purposes as exceptions from a general prohibition under a comprehensive test ban; and it endorsed the opinion expressed by the nonaligned nations of the

ENDC linking a comprehensive test ban with the problem of peaceful nuclear explosions.

Finally, the conference invited the General Assembly to consider the best ways and means of implementing its decisions, including the convening of a second Conference of Non-Nuclear-Weapon States.

The Failure To Implement Its Decisions

At the General Assembly in the fall of 1968, one of the principal subjects of discussion was the question of establishing an *ad hoc* committee to oversee the implementation of the resolutions of the conference. Brazil, Italy, and Pakistan were among the leaders in urging the creation of such a committee, but it was opposed by the nuclear powers, who held that there was no need to set up a special body for that purpose. A compromise solution was worked out by which the General Assembly endorsed the declaration and took note of the decisions of the conference; requested that the declaration and resolutions be transmitted to the members of the United Nations, and to members of the IAEA and the other international bodies concerned; invited those international bodies to report to the Secretary-General on actions taken concerning the resolutions; invited the UNDP, the IBRD, and the IAEA to continue to study the recommendations of the conference; and requested the Secretary-General to submit a comprehensive report on progress in the implementation of the resolutions and also to appoint a group of experts to prepare a full report on all possible contributions of nuclear technology to the economic and scientific advancement of the developing countries. The United States supported this resolution, but the Soviet Union voted against it. Another resloution adopted by the Assembly, but without the support of any of the nuclear powers, requested the Secretary-General to prepare a report on the establishment within the framework of the IAEA of an international service for peaceful nuclear explosions under international control.

At the General Assembly in the fall of 1969, the Secretary-General submitted the three reports called for at the preceding session. The first report, on progress in the implementation of the resolutions of the CNNWS, was based on reports submitted to the Secretary-General by the various bodies concerned, including the IAEA and the IBRD. The Secretary-General concluded that the most promising and possibly the only way to solve the complex political, economic, financial, and technical problems involved in implementing the conference decisions lay in maximum international cooperation and the fullest possible utilization of the U.N., the specialized agencies, and other competent bodies.

The second report, on possible contributions of nuclear technology to the developing countries, recommended among other things, "that the advanced countries provide training in nuclear technology to personnel from developing countries and establish national or regional nuclear centers; [that] when a strong cadre of research scientists is available, consideration could be given to providing these countries with nuclear research reactors; that more intensive exploration for uranium in the developing countries be promoted; that development of medium-sized nuclear power plants suitable for developing countries be encouraged; that the construction of large desalination plants, or combined nuclear power and desalination complexes, be considered for arid areas, when such construction could be justified; that all possible aid be given to developing countries for many uses of radio-isotopes and ionizing radiation; that the development of nuclear explosions for peaceful purposes, which involved many uncertainties, be kept under constant review by the IAEA; that the IAEA and UNDP increase their technical cooperation projects; [that] since the financing of nuclear power plants seemed beyond the abilities of the IAEA, the IBRD review its position on the conditions for supporting major nuclear projects, and that the General Assembly and other organizations seek appropriate solutions to the financial problems involved."

The third report, dealing with the establishment of an international service for peaceful nuclear explosions, contained the texts of the replies from almost fifty governments to a request for their views on this subject, and the text of the report on the subject by the IAEA. The Secretary-General concluded that the IAEA should take on the role of such an international service, but he considered that the specific functions to be included in the service would evolve gradually after continued international discussion in the IAEA, the United Nations, and other organizations.

Additional resolutions were adopted by the General Assembly that year and in the following years calling for the implementation of the decisions of the CNNWS and for further reports in that regard. After 1970, no further special reports were made, but the Assembly requested the IAEA to report on its activities in this regard in its annual report to the General Assembly.

In sum, the General Assembly failed to implement the decisions of the CNNWS, except in minor respects and in calling for studies and reports. This was due basically to the lack of interest and enthusiasm on the part of the nuclear powers in matters of security assurances, nuclear disarmament, and the promotion of the peaceful uses of nuclear energy for the benefit of developing countries. They showed real interest and drive only in developing the safeguards system and in urging countries to sign and ratify the NPT. Moreover, the failure of the non-nuclear states to set up any continuing supervisory machinery such as a special committee or periodic meetings of the CNNWS, meant that there was no organ fixed with the responsibility of following up conference decisions and pressing for their implementation. Just as the non-nuclear powers were outmaneuvered by the nuclear powers in not insisting on holding their conference before the NPT was completed and signed, so were they again outmaneuvered by the nuclear powers who successfully opposed the creation of some machinery for implementing the decisions of the conference.

The net result was that, after a number of studies and special reports and a number of general appeals by the General Assembly for implementation of the decisions of the conference, no concrete action was taken and the efforts at implementation simple petered out. Since the decisions of the CNNWS were intended to elaborate, give concrete meaning to, and implement the pledges contained in the NPT, this is another way of saying that there was no real implementation of the pledges contained in that treaty. The failure to implement Articles IV, V, and VI of the treaty is described in Chapters 12, 13, and 14.

Thus, the Conference of Non-Nuclear-Weapon States, which had been conceived in high hopes, had, within the space of three years, become a "Forgotten Conference." But the problems and concerns that motivated the non-nuclear-weapon states at that conference were not forgotten. In fact, the failure to implement the decisions arrived at there added to the resentment of some of the non-nuclear powers that existed at the time of the holding of the conference.

Chapter 10.   Has the Security of Non-Nuclear
States Been Ensured?

The Complexity of the Problem

The problem of providing security assurances or guarantees to non-nuclear countries is an extremely complex one. The problem is relatively simple as regards those nations that are aligned with either the United States or the Soviet Union in some defense agreement such as NATO or the Warsaw Pact, or bilaterally in the case of Japan; all of them are under the nuclear umbrella of one of the two superpowers. The problem becomes vastly more difficult, however, in the case of states that are non-aligned and wish to remain so.

The problem first received wide public attention after the first Communist Chinese nuclear test, in October 1964. Immediately after the explosion, on October 16th, China declared that it would "never be the first to use nuclear weapons." It proposed a world summit conference to discuss the "complete prohibition and thorough destruction of nuclear weapons." As a first step, the "Summit Conference should reach an agreement to the effect that the nuclear powers and those that may soon become nuclear powers undertake not to use nuclear weapons."

President Johnson reacted immediately to the fears of other nations, with India chiefly in mind. He declared at the time that nations that did not seek nuclear weapons could be sure that "if they need our strong support against some threat of nuclear blackmail, then they will have it." This was a positive assurance of support, but one cast in vague and general terms.

India also reacted immediately to the Chinese test, by strongly criticizing it. Later, on December 4th, Prime Minister Lal Bahadur Shastri told a news conference that all non-nuclear countries needed a nuclear guarantee by the existing nuclear powers against nuclear attack. He added that it would be "very wise" for the nuclear powers "to give serious thought to this aspect of the problem."

As the preliminary discussions leading toward the Non-Proliferation Treaty continued, the question of security guarantees or assurances took on increasing prominence. The first concern of every government is for the security of its country. As discussions about non-proliferation became more serious, so too did the attention which governments devoted to the question of the security of their countries and to the relative advantages and disadvantages of going nuclear or of renouncing nuclear weapons. Consultations within governments, as well as bilateral and multilateral discussions, were undertaken. It became clear that, when any country went nuclear, the security of all its neighboring countries was immediately affected.

The question of whether to acquire nuclear weapons is itself a whole complex of many questions, including not only military considerations and the economic cost of manufacturing nuclear weapons but more intangible factors such as prestige and the enhanced political stature that might be involved. On the other hand, it is obvious that a country that has nuclear weapons automatically by that very fact becomes a nuclear target. Smaller and poorer countries can never hope to be able to compete with or stand up to the greater nuclear powers, not to speak of the two superpowers. While going nuclear might give a country a great military advantage over its neighbors or in its region, this advantage might turn out to be short-lived as one or more neighboring countries felt compelled to go nuclear also. A costly and dangerous nuclear arms race, which could weaken all of the participants economically and also reduce rather than increase their security, might result. Each country, if it had only a small and vulnerable nuclear arsenal, might find itself living in a constant state of fear of nuclear attack and on a hair-trigger alert lest one of the other countries be tempted to strike first at a moment of high tension.

Clearly, if all of the countries in any region decided not to go nuclear, the security of all of them would be enhanced. But what of the neighbors of a country that was already a nuclear power? To take only one recent example, how could the security of China's neighbors be increased? Would India, Japan, Korea, Taiwan, Indonesia, and Australia feel more secure if they acquired their own nuclear deterrent or if they received a guarantee from one or more nuclear powers? If France did not feel entirely safe under the American nuclear umbrella and the American commitment under the North Atlantic Treaty, how could any country rely on the promises of another to guarantee its security against nuclear threat or attack? If the United States might think twice before risking the existence of Washington or New York for the sake of Paris or Rome, how many times would it think before risking them for New Delhi or Tokyo? Would *any* guarantee be credible, and *could* any one be really effective? If there were no completely reliable or permanent guarantees, could less absolute assurances be adequate? Could there be some intermediate guarantees or assurances between becoming the protectorate of one or more nuclear powers and merely relying on the United Nations Charter and possible action by the Security Council? Every government is conscious to a greater or lesser degree of Palmerston's dictum that a great power has no permanent friends and no permanent enemies, only permanent interests. There is no real, in the sense of absolute, guarantee of security for any country; perhaps all countries must be content with trying to achieve the maximum degree of security that is possible in the light of its needs and the existing circumstances.

At the 1965 meetings of the United Nations Disarmament Commission, the security question was raised by several delegations. India suggested an "integrated solution" consisting of five points (see Chapter 5, p. 65) covering the entire problem of the proliferation of nuclear weapons. The third point was "an undertaking through the United Nations to safeguard the security of countries which may be threatened by powers having a nuclear weapons capability or about to have a nuclear weapons capability." Nigeria specifically agreed with the Indian view that a non-proliferation treaty should provide for the security of non-nuclear states.

At the ENDC meeting in August 1965, India reaffirmed its five-point program. Canada stated that non-nuclear countries "should have some assurances for the future that they will have a degree of security against nuclear attack." Brazil stated that the non-proliferation treaty should take into account the security of non-nuclear states. Nigeria warned that a country might find itself under popular pressure to acquire nuclear weapons in order to achieve security from external threats. No non-proliferation treaty would last, according to Nigeria, unless the following conditions were met: (1) the great powers refrain from nuclear blackmail against smaller states; (2) the United Nations was able to guarantee the territorial integrity of all states; and (3) the nuclear powers foreswore the use of nuclear weapons or at least gave categorical assurances that they would not use them against non-nuclear states or be the first to use them against each other. Nigeria added that "unless and until the nuclear powers take positive steps to allay [the non-nuclear powers'] fears, it will be impossible to prevent the spread of nuclear weapons and vain to think that any agreement could, in the long run, stop it." Sweden, however, which was committed to a policy of neutrality and nonalignment, doubted that security guarantees were desirable.

At the General Assembly that Fall, the United States repeated President Johnson's assurances of support to non-nuclear countries against nuclear blackmail, and added that action by the General Assembly could be a "useful part of such assurance" and that the United States was prepared to work for such action. The UAR, however, opposed bilateral guarantees to non-nuclear countries for fear that other nuclear powers would offer such guarantees to other non-nuclear states and the world would find itself divided into nuclear trusteeships of one or another nuclear power.

Neither the American draft treaty or non-proliferation of August 17, 1965, nor the Soviet draft of September 24, 1965, contained any references to security assurances. On January 27, 1966, President Johnson stated in a message to the ENDC: "So that those who foreswore nuclear weapons may forever refrain without fear from entering into the nuclear arms race, let us strive to strengthen United Nations and other international security arrangements. Meanwhile the nations that do not seek nuclear power can be sure that they will have our strong support against threats of nuclear blackmail." Once again, the United States was proposing an imprecise formula for security assurances.

The Kosygin Proposal

In his message to the ENDC on February 1, 1966, Soviet Premier Kosygin made a new proposal. He offered to include in a non-proliferation treaty "a clause on the prohibition of the use of nuclear weapons against non-nuclear states parties to the treaty which have no nuclear weapons in their territory." This proposal for a "negative" type of security assurance came to be known as the "Kosygin Proposal" or the "Kosygin Formula."

Canada thought that there might be a problem in verifying that a country had no nuclear weapons on its territory, but it held that the positive American and the negative Soviet approaches were not mutually exclusive. The United Kingdom suggested that the nonaligned countries themselves should inform the ENDC of their needs and felt that a compromise might be found between the American and Soviet approaches and that the nonaligned nations might accept a multilaterial guarantee. Brazil also hoped that the American and Soviet proposals could be brought closer together. Burma, Mexico, Nigeria, India, and the United Arab Republic welcomed the Kosygin offer. Sweden asked for clarification of it.

On August 22 of that year, Ethiopia submitted a memorandum proposing a ban on the use of nuclear weapons against denuclearized areas, the denuclearization of non-nuclear-weapon countries and regions, and an appropriate guarantee agreement by the nuclear powers of such arrangements, "jointly or severally."

At the General Assembly that fall, a resolution sponsored by nonaligned countries was adopted which, among other things, called on nuclear-weapon powers to refrain from the use or the threat of use of nuclear weapons against states which may conclude regional treaties for nuclear-free zones, and requested the ENDC "to consider urgently the proposal that the nuclear-weapon powers should give an assurance that they will not use, or threaten to use, nuclear weapons against non-nuclear-weapon States without nuclear weapons on their territories, and any other proposals that had been or may be made for the solution of this problem."

At the 1967 session of the ENDC, Nigeria stated that it would be unfair to ask any responsible government to adhere to a non-proliferation treaty without guarantees, and maintained that the treaty should provide for an "international deterrent system against nuclear blackmail." Brazil agreed and added that non-nuclear states which signed a non-proliferation treaty would be surrendering "the most important means they might otherwise have at their disposal to counter possible aggression."

In India, the external affairs minister told Parliament that India had a "special problem of security against nuclear attack or nuclear blackmail," and later he stated that the non-proliferation treaty would put India in a worse position than Communist China. If India was not to go nuclear, he said, it must have a "'credible guarantee" for her security. India also complained that the great powers had not yet given "any effective and credible consideration to the security needs of the non-nuclear countries, and particularly the nonaligned countries."

After the Soviet Union and the United States submitted their identical drafts of a non-proliferation treaty containing no provision for security assurances, in August 1967, the U.A.R. and Romania proposed treaty languages specifically incorporating the Kosygin Proposal, and Switzerland made a similar suggestion. Nigeria proposed a more positive guarantee, namely that "each nuclear-weapon State party to this treaty undertakes, if requested, to come to the aid of any non-nuclear-weapon State which is threatened or attacked with nuclear weapons." Canada thought that security assurances should be provided outside of the treaty and that the Kosygin Proposal created problems in connection with members of alliances who might have nuclear weapons on their territory even though they were non-nuclear-weapon states. Canada hoped that there could be parallel declarations by the nuclear powers recording their intention to assist non-nuclear parties subject to or threatened by nuclear attack; the nuclear powers might also undertake not to use nuclear weapons against non-aligned, non-nuclear parties. There could also be a United Nations resolution incorporating similar assurances.

The revised draft treaties that were submitted by the United States and the Soviet Union to the ENDC on January 18, 1968, still did not contain any security assurances for the non-nuclear nations. A number of ENDC members regretted the absence of any provision in this regard. West Germany also stated, in a memorandum that it circulated on March 6, 1968, that the treaty should ban nuclear blackmail against non-nuclear-weapon nations. Romania again asked for the inclusion of an undertaking along the lines of the Kosygin Proposal. The United States replied that the draft treaty did not include security assurances because the question was "too difficult and complicated to be reduced to a treaty provision."

Tripartite Proposal on Security Assurances, March 7, 1968

On March 7, 1968, the United States, the Soviet Union, and the United Kingdom submitted to the ENDC the draft of a Security Council resolution on security assurances which they were prepared to submit and support in the Security Council. The draft resolution read as follows:

> The Security Council
>
> Noting with appreciation the desire of a large number of States to subscribe to the Treaty on the Non-Proliferation of Nuclear Weapons, and thereby to undertake not to receive the transfer from any transferor whatsoever of nuclear weapons or other nuclear explosive devices or of control over such weapons or explosive devices directly, or indirectly; not to manufacture or otherwise acquire nuclear weapons or other nuclear explosive devices; and not to seek or receive any assistance in the manufacture of nuclear weapons or other nuclear explosive devices,
>
> Taking into consideration the concern of certain of these States that, in conjunction with their adherence to the Treaty on the Non-Proliferation of Nuclear Weapons, appropriate measures be undertaken to safeguard their security,
>
> Bearing in mind that any aggression accompanied by the use of nuclear weapons would endanger the peace and security of all States,
>
> 1. Recognizes that aggression with nuclear weapons or the threat of such aggression against a non-nuclear-weapon State would create a situation in which the Security Council, and above all its nuclear-weapon State permanent members, would have to act immediately in accordance with their obligations under the United Nations Charter;
>
> 2. Welcomes the intention expressed by certain States that they will provide or support immediate assistance, in accordance with the Charter, to any non-nuclear-weapon State Party to the Treaty on the Non-Proliferation of Nuclear Weapons that is a victim of an act or an object of a threat of aggression in which nuclear weapons are used;
>
> 3. Reaffirms in particular the inherent right, recognized under Article 51 of the Charter, of individual and collective self-defence if an armed attack occurs against a member of the United Nations, until the Security Council has taken measures necessary to maintain international peace and security.

The three nuclear powers stated that their governments would make declarations of intention to support the principles enunciated in the Tripartite Resolution. The United States also outlined the Declaration that it was prepared to make in the Security Council together with the two other nuclear-weapons nations planning to sign the non-proliferation treaty. The declaration by the United States read as follows:

> Aggression with nuclear weapons, or the threat of such aggression, against a non-nuclear-weapon State would create a qualitatively new situation in which the nuclear-weapon States which are permanent members of the United Nations Security Council would have to act immediately through the Security Council to take the measures necessary to counter such aggression or to remove the threat of aggression in accordance with the United Nations Charter, which calls for taking "effective collective measures for the prevention and removal of threats to the peace, and for the suppression of acts of aggression or other breaches of the peace." Therefore, any State which commits aggression accompanied by the use of nuclear weapons or

which threatens such aggression must be aware that its actions are to be countered effectively by measures to be taken in accordance with the United Nations Charter to suppress the aggression or remove the threat of aggression.

The United States affirms its intention, as a permanent member of the United Nations Security Council, to seek immediate Security Council action to provide assistance, in accordance with the Charter, to any non-nuclear-weapon State party to the treaty on the non-proliferation of nuclear weapons that is a victim of an act of aggression or an object of a threat of aggression in which nuclear weapons are used.

The United States reaffirms in particular the inherent right, recognized under Article 51 of the Charter, of individual and collective self-defense if an armed attack, including a nuclear attack, occurs against a Member of the United Nations, until the Security Council has taken measures necessary to maintain international peace and security.

Communist China attacked the Tripartite Proposal as another step in an American–Soviet alliance against China and the people of the world. They charged that the proposal and the non-proliferation treaty were part of a conspiracy designed to turn the non-nuclear countries into "protectorates" and their peoples into "nuclear slaves" who would never be able to acquire nuclear weapons to resist the "nuclear threat" from United States imperialism and Soviet revisionism.

Security Council Action on the Tripartite Assurances

On the same day that the General Assembly Resolution commending the Non-Proliferation Treaty was approved, the United States, the United Kingdom, and the Soviet Union submitted to the Security Council their proposal of March 7th on security assurances. At the Security Council Meeting of June 17, the United States, the United Kingdom, and the Soviet Union made declarations of intention substantially identical to that set out above.

France abstained from voting on the resolution, as it did not believe that the nations of the world would receive the security guarantees to which they were entitled until nuclear disarmament had been achieved. India also abstained. It agreed with the French view that nuclear disarmament was the real hope for security, and it also objected to the resolution and the declaration on the grounds that it was the responsibility of the nuclear members of the Security Council to aid any state that was subject to nuclear attacks or threats and not merely parties to the Non-Proliferation Treaty. Algeria, Brazil, and Pakistan also abstained on the grounds, among others, that the security assurances were inadequate and that they were discriminatory in applying only to parties to the treaty.

The other members of the Security Council supported the Tripartite Draft Resolution and the Declarations made by the nuclear powers on the grounds that the assurances contained therein seemed the best possible obtainable in the prevailing international situation and were preferable to no guarantee at all.

On June 19, 1968, the Tripartite Draft Resolution was adopted by the Security Council by a vote of 10 to nothing with 5 abstentions, as Resolution 255.

The Effect of the Security Council Action

Security Council Resolution 255 specifically welcomed the declarations of intention on the part of the U.S., the U.S.S.R., and the U.K. that they would provide "immediate assistance in accordance with the Charter" to any non-nuclear party to the NPT subject to nuclear aggression or the threat of nuclear aggression. In this manner the declarations were incorporated into the resolution.

In actual fact, the declarations, although they are merely declarations of intention and not binding legal obligations such as would arise from a treaty commitment, can be regarded as more important than the Security Council resolution. As an organ of the United Nations, the Council can adopt decisions and take action only in accordance with the provisions of the Charter—i.e., if nine members of the Council support the decision and the action and it is not opposed (vetoed) by any of the five permanent members (China, France, the U.S.S.R., the United Kingdom, and the United States). Any of the nuclear powers, however, could, under the inherent right of individual or collective defense provided for in Article 51 of the Charter, come to the defense of any member of the United Nations subjected to armed attack.

But neither the Security Council resolution nor the declarations increase the commitments already undertaken in the Charter by every member of the Security Council. The "immediate assistance" promised is to be only "in accordance with the Charter." At most, the declarations of intention would require the nuclear powers concerned to call the attention of the Security Council to any act or threat of nuclear aggression and to do so immediately. The powers concerned have given up only the right or option to do nothing in the event of such an act or threat. While they have also stated their *intention* to "provide or support" immediate assistance, they are not legally committed to do so, and any of them can unilaterally change its mind at any time.

This was made unmistakably clear by Secretary of State Dean Rusk in his testimony to the Senate Foreign Relations Committee during its hearings on the NPT for the purpose of advising the Senate with respect to ratifying the treaty. Rusk told the Committee that "as a matter of law and as a matter of policy there were no additional obligations assumed by the United States under the security guarantee resolution," and that "any action the United States would take as a result of United Nations decisions . . . would not be taken by the United States because of any new obligations assumed under the resolution." He emphasized:

> The decision itself [to act on any Security Council decision] would have to be made at the time in terms of the total interests of the United States and the judgment of the President, in consultation with leaders of the Congress, as to what is required in our own interests at that time.

Because of the confusion and growing debate in the United States at that time about the wisdom and legality of the American commitment to South Vietnam, the Senate was very sensitive to any suggestion that new or additional commitments might arise from the U.S. declaration and the Security Council resolution. In its report on September 26, 1968, the Committee recorded

> its firm conclusion, reached after extensive testimony, that the Security Council resolution and security guarantee declaration made by the United States in no way either ratify prior national commitments or create new commitments.

It can be assumed that the U.S.S.R. and the United Kingdom also assumed no new commitments. The message both to parties to the NPT and to non-parties was thus made very clear. The security assurances of the three nuclear powers had little, if any, meaning. They certainly did not provide any clear or binding security guarantee or even any reliable or credible assurance. The three nuclear powers were not legally bound to do anything more than they were already committed to do by the Charter.

The actions of the nuclear powers in the Security Council since the time of their declarations of intention and the adoption of the Security Council resolution have not been such as to create much confidence in the non-nuclear states that *their* security is in any way enhanced. Although such armed conflicts as those that have occurred since 1970 in Bangladesh, in the Middle East, and in Cyprus were limited to conventional and not nuclear attacks, and no finding of aggression was made, there is no evidence that events would have taken a different course if there had been any threat of nuclear attack.

If the security assurances do not embody any obligations beyond those already contained in the United Nations Charter, they have no special significance whatsoever. If they do intend to embody obgligations going beyond those already provided for in the Charter, then they are so vague and ambiguous as to be meaningless. And with the People's Republic of China now occupying a permanent seat in the Security Council, they are virtually worthless. Whatever persuasive influence they might have had at the time of their adoption by the Security Council in 1968 has, by now, completely vanished.

American–Soviet Agreement on the Prevention of Nuclear War

At the Nixon–Brezhnev Summit Conference in Washington in June 1973, the Soviet Union and the United States entered into an "Agreement on the Prevention of Nuclear War." Article IV of that agreement provides as follows:

> If at any time relations between the Parties or between either Party and other countries appear to involve the risk of a nuclear conflict, or if relations between countries not parties to this Agreement appear to involve the risk of nuclear war between the United States of America and the Union of Soviet Socialist Republics or between either Party and other countries, the United States and the Soviet Union, acting in accordance with the provisions of this Agreement, shall immediately enter into urgent consultations with each other and make every effort to avert this risk.

The avoidance of nuclear war, or the risk of such war, involving either or both of the superpowers is obviously in the interests of all countries and, as such, can be regarded as improving world security generally; but this agreement adds nothing in the way of security assurances to the non-nuclear parties to the NPT. On the contrary, since the agreement is clearly aimed at enhancing the security of the two superpowers, and since whatever increase in world security that results therefrom applies to all countries alike, both nuclear and non-nuclear and whether parties to the NPT or not, it could conceivably create some resentment among non-nuclear treaty parties that no heed was paid to their special needs or claims for additional security assurances, as countries that have renounced nuclear weapons. They might easily conclude that the nuclear powers are interested only in their own security, whether under the NPT or otherwise.

A Modest Proposal for Improved Security Assurances

The absence of any credible or effective security assurances to non-nuclear parties to the NPT obviously has a negative effect on the credibility of the treaty and has unquestionably served to weaken it. It seems most unlikely that the superpowers would at the present time be prepared to give any greater positive security assurances, either jointly or separately, to the non-nuclear states than they were prepared to give in 1968. It is clear that there is no fully satisfactory solution to the problem of security assurances, but it is possible to provide some better form of security assurances than is embodied in the present Security Council Resolution No. 255 and the Tripartite Declarations. Some form of negative assurance not to use or threaten to use nuclear weapons against non-nuclear states is certainly called for. Such a negative form of assurance would also be more credible than any pledges of positive assistance.

At the time the NPT was negotiated in 1967 and 1968, the United States was adamantly opposed to any declaration or undertaking regarding the nonuse or non–first use of nuclear weapons. As recently as the summer of 1975, President Ford and Secretary Schlesinger reaffirmed that the United States still stood by the policy of first use of nuclear weapons, whether against nuclear or non-nuclear states. Nevertheless, it is possible that with increasing pressure from the non-nuclear countries and with the further development of détente between the U.S. and U.S.S.R., the United States might be willing to reconsider its position on this matter. At an unofficial conference on the NPT organized by the Arms Control Association and the Carnegie Endowment for International Peace (both American bodies) in Divonne, France, in September 1974, the following recommendation was made:

> As the U.N. Security Council Resolution 255 and the associated declarations on security assurances are widely regarded as inadequate, and, in the opinion of many states, meaningless, the nuclear powers should be prepared to take more meaningful action, including at least an offer along the lines of a pledge of an appropriate type not to use or threaten to use nuclear weapons against a non-nuclear party to the Treaty. Regional moves toward nuclear-free zones patterned along the lines of the Treaty of Tlatelolco should also be encouraged as another means of allaying fears of nuclear threats.

When the United States ratified Protocol II of the Treaty of Tlatelolco on June 11, 1971, its ratification was subject to the understanding, among other things,

> That as regards the undertaking in Article 3 of Protocol II not to use or threaten to use nuclear weapons against the Contracting Parties, the United States Government would have to consider that an armed attack by a Contracting Party, in which it was assisted by a nuclear-weapon state, would be incompatible with the Contracting Party's corresponding obligations under Article I of the treaty.

Thus the United States, in effect, undertook not to use or threaten to use nuclear weapons against a party to the Treaty of Tlatelolco unless that party was engaged in an armed attack in which it was assisted by a nuclear-weapon state.

If the U.S. was prepared to give that assurance with regard to the Latin American nuclear-free zone, there are solid grounds for urging that it should give some similar type of assurance to non-nuclear parties to the NPT. Since the Soviet Union was prepared to go even further in the Kosygin Proposal, it is possible that it would agree to some form of negative security assurance.

Even though such an assurance might be regarded as less than fully credible and adequate, it would be better than none at all. Certainly, continuing failure to give such an assurance in the light of the many calls for it by the nonaligned, non-nuclear powers would serve only to further weaken the credibility and viability of the Non-Proliferation Treaty. While the giving of such an assurance might not be sufficient to attract any new adherents to the treaty, it might provide some inducement to the present parties to continue to abide by it.

The NPT Review Conference, 1975

The question of providing security assurances to the non-nuclear powers was, as expected, one of the major issues at the NPT Review Conference. Romania, which was the only member of the Warsaw Pact or NATO to "break ranks" on this issue, joined the third world non-nuclear countries in putting forward specific proposals for improved security assurances. (See Chapter 18.)

The two superpowers refused to negotiate on this question, however, and rejected the various proposals for specific security assurances. Not only did the United States fail to move forward in any way on this matter, but, to the great surprise and disappointment of the non-nuclear countries, the Soviet Union moved backward. It abandoned the Kosygin Formula and confined itself to reiterating its continuing support for Security Council Resolution 255 and repeating the obligation expressed in the U.N. Charter to refrain from the threat or use of force involving either nuclear or non-nuclear weapons.

The vague and general exhortations contained in the Final Declaration of the Review Conference, which was adopted by a wholly artificial consensus, failed to meet in any respect the demands for better security assurances. Thus, after five years of the NPT and the holding of a conference of the parties to review how the purposes of the treaty were being realized, the non-nuclear parties are no further ahead, and have in fact lost ground, in their efforts to obtain any adequate or even meaningful form of security assurances.

Chapter 11. How Good Are International Safeguards?

From the dawn of the nuclear age, it was said that nuclear energy must be subject to safeguards to ensure that it was used solely for peaceful purposes and that none of it was diverted to military purposes. The word "safeguards" is not a very precise term, and it has been used to describe a broad range of activities, international and national, including the Baruch Plan concept of international ownership, management, and control; a worldwide system of reporting and occasional inspections under the IAEA; and national safety regulations involving the use of guards and other measures to ensure the physical security of nuclear facilities and materials. The term is also used to describe the regulations and restraints that a nuclear supplier country imposes on its exports of nuclear materials and equipment.

Before the IAEA was created, the United States entered into bilateral agreements to provide nuclear assistance and materials to other states. All these agreements contained provisions for safeguards as required by the McMahon Act. After the IAEA was established and its safeguards system set up, the U.S. and many of these other states replaced bilateral agreements with new trilateral ones, with the IAEA as the third party, whereby the agency took over the safeguarding functions previously carried out by the United States under the bilateral agreements.

It must be remembered that the primary purpose of the IAEA was to promote and facilitate the peaceful uses of atomic energy for the welfare of mankind. International safeguards were intended not to be an end in themselves but only as a means to ensure that the nuclear assistance provided by or through the IAEA would not be misused for military purposes.

Both the provision of assistance in the peaceful nuclear field and the development of a safeguards system proceeded very slowly. For example, the total amount of technical assistance provided by the agency in the ten years from 1964 to 1973 added up to only $42,485,000. Until the entry into force of the NPT in 1970, the agency's safeguarding activities were also

147

extremely modest. Since the entry into force of the NPT, however, the agency's safeguarding functions have grown steadily though slowly. For example, in 1970, when the IAEA was applying safeguards in 32 states, it had less than ten fulltime inspectors on its staff. By 1975, when it was applying safeguards in 53 states under 59 agreements, its inspectors numbered sixty-nine, and the total budgetary cost of safeguards was over $5,000,000, almost one fifth of the total budget of the agency. As the 96 NPT parties continue to enter into safeguards agreements with the IAEA, this aspect of the agency's work will expand rapidly. Thus the IAEA's functions are now undergoing a transformation—a process likely to accelerate in the future—from what are basically positive peaceful development purposes to what are predominantly negative safeguarding tasks.

A detailed description and analysis of the IAEA's safeguarding responsibilities are beyond the scope of this book, which is concerned solely with an assessment of the effectiveness of the international safeguards system in preventing the proliferation of nuclear weapons. Those who wish to delve more deeply into the subject might find it useful to look at three books dealing specifically and in detail with the subject of safeguards. They are: *Atomic Safeguards: A Study in International Verification*, by Allan McKnight (the first Inspector-General of the IAEA), published by UNITAR, New York, in 1971; "*The Law and Practices of the International Atomic Energy Agency*," by Paul C. Szasz, published by the IAEA, Vienna, in 1970; and "*Safeguards against Nuclear Proliferation*," by Benjamin Sanders, published by SIPRI, Stockholm, and the MIT Press, Cambridge, Mass., in 1975.

IAEA Safeguards

Article II of the IAEA's statute sets out the agency's objectives as follows:

> The Agency shall seek to accelerate and enlarge the contribution of atomic energy to peace, health and prosperity throughout the world. It shall ensure, so far as it is able, that assistance provided by it or at its request or under its supervision or control is not used in such a way as to further any military purpose.

Article III, A, 5 of the statute sets out the agency's functions in regard to safeguards. It authorizes the agency

> To establish and administer safeguards designed to ensure that special fissionable and other materials, services, equipment, facilities, and information made available by the Agency or at its request or under its supervision or control are not used in such a way as to further any military purpose; and to apply safeguards, at the request of the parties, to any bilateral or multi-

lateral arrangement, or at the request of a State, to any of that State's activities in the field of atomic energy.

It will be noted that the statute does not *require* any member state of the agency to submit to safeguards. It does not even require that members subject their provision of international assistance in the nuclear field to the agency's controls. In a world of sovereign states, any limitation of sovereignty, including the acceptance of any system of controls, must be based on the consent of the states concerned, which is usually strictly defined and expressed in treaties. The statute merely provides an instrument for the establishment of controls but leaves it to each state to decide whether to submit to such controls and to what extent. Such decisions are also expressed by agreement between the states concerned and the agency.

The IAEA Statute and its safeguards system do not prevent or prohibit states from acquiring nuclear weapons or material and the equipment to make them. France and India, for example, were members in good standing when they first exploded nuclear devices, as the United States, the Soviet Union, and the United Kingdom are all members who are continuing their explosions. (The People's Republic of China has never participated in the IAEA, although Nationalist China [Taiwan] was excluded in 1971. The People's Republic has protested the inclusion of references to Nationalist China, with which the IAEA has safeguards agreements, in the agency's reports.)

The statute and safeguards system are intended only to ensure that specific projects, facilities, and nuclear material are not diverted to military uses. The NPT, the Treaty of Tlatelolco, and the 1954 Western European Union Treaty (which forbade West Germany to manufacture atomic weapons in its territory) are the only multilateral instruments that expressly forbid the acquisition of nuclear weapons. A number of bilateral agreements—for example, the Indian–Canadian agreement of 1956—also contain similar provisions. All bilateral American agreements to provide nuclear assistance contain an obligation by the recipient to use the assistance solely for peaceful purposes.

It will be noted that the agency's mandate, while not as specific as that of the above-mentioned three treaties, is somewhat broader in scope, in that it forbids the use of such assistance "in such a way as to further any military purpose," which is not defined. While it is not entirely clear, this would presumably prohibit the use of such assistance not only for the manufacture of nuclear weapons but also for building power plants for the propulsion of naval submarines or other warships or military means of transportation, whereas such activities are not prohibited by the three treaties.

Article III of the NPT provides that the IAEA system of safeguards is to be accepted by all non-nuclear-weapon parties to the treaty "with a view to *preventing* diversion of nuclear energy from peaceful uses to nuclear weapons or other nuclear explosive devices" (emphasis added). The article reads:

1. Each non-nuclear-weapon State Party to the Treaty undertakes to accept safeguards, as set forth in an agreement to be negotiated and concluded with the International Atomic Energy Agency in accordance with the statute of the International Atomic Energy Agency and the Agency's safeguards system, for the exclusive purpose of verification of the fulfillment of its obligations assumed under this Treaty with a view to preventing diversion of nuclear energy from peaceful uses to nuclear weapons or other nuclear explosive devices. Procedures for the safeguards required by this article shall be followed with respect to source or special fissionable material whether it is being produced, processed or used in any principal nuclear facility or is outside any such facility. The safeguards required by this article shall be applied on all source or special fissionable material in all peaceful nuclear activities within the territory of such State, under its jurisdiction, or carried out under its control anywhere.

2. Each State Party to the Treaty undertakes not to provide: (a) source or special fissionable material, or (b) equipment or material especially designed or prepared for the processing, use or production of special fissionable material, to any non-nuclear-weapon State for peaceful purposes, unless the source or special fissionable material shall be subject to the safeguards required by this article.

3. The safeguards required by this article shall be implemented in a manner designed to comply with article IV of this Treaty, and to avoid hampering the economic or technological development of the Parties or international cooperation in the field of peaceful nuclear activities, including the international exchange of nuclear material and equipment for the processing, use or production of nuclear material for peaceful purposes in accordance with the provisions of this article and the principle of safeguarding set forth in the Preamble of the Treaty.

4. Non-nuclear-weapon States Party to the Treaty shall conclude agreements with the International Atomic Energy Agency to meet the requirements of this article either individually or together with other States in accordance with the Statute of the International Atomic Energy Agency. Negotiation of such agreements shall commence within 180 days from the original entry into force of this Treaty. For States depositing their instruments of ratification or accession after the 180-day period, negotiation of such agreements shall commence not later than the date of such deposit. Such agreements shall enter into force not later than eighteen months after the date of initiation of negotiations.

The IAEA actually has two safeguards systems in operation. The first, which is contained in the agency's document INFCIRC/66 and revisions thereto and was adopted in 1965, is referred to as the agency's safeguards system. The second is the agency's safeguards system under the NPT, which was worked out and adopted in 1971 and appears in agency document INFCIRC/153, entitled "The Structure and Content of Agreements between the Agency and States Required in Connection with the Treaty on the Non-Proliferation of Nuclear Weapons" and commonly referred to as the "Blue Book." This second system is known as the IAEA/NPT safeguards.

The agency's 1965 safeguards system was based upon the idea of safeguards for specific projects. If a country wished to obtain assistance from the agency in developing the peaceful uses of nuclear energy, e.g., for a nuclear reactor, it would apply for approval of that specific project and would have to submit to safeguards established by the agency to ensure that the nuclear material would be used only for peaceful purposes. In addition, any safeguards agreements which had been entered into on a bilateral basis between states could be transferred to the IAEA, and any state could unilaterally submit any of its activities in the field of atomic energy to the agency's safeguards system. Thus, a state might have one facility under agency safeguards while retaining, unsafeguarded, all or part of a nuclear fuel cycle.

IAEA/NPT Safeguards

The agency's safeguards under the NPT, unlike the 1965 safeguards under the IAEA Statute, are designed to apply to *all* nuclear material in *all* peaceful nuclear activities within a state, as required by Article III (1) of the NPT, to ensure that such material is not diverted to nuclear weapons or other nuclear explosive devices.

The IAEA/NPT safeguards, like those of the 1965 system, are intended to be as nonintrusive as possible, but in this case the Blue Book specifically states that they should be implemented in a manner designed to avoid hampering the economic and technological development of states and to avoid undue interference in nuclear activity. It also states that the objective of safeguards is the timely detection of diversion of significant quantities of nuclear material from peaceful nuclear activities to the manufacture of nuclear weapons or of other nuclear explosive devices or for purposes unknown, and, hence, deterrence of such diversion by the risk of early detection.

A basic and novel feature of the IAEA/NPT safeguards is the formal requirement for each state to establish its own system of accounting for and controling all nuclear material to be subject to safeguards. The use of material accountancy is the fundamental safeguard measure and the NPT safeguards are applied in such a way that, in effect, they verify the findings of the state's own system. In addition, the agency's verification rights include independent measures of containment (the use of locks, seals, etc.) and surveillance (monitoring by cameras, television, and other automatic devices), as well as inspections conducted in accordance with specified procedures.

It is noteworthy that, although the safeguards are to apply to all nuclear material in all peaceful nuclear activities, the agency's verification procedures are limited to those locations which have been declared as having nuclear material. The safeguards are concentrated on key measurement points at which the flow or inventory of nuclear material may be easily determined.

An allowance is made for material which unaccountably disappears as a result of operational losses or "shrinkage." During the course of its flow through the fuel cycle the nuclear material undergoes many changes in nature and composition, and the analysis of the fissionable material is subject to small variations, so that there is often a discrepancy between the physical inventory and the book inventory of such material, which may amount to about 2 percent. In the United States, an official of the Atomic Energy Commission said that there was "a long way to go" before they could measure scrap effluents, products, inputs, and discards to a 1-percent accuracy, but now the goal is a level of accuracy of one-half of 1 percent. This missing material resulting from normal operational losses is called "material unaccounted for," or "MUF." The amount of MUF is closely watched to see whether it falls within the normal limits or exceeds them. While the MUF is quite small, it could become a possible basis for diversion of significant quantities of fissionable material over a period of time, particularly in large-scale operations. If by 1985 the annual amount of plutonium produced in the world is about 75,000 kg., then one-half of 1 percent of that amount would be sufficient to make one nuclear bomb every week, or more than 50 per year. Similarly, the MUF (one-half of 1 percent) of the cumulative total of plutonium produced by that time (350,000 kg.) would be sufficient to make some 300 nuclear bombs.

The IAEA/NPT safeguards also provide for reporting all exports of nuclear material. In order to facilitate arrangements in this regard, the governments of the United Kingdom, the Soviet Union, and the United States announced in June 1974 that they would, in the future, provide the agency on a continuing basis with information regarding exports and imports of nuclear material out of or into their three respective countries. The agency, however, has no responsibility for verifying the requirement in Article III (2) of the NPT whereby all parties to the treaty assume the obligation not to export source or special fissionable material or equipment therefor to any non-nuclear-weapon state unless the material involved is subject to agency safeguards. This matter is left to the exporting states under the NPT, and the agency becomes involved only when safeguards are applied in the territory of the importing state under an agreement entered into with the agency.

Because the safeguards were intended to be as nonintrusive as possible, there are a number of provisions which make it possible for a state wishing to do so to delay, hinder, or even, perhaps, evade the effective operation of the safeguards system. These include such matters as the normal requirement for advance warnings of inspections (although provision is made for surprise inspections); the necessity for the inspected or safeguarded state to accept the designated inspector or inspectors and to agree on the defined areas or strategic points to be inspected; and the fact that the safeguards are to apply only to declared facilities. The state in question can also lay down its own rules concerning health and safety matters. Finally, several months can elapse between inspections, and there can be a time gap between a state's reported inventory and its current inventory.

A more serious problem is that regarding the actual physical security of the nuclear material, which is not subject to international safeguards but rather is left exclusively to individual states. The responsibility for physical protection of safeguarded material in the case of international transfers is also a matter for agreement between the states concerned and is not subject to agency safeguards. However, the agency has assumed an advisory role in this area, and it has drawn up "Guidelines for the Physical Protection of Nuclear Material against Loss, Theft, etc." These recommendations have been published and made available to interested states.

There are no real measures of sanction or enforcement in case of noncompliance or violation by any state. National enforcement measures provide fines or other penalities in case of violations. In the case of the IAEA, however, the only recourse is under the provisions of Article XII C of the agency's statute. This provides merely that the Board of Governors can give publicity to the violation by reporting it to the members of the agency and to the Security Council and General Assembly of the United Nations. In addition, the Board may direct the curtailment or suspension of any assistance being provided by the agency, and the agency may suspend any noncomplying member from membership.

In sum, the IAEA/NPT safeguards system can only be as effective as the accounting and physical security safeguard techniques of each state permit and as that state is willing to cooperate with the agency. Within the limitations provided in Article III of the NPT and those imposed by governments jealous of their national sovereignty, the agency has provided a workable safeguards system. It can be fully effective, however, only if there is full cooperation from governments. If a state regards the safeguards as contrary to its national interest at any time, it is very doubtful that it would enforce them or accept, for example, international surveillance or inspections. If any state should decide at any time that it wished to divert nuclear materials to the manufacture of weapons or nuclear explosive devices it would not be very difficult for it to circumvent the safeguards, without going to the extent of actually falsifying its records.

It has been suggested that, irrespective of the rather large possibilities for circumventing or evading the agency's safeguards, there is a very great likelihood that the clandestine intelligence agencies of the nuclear powers would undoubtedly get wind of any attempts at illegal diversion. Governments could then intervene privately and directly with the offending state or could alert the IAEA and its inspectors so that they could pursue the matter. Such possibilities can undoubtedly serve to bolster and reinforce the effectiveness of the agency's safeguards.

It has also been suggested, however, that a government wishing to evade its commitments could do so in a relatively open manner. For example, one can visualize a scenario whereby the government of a country announces one day that 50 kilograms of plutonium has been stolen or hijacked while in transit, and that all of the nation's resources are being mobilized to track down the culprits and recover the stolen material. After a year, the government announces that all its efforts have proved fruitless —it has failed to recover the material or even obtain any good leads. It states that it will continue to pursue the matter with due diligence and asks all citizens to bring any information or suspicious activities to its attention. It then retains the 50 kilograms in a safe and secret place for its own use or secretly sells it to some other government to fabricate into nuclear weapons. While this scenario seems rather far-fetched, it is far from impossible, and there would be little or no recourse if it were followed.

Another possibility is that a government, not willing to engage in clandestine diversion from its own facilities, may either go into the black market to purchase material for weapons or else enter into an arrangement with some criminal group to procure a nuclear weapon or material for one.

Finally, a state wishing to free itself from its commitments need not engage in any clandestine or prohibited activities or even go into the black market to acquire nuclear materials and equipment; it can, if it chooses to do so, openly withdraw from the NPT and be free to do what it wishes. This might, of course, give rise to delicate political problems which the state would have to balance against its perception of the benefits of withdrawal.

We have seen that the IAEA/NPT safeguards system is a system for detection rather than prevention of diversion, which seeks to deter such diversion only by the risk of early detection. The credibility and viability of such a system of safeguards depends on the moral climate and on the strength of the entire non-proliferation regime. It is highly unlikely that the nations of the world would confer sufficient police powers or authority on any international body to actually prevent diversion of nuclear material. In the final analysis, even domestic law, which is much more effective since it can be enforced by police power and a system of penalties, depends for its observance on the prevailing climate of opinion and on the respect with which the laws are held. If they fall into disrepute, they are honored more often in their breach than in their observance. The same applies, to a large extent, to the NPT. The respect accorded the treaty, and the observance of its obligations by the parties to it, may have more to do with the effectiveness of its safeguards system than the actual measures and procedures themselves.

The Nuclear "Suppliers Club"

The United States—the chief supplier state of nuclear materials and equipment—and other supplier states have continued to supply source or special fissionable material and equipment therefor to non-nuclear states that are not parties to the NPT without insisting that *all* the nuclear material and *all* nuclear activities of the receiving states be subject to the safeguards required by the article, that is, to IAEA safeguards. From 1970 to 1975, the United States continued to supply fissionable material to such countries as the members of Euratom, India, Japan, and other non-parties to the NPT without their being subject to IAEA safeguards.

While such sales may not, strictly speaking, constitute actual legal violations of the treaty, they make a mockery of the treaty by providing more favorable terms to non-parties than to parties.

Only partial measures have been taken to remedy the situation. In August 1974, the United States joined the other chief supplier states, including the United Kingdom, the Soviet Union, Australia, Canada, and West Germany, in a sort of "suppliers club." These countries entered into public undertakings in letters to the IAEA stating that they would not provide source or special fissionable material or equipment and material therefor to any non-nuclear-weapon state unless the material were subject to safeguards under an agreement with the IAEA. The letter contained detailed lists of the material and equipment that would be covered by the embargo. The U.S. and the Soviet Union also announced that the safeguards would also verify that the nuclear material was not used for any nuclear explosive device. However, unless both nuclear and non-nuclear parties to the treaty insist on the strict application of the safeguards to all nuclear material and activities, the new restraints will have only a minor effect on preventing the diversion of materials to nuclear explosives. The loophole that remains is large enough to permit, or even facilitate, the acquisition of nuclear weapons by countries that are not parties to the NPT. In fact, the new restraints announced by the members of the suppliers club maintain, and indeed, sharpen, a discriminatory and most anomalous situation. Non-nuclear countries that are not parties to the NPT continue to be subject to fewer safeguards than are parties. Under the provisions of Article III, all non-nuclear parties to the NPT must place all their source and special fissionable material in all their peaceful nuclear activities under IAEA safeguards. Under the embargo announced by the suppliers club, however, non-nuclear countries that are not parties to the NPT need accept IAEA safeguards only on their new and future supplies of nuclear material and equipment. Whatever unsafeguarded nuclear supplies and equipment they have received in the past or that they themselves acquire from indigenous or other sources in the future remain free of safeguards, and they can use them as they will. Thus, for example, Canada and Sweden must accept IAEA/NPT safeguards on all their nuclear material, equipment, facilities, and activities, while Argentina, Brazil, Japan, Pakistan, South Africa, Spain, India, and all other nonparties to the NPT need accept them only for new supplies. Thus, parties to the NPT are at a distinct disadvantage by comparison with nonparties with respect to safeguards. This situation can hardly be regarded as offering any incentive to nonparties to sign or ratify or otherwise adhere to the NPT.

In any case, there is some doubt as to how effective the embargo of the suppliers club really is even with respect to new supplies. For an embargo to be fully effective, it must close off all sources of supply. But some important supplier states that are not NPT parties, such as France and South Africa, have not joined in the suppliers club nor offered any equivalent undertaking. Whether they will agree to abide by a similar unilateral embargo or restraint is far from clear. Given the growing commercial rivalry among supplier countries to sell nuclear reactors, material, and equipment, there are solid grounds for doubting the effectiveness of an embargo by supplier countries, whether members of the suppliers club or not. In fact, a French commercial corporation is now in the market to sell complete chemical separation plants for reprocessing plutonium, albeit under safeguards.

As a result of its unfortunate experience with India, Canada has now unilaterally announced the imposition of the strictest export regulations of any nuclear supplier country. On December 20, 1974, Canada announced that it would in the future require that international safeguards to ensure against the development of any nuclear explosive device cover (1) all nuclear facilities and equipment supplied by Canada; (2) all nuclear facilities and equipment using Canadian-supplied technology; (3) all nuclear material—uranium, thorium, plutonium, and heavy water—supplied by Canada and all fissionable material produced from or with these materials; and (4) all nuclear materials, whatever their origin, produced or processed in facilities supplied by Canada.

But even these strict regulations can be evaded. A country, (such as India or Argentina) that is not a party to the NPT, that has obtained a research or power reactor using natural uranium can copy it or build its own and can operate it with its own natural uranium, since most countries have access to their own resources of uranium ore or to foriegn sources of uranium and thorium ore. If it buys or builds a small reprocessing plant, it can acquire its own stockpile of plutonium. Thus a country subject to the Canadian safeguards and abiding strictly by them can still manufacture its own nuclear explosive devices. Only the NPT requires that *all* nuclear material in *all* peaceful nuclear activities of a country be placed under international safeguards. Anything short of that can inhibit or delay but not prevent a country from going nuclear.

Moreover, even the Canadian regulations, since they do not insist that all of a recipient's nuclear materials and activities be put under IAEA safeguards, still permit the invidious discriminatory situation wherein countries that are not parties to the NPT can obtain nuclear materials, equipment, and technology on more favorable terms (i.e., under less strict conditions) than parties.

Euratom and Tlatelolco Safeguards

A word needs to be said about the safeguards systems of Euratom and of the Treaty of Tlatelolco. Both the Euratom and the Tlatelolco treaties provide for their own systems of safeguards, although the latter makes specific provision that the safeguards system of the IAEA should apply to the countries in the Latin American nuclear-free zone. (The Tlatelolco treaty also has a much wider and more intrusive system of control and verification to supplement the IAEA safeguards.) Euratom and the Euratom countries have entered into an agreement with the IAEA by which Euratom and its member countries in effect agree to accept the IAEA/NPT system of safeguards. A compromise was worked out whereby Euratom would work together with the agency in carrying out the agency's safeguards system. The Tlatelolco treaty likewise envisages agreements between its parties and the IAEA, and it is expected that the IAEA/NPT safeguards will also apply to the member states of the Latin American nuclear-free zone. Accordingly, it seems that the IAEA/NPT system is extending its sway and is establishing itself as the standard system for safeguarding, not merely with respect to the NPT itself, but for the entire non-proliferation regime.

Evaluating Safeguards

As we have seen, the safeguards system of the IAEA is a system for keeping track of nuclear material primarily on the basis of auditing the accounts of a national government or of its nuclear facilities, supplemented by automatic instrumental checks and by inspections. In some ways, the process is similar to that of the auditors of a bank, but the IAEA inspectors have much less authority than do bank auditors. Even if the IAEA inspectors had the same authority as bank auditors, their task would be much more difficult. In a bank, the flow of dollars and securities in and out of the system can be readily checked. (And even under those circumstances, banks make mistakes or are victims of theft by outsiders or embezzlement by insiders.)

In the case of fissionable material, however, whether it is natural or enriched uranium, thorium, or plutonium, the composition of the material itself changes in a nuclear reactor. For example, either natural or enriched uranium is converted into several different isotopes of plutonium. The difficulties involved in keeping track of each isotope are compounded by the problem of MUF (material unaccounted for). In addition, there have been instances in the United States where thousands of kilograms of plutonium, far above the normal MUF loss, have simply disappeared without any known reason. For example, one American corporation was unable to account for 100 kilograms of missing weapons-grade nuclear material—6 percent of the material it had handled over several years. For all anyone knows, it may already have found its way to a reported black market in Europe. These disappearances or shortages have occurred within a national jurisdiction where the domestic authorities have far greater power than any international authority possesses. Within a country, the authorities can exercise police powers, either through direct contracting or licensing arrangements or by the laws and regulations of the country, and they have the power of imposing fines and penalties in case of violations. No existing international authority has such power. All it can do is alert the world community to a breach or suspected breach of a contract or treaty. If it is not possible for a national authority to prevent all diversions or even detect them and account for them at an early stage, it is clearly impossible for an international authority to do so.

Nevertheless, despite the obvious shortcomings of any safeguards system, the stricter the safeguards, whether national or international, the more effective they are likely to be. Viewed in the context of a system or regime for the non-proliferation of nuclear weapons, safeguards can be regarded as reinforcing or supporting mechanisms of a political and symbolic significance. Even if their effect is merely to deter or discourage diversion of nuclear material from peaceful uses to weapons production or place impediments in the way of diversion, they play a useful role. A safeguards system may help to create a standard of legitimacy and norms of conduct and have an inhibiting effect on those who might contemplate the possibility of diversion or theft. It is said that locks on doors to private homes and establishments are necessary and useful in order to deter, or inhibit, or remove temptation from, normally honest persons rather than to keep out thieves and burglars, who can, if they set out to do so, find some way to get around them. But better locks and burglar-alarm systems help to discourage or deter even professional burglars. In similar fashion, the stricter the safeguards and controls the more likely they will be to minimize the possibilities of diversion or theft, and even to delay or postpone a decision by a country to go nuclear. If a country delays or postpones its decision, whether for two years or ten, that can be useful. The longer the delay can be stretched, the better the chances are that, as events occur and as a better understanding of all circumstances develops, the decision can be postponed indefinitely. In many cases international problems die a natural death or simply disappear in time. So, too, may the desire or perceived necessity for going nuclear.

It is interesting that Article III (1) of the NPT contains an undertaking on the part of each non-nuclear-weapon party to the NPT "to accept safeguards . . . with a view to *preventing* diversion of nuclear energy from peaceful uses to nuclear weapons or other nuclear explosive devices" (emphasis added). In view of the extensive consideration given to the preparation of the entire NPT and in particular to Article III, it must be assumed that the word "preventing" was included in the text not as a result of careless drafting but as a result of careful intention. If that is the case, it provides sound legal grounds for urging the parties to go beyond a system of mere detection and deterrence and to attempt to elaborate a system of prevention of diversion. While it is, of course, true that the problem is not in its essence a legal problem but rather a political and perhaps even a psychological problem, nevertheless, if the two superpowers and the other great industrial powers are convinced of the overriding importance of ensuring the success of the non-proliferation regime, they could and should take the lead in establishing the most stringent possible regulations for the supply of material and equipment and in giving some far-reaching authority and powers to the IAEA or some other international agency. It may be that such a revolutionary approach to the problem of preventing the proliferation of nuclear weapons is the only way that such proliferation can, in practice, be prevented. Certainly, present practices seem hardly likely to achieve that aim.

As we indicated earlier, although possibilities exist for doing so, there is not much likelihood of countries clandestinely violating their obligations by attempting, in secret, to divert nuclear material from peaceful to military purposes. The main danger stems from the fact that, on the one hand, some important countries are not parties to the NPT—some potential nuclear states have not signed the NPT; others have signed but not yet ratified—while, on the other hand, those who have signed and ratified may decide to withdraw from the treaty. The dangers in this regard have nothing to do with the adequacy or inadequacy of the safeguards system. In any case, no system of safeguards can prevent a country from going nuclear if it decides that it is in its vital interest to do so. Any decision in this respect will depend on a country's views concerning its security requirements and on a complex of larger questions involving military, political, economic, and prestige considerations.

It is a matter of considerable significance and a noteworthy international achievement that the NPT now has nearly 100 parties and that more than a dozen other states have signed but not yet ratified it. Since the treaty is inherently discriminatory in nature as regards the obligations assumed by the nuclear-weapon states and the non-nuclear-weapon states, it can be assumed that all the non-nuclear-weapon states that have become parties to the treaty have reached a consensus with the nuclear-weapon states that it is not in the interest of any of them to permit or acquiesce in the further proliferation of nuclear weapons. Such a consensus does tend to establish the idea of the illegitimacy of the further proliferation of nuclear weapons. But if this idea is to succeed, it must be reinforced and strengthened and not allowed to erode or become weakened. And safeguards alone cannot ensure the success of the concept or of the non-proliferation regime.

Proposals for Improving Safeguards

There are a number of things that can be done to strengthen the non-proliferation regime by eliminating or reducing the discriminatory aspects of safeguards. The safeguards system applies only to the non-nuclear-weapon states, as provided in Article III of the NPT. However, as an inducement to some of the near-nuclear or potential nuclear states to join the NPT, the United States and the United Kingdom voluntarily agreed to submit their peaceful nuclear facilities and programs to IAEA safeguards. It would certainly help to improve the situation if both these countries were to enter into early agreements with the IAEA for the application of the safeguards system to them. It would also be important for the U.S.S.R. to likewise agree to voluntarily accept IAEA safeguards over its peaceful programs and facilities.

Moreover, since the superpowers already have more than enough weapons-grade U235 and Pu239 for any conceivable military use, they should agree to halt the production of all fissionable material for military purposes. This would mean that *all* their future production of fissionable material would be solely for peaceful purposes. They could and should, therefore, agree to put the entire fuel cycle of their plants and facilities under international safeguards.

The author makes the following other recommendations for strengthening safeguards:

1. All nuclear-weapon parties to the NPT should agree to accept IAEA safeguards over *all* their peaceful nuclear activities.
2. The nuclear-weapon states and supplier states should agree to make no sales and provide no nuclear material or equipment to any nuclear or non-nuclear country unless that country agrees either to become a party to the NPT or to accept equivalent restraints and to place *all* of its nuclear material and facilities, including re-exports, under IAEA safeguards.
3. The supplier states should make a public declaration, along with the Board of Governors and the General Conference of the IAEA, that peaceful nuclear explosions under national control are incompatible with the peaceful utilization of nuclear energy. (See Chapter 13.)
4. The IAEA/NPT safeguards system should be strengthened by, for

example, including measures provided for in the agency's statute whereby inspectors could have free access not merely to declared or reported facilities but to all nuclear facilities or material in the possession of any party; providing that no nuclear material can be withdrawn for any military uses other than the manufacture of weapons or explosive devices; and instituting a more active program of research on the development of better safeguards and better instruments and technical means of safeguarding. The goal should be, in general, to work towards the removal of those procedures which enable a safeguarded state to delay or hamper inspections or other applications of safeguards.

5. All spent fuel should either be returned to the supplier country for reprocessing (or for storing, if reprocessing is not required), or be sent to some internationally operated and safeguarded plant for reprocessing at cost, and thereafter returned as fuel for identified peaceful purposes to the country from which it originated. If reprocessing is done at cost, or better still without charge, it would provide a substantial inducement to countries not to acquire or use their own reprocessing plants.

6. The proposal for the establishment of regional, multinational, or international fuel cycle centers for uranium enrichment, fuel fabrication, reprocessing, spent fuel storage, and waste management should be implemented. Such centers would minimize the number of shipments of nuclear material and the risks of diversion or theft and would improve the effectiveness of the safeguards system. They would also help to prevent the acquisition of fissionable material for explosive devices by any individual national government.

7. Once the above international services are available, nuclear supplier countries should not export any chemical separation plant for plutonium reprocessing which might come under national control. Nor should they export any nuclear material, equipment, or technology to any non-nuclear country that has or that acquires any reprocessing plant under national control.

8. The supplier countries should work towards the adoption of physical security systems, both national and international, which would prevent the theft of nuclear material by terrorists and criminal elements, either at nuclear facilities or during transport of nuclear materials. (See Chapter 19.)

9. The nuclear supplier countries should adopt effective sanctions providing for the immediate withholding of *all* nuclear assistance by *all* suppliers not only for future contracts but also under previous or existing contracts, from countries that violate any of the above measures.

Even such nuclear powers as France and supplier or potential supplier states such as South Africa and India, none of which is a party to the

NPT, ought to regard the prevention of the further spread of nuclear weapons as in their interest. Hence it is possible that they too might be willing to support and subscribe to those measures in the above list that are not dependent on or related to adherence to the NPT.

As we explain in Chapter 18, the NPT Review Conference reached a large measure of agreement on desirable technical measures for improving and strengthening the system of safeguards. These measures included general endorsement of the above list of measures, excepting items 2 and 9, but fell short of specific support for all of them. The conference favored the improvement and universal application of IAEA safeguards, the extension of safeguards to all peaceful nuclear activities in states not party to the NPT, the elaboration of effective national and international measures for the physical protection of all nuclear material, undertakings by non-nuclear states not to conduct their own peaceful nuclear explosions, and the establishment of regional or multinational nuclear fuel cycle centers for the construction and operation of fuel fabrication plants, chemical reprocessing plants, waste management installations, and spent fuel storage. The conference did not, however, go so far as to insist on the absolute necessity of such measures—in particular of a ban on exports to any country that did not place all of its nuclear activities under IAEA safeguards or that operated a chemical reprocessing plant under its national control. Nor did it venture into the area of sanctions in case of violations. In sum, while moving in the right direction as regards technical measures for improving safeguards, the conference did not go far enough to make safeguards really effective.

In any case, as we point out in Chapter 18, improved technical measures alone will not achieve the desired objective. Only a combination of both political and technical measures can succeed in providing the required credibility and viability for the non-proliferation regime. The combination of the necessary minimum political and technical measures is set forth in Chapter 18.

While the above suggestions for technical measures to strengthen the safeguards system are far-reaching in nature, they are no more radical than is the concept of non-proliferation itself or, for that matter, the Non-Proliferation Treaty. If the nuclear-weapon states and the supplier states would agree to accept and implement them, the non-nuclear states might be persuaded to do likewise. And if the two superpowers were to lead the way in this regard, they could help to create a momentum and community of interest in favor of the adoption of such a strengthened and expanded safeguards system similar to that which they succeeded in achieving when they worked out the provisions of the Non-Proliferation Treaty and obtained the commendation of the United Nations by an overwhelming majority. Agreement on the implementation of these technical measures would also help to facilitate agreement on the necessary political measures outlined in Chapter 18.

Chapter 12. Have the Peaceful Uses of Nuclear Energy Been Facilitated?

The Promise

It was as a result of the demands and pressures of the non-nuclear states, and especially of the developing countries, that Article IV was written into the NPT. It was also on their insistence that each succeeding draft of the text of the article was strengthened until it attained its present form. The article calls on all the parties to the treaty "to facilitate . . . the fullest possible exchange of equipment, materials, and scientific and technological information." Parties "in a position to do so shall also cooperate in contributing . . . to the further development of the applications of nuclear energy for peaceful purposes." These peaceful uses were to be promoted "especially . . . in non-nuclear states parties" and with "due consideration for the needs of the developing areas."

In plain words, Article IV amounted to a firm pledge by the nuclear powers and other supplier countries of aid to the non-nuclear countries, with the developing ones singled out for special consideration. As indicated in earlier chapters, this was part of the bargain negotiated by the non-nuclear powers for giving up their right to go nuclear. In exchange for their foreswearing the acquisition of nuclear weapons, they were to receive increased benefits from the peaceful application of nuclear energy, which would also include the potential benefits of peaceful nuclear explosions. (This question is dealt with in the next chapter.)

That this pledge was an important part of a "deal" between the nuclear and the non-nuclear nations is confirmed by the Senate Foreign Relations Committee report of September 26, 1968, in which the committee advised ratification of the NPT. The report stated: "The compensation for such an important act of self-denial" by the non-nuclear-weapon states, who were denying by the NPT what the United States and the Soviet Union consider essential for their own security, "is the pledge of nuclear-weapon states to make available to the non-nuclear-weapon states which are signatories the benefits of peaceful nuclear programs. . . ."

The intent and the language of Article IV were clear. Its implementation rapidly became unclear.

The Performance

The interest of the non-nuclear countries in obtaining the benefits of the peaceful uses of nuclear energy under Article IV of the NPT was registered in considerable detail and in practical terms at the Conference of Non-Nuclear-Weapon States, which was discussed in Chapter 9 above. Despite the many specific recommendations for concrete action at that conference, its energies were soon dissipated. Instead of action by the nuclear and other supplier states to implement their treaty obligations in this regard, what followed were studies and reports by the Secretary-General, by groups of experts, by the IAEA, and by various other international agencies—a diffusion of efforts which in the final result added up to very little, if anything, in practical terms.

In September 1971, the Fourth International Conference on the Peaceful Uses of Atomic Energy was held at Geneva. The conference was held under the aegis of the United Nations and with the full participation of the IAEA. It focused on one main theme, the rapid rise of nuclear power as a major source of energy in the world. The conference confirmed that nuclear power would account for about one-fourth of the total installed electrical generating capacity in the world by 1985 and about one-half by the year 2000. It considered reports describing progress in nuclear fusion and the applications of radio isotopes and radiation in agriculture, hydrology, medicine, and industry. It devoted attention to the problems of education and training of scientists and engineers in the nuclear field. Both that conference and the General Conference of all of the members of the IAEA held later in the same month recommended that efforts be intensified to assist developing countries in planning for nuclear power.

In a report prepared by the IAEA in 1974 for the Review Conference of the NPT held in May 1975, figures were given on the distribution of money and resources in kind by the IAEA for peaceful uses of nuclear energy by way of technological assistance, including grants from the UNDP. The figures compared the amount of such resources and aid given during the five-year periods before and after the holding of the Conference of Non-Nuclear-Weapon States. From 1964 to 1968, the *total* amount of such assistance came to $15,941,000. In the period from 1969 to 1973 the aid totaled $26,544,000. While this represents an increase of about 66.6 percent, the sum involved is minuscule. Of this sum, roughly one-third went for experts, one-third for the provision of fellowships, and one-third for the provision of equipment. One can appreciate how insignificant was the five-year outlay for all recipients when one remembers that the cost of building a single nuclear power reactor varies from about $300 million for a 200-megawatt plant to over $1 billion for a 1,000-megawatt plant.

The IAEA also reported that it had increased its programs for the exchange of scientific and technological information and had established an International Nuclear Information System (INIS); it noted that the number of UNDP projects executed by the agency had increased from nine in 1973 to fifteen in 1974.

And it stated that not only parties to the NPT but also nonparties had increased their participation in the IAEA's activities. It summed up the situation by noting that "it is difficult to estimate how much of the growth and development of these various programs are attributable to the implementation of Article IV of the NPT and how much is due to the normal evolution of the IAEA work, including increased program participation by states not parties to the NPT."

The Conference of Non-Nuclear-Weapon States had called for the establishment of a "Special Nuclear Fund" by the IAEA, of a "Nuclear Technology Research and Development Program" by the United Nations Development Program, and of a "Program for the Use of Nuclear Energy in Economic Development Projects" by the International Bank for Reconstruction and Development, for the benefit of non-nuclear-weapon states and in particular of developing countries, and had invited the nuclear-weapon states to support such undertakings. The IAEA reported that France, the Soviet Union, the United Kingdom, and the United States had indicated that special fissionable materials would be made available through the agency on the same terms and conditions as they were available through bilateral channels. These countries also drew attention to the fact that the special fissionable materials available to the agency before 1960 were still very largely intact and had not been used up. It is worth noting here that the main reason why this fund of special fissionable materials was not used up was that there were not enough reactors able to use the material in the hands of developing countries.

In the same 1974 report, the IAEA noted that in earlier years its programs were mainly directed to helping developing states to use research reactors and to apply radioisotope and radiation techniques in medicine, agriculture, hydrology, and so forth. The present programs, however, were increasingly focusing on helping these countries to apply large-scale nuclear technology, to discover and develop nuclear fuel (uranium) resources, and to introduce nuclear power. The agency summed up its report by stating that the problems that had to be solved in achieving a rapid growth of nuclear capacity would require additional resources and continued willingness on the part of the industrially advanced member states to make available both expertise and hardware—that is, equipment, facilities, and fuel.

It is true that the amount of aid and technical assistance given to facilitate and promote the peaceful uses of nuclear energy has increased since the approval of the NPT but, as we mentioned, the amount involved is pitifully small. This is owing to no fault of the IAEA, which keeps calling repeatedly, but without notable success, for more assistance. The supplier states—the nuclear powers and the other developed, industrialized states with advanced nuclear programs—have simply not given much in the way of aid to the non-nuclear and in particular the developing countries. West Germany gave a training reactor to Argentina and one to Mexico. But not one single reactor for power or desalination was given or sold to any country as a direct result of Article IV that would not have been given without it. In fact, none whatsoever was given to any developing country. Such international aid and trade as did take place in the nuclear field were almost exclusively bilateral and were commercial sales by supplier states mainly to rich industrial countries.

There may be some truth in the argument made by the nuclear powers and other supplying states that the developing countries are not yet ready to receive nuclear reactors for power or desalination in that they are not yet capable of using this technology. But the answer is, of course, that many of these countries could have been ready by now if sufficient effort and aid had been invested for that purpose. Twenty-two years have gone by since President Eisenhower made his "Atoms for Peace" speech at the United Nations, and seven years since the NPT was signed. Moreover, there are, in fact, several developing countries that are both ready for and capable of using nuclear power reactors. The IAEA made a survey of fourteen interested countries in Asia, Southeast Europe, and Latin America in 1972–73 to determine appropriate and economically justifiable size and timing for nuclear power plant installation during the 1980s. The survey showed that at the time only plants of 600 to 1,000 megawatts would be economical even for developing countries. After the energy crisis of 1973, however, with the quadrupling in the price of oil, the IAEA estimated that plants of 200 to 400 megawatts in size, or even smaller, would be economical. Given past experience, however, it is questionable to what extent the developing countries, except for some of the oil-rich ones, will benefit from this new situation.

Future international trade and dealings in the peaceful nuclear field will increasingly be undertaken by industrial and commercial enterprises, mainly multinational corporations. They will be carried out according to the normal rules and competition governing such commerce. The main interest of the corporations involved will naturally be directed toward the more developed and industrialized countries, where there are huge potential markets, rather than toward the developing countries, with their rather restricted markets and all the problems and uncertainties that affect them. The developing countries, except for a few of the more advanced and oil-rich ones, will be regarded more as a source of uranium and other natural resources required by the nuclear industry than as a market for nuclear reactors and technology.

During the past decade there was a very marked increase in the spread of nuclear technology and in the proliferation of nuclear power reactors. This increase took place almost exclusively in the territories of the nuclear powers and the advanced industrial countries; very little took place in the developing countries. In fact, the gap between the rich and poor countries in the nuclear field was particularly noticeable and increased at a greater rate than in other fields. In the absence of a conscious and concerted effort by the nuclear supplier states, the gap between the rich and poor countries in the field of nuclear energy will continue to widen and will cause increasing resentment.

Most developing countries would prefer that assistance in the nuclear field, as in others, be channeled through an international organization; they feel at less of a negotiating disadvantage than in bilateral dealings. The nuclear powers prefer that requests for nuclear assistance be dealt with through the IAEA, first because the nuclear powers have voting control in the Board of Governors and can thus keep a close watch on the activities of the agency, and second, because by internationalizing the responsibility for such aid the nuclear powers can reduce the direct pressures on themselves.

An enormous potential world market has developed for nuclear power, amounting to billions of dollars a year. As we indicated, this market has developed mainly in the more advanced and industrialized developed nations. Now the oil-rich countries, with their concern for the maximum possible conservation of their petroleum resources, are becoming increasingly interested in nuclear power and technology. At the present time, for example, Iran is engaged in negotiations to acquire ten or twelve large nuclear reactors. This market has developed not as a result of the pledge in Article IV of the NPT and not as a result of cooperation among the nuclear powers, but because of the tremendous increase in the cost of fossil fuels, the growing interest of the richer developing countries in nuclear energy and the intense competition among the nuclear powers and a few other supplier states, such as Canada and West Germany, for profits and foreign exchange.

We have already noted that the IAEA itself came to a somewhat similar conclusion, expressed in the characteristically restrained and cautious language of secretariats of international organizations, in its report on its activities under Article IV of the NPT. Dr. Bernard Goldschmidt, the Director of External Relations and Planning of the French Atomic Energy Commission and an internationally known and respected figure in the field of nuclear energy stated a substantially similar conclusion in more pungent and dramatic language. He wrote in the 1974 SIPRI publication *Nuclear Proliferation Problems*:

> Under present circumstances, Article IV is no more than a pious vow having no practical application, which tries to present in more palatable terms a treaty not always subscribed to with enthusiasm.

Nearly all of the developing countries would agree with his assessment. Many of them, in fact, consider that they have been misled or duped by the nuclear powers.

The NPT Review Conference, 1975

The NPT Review Conference did little beyond reaffirming the undertakings set forth in Article IV of the treaty. The developing countries again pressed for concrete action by the nuclear powers and the rich industrialized non-nuclear countries to provide preferential treatment and concessional terms to them in the acquisition of research reactors and nuclear materials, equipment, and technology. They called for the creation of a Special Fund under the IAEA to provide nuclear research reactors and fuel, and for a Special Nuclear Fund, under an international organization or third world regional body, to provide financing under concessional terms for nuclear projects in the territories of developing NPT parties.

The nuclear powers and the industrialized non-nuclear countries opposed these specific proposals and limited themselves to saying that they would "consider" taking measures, making contributions, and establishing programs to provide special assistance to the developing parties, and would "give weight" to adherence to the treaty on the part of recipient states. In addition, they supported studies by the IAEA concerning the establishment of regional or multinational nuclear fuel cycle centers in specific geographical areas.

Because of their failure to achieve any results from their previous proposals, put forth at the Conference of Non-Nuclear-Weapon States in 1968, to obtain significant assistance in developing the peaceful uses of nuclear energy, the developing countries regarded such vague generalities as being totally inadequate and as tending to confirm their worst suspicions.

Proposals for the Future

Unless some new attitudes and policies are adopted by the nuclear powers and some more effective machinery for implementation of Article IV is devised, either by improving existing institutions or by creating new ones, the promise of this article of the NPT will be unfulfilled. The failure of the nuclear powers to live up to their commitment will become an additional factor weakening the NPT and exacerbating the discontent between the rich and poor countries.

There are risks in providing countries with nuclear equipment, materials, and technology for peaceful purposes. This was recognized at the time that the "Atoms for Peace" program was first conceived and has been the object of a great deal of thought ever since, particularly at the time that Article IV of the NPT was being negotiated.

What must be recognized, however, is that there are also risks in *not* helping other countries to acquire capability in the peaceful nuclear field. Each of the six nuclear powers acquired a nuclear explosive capability as a result of its own efforts, although some of them received some assistance from the U.S. or Canada, and it is likely that China received some help from the U.S.S.R. in the 1950s. Today the open, published literature contains all the information necessary for any nation or group of scientists to manufacture peaceful reactors or nuclear explosives. The only stronghold of secrecy left is with respect to the process of enriching uranium, and this knowledge, too, is rapidly becoming diffused. There is nothing secret about the production of fissionable plutonium. Consequently, any country that decides to go nuclear can do so, with or without receiving aid from the nuclear countries. The receipt of nuclear assistance merely hastens and facilitates the process. The question, then, is whether and in what way nuclear assistance should be given in order to maximize the probabilities that it will be used only for peaceful purposes and to minimize the likelihood of its being diverted to the manufacture of nuclear explosives.

We have seen that the nuclear supplier states are capable of coming together to ensure that aid will be given only to those countries that agree to place all of their future supplies of nuclear material and equipment under IAEA safeguards. In fact, since December 20, 1974, Canada has taken a position that in effect requires any recipient of Canadian nuclear assistance to place all current and future supplies of nuclear material, equipment, and technology under such safeguards.

If it was possible for the supplier countries to reach agreement on the application of safeguards, which is bound to cost them something in terms of reduced sales, it should not be beyond their wisdom and ability to come together for the purpose of furnishing nuclear assistance, including loans and grants for nuclear power reactors, to non-nuclear states and in particular the developing ones. Such assistance could be channeled through existing agencies such as the UNDP, the World Bank, and the IAEA.

In this regard, there is an increasing number of voices being raised among the developing countries in favor of the establishment of some new bodies for promoting the peaceful uses of nuclear energy, either under the United Nations or as separate, specially created agencies. There are two reasons for this. First, there is the suspicion that the IAEA is dominated by the two superpowers, who control and manipulate the agency mainly in their own interests. Second, there is the fear that the growing safeguarding functions of the agency are tending to overshadow its other peaceful activities and that soon the "tail will wag the dog."

A word of caution is necessary. While the full implementation on the part of the supplier states of their commitments under Article IV of the

NPT would be a commendable thing in itself and would help strengthen the NPT, it would not *alone* suffice to give viability and credibility to the treaty. For that, it would be necessary to implement all of the provisions of the treaty, particularly Article VI on disarmament, and to provide more adequate security assurances.

Chapter 13. What About Peaceful Nuclear Explosions?

The Promise

Since the Non-Proliferation Treaty banned peaceful nuclear explosions for non-nuclear-weapon states but not for nuclear states, the non-nuclear states, both developed and developing, feared that they would be at a great disadvantage. They insisted on a positive commitment in the treaty on the part of the nuclear states to make the benefits of peaceful nuclear explosions available to them. Such a commitment was written into the treaty in Article V.

As in the case of Article IV, each succeeding draft of the NPT had a strengthened Article V. Under Article V in its final form, the nuclear powers undertook to ensure that the "potential benefits" from peaceful nuclear explosions "will be made available to non-nuclear-weapon States Party to the Treaty on a non-discriminatory basis" at as low a cost as possible. The cost would not include any payments for any of the very large expenses incurred for research and development. Thus the treaty could provide very significant advantages to non-nuclear nations in the event that peaceful explosions became practical. The article further provided that the non-nuclear countries could obtain these benefits pursuant to "a special international agreement or agreements, through an appropriate international body with adequate representation of non-nuclear-weapon states." This provision was inserted in order that non-nuclear states would not have to rely on bilateral agreements (which were also permitted by the article) and to ensure that there would be no discrimination. The article also provided that negotiations on this subject would commence "as soon as possible after the Treaty enters into force."

Ever since the discovery of nuclear fission, high hopes—in fact, exaggerated ones—have been held out for the blessings that could be conferred on mankind through the peaceful uses of nuclear energy and technology. These hopes were nourished by President Eisenhower's

"Atoms for Peace" address to the United Nations in 1953, although he made no mention of the possible benefits from peaceful nuclear explosions; at that time, nobody was considering undertaking such explosions. Although Andrei Vishinsky, the Soviet Foreign Minister, stated after the Soviet Union's first explosion of an atomic bomb in 1949 that the Soviet Union intended to use nuclear explosions for moving mountains and excavating canals and roads, nobody took the idea very seriously. Attention was at first devoted to the use of nuclear isotopes in medicine, industry, agriculture, and hydrology and to the important benefits that could be conferred upon all states, in particular the developing ones, by the use of cheap nuclear power from nuclear reactors. It was the potential of nuclear power that was the dominant theme at the four Conferences on the Peaceful Uses of Atomic Energy, held in Geneva in 1955, 1958, 1964, and 1971. It was only after the United States launched its Plowshare Program in 1957 and conducted its first underground nuclear test in September of that year that the idea of peaceful nuclear explosions first attracted any significant public attention.

The Plowshare Program was conceived and launched by a number of the scientists at the Lawrence Radiation Laboratory in Livermore, California, now called the "Lawrence Livermore Laboratory," who had spent their lives designing nuclear weapons and who now wished to continue nuclear testing. The public campaign to stop nuclear tests began to make headway in 1954, after the Japanese fishermen in the "Lucky Dragon" had been contaminated with radioactive fallout from the huge American thermonuclear test at Bikini in March of that year (see p. 48) and after Prime Minister Nehru had begun his public appeals to suspend nuclear testing. By way of response, the scientists working for the Atomic Energy Commission, led by Dr. Edward Teller, and its chairman, Admiral Lewis Strauss, first announced the development of "clean" bombs. While it is true that they had developed "cleaner" bombs, there was no such thing as a "clean" nuclear bomb, and the campaign to allay public fears of fallout did not succeed. It was only then that the same scientists and the Atomic Energy Commission shifted their attention to the potential benefits that might accrue from peaceful nuclear explosions. Many members of the American arms control community believed that both the notion of clean bombs and that of underground peaceful nuclear explosions were invented by these scientists because of their fears that nuclear tests might be halted and permanently ended. In 1958 the Soviet Union and the United States did in fact agree to a voluntary moratorium on nuclear testing, which lasted until 1961.

A large-scale campaign was launched on behalf of the Plowshare Program. Four national symposia were held in the United States in 1957, 1959, 1964, and 1970. The concept of peaceful nuclear explosions was first brought up internationally at the Second Conference on the Peaceful Uses of Atomic Energy, held in 1958. At that conference American scientists outlined a number of potential peaceful uses of nuclear explosions that created much interest and were, in fact, welcomed by the conference. The ideas were further developed at the Third Conference in 1964 and at the Fourth in 1971. At all of these conferences, the potential benefits from peaceful nuclear explosions were described in glowing terms. It is not surprising, therefore, that both the rich and the poor countries were dazzled by their promise.

From the time it was launched in 1957, the idea of peaceful nuclear explosions was also promoted in arms control negotiations. At the Conference on the Discontinuance of Nuclear Weapon Tests that took place in Geneva from 1958 to 1961, the United States and the Soviet Union each put forward specific proposals for the conduct and observation of peaceful underground nuclear explosions. The Partial Test Ban Treaty that was concluded in 1963 made no mention of peaceful nuclear explosions, but it did sanction underground nuclear tests, provided that the explosions did not cause the dissemination of radioactive debris outside of the territory of the state where the explosion was conducted. The Treaty of Tlatelolco, which was signed in February 1967, made specific provision (in Article 18) for the conduct of peaceful explosions, provided that such explosions did not amount to a test of a nuclear weapon.

The Conference of Non-Nuclear-Weapon States, which was held in September 1968 after the opening for signature of the NPT, adopted a resolution noting that important benefits might be dervied from the peaceful uses of nuclear explosives and that the existing situation was discriminatory in allowing nuclear-weapon states to conduct nuclear explosions while other states could obtain the benefits from them only in an indirect way under Article V of the NPT, and stressing the urgent need to obtain a comprehensive test ban treaty and to create by a separate international instrument a separate international regime for conducting all peaceful nuclear explosions. It also endorsed the views of the non-aligned members of the Geneva Disarmament Conference calling for a universal and comprehensive solution of the problem of peaceful nuclear explosions compatible with a comprehensive test ban treaty.

The Performance

The CNNWS failed, however, to achieve the necessary two-third's majority required to adopt another resolution, proposed by fourteen Latin American States (including Argentina, Brazil, and Mexico), calling for a special international agreement to establish an "International Service for Nuclear Explosions for Peaceful Purposes" within the framework of the IAEA, and requesting the General Assembly to consider convening a special conference for that purpose. Only West Germany, Italy, and Spain among U.S. allies supported the proposal; all the other U.S. allies and all the Soviet Union's allies either voted against it or abstained. The Soviet Union and the United States, although they did not speak and could not vote at the CNNWS, were not sitting idle in the lobbies.

One reason for Soviet and American opposition could be found in the report on the NPT of the Foreign Relations Committee of the U.S. Senate, made public in the same month, which recorded the committee's "concern at the open ended commitment implied in Article V." The committee "specifically rejects any suggestion that Article V constitutes an across-the-board pledge by the United States to support foreign and domestic commercial research and development projects." Both nuclear services and research and development projects were to be undertaken "only after the public interest had been carefully defined by the appropriate congressional committees."

The General Assembly meeting in the fall of 1968 requested the Secretary-General to prepare a report on the establishment, within the framework of the IAEA, of an international service for conducting nuclear explosions for peaceful purposes under appropriate international control. The Secretary-General's report was prepared by a group of experts, who summarized their views on peaceful nuclear explosions as follows:

> The Group notes that while this new branch of technology holds much promise for the future, especially for very large-scale civil engineering works as well as for developing underground mineral resources or providing storage space for them, it is still at an early stage of development. Many uncertainties must be resolved before it can be put to industrial uses on a wide scale. The Group considers that, in the international field, the first need is to obtain and systematically disseminate more information about the potential of this new technology as well as its technical limitations and costs. . . . The Group recommends that developments in this technology be kept under constant review by IAEA in cooperation with those United Nations agencies which may be interested in their economic application and their effects upon the environment.

A second report by the Secretary-General, which presented the views of different members of the United Nations on the subject of establishing an international service for conducting peaceful nuclear explosions, concluded that the technical expertise of the IAEA favored its assuming the functions of such an international service. The Secretary-General considered, however, that the specific functions to be included would evolve gradually after continued international discussion in the IAEA, the United Nations, and possibly other organizations.

Beginning in 1969, the United States and the Soviet Union held several bilateral technical discussions with respect to peaceful nuclear explosions. The IAEA convened a series of international panels to compile and evaluate information on the present status of the technology of peaceful nuclear explosions. The agency made a decision in 1969 that it had the technical competence and statutory authority to fill the role outlined for the international body provided for in Article V; in 1972 it also adopted guidelines for its observation of nuclear explosions for peaceful purposes.

The possible potential uses of peaceful nuclear explosions, could be divided into two main categories.

1. Mining operations for the recovery of natural resources. Among the various uses envisaged were: the fracturing of oil- and gas-bearing rock in order to stimulate oil and gas recovery; the blasting out of cavities to store gas or oil or nuclear wastes from spent fuel; the leaching of copper and other minerals from ore-bearing rock; the crushing and fracturing of ore; the removal of overburden and uncovering of mineral rock for strip mining; and putting out run-away oil- and gas-well fires by sealing them off with an underground explosion.

2. Excavation operations and earth moving by cratering explosions. Among the operations envisaged here were the excavation of canals, harbors, mountain passes, and highways; the diversion of rivers; and the building of dams and water reservoirs.

While these various ideas were being developed, other scientists were pointing out some of the shortcomings. They pointed out that peaceful nuclear explosions must prove to be of economic value, i.e., that not only should the return exceed the cost, but the cost should be cheaper than that of conventional explosives. In addition, they urged that there should be no deleterious environmental effects, such as radioactive contamination of the atmosphere from cratering explosions or venting of underground explosions, from the triggering of earthquakes and tidal waves, and from the radioactive contamination of underground streams and water. They also pointed to the ever-present danger of accidents. But above all, they pointed to the dangers that were posed with respect to the proliferation of nuclear weapons by the development of peaceful nuclear explosions. They argued that this was the greatest danger of all and that it might amount to a case of "beating plowshares into swords."

When the Plowshare Program was first launched in the United States, the main interest was in great engineering projects such as the digging of canals, harbors, dams, and so forth. These ideas were soon discarded by the United States when the dangers of radioactivity from surface or cratering explosions became apparent. The U.S. abandoned the idea of a second "Panama Canal" through Central America and a harbor in Alaska, and Australia quickly gave up the idea of blasting a harbor on its west coast. In the U.S., interest then turned to the idea of fracturing oil- or gas-bearing rock by contained underground nuclear explosions in order to stimulate the flow of oil and gas; blasting underground cavities for their storage; and leaching minerals, such as copper. But none of the U.S. underground explosions has been successful in achieving any of these goals. It has become apparent that to succeed in fracturing ore to produce quantities of oil and gas, not one or two but hundreds of explosions would be required. It has been estimated that for the Rio Blanco field (in Colorado) alone, more than 1,000 explosions would be necessary—which is more than the total of *all* military tests conducted to date. These would be extremely costly as well as hazardous, and no practical or economical way of dealing with the resulting radioactive tritium and other radioactive by-products has yet been discovered.

Curiously enough, as American nuclear scientists and experts began to lose interest in the peaceful uses of underground explosions and to doubt whether such explosions had any practical purpose that could not be achieved as well or better by ordinary high explosives, their counterparts in the Soviet Union began to evince greater interest in them. They promoted the same ideas as had the Americans at an earlier stage and added some new ones of their own. In the last few years they have suggested diverting water flowing to the Arctic Ocean by means of a Pechora–Kama Canal to the Volga River and the Caspian Sea. This would require 250 to 400 cratering explosions over a distance of 65 kilometers, with all the attendant dangers of releasing massive radioactivity. The Soviet Union was successful in building a dam to create a lake and also in putting out, by means of underground explosions, two runaway gas-well fires that had been out of control for more than a year; but here, too, it is not clear whether the jobs could not have been done better by high explosives. Apparently the Soviet Union has been no more successful than the United States in increasing the flow of oil and gas or extracting minerals by means of nuclear explosions.

Within the past year or two there is increasing evidence that a number of experts in the Soviet Union are also becoming disillusioned by the inability to fulfill the expectations once held for nuclear explosions. Professor Vassily Emelyanov, the noted Soviet scientist and expert, in an article entitled "On the Peaceful Use of Nuclear Explosions" which appeared in the 1974 SIPRI publication *Nuclear Proliferation Problems,* drew the following conclusions:

> Despite successful experiments by the USA and USSR on the use of nuclear explosions for gas recovery stimulation, underground gas reservoir construction and excavation works, the main problem hindering wide use of peaceful nuclear explosions is the danger of radioactive contamination of the environment with fission products, and this has not yet been resolved.
>
> Therefore it seems that the peaceful use of nuclear explosions today can be considered advisable only in exceptional cases, when an urgent problem crops up which cannot be solved by alternative means. Nuclear explosions may be used mainly for experimental production purposes under close scientific observation.
>
> Only when nuclear explosives are developed to be truly clean and avoid triggering fission devices which produce radioactive fission products can

they be put to wide use. As it has already been said, this problem is not yet solved and it is not even known when the solution can be found.

In private, Soviet scientists are stating quite freely their opposition to underground peaceful nuclear explosions on account of their harmful rather than beneficial potential. Ambassador Alexei Roschin, the Soviet representative to the Conference of the Committee on Disarmament in Geneva, stated officially and publicly on August 8, 1974:

> On the question of peaceful nuclear explosion, Mrs. Thorsson, the representative of Sweden, said that the Treaty's provisions with respect to such explosions had so far not been implemented. We should like to point out in this connexion that at present, when peaceful nuclear explosions still have no practical application because of inadequate technology, there are no grounds for speaking of failure to implement that part of the Treaty. It would be more accurate to say that the Treaty's provisions with regard to such explosions have not so far been implemented, since there has been no practical need for such explosions.

In the United States, the process of disenchantment with these explosions seems to have gone even further. No additional monies have been voted by Congress for carrying on any further underground nuclear explosions under the Plowshare Program. Furthermore, the director of the U.S. Arms Control and Disarmament Agency, Dr. Fred Ikle, stated to a House of Representatives subcommittee in 1974:

> From an arms control point of view, peaceful nuclear explosions are a diabolical invention. They pretend to make a distinction where there can't be one and make it easier for governments to move in the direction that could lead to weapons production.

Whatever the reasons, the fact is that the nuclear powers have not taken any initiative to begin any negotiations to create the international regime for conducting peaceful nuclear explosions required by Article V of the NPT, and in this respect they are in breach of the treaty. Even though it may be reasonably argued that it is premature to set up any international service for peaceful nuclear explosions until their practical value is established, it can also be argued that if the international regime is created and is on the books awaiting proof of the practicality of such explosions, there will be less incentive for non-nuclear states to attempt to develop their own peaceful nuclear explosions. It would be much more difficult for any government to justify to its domestic public opinion and to international opinion the need to undertake its own peaceful nuclear explosion, with all of the problems which that entails and creates, if there were available to all nations an international service for conducting such explosions. India is not a party to the NPT, and thus presumably would not be entitled to all of the privileges provided by Article V for parties to the treaty. Nevertheless, if there had been an international service under the IAEA for conducting such peaceful nuclear explosions for all members of the IAEA (and India is an active participant in all IAEA activities), it is possible that those persons and groups in India which were opposed to India's peaceful nuclear explosion might have been strengthened in their opposition and might have prevailed in the internal debate in India preceding its explosion of May 1974.

Unfortunately, the United States and the Soviet Union, instead of proceeding to establish an international regime for peaceful nuclear explosions as required by Article V, instead signed on July 3, 1974, the extraordinary Threshold Test Ban Treaty. This treaty not only permitted the parties to continue unrestricted underground tests of whatever size they wish until March 31, 1976, but thereafter "limits" them to tests of 150,000 tons each, which is about ten times larger than the bomb which obliterated Hiroshima. What is worse is that Article III of the Threshold Test Ban Treaty envisages the continuation of underground nuclear explosions for peaceful purposes. It states that such explosions are exempt from the treaty and adds:

> Underground nuclear explosions for peaceful purposes shall be governed by an agreement which is to be negotiated and concluded by the parties at the earliest possible time.

There is no restriction in the Threshold Test Ban Treaty on peaceful nuclear explosions of any size. India can claim that its peaceful explosion in no way differs from those permitted the two superpowers. The Threshold Test Ban Treaty certainly does not put the two superpowers in any moral position to urge other powers not to conduct peaceful nuclear explosions or to denounce those who do.

The NPT Review Conference, 1975

In the case of Article V, as in the case of other articles of the Non-Proliferation Treaty, the 1975 Review Conference did little more than reaffirm the provisions of the treaty. It did, however, also affirm that peaceful nuclear explosions might be made available to non-parties to the treaty. And it stated that the IAEA should study the legal and all other aspects of peaceful nuclear explosions and should play a central role in providing services for such explosions.

The nuclear powers and their allies rejected a proposal by third-world countries that the three nuclear powers take steps toward holding a meeting to conclude the special international agreement called for by Article V, and insisted on leaving the matter to the IAEA.

Proposals for the Future

One can conceive of an international regime for the conduct of peaceful nuclear explosions whereby all parties, including nuclear-weapon powers, would agree not to conduct such explosions themselves, and any such explosions would be conducted either by some international authority composed of nuclear-explosive powers or by some designated nuclear powers, only after the project in question had been examined and approved by some international body. If nuclear proliferation is made less possible and less likely by all powers, including the nuclear powers, giving up the right to conduct such explosions themselves, the costs of foregoing this technology would be very small or insignificant. On the other hand, if the nuclear powers do not arrange to set up the international regime they pledged to create under Article V of the NPT, there may be some incentive or excuse for the nonnuclear powers to develop their own explosive devices as India did.

It might even be in the interests of all the nuclear-explosive powers to agree to undertake any approved project free of charge. The costs are relatively small (from $150,000 to $600,000 per explosion), and if these services were free, it might provide some inducement to developing countries not to seek to acquire their own capability.

Because of opposition to the NPT, and in order to attract some of the states that are not parties to the NPT, it might be better if the international regime were set up by the United Nations outside of the NPT. I recognize, of course, that there will be real problems in obtaining the support of the United States Congress for such "giveaway" programs. But if only a fraction of the many millions of dollars spent by the American government in publicizing the potential benefits of peaceful nuclear explosions and in conducting underground tests were devoted to publicizing the benefits of a free Plowshare Program for poor countries, it is not at all inconceivable that such a program would receive the requisite support. Moreover, unless and until such explosions can be demonstrated to be both practical and cheaper than conventional explosives, there may never be any need to provide the service at all.

Article 18 of the Treaty for the Prohibition of Nuclear Weapons in Latin America (The Treaty of Tlatelolco) which provides a system for carrying out peaceful nuclear explosions, under previously advertised safeguards, by nuclear devices, so long as these devices do not constitute nuclear weapons, might provide a useful precedent for an international regime that would provide explosive services.

While the establishment of an international regime would appear to be technically and legally feasible, it is far from clear whether it would be politically acceptable, either to the nuclear powers or to those nonnuclear states who might wish to acquire their own explosive capability. Nevertheless, the idea is worth exploring. Certainly, in order to fulfill their commitment under Article V of the NPT—or at least help defuse the complaint of the non-nuclear states that they are not living up to this commitment—the nuclear powers ought to undertake negotiations "as soon as possible."

It is worth noting that the full implementation of this article, unlike that of Article IV, would reduce rather than possibly increase the risks of nuclear proliferation.

An immediate step that might be undertaken is to have a moratorium on all peaceful nuclear explosions by all powers, pending the examination of the idea of an international regime for such explosions. If the nuclear-weapon states would agree to such a moratorium, even if only for a limited period of time, it might be possible to obtain the agreement of India and of all the other potential nuclear powers while the question was being studied. And the other potential nuclear powers would have little to lose by agreeing to the delay. But once again, as in all nuclear matters, the nuclear-weapon states would have to lead the way. It would clearly be in their interests to do so. It would remove charges of discrimination as well as an obvious excuse for other non-nuclear powers to embark on their own programs.

Chapter 14. Stopping the Nuclear Arms Race?

The Promise

The Non-Proliferation Treaty is in essence a compact between the nuclear and the non-nuclear states that negotiated it and became parties to it. It is true that it was not solely a contract between the nuclear and non-nuclear parties; it was also a political act of far-reaching importance. As with all contracts and political instruments, there must be a perceived mutual benefit for each of the parties. In the case of the NPT there was the basic assumption that all parties, both nuclear and non-nuclear, had a common, though not necessarily equal, interest in preventing the further spread of nuclear weapons, which could lessen the security of the non-nuclear as well as the nuclear powers.

The obligations accepted by the non-nuclear countries are contained in the first three articles of the treaty. Although Article I commits the nuclear powers not to help others acquire nuclear weapons or explosive devices or control over them, this is in reality a limitation more on the rights of non-nuclear parties than on those of the nuclear parties, as the latter in any case did not and do not want or intend to help other powers acquire nuclear capability. Article II contains the pledge on the part of the non-nuclear states not to acquire nuclear weapons or other explosive devices or control over them. And Article III sets out their obligation to subject themselves to IAEA safeguards to ensure that they live up to their commitments. There is no safeguard provision to ensure that the nuclear powers live up to their commitment, since it was assumed that it was in their interest not to allow nuclear weapons to proliferate and that no assurances were necessary in this regard.

The obligations of the nuclear powers, which constitute the quid pro quo, are contained in Articles IV, V, and VI of the treaty. Article IV provides for the promotion of the peaceful uses of nuclear energy especially in the territories of nonnuclear states. Article V provides that the benefits of peaceful nuclear explosions should be made available to non-nuclear states through international machinery on a nondiscriminatory and inexpensive basis. And Article VI contains the obligation on the part of the nuclear powers to work for a cessation of the nuclear arms race at an early date and for nuclear disarmament.

Prime Minister Harold Wilson summed up the situation on March 5, 1970, at a ceremony marking the entry into force of the treaty: "We know that there are two forms of proliferation, vertical as well as horizontal. The countries which do not possess nuclear weapons and which are now undertaking an obligation never to possess them, have the right to expect that the nuclear-weapon states will fulfill their part of the bargain."

It is not surprising that the nuclear powers tend to emphasize the importance of the first three articles of the treaty and the non-nuclear powers that of the second group of three articles.

Article VI is, of course, the most important of the provisions defining the responsibilities of the nuclear powers. It is the only provision of the treaty referred to in the operative part of General Assembly Resolution 2373 (XXII) of June 12, 1968, which approved the treaty and called on the ENDC and the nuclear powers "urgently" to pursue disarmament negotiations (see pp. 83–84). The article reads as follows:

> Each of the Parties to the Treaty undertakes to pursue negotiations in good faith on effective measures relating to cessation of the nuclear arms race at an early date and to nuclear disarmament, and on a treaty on general and complete disarmament under strict and effective international control.

The language is not quite as clear and categorical as it might be. It places the obligation on "each of the Parties," which includes the non-nuclear powers. All the parties are formally bound only "to pursue negotiations" and not necessarily to make them succeed, although these negotiations must be "in good faith" (a most extraordinary qualification, added at the insistence of the non-nuclear states). Moreover, the negotiations are not specifically for a cessation of the nuclear arms race at an early date and for nuclear disarmament, but only on "effective measures relating to" these objectives.

Nevertheless, the intent and meaning of the article are clear enough when read in conjunction with the Preamble—in particular, the eighth, ninth, tenth, and eleventh preambular paragraphs. These read as follows:

> [The Parties to the Treaty]
> Declaring their intention to achieve at the earliest possible date the cessation of the nuclear arms race and to undertake effective measures in the direction of nuclear disarmament,
>
> Urging the co-operation of all States in the attainment of this objective,
>
> Recalling the determination expressed by the Parties to the 1963 Treaty banning nuclear weapon tests in the atmosphere, in outer space and under water in its Preamble to seek to achieve the discontinuance of all test explosions of nuclear weapons for all time and to continue negotiations to this end,

Desiring to further the easing of international tension and the strengthening of trust between States in order to facilitate the cessation of the manufacture of nuclear weapons, the liquidation of all their existing stockpiles, and the elimination from national arsenals of nuclear weapons and the means of their delivery pursuant to a treaty on general and complete disarmament under strict and effective international control.

[Have agreed as follows:]

In short, though as an oversimplification, it can be said that the non-nuclear states undertook to halt the "horizontal" proliferation of nuclear weapons (i.e., their spread to additional countries) in exchange for the promise on the part of the nuclear powers to halt the "vertical" proliferation (i.e., their further development, accumulation, and deployment). While the obligation of the non-nuclear states not to acquire nuclear weapons went into effect immediately, that of the nuclear powers to halt and reverse the nuclear arms race could only take effect more gradually.

This chapter describes and evaluates the extent of the performance by the parties of their respective promises in the seven years since the signing of the treaty on July 1, 1968, and the five years since its entry into force. Certainly the non-nuclear parties have fulfilled their essential commitment in that they have not manufactured or otherwise acquired nuclear weapons or other explosive devices or acquired control over them. It is true that the vast majority of them have almost no potential for going nuclear in the foreseeable future and have therefore given up nothing, but the few who do have the capability of acquiring nuclear weapons in the near future have lived up to their commitment in forgoing the option of doing so. But to what extent have the nuclear powers implemented their basic pledges?

It is clear that there has not been any nuclear disarmament nor a cessation of the nuclear arms race. But have there been negotiations in good faith on effective measures relating to these goals? To answer this question in a considered way, it is necessary to examine the record in some detail.

First it is necessary to define the terms. A "cessation of the nuclear arms race" must mean a halt to the quantitative accumulation of nuclear weapons and to their qualitative development or improvement. Stopping either one alone could affect the pace or nature of the arms race, but only an end to both of these aspects of the arms race could amount to a stopping or halting of that race. As for "nuclear disarmament," while it might be argued that this term could encompass the elimination of nuclear weapons, it will be noted that the Preamble refers to the "elimination" of these weapons "pursuant to a treaty on general and complete disarmament." On the other hand, the Preamble, in addition to referring to a comprehensive test ban, also mentions "the cessation of the manufacture of nuclear weapons" and "the liquidation of all of their existing stockpiles" (the latter being practically tantamount to the elimination of these weapons). The cessation of manufacture would amount to the freezing of nuclear armaments at their present quantitative and qualitative levels and would mean the cessation of the nuclear arms race but would not actually constitute nuclear disarmament. Hence it would seem logical to regard the term as meaning a substantial reduction of nuclear armaments such as would amount to a reversal of the nuclear arms race, even if it meant something less than the liquidation of all stockpiles.

An indication of what the nuclear powers had in mind as constituting "effective measures relating to the cessation of the nuclear arms race at an early date and to nuclear disarmament" is found in the comprehensive provisional agenda adopted by the Conference of the Eighteen-Nation Disarmament Committee (ENDC), the predecessor of the present Conference of the Committee on Disarmament (CCD), on August 15, 1968. The draft of this agenda was worked out by the Soviet Union and the United States and was proposed by them for adoption. After the agenda item "Further effective measures relating to the cessation of the nuclear arms race at any early date and to nuclear disarmament" is written:

> Under this heading members may wish to discuss measures dealing with the cessation of testing, the non-use of nuclear weapons, the cessation of manufacture of weapons, and reduction and subsequent elimination of nuclear stockpiles, nuclear-free zones, etc.

Some indication of what the non-nuclear powers considered to be the purpose of Article VI is found in the proceedings of the Conference of Non-Nuclear-Weapon States. One of the resolutions adopted at that conference reads as follows:

> The Conference of Non-Nuclear-Weapon States,
> Having discussed the question of "Effective measures for the prevention of further proliferation of nuclear weapons, the cessation of the nuclear arms race at an early date and nuclear disarmament,"
> Bearing in mind that the achievement of the goal of nuclear non-proliferation necessitates the adoption of measures to prevent both horizontal and vertical proliferation,
> Recognizing the growing concern of world opinion at the continuous expansion of research and development relating to new nuclear weapons, . . .
> Requests the United Nations General Assembly . . . to recommend that the Conference of the Eighteen-Nation Committee on Disarmament should begin, not later than March 1969, to undertake negotiations for:
>
> (a) The prevention of the further development and improvement of nuclear weapons and their delivery vehicles;
> (b) The conclusion of a comprehensive test-ban treaty, as an important step in the field of nuclear disarmament, and as a matter of high priority;
> (c) Reaching agreement on the immediate cessation of the production of fissile materials for weapons purposes and the stoppage of the manufacture of nuclear weapons;

(d) The reduction and subsequent elimination of all stockpiles of nuclear weapons and their delivery systems.

The Performance

A Comprehensive Test Ban

No other question in the field of arms control and disarmament has been the subject of so much study and discussion as that of stopping nuclear weapons tests. Ever since Prime Minister Nehru, in April 1954, called for a halt to such tests, the subject has been at or near the top of the disarmament agenda.

By the Partial Test Ban Treaty of August 5, 1963, the nuclear powers undertook to seek "to achieve the discontinuance of all test explosions of nuclear weapons for all time" and expressed their determination "to continue negotiations to this end." As indicated earlier, this commitment was repeated in the Non-Proliferation Treaty in 1968. One measure of the implementation of this commitment may be found in a comparison of nuclear weapons tests before and after the signing of the Partial Test Ban Treaty. In the eighteen years between 1945 and 1963 the Soviet Union conducted some 164 nuclear weapons tests (of which 3 were underground), and the United States some 282 tests (of which 89 were underground); in the decade August 1963–June 1973, the Soviet Union conducted 121 tests and the United States 259 tests, all of them underground. This indicates a considerable increase in the rate of testing—of 33 percent by the U.S.S.R. and 60 percent by the U.S.

After the signing of the Partial Test Ban Treaty there were, in fact, no negotiations between the two main nuclear powers on an underground test ban until the preparations for the June 27–July 3, 1974 Summit meeting in Moscow. The Soviet Union during all this period of time has stated that it is prepared to stop all tests on the basis of "national means of verification," that is, without any on-site inspection of its territory and without any international control. The United States has continued to insist that some on-site inspections are necessary (it has not officially departed from the figure of 7 put forward in 1963) to verify compliance with a test ban. Most scientists and experts are not convinced of this argument. On the contrary, they appear to consider that recent improvements in long-range seismic means of detection and identification of underground tests, together with the remarkable capabilities of satellite surveillance and electronic and telecommunications monitoring as well as traditional covert methods of acquiring military intelligence, are more than sufficient to deter any attempts at clandestine testing. While some differences of opinion concerning the effectiveness of seismic methods still remain, it is generally agreed that it is now possible to identify practically all underground explosions down to the level of a very few kilotons by seismic means alone, and that even if a few such tests should escape detection, it is most unlikely that a series of them could do so. Secretary-General Waldheim has stated that "all the technical and scientific aspects of the problem have been so fully explored that only a political decision is necessary in order to achieve final agreement" on an underground test ban. He has called for a moratorium on further underground tests pending a permanent agreement, as has the United Nations General Assembly itself. In any case, nearly all authorities, other than those who are members of the United States government, agree that the risks of further testing far outweigh the risks of stopping all testing.

Since the Partial Test Ban Treaty, the General Assembly has adopted more than a dozen resolutions calling for a comprehensive test ban. The non-nuclear powers appear to regard the conclusion of an underground test ban as a litmus test of the seriousness of the two nuclear superpowers' intentions to stop the nuclear arms race. While such a halt would not by itself end the further technological improvement of nuclear weapons, it would be an important step in that direction. There is an increasing conviction among the nations of the world that an underground test ban is the single most important measure, and certainly the most feasible one in the near future, toward halting the nuclear arms race, at least as regards its qualitative aspects. They also seem to regard an underground test ban by the U.S. and the Soviet Union as possibly having a beneficial effect on persuading China and France to curb and ultimately halt their testing. A test ban would also put the superpowers in a better moral position to urge those non-nuclear countries who are capable of going nuclear to resist the temptation to do so.

In light of these considerations, most nations (and most people) find it very difficult to understand the further delays by the two superpowers in banning their underground tests, and regard their failure to do so as an indication of their lack of seriousness (or failure of will) with regard to halting the nuclear arms race. Increasingly, statements are being made by near-nuclear countries that unless the nuclear powers stop their vertical proliferation, it will not be possible for long to prevent the horizontal proliferation of nuclear weapons.

The extraordinary Threshold Test Ban Treaty concluded by the U.S.S.R. and the U.S. in Moscow on July 3, 1974, permits the two parties, as we have noted, to continue unrestricted underground tests of whatever size they wish until March 31, 1976; thereafter they will "limit" their tests to a magnitude of 150,000 tons each—which is about ten times larger than the bomb which obliterated Hiroshima and which exceeds in size all but a few of the tests conducted by the two powers in recent years. And there is no restriction whatsoever on peaceful nuclear explosions, which, in the absence of stringent controls, can be used for improving nuclear weapons. This is not just a "cosmetic" agreement; it is a mockery of a test ban treaty. It would not help to curb the technological or qualitative improvement, testing, and development of new nuclear weapons—nor, therefore, the nuclear arms race. Nor would it serve to alleviate the concerns of the non-nuclear powers or provide any cogent reasons for them to forgo testing. Just as the ban on atmospheric tests resulted in an increase in underground tests, so a ban on underground tests above 150 kilotons may result only in increasing the pace of testing below that magnitude. Moreover, such a ban may open the door to considerable confusion and possible charges of violation as to whether a given test was or was not below the permitted threshold. The entire process of verification may be more difficult and expensive than under a comprehensive ban. Most important of all, this delayed threshold ban may be used by the superpowers as a pretext to resist the pressures for a complete ban and thus to postpone indefinitely, or for a long time, a comprehensive test ban. If that should, in fact, be the case, the threshold treaty would be worse than no treaty at all. It can, indeed, be harmful to the cause of nuclear non-proliferation.

The irony, if not the tragedy, of the situation is that Mr. Brezhnev renewed the Soviet offer of a total ban on underground weapons tests without on-site inspection and that he favored their complete cessation according to an agreed-upon timetable. According to press reports (*New York Times*, June 16, 1974), there was almost no chance for a total ban because of the strong opposition of the staff men in the United States military and the Atomic Energy Commission. Consequently, the delayed threshold ban may lead the non-nuclear powers to conclude that once again they are being deceived or misled by the nuclear superpowers and that there is no early prospect of any real action to stop the nuclear arms race.

Denuclearization of the Seabed

On February 11, 1971, there was signed the "Treaty on the Prohibition of the Emplacement of Nuclear Weapons of Mass Destruction on the Seabed and the Ocean Floor and in the Subsoil Thereof," commonly referred to as the Seabed Treaty. The treaty entered into force on May 18, 1972. Its main provision is set forth in Article I, paragraph 1, which reads as follows:

> The States Parties to this Treaty undertake not to emplant or emplace on the seabed and the ocean floor and in the subsoil thereof beyond the outer limit of a seabed zone, as defined in article II, any nuclear weapons or any other types of weapons of mass destruction as well as structures, launching installations or any other facilities specifically designed for storing, testing or using such weapons.

The Soviet Union and the United States at first resisted a number of amendments that were put forward by the coastal states and other non-nuclear countries insisting on explicit recognition of the rights of coastal states, on some procedures for international rather than mere adversary verification, and on an undertaking for further arms limitation measures. After much discussion and the failure of the United Nations to approve the original American/Soviet draft treaty, the two superpowers agreed to a number of revisions, including the addition of Article V, which reads as follows:

> The Parties to this Treaty undertake to continue negotiations in good faith concerning further measures in the field of disarmament for the prevention of an arms race on the seabed, the ocean floor and the subsoil thereof.

It is often claimed by the nuclear powers that this treaty represents a partial implementation of Article VI of the NPT. This claim is not accepted by the other powers, many of whom feel that the treaty constitutes a non-armament agreement of minor importance that is more significant for cosmetic than for arms control purposes. Some claim that the treaty was put forward because there were no other measures in the field of nuclear arms control which the two powers were prepared to negotiate at that time. Moreover, they say, the seabed and ocean floor are not nearly as useful for military purposes as the ocean space itself, and any military activities, nuclear or otherwise, can be conducted more efficiently and less expensively from the surface and subsurface of the seas and the oceans than from the seabed or ocean floor. They note the failure of the two superpowers to make any proposal whatsoever for the prevention or limitation of an arms race, nuclear or conventional, in the seas and oceans themselves. In any case, they say, since there are only two powers who could conceivably exploit the seabed and ocean floor for nuclear weapons purposes in the foreseeable future, the treaty could have been concluded as a bilateral agreement without bothering to have other states as parties.

The only real significance in having other states besides the two superpowers as parties to the treaty lies in the undertaking to continue negotiations for further measures. In this regard, a number of non-nuclear countries have pointed out that no negotiations whatsoever, in good faith or otherwise, have taken place in pursuance of the commitment made in Article V.

SALT

Proposals concerning the limitation and reduction of offensive and/or defensive strategic nuclear weapons and delivery vehicles had been put forward at various times during the 1960s by the United States. During this same period, the Soviet Union repeatedly proposed the complete elimination of such weapons. In 1963 the Soviet Union put forward what came to be known as the Gromyko Proposal for a "nuclear umbrella" whereby the two powers would reduce their nuclear delivery systems to a small fraction of their existing strengths.

In 1964, President Johnson formally proposed a verified freeze on offensive and defensive strategic nuclear weapons systems that would limit these weapons to existing levels and types. The Soviet Union regarded the proposal as inadequate since it allowed the retention of the existing "overkill" capacity of the United States. In 1966 the Soviet Union proposed the destruction of all stockpiles of nuclear weapons and delivery vehicles and a ban on their further production.

On July 1, 1968, the day of the signing of the NPT, it was finally announced that the United States and the Soviet Union would begin bilateral discussions on the "limitation and reduction of both offensive and defensive strategic nuclear weapon delivery systems." These strategic arms limitation talks (SALT) did not actually begin until November 1969. The course of the negotiations and the various agreements arrived at are outlined in Chapter 2.

One effective measure of to whether or not the arms race is being brought under control is the level of national military expenditures. In January 1973, President Nixon proposed an increase in the U.S. military budget from $76 to $81 billion; the total U.S. military budget approved in 1973 was $84.2 billion. In January 1974 the President proposed a further increase of military expenditures for the forthcoming year to $99.1 billion. In February 1975, President Ford asked for a defense budget of $92.8 billion, but the total amount of defense expenditures to be appropriated came to more than $104 billion. One thing is certain: no matter how many or what kinds of agreements for arms limitation or disarmament are achieved, if military expenditures increase rather than decrease, as has been the case despite the SALT agreements, there is no cessation of the arms race.

The SALT agreements may have been a diplomatic success. They do tend to stabilize a state of deterrence between the two superpowers, at least for the present, on the basis of each side retaining a second-strike capability. They have also helped to promote the spirit of détente. But they have not served to achieve a cessation or any real limitation of the nuclear arms race, far less nuclear disarmament. In fact, many critics of SALT say that these negotiations have served only to replace the quantitative nuclear arms race with a more dangerous qualitative one. Each successive SALT agreement has raised the numerical ceiling for nuclear weapons and, up to the time of writing, has imposed no qualitative or technological limitations on offensive weapons. The action–reaction process that formerly fueled the nuclear arms race has now been largely transformed into an internal domestic technological competition for the improvement (if that is the right word) of the accuracy, variety, and lethality of weapons—a competition that proceeds by a dynamic of its own. It seems that the agreements already concluded, and indeed those now being nego-

tiated, are designed not to halt or reverse the arms race, but rather to institutionalize it and regulate it so that it may continue within each country
on its own momentum under conditions of relatively less instability and
insecurity for the two great powers. The SALT agreements have become
blueprints for the continuation of the nuclear arms race by the two superpowers under agreed terms and conditions.

The depressing picture that emerges from these agreements is hardly
likely to reassure the other nations of the world, nuclear as well as non-
nuclear that the nuclear arms race is being brought under control or that
their security is being enhanced.

The failure of the July 1974 summit to agree on any limitation or reduction of offensive strategic nuclear weapons, the mockery of the Threshold Test Ban Treaty, and the expansion of the arms race that will result
from the Vladivostok agreement (see Chapter 2, pp. 29–33) will serve
only to confirm the fears of the non-nuclear states that the nuclear powers
are unwilling or unable to halt the nuclear arms race.

The continuing credibility and viability of the NPT was in question
even before India exploded a nuclear device. The failure of the superpowers to live up to their commitments under Article VI of the NPT is
likely to give added force to the arguments of those in the near-nuclear
countries who argue that they too must go nuclear in order to have at
least some restraining or deterring effect on the nuclear powers. It will
make it easier for them to repeat the earlier Indian warnings that the
nuclear powers must begin to reduce their nuclear arsenals if they want
to ensure that the non-nuclear powers do not start building their own.
Japan, too, warned in 1968, when the NPT was being approved, that
"unless the nuclear-weapons-States keep their part of the bargain, the
balance of obligations will be upset and the treaty will lose its moral basis."

Cessation of Production of Fissile Material
for Military Purposes

The United States has for many years proposed a cutback of production of fissile material for military purposes, the closing down of plants
for such production, and the transfer of a portion of the existing stocks
to civilian purposes. The Soviet Union has rejected the American proposals, without making any counter-proposals, on the grounds that they
would not result in any reduction in military capabilities and were designed more for appearances than as having any practical significance.

Nuclear-Free Zones

The only existing nuclear-free zone in any inhabited part of the world
is that established for Latin America by the Treaty of Tlatelolco in 1967.

Protocol II of this treaty, whereby the nuclear powers pledge to respect the nuclear-free zone and not to use or threaten to use nuclear weapons against the countries in the zone, has been signed by the United Kingdom, the United States, China, and France (in that order), but not by the Soviet Union, despite a number of resolutions of the General Assembly calling on all the nuclear powers to sign the Protocol.

A proposal to create a peace zone in the Indian Ocean and its littoral and hinterland states, supported by all the littoral states of the Indian Ocean, is still in an early stage. The proposal envisages maintaining the area as a nuclear-free zone and preventing a military and naval arms race by the great powers in the area. China and Japan support the proposal, but up to now the U.S.S.R., the United States, the United Kingdom, and France have withheld their support.

The whole question of nuclear-free-zones is dealt with in greater detail in the next chapter.

General and Complete Disarmament

No proposals or negotiations in regard to general and complete disarmament have been put forward or been the subject of negotiations between the nuclear powers since the abandonment of the discussions concerning a treaty for general and complete disarmament in 1963. A number of the non-nuclear powers have, from time to time, urged that renewed consideration be given to this item and have in fact requested the U.S.S.R. and the U.S. to revise and update their 1962 draft treaties for general and complete disarmament. There has been no response from either of the two powers.

In December 1969, the General Assembly adopted Resolution 2499, which declared the decade of the 1970s a Disarmament Decade. In the same resolution, it requested the CCD,

> while continuing intensive negotiations with a view to reaching the widest possible agreement on collateral measures, to work out at the same time a comprehensive program, dealing with all aspects of the problem of the cessation of the arms race and general and complete disarmament under effective international control, which would provide the Conference [the CCD] with a guideline to chart the course of its further work and its negotiations, and to report thereon to the General Assembly at its twenty-fifth session.

No comprehensive program was worked out by the CCD, although the Netherlands and Italy each submitted working papers on such a program and a draft of a comprehensive program was submitted by Mexico, Sweden, and Yugoslavia. The latter draft was revised at the General Assembly during its 1970 session, and the Assembly recommended that the CCD take this revised comprehensive program into account. Despite the efforts of the sponsors of the draft and of other countries to have the CCD give serious attention to this comprehensive disarmament program, it has, in the absence of any willingness by the nuclear powers to enter into serious discussions, remained a dead letter.

As a result of the initiative of the U.S.S.R. in 1971, the General Assembly has been discussing the convening of a World Disarmament Conference (WDC) to deal with all aspects of disarmament. The conference would seek the prohibition and destruction of nuclear weapons and the reduction of conventional weapons.

China said that such a conference would be useless and would only delude the peoples of the world unless all the nuclear powers agreed to two preconditions before the conference was held: viz., to undertake not to be the first to use nuclear weapons and to liquidate all their foreign military bases. Faced with the virtually unanimous desire of the Third World and of non-nuclear countries for the holding of a WDC, however, China has joined the other nuclear powers in supporting unanimously adopted U.N. resolutions from 1972 to 1975 calling for a study of the matter. Most observers think China is merely trying to delay the holding of such a conference until it has built up its own nuclear arsenal.

The United States opposed a World Disarmament Conference and was the only country to abstain on the 1971 Assembly resolution. In 1972 it stated in the General Assembly that it was even opposed to any preparations for holding such a conference and would not participate in them. It stated that it preferred to work through SALT, the CCD, and other small negotiating bodies, and that it believed that a conference attended by some 140 countries would be counterproductive and could lead to great disappointment among the nations and peoples of the world. Nevertheless, earlier, at the 1972 Summit meeting in Moscow, and at the Summit meetings in June 1973 and July 1974 the United States did agree with the Soviet Union to the holding of such a conference at the "appropriate time," although it has never explained what it would regard as the appropriate time.

France and the United Kingdom have supported the idea of a World Disarmament Conference provided that all the nuclear powers participate in it. Together with the U.S.S.R., they participate in the meetings of the *Ad Hoc* Committee on the World Disarmament Conference, consisting of forty non-nuclear states, created by the General Assembly in December 1973 to examine all governmental views and suggestions relative to a WDC and the conditions for its realization. China and the United States do not participate in the work of the *Ad Hoc* Committee but have agreed "to cooperate or maintain contact" with it.

With the United States opposed to the holding of a WDC, it is clear that no such conference is likely in the near future. The opposition of China makes it easier for the U.S. to maintain its own negative position. All countries are agreed that the participation of all nuclear countries is an essential condition for holding a WDC. If the U.S. were to change its position to one of support, it is quite possible that China would not wish to remain isolated and would also agree.

Chemical and Biological Weapons

It might be argued that the negotiations on chemical and biological weapons are a step toward general and complete disarmament. It has, in fact, been urged by the United States and the Soviet Union and some of their allies that the Biological Convention (formally, the Convention on the Prohibition of the Development, Production, and Stockpiling of Bacteriological (Biological) and Toxin Weapons and on their Destruction), signed in 1971, was the first real disarmament treaty, as distinct from the previous treaties which were agreements for nonarmament or the limitation of armaments, since it provides for the destruction of existing weapons. Some of the non-nuclear powers have argued, however, that the treaty is of little significance since the United States had, in any case, unilaterally given up these weapons in 1969 and had ordered their destruction two years before the conclusion of the treaty. Moreover, it was argued, biological weapons were too dangerous to use, since ultimately they could do as much damage to the country using them as to the country against which they were used.

The CCD has been bogged down for five years in its discussions of a ban on chemical weapons. The Soviet Union wants a comprehensive ban similar to the Biological Convention; the United States appears to favor a more limited first-step agreement but has failed to put forward any concrete proposal of any kind in this field. At the Summit III meeting, however, the two parties agreed "to consider a joint initiative in the CCD with respect to the conclusion, as a first step, of an international convention dealing with the most dangerous lethal means of chemical warfare."

The Conference on Security and Cooperation in Europe, and the Conference on Mutual Reduction of Forces and Armaments in Central Europe

It might also be argued that the measures considered by these two conferences are steps toward general and complete disarmament. In essence, however, they are regional matters relating to the security of the European countries participating in the discussions and the overall military postures of the U.S. and the U.S.S.R., and can have only a marginal effect as measures of arms control or steps toward general and complete disarmament.

The Conference on Security and Cooperation in Europe was concluded with the signing of a Declaration at Helsinki, Finland, on August 1, 1975, by 35 states including the United States and Canada. The Declaration contained a provision for announcement twenty-one days in advance of large-scale military maneuvers in Europe and for invitations to interested observers, which are not measures of major significance.

At the time of this writing, the Vienna Conference on Mutual Reduction of Forces and Armaments is making very slow progress. It is not yet clear whether the conference will deal with tactical nuclear weapons. In any case, the conference is discussing only the withdrawal of a small percentage of the forces and armaments from Central Europe and not the demobilization of forces or destruction of armaments.

Environmental Warfare

At the summit meeting in Moscow on July 3, 1974, General Secretary Brezhnev and President Nixon signed a joint statement agreeing to advocate measures to overcome the danger of environmental warfare. In December the U.N. General Assembly called for agreement on a convention to prohibit action to influence the environment and climate for military and other deleterious purposes. In August 1975 the U.S.S.R. and the U.S. each presented in the CCD identical draft conventions on the Prohibition of Military or Any Other Hostile Use of Enviromental Modification Techniques. These techniques were defined as the deliberate manipulation of natural processes for changing "the dynamics, composition or structure of the earth . . . so as to cause such effects as earthquakes and tsunamis [tidal waves], an upset in the ecological balance of a region, or changes in weather patterns, . . . in the state of the ozone layer or ionosphere, in climate patterns, or in ocean currents."

It is quite likely that agreement will be reached in the near future on the text of such a convention. While it is, of course, useful to prevent the possible development of such bizarre methods of waging war in the future, it should be noted that these methods are not very efficient means of warfare and would have little value as compared to already existing weapons systems. A convention barring such future developments would constitute another "non-armament" step rather than a disarmament measure. It has more to do with the environment than with war; it fails to come to grips with—and perhaps sidetracks the efforts to deal with—the much more serious dangers of nuclear and other weapons of mass destruction that pose clear and present threats to humanity.

Consequences of the Failure of the Nuclear Powers To Implement Article VI

All during 1966 and 1967 the non-nuclear powers had stressed the importance of the nuclear powers undertaking a number of tangible steps to halt the arms race and to limit, reduce, or eliminate stocks of nuclear weapons and their means of delivery. The eight nonaligned members of the ENDC had proposed a number of specific measures in a joint memorandum in 1966 which put primary emphasis on the necessity for an acceptable balance of mutual responsibilities and obligations between nuclear and non-nuclear states, in accordance with General Assembly Resolution 2028 adopted in 1965. Among the measures proposed in the memorandum were:

a comprehensive nuclear test ban;
a complete cessation of the production of fissionable material for weapons purposes;
a freeze on, and a gradual reduction of, nuclear weapons stocks and means of delivery;
a ban on the use of nuclear weapons; and
security assurances to the non-nuclear states.

It is noteworthy that countries such as Brazil and India, who did not sign the NPT, joined in these demands. Those countries, along with others, criticized the various drafts and the final text of the NPT as being discriminatory against non-nuclear states. The same two countries, together with Pakistan, were also leaders at the Conference of Non-Nuclear-Weapon States in 1968.

At this late date, and in light of the Indian nuclear test explosion of May 18, 1974, one can only speculate as to whether a more active and determined approach by the nuclear powers to live up to their obligations under Article VI of the NPT might have led Brazil, India, and Pakistan, along with other countries such as Argentina, Israel, Spain, and South Africa, to sign the NPT. It is quite likely that other, primarily domestic, considerations would have been the overriding factors in the attitude of these countries, but one never knows in advance how things may develop on the international scene. What can be said with some degree of assurance is that the efforts undertaken by the two nuclear powers were far from sufficient to convince the non-nuclear powers of their seriousness of purpose in living up to their obligations. Certainly many of the non-nuclear powers felt that the nuclear powers were in breach of their obligations under both the 1963 Partial Test Ban Treaty and the NPT. No negotiations whatsoever took place for ten years on an underground test ban or for the cessation of production of fissionable material for weapons purposes, for the reduction of production of nuclear weapons and their delivery systems (much less for its cessation), for steps leading to general and complete disarmament, or even for a ban on the use of nuclear weapons against non-nuclear powers.

At most it can be said that the two superpowers did pursue negotiations at SALT for a limitation on offensive and defensive strategic nuclear-weapons systems. Even in the agreements achieved at SALT I, however, quantitative limitations are established at higher than existing levels, and there are no qualitative limitations on the ongoing nuclear arms race in offensive weapons. The two superpowers refused at first even to officially communicate the SALT I agreements to the CCD or the General Assembly. They agreed to communicate to the General Assembly the agreements reached at the summit meeting in Washington in June 1973 only when faced with the threat that other powers would request their circulation as Assembly documents, as Mexico had done in 1972 with the SALT I agreements.

The failure of the two superpowers to agree on any reduction of strategic nuclear weapons or on any qualitative limitation whatsoever on their mind-boggling and still growing overkill capacity led to suspicions by the non-nuclear powers that the superpowers intend to continue and intensify, rather than end, the nuclear arms race.

As we explain later in this chapter and in Chapter 18, the NPT Review Conference also did nothing to allay the suspicions of the non-nuclear members that the nuclear powers have no plans for, and are in fact extremely reluctant even to give serious consideration to, really effective measures that would lead to the cessation of the nuclear arms race and to nuclear disarmament, let alone to general and complete disarmament. The three nuclear parties to the NPT opposed every concrete proposal for an underground test ban and for a reduction in their nuclear arsenals.

The non-nuclear states are rapidly losing, indeed may have already lost, confidence in the desire and intention of the nuclear states to achieve a cessation of the nuclear arms race and nuclear disarmament. They fear that the gap between the powers' promises and their performance is indicative of the absence of any true will on their part to implement their commitments. They sense that the two superpowers are quite comfortable in their dealings with each other and that their efforts are designed more toward establishing a balance between themselves than toward ending the arms race—in other words, merely to regulate and make safer the continuation of the nuclear arms race.

Yet, in the words of Prime Minister Harold Wilson, the non-nuclear powers not only expect the nuclear powers to fulfill their part of the bargain and halt the vertical proliferation of nuclear weapons, but "have the right to expect" so.

It is possible, of course, that the failure of the nuclear powers to live up to their commitments in the Preamble and in Article VI of the NPT can be and has been exaggerated as a factor that may lead to the further spread of nuclear weapons to non-nuclear countries. It is even possible that non-nuclear countries that want to go nuclear have used and are continuing to use this failure as an excuse or pretext for doing what they would do in any event, whether or not the nuclear powers lived up to their commitments.

As we indicated earlier, whether a country decides to go nuclear or not depends on reasons that are of particular importance to that country.

These reasons are primarily related to how a country sees its security needs and to the pressures of domestic public opinion in that country. A country will evaluate its security position not so much by what the great powers do or do not do in the fields of nuclear armament and disarmament, but by what it regards as threats or potential threats from its neighbors or from other countries in its region of the world. Thus, Pakistan is obviously much more concerned by its fears of what India may or may not do than it is about what the nuclear powers may do about the nuclear arms race. The same applies to Israel and the Arab states, South Africa and the other African states, Argentina and Brazil, and others. The governments of these countries will also be responsive to the reactions and pressures of public opinion in their own countries, which will be shaped by developments in neighboring countries rather than by developments in the policies and actions of the nuclear powers that do not directly affect them.

Within each country there is no single or unified view as regards nuclear weapons, but rather a whole spectrum of competing and often conflicting opinions, with different groups struggling to make their point of view prevail. It can usually be expected that the "military–industrial complex," scientists and bureaucrats associated with it, and the more conservative elements in the country will favor the acquisition of nuclear weapons, while the more liberal elements, peace groups, and scientists in universities and other academic institutions will oppose that course of action. Public opinion also changes over time within a given country. Even in such secure and stable countries as Sweden and Switzerland there were lively debates on the subject of nuclear weapons, with the respective military establishments arguing in favor of going nuclear, or at least retaining the option to do so. At times the outcome seemed in doubt, but finally the issue was decided in favor of not going nuclear.

Nevertheless, what the nuclear powers and other great powers do determines not only the military but also the political and moral climate in the world. If the superpowers demonstrate that they intend to halt and reverse the nuclear arms race and are, in fact, engaged in doing so and in living up to their legal and moral obligations, they will create a climate that favors nuclear arms restraint and that discourages or weakens the elements within other countries that want to go nuclear. Their cessation of the nuclear arms race would have a positive effect on world security and would begin to diminish the aura of prestige that is attached to the possession of vast stockpiles of nuclear weapons. It might also release human and material resources for scientific and technological development of the peaceful uses of nuclear energy and for making them more safe. It would begin to lessen the central role that these weapons play in the defense systems and power positions of the nuclear states and reduce their psychological involvement and preoccupation with nuclear weaponry. Above all, it would enhance the moral position of the nuclear powers and put them in a better position to urge other states not to go nuclear.

Some success on the part of the nuclear powers in moving toward real nuclear disarmament could at least help to postpone the decisions of non-nuclear countries to acquire a nuclear option and capability. Any time gained in this respect will make possible further debate and reflection; it will allow more time for wiser counsels to prevail and for taking action to manage and shape events so as to reduce the pressures for going nuclear. In short, the achievement of substantial progress toward nuclear disarmament by the nuclear powers would provide incentives and pressures for the non-nuclear countries to refrain from going nuclear.

On the other hand, the continuing failure of the nuclear powers to stop nuclear tests, to halt the nuclear arms race, and to achieve measures of nuclear disarmament will provide, if not genuine reasons, then at least excuses for other countries to go nuclear. It will certainly strengthen the arguments and positions of the nuclear hawks and weaken those of the doves in the non-nuclear countries. As the nuclear powers militarize the world, not merely by the increasing accumulation and deployment of nuclear weapons but also by the continuing and increasing proliferation and dissemination of conventional armaments, the development of regional arms races and of an "arms race climate" in the world becomes inevitable. And such an arms race climate will not stop with the acquisition of conventional armaments. The same cost-effective arguments of a "bigger bang for a buck" that proved so persuasive with the nuclear powers may also be decisive for nonnuclear powers.

Even the concept of nuclear deterrence has a pernicious effect on the possibilities of nuclear proliferation. Apart from whatever other motivations may induce non-nuclear countries to "go nuclear," the very idea of nuclear deterrence espoused by the superpowers tends to encourage other countries to acquire nuclear weapons to deter any attack. If deterrence is considered a sound doctrine by the great nuclear powers, it will be considered by smaller powers as having some validity for them as well.

Accordingly, even if the link between vertical and horizontal proliferation has been exaggerated or even exploited, by the non-nuclear powers, there can be no doubt that maintaining the legitimacy of nuclear weapons and of the nuclear arms race will facilitate the further spread of these weapons.

It may be difficult or even impossible to prove that, if the nuclear powers completely fulfilled all of their obligations concerning nuclear disarmament, it would necessarily or even to any important extent prevent other countries from going nuclear. The non-nuclear powers might fall back on other arguments or excuses relative to their security, their prestige, their economic and technological development, or the discriminatory nature of the NPT. On the other hand, it is easier to provide evidence that the failure of the nuclear powers to implement their nuclear disarmament pledges has been a factor in damaging or weakening the NPT. There have been countless statements and warnings by near-nuclear and other non-nuclear powers that they can not or will not give up their option of going nuclear so long as the nuclear powers do not give up the vertical proliferation of these weapons. The constant repetition of this argument, irrespective of how sincerely it is meant, makes it easier for the non-nuclear states to stand apart from the NPT. It might also provide a ready excuse some day for any of the non-nuclear parties to the NPT to withdraw from the treaty under the procedure provided for.

It would seem to be quite evident, therefore, that the failure of the nuclear powers to live up to their commitments under Article VI of the NPT has had and will continue to have a clearly negative effect on the treaty and on the entire regime and concept of non-proliferation.

The NPT Review Conference, 1975

As was to be expected, the two superpowers came under heavy criticism at the 1975 NPT Review Conference for their failure to implement their commitments under Article VI of the treaty. This, in fact, was a main issue dominating the debates. As we explain in greater detail in Chapter 18, the third world non-nuclear countries put forward concrete proposals for the immediate suspension and eventual permanent cessation of underground nuclear weapons tests, the drastic reduction of strategic nuclear delivery vehicles, and the adoption of a comprehensive approach to disarmament.

The superpowers refused to consider any of these proposals, however, and insisted that the recent SALT agreements, the Threshold Test Ban Treaty, and the other recent multilateral treaties went at least some way towards fulfilling their commitments. They stressed that Article VI also placed responsibility on non-nuclear powers to make progress on conventional disarmament, which some non-nuclear countries claimed was an attempt to reverse the legal as well as the strategic and disarmament priorities.

The Final Declaration of the conference expressed its serious concern that the arms race, in particular the nuclear arms race, was "continuing unabated," and called on the superpowers to take the lead towards a comprehensive test ban by agreeing to halt their tests for a specified period of time pending a universal and comprehensive ban. It also called for further limitations and significant reductions of their strategic arms following the Vladivostok agreement.

Neither the non-nuclear nor the nuclear powers were satisfied with the Declaration, and both superpowers expressed reservations. The Soviet Union stressed that both nuclear disarmament and a comprehensive test ban could be achieved only with the participation of all the nuclear powers, which is the euphemism it uses to refer to China. Nearly all participants in the conference felt, however, that the superpowers were so far ahead of China that they could suspend all further vertical nuclear weapons proliferation for a decade or more without fear of China catching up to them. The United States emphasized that it was opposed to any comprehensive test ban agreement without adequate verification and a solution to the problem of peaceful nuclear explosions. In this case, too, most partcipants felt that the United States was creating artificial obstacles to a comprehensive test ban.

Proposals for the Future

There are many ways whereby the nuclear powers could demonstrate their "good faith" and the seriousness of their intentions to stop the nuclear arms race "at an early date," as pledged by them in Article VI of the NPT. The list of measures discussed below is not intended to be exhaustive; it merely indicates a number of nuclear arms control measures, some of which are meaningful and important, that the author regards as both logical and feasible in a world of relatively stable, bipolar mutual nuclear deterrence and of developing détente between the superpowers. The nuclear disarmament measures are the most important and are given priority, but conventional disarmament is also a necessary part of any program. The nuclear and conventional measures will have a mutually reinforcing effect.

1. The most important and probably the easiest step would be for the superpowers to agree on an *underground test ban*. As proposed in Chapter 13, it would be best if all underground nuclear explosions, whether for military or peaceful purposes, were banned, until an international regime was set up that would authorize or license the nuclear powers to conduct peaceful nuclear explosions either for themselves or for non-nuclear powers. A moratorium for a year or longer on all underground explosions, pending the working out of a treaty for such an international regime, would have a beneficial effect and would indicate the good faith and goodwill of the superpowers. It would also make an important impression if the three nuclear powers that are parties to the NPT would announce that they were beginning immediate negotiations to draft a treaty banning all underground tests for military purposes, with a view to completing the treaty within six months to a year.

2. The nuclear powers that are parties to the NPT should agree on the immediate *cessation of the production of fissionable material for weapons purposes* and the earmarking of all future production of enriched uranium and plutonium for peaceful purposes. In fact, each of the three nuclear powers could unilaterally announce its intention to take these steps. Back in 1964, all three unilaterally cut back their production of fissionable material for weapons purposes without any talk of verification

and inspection, and there were no charges nor any suspicion of evasions. Each of the three nuclear powers has more than sufficient nuclear weapons and fissionable material for weapons than they can use, and they have been unilaterally cutting back their production as it is; there is no reason why they could not announce a complete cutoff of such production. While it would not be a very significant limitation, it would at least have the merit of meeting one of the long-standing demands of the non-nuclear powers and, if made permanent by treaty, would signify the intention of the nuclear powers to deemphasize weapons and shift their interest to the peaceful, civilian uses of fissionable materials. It would also make it possible for them to accept IAEA safeguards over all their peaceful nuclear activities, including the entire fuel cycle, and put them on an equal basis with other NPT parties.

3. The two superpowers should begin immediate negotiations to *reduce and phase out all land-based ICBMs* with a view to their elimination within a fixed period of time, say six to ten years. Instead of each building up to the ceiling of 2,400 strategic arms (1,320 of them MIRVs) by 1985, as permitted by the Vladivostok agreement, they would announce instead that their objective was to eliminate the 1,618 Soviet and 1,054 American ICBMs by that date. Because of the remarkable and increasing accuracy of missiles, the fixed land-based missiles are becoming increasingly vulnerable to attack and are rapidly becoming obsolete as second-strike weapons. Early in 1974, in fact, the Federation of American Scientists issued a call to eliminate all ICBMs in three stages of five years each. Several American officials, including the director of the Arms Control and Disarmament Agency, saw merit in the proposal. Since missile silos are easily subject to surveillance by satellite, the complete elimination of ICBMs would obviate the difficult problem of verification that would arise under the Vladivostok agreement, which would require that the number of MIRVed missiles be verified. If it would help to obtain Chinese and French participation in an agreement, some provision might be made for them to make and retain a very limited number of ICBMs, say about 50.

4. The two superpowers should also begin immediate negotiations to *reduce their SLBMs (submarine-launched ballistic missiles) drastically.* If the concept of stabilizing the deterrent on the basis of mutual assured destruction—i.e., by each side's retaining a second-strike capability—has any validity, its effectiveness would be greatly increased by each side's agreeing to limit its strategic nuclear forces to sea-based missiles and at a much lower, balanced level. Each side now has a tremendous, useless overkill capability which it attempts to justify on the basis of matching the other side in order to deter or cope with a counterforce strike. The security of both superpowers and of the whole world would be vastly enhanced if the superpowers were to stabilize their deterrents on the basis of a small number of SLBMs, which will continue to be practically invulnerable to attack for as far ahead as anyone can see. This, of course, raises

the question of how much assured destruction capability is enough to deter an attack. In the author's opinion, 10 percent of the missile-firing submarines permitted by the 1972 SALT agreements (see Chapter 2, pp. 28–29) would be more than sufficient for any conceivable rational purpose. If the Soviet Union were permitted to retain, say, 7 missile-firing submarines (with 112 SLBMs) and the United States, say, 5 submarines (with 80 SLBMs), it should be more than enough to ensure mutual deterrence on a more stable basis than at present. Such an agreement might also ban the construction and deployment of the Trident submarines, which would have 24 missiles with up to 20 or 24 warheads each instead of the 16 missiles with 10 warheads each on Poseidon submarines. As indicated in Chapter 2, the author believes that both the United Kingdom (with 4 nuclear-missile submarines) and France (which will have 5 such submarines), although without MIRVed missiles, have a very credible deterrent capability—even if only half of their submarines are normally at sea at any one time.. When one contemplates the fact that the Poseidon missiles are MIRVed with 10 warheads each, it can be argued that even the limited number of SLBMs suggested here, with the United States having some 800 warheads and the Soviet Union (if it also builds 10 warheads for each missile) having 1,120 warheads, is much more than would be required for mutual deterrence. Their numbers could, of course, be reduced further in subsequent negotiations. Since the submarines and their launchers can easily be photographed by "spy satellites," which are the "national technical means of verification" officially sanctioned by the 1972 SALT agreements, no problems of verification or of international inspection would arise.

5. Each of the two superpowers has unilaterally reduced the number of its long-range bombers over the past decade to 432 for the United States and 135 for the Soviet Union, as will be seen from Table 2–2. Many authorities are convinced that the day of the bomber is past and that these strategic arms are obsolescent. Although military establishments still argue the necessity of a "triad" of strategic arms (ICBMs, SLBMs, and bombers) for greater flexibility, many experts regard this attitude as having more to do with interservice rivalry than with defense needs. In any case, if both superpowers were to agree to *reduce and eliminate their strategic bombers,* the balance of deterrence would be preserved and net security enhanced. In this case, too, since bombers are difficult or impossible to hide, verification would not be an obstacle.

6. The two superpowers should also begin immediate negotiations to *ban the testing, manufacture, and deployment of new strategic nuclear-weapons and delivery systems.* While it is practically impossible to ban research and development of new nuclear weapons because of the difficulties of verification, it is easy to monitor a ban on their testing and deployment. If they cannot be tested and deployed, there is not much likelihood of their being manufactured, either openly or secretly. A ban

of the nature proposed here should begin with a prohibition on the flight testing of missiles and other nuclear delivery vehicles including long-range bombers, which is easy to verify. Such a ban, coupled with that on all underground nuclear testing (as proposed in item 1), would put a very effective limitation on the development of new nuclear-weapons systems and on the technological strategic nuclear arms race. It would mean ending the program for the Trident submarine, MARVs, cruise missiles, mobile land-based missiles, and new types of long-range bombers. It would mark a giant step toward the objective of a "cessation of the nuclear arms race at any early date." It would also represent a major increase in international security by removing the fears (and the possibility) of either side's achieving a breakthrough in nuclear weaponry that could threaten the stability of mutual deterrence.

7. While it would be much more difficult to verify a *ban on new tactical nuclear weapons and "mini-nukes,"* the superpowers could begin negotiations for *pulling them back* from frontier and border areas separating the NATO and Warsaw Pact forces in Europe and drastically reducing their numbers. The United States, with over 20,000 tactical nuclear weapons, of which some 7,000 are in Europe, could start a unilateral cutback immediately. A unilateral beginning followed by a bilateral agreement would give real military significance to the Vienna negotiations for force reductions in Central Europe.

8. All the nuclear powers should declare that they will respect all regional treaties creating *nuclear-free zones* or peace zones, and accept binding legal obligations to do so. Such declarations would merely be variants of a pledge not to use or threaten to use nuclear weapons against any non-nuclear party to the NPT that has no nuclear weapons on its territory. All the nuclear-weapon states except the U.S.S.R. have already given such formal legal pledges by signing and ratifying Protocol II of the Treaty of Tlatelolco. If the U.S.S.R. does so, and all the nuclear powers make such declarations, it would provide real impetus and encouragement to the negotiation of other nuclear-free zones and peace zones.

9. The two superpowers should undertake to present, within a specified period of time (say one or two years), *new draft treaties for general and complete disarmament.* Both of them have paid lip service to the idea of general and complete disarmament ever since the unanimous adoption of the United Nations resolution approving it in 1959, and both have voted in favor of many resolutions over the years calling for concrete progress toward this goal. Neither one, however, has shown much interest in revising or updating its 1962 draft treaty outlining a disarmament program. While it would be highly unrealistic to expect that general and complete disarmament would be attained at any time in the foreseeable future, the very efforts of each of the two superpowers to work out new programs, and the negotiations on such programs, might have a very salutary effect on all disarmament efforts, conventional as well as nuclear, regional as

well as global. They could help to revive and give much-needed impetus to the whole range of negotiations on arms control and disarmament, which are bogged down in discussions of relatively minor measures and incremental steps of relative insignificance.

10. During the past twelve years there have been seven multilateral arms control agreements, starting with the Partial Test Ban Treaty in 1963, and eight bilateral Soviet–American agreements, beginning with the Hot Line agreement in 1963 and including the various SALT agreements. During the same period of time, world military expenditures have increased from some $130 billion in 1962 to some $190 billon in 1968, when the NPT was signed, to some $260 billion in 1974. Thus, military expenditures have doubled in absolute figures and increased by about one-fourth in constant dollars. All the arms limitation and disarmament agreements have failed to bring about any reduction whatsoever in military expenditures. The increasing level of military expenditures makes it clear that, despite the many agreements achieved, the arms race continues to escalate at a frantic rate. The two superpowers, who, together with their NATO and Warsaw Pact allies, are responsible for more than 80 percent of these expenditures, should take the lead in first *freezing and then reducing their expenditures*. If they would agree to freeze their military expenditures, it would in fact amount to an actual reduction because of inflation. They could even begin the process by reducing their military expenditures unilaterally, as both powers did in 1963–64. The implementation of the nuclear arms limitations outlined above would lead to substantial reductions.

Unless and until states begin to reduce their military budgets, all arms limitation agreements are, if not meaningless, then illusory. They merely give the illusion of progress toward disarmament, whereas the reality is that the course of the arms race is merely being shifted to new and probably more dangerous channels.

11. The two superpowers possess the overwhelming proportion of conventional armaments and armed forces in the world. They are also by far the largest suppliers of conventional armaments to other countries, including those of the third world as well as their own allies in NATO and the Warsaw Pact. The superpowers should take the lead in *reducing their armed forces and conventional armaments,* as they have done by unilateral action at various times in the past. Some unilateral actions can be undertaken on a permanent basis, but others may have to be on a temporary or trial basis pending reciprocal action by the other side.

The superpowers should also agree to *reduce drastically their sales and transfers of arms to third-world countries,* in particular to the Middle East and Southeast Asia. If they were to take these steps, they would be in a much stronger moral and political position to urge the developing countries not to squander their very limited material and trained human resources on useless local or regional arms races. They would also thereby help to facilitate a better climate of security and confidence in the whole world.

12. Related to the matter of general disarmament is the question of *convening a World Disarmament Conference*. The Soviet Union was responsible for reviving this idea in 1971, and it was taken up by the non-aligned countries and has received the official blessing of the United Nations. The United Kingdom and also France favor the idea. The United States is the only nuclear party to the NPT that is opposed. If the U.S. were to announce its support for holding the conference at the earliest possible date, say within one or two years, it would very probably become a reality and might well achieve universal participation, including that of China. Except for the measures of nuclear disarmament outlined in items 1 to 6 above, nothing could be more calculated to give renewed life and momentum to progress in disarmament than the holding of a World Disarmament Conference. The conference would deal with all aspects of disarmament, including nuclear, conventional, chemical, environmental, and all other forms of warfare.

The question of control and verification, which had in the past posed serious obstacles to agreement on substantial measures of disarmament, no longer constitutes an insuperable problem. The truly remarkable technological advances in satellite surveillance and electronic and telecommunications monitoring during the last decade or so, in addition to the traditional secret means of gathering intelligence, make it almost impossible for any country to undertake clandestine activities that could provide it with an important advantage or that could affect the basic balance of power.

The author is not so naive as to think that the above program of measures, whether as a means to implement the obligations of the nuclear powers under the NPT or as a sensible approach to avoiding a global nuclear holocaust, is likely to be achieved within the predictable or foreseeable future. Even the adoption of this list of items as an agenda for negotiation in the immediate future seems a remote possibility at this time. Nevertheless, the measures proposed are neither unreasonable nor utopian. In a world in which great powers behaved rationally, they would appear so logical as to be obvious on their face. Unfortunately, the military–industrial–scientific–bureaucratic complex in the U.S. and the military–bureaucratic–scientific complex in the U.S.S.R. will oppose these proposals with every political and propaganda weapon in their formidable arsenals.

While the superpowers are undoubtedly aware that only prompt and drastic action by them will prevent the deteriorating non-proliferation regime from eroding further and the NPT from crumbling, they seem unable or unwilling to take the steps necessary to salvage the situation. Unless the superpowers are able to generate the political will that is essential in order to undertake at least some of the proposed measures, the outlook for the NPT and for preventing the further spread of nuclear weapons is discouraging.

One collateral measure that could help promote the cessation of the arms race and disarmament can be undertaken by individuals without waiting for action by governments. Since all inventions in the field of nuclear and other weapons of mass destruction have been conceived in the fertile brains of scientists and engineers, they have an awesome responsibility in this regard. Perhaps they have a special duty to examine their activities in the light of the human and social implications of their work.

I would urge scientists and engineers to stop all further work in the research and development of military weapons and delivery systems. In any case of doubt they should check their work with other scientists who have competence in social, environmental and other related fields. They should create some organizations authorized to evaluate their research and to bar weapons work. They should also refuse to undertake any secret work and insist on their right to publish freely and openly the results of all their research. They should refuse to work in any stage of the nuclear fuel cycle that is not under international safeguards.

In the public sector, scientists and engineers should become more fully engaged in activities for alerting public opinion, the mass media and members of legislatures and governments to the dangers of the continuing arms race. They should also become more actively involved in political efforts to achieve disarmament and in educational work in schools and universities. Such activities can and should be undertaken by all men of goodwill who have a social conscience. But scientists and engineers are better equipped to do so because they are more cognisant of the dangers and, for that reason, more weight may be given to their views.

If scientists were to take the initiative in this respect, then governments would have to take their own responsibilities more seriously.

Chapter 15.   Nuclear-Free Zones

As we indicated in Chapter 4, the Treaty of Tlatelolco created the only nuclear-free zone established specifically for that purpose and as a conscious step toward preventing the spread of nuclear weapons. Other nuclear-free zones were created for Antarctica, outer space, and the seabed by international treaties, but these zones did not cover populated areas and the agreements in question did not require the consent of any local governments. While these zones were created in part for the purpose of arms limitation, they were also part of the efforts of the world community to regulate the use of these still unexplored and unexploited environments; unlike the Treaty of Tlatelolco, there was no specific objective of establishing nuclear-free zones.

The NPT does not actually support the creation of nuclear-free zones. It merely provides, in Article VII, that

> Nothing in this treaty affects the right of any group of states to conclude regional treaties in order to assure the total absence of nuclear weapons in their respective territories.

This provision was inserted in the NPT at the request of the Latin American states, who wished to make it clear that the Treaty of Tlatelolco would not be affected by either the success or failure of the NPT.

Nuclear-free zones had been proposed at different times for a number of inhabited regions of the world, including the Balkans (proposed by Romania), the Mediterranean (proposed by the U.S.S.R.), the Nordic countries (proposed by Finland), and Asia and the Pacific region (proposed by China), but no formal and detailed proposals were put forward and plans for these zones were not persistently pursued. The most recent proposal was put forward in 1975 by Fiji and New Zealand for the establishment of a nuclear-free zone in the South Pacific. On the other hand, formal plans were presented for nuclear-free zones in Central Europe (by Poland), for Africa (by a number of African states), for Latin America (by a number of Latin American states), for the Middle East (by Iran and Egypt), and for South Asia (by Pakistan). These are discussed below.

In general, the Soviet Union and its allies have favored the creation of nuclear-free zones in various parts of the world, but they have placed particular emphasis on Central Europe and on those regions where the two great-power blocs confronted each other (Central Europe and the Mediterranean), where the danger of nuclear conflict seemed greatest. The purpose of such zones, for them, was to reduce the American nuclear presence and its potential threat to them. The United States and its allies, however, considered that these proposals would give some military advantage to the Soviet Union. They conceived of such zones chiefly in the context of preventing the spread of nuclear weapons and laid down certain principles regarding their creation:

1. that they should not upset the existing military balance;
2. that they should be initiated by the states concerned in the region;
3. that they should include all the countries of the area, if possible, and at least those with significant military power; and
4. that they should be subject to verification to ensure that the zone would remain nuclear-free.

As a result of the growing doubts in 1974, after the Indian explosion and in light of the rapidly growing importance of nuclear energy, about the continuing credibility and viability of the Non-Proliferation Treaty, there has been a revival of interest in the whole concept of nuclear-free zones as providing an alternative way of preventing the proliferation of nuclear weapons. Not only can such zones prevent the acquisition of nuclear weapons or explosive devices by the non-nuclear countries in the zone, but they can also prevent the deployment of such weapons in the area by the nuclear powers, and, very importantly, the use or threat of use of nuclear weapons against the countries in the zone by the nuclear powers. The NPT, it will be noted, provides only the first of these benefits. Moreover, a nuclear-free zone created on the initiative of the countries of a region differs radically from the NPT, which, by its very nature, is discriminatory, involving the nuclear powers imposing restrictions or limitations on the non-nuclear powers without accepting any on their own freedom of action.

Central Europe

In 1957, Mr. Adam Rapacki, the foreign minister of Poland, proposed a plan for a nuclear-free zone in Central Europe that came to be known as the "Rapacki Plan." Czechoslovakia and East Germany endorsed the plan, and it was formally put forward in 1958. According to the plan, no nuclear weapons would be manufactured, stockpiled, or installed on the territory of Poland, Czechoslovakia, and East and West Germany; the use of nuclear weapons against the four countries would be banned; the Soviet Union, the United States, the United Kingdom, and France would undertake to respect the nuclear-free status of the zone; a system of ground and air control with inspection bases would be set up to verify the observance of the commitments undertaken and the zone could be established by binding unilateral declarations in order to avoid the complications of negotiating a formal treaty.

The plan was unacceptable to the Western powers, who regarded it as an attempt to weaken their military and political position in Central Europe, since it contained no limitations on conventional arms and forces and would, in effect, amount to a form of recognition of East Germany, which the Western powers were not willing to give at that time, as they were pressing for a reunified Germany.

In order to meet some of the objections, Rapacki submitted a revised plan which would be implemented in two stages; first, a freeze of nuclear armaments in the proposed zone; and second, a reduction of conventional forces, to be carried out together with the complete denuclearization of the zone. A third version of the plan, submitted by Poland in 1962, envisaged that the proposed zone would be open to any other European states wishing to accede to the plan. This version was also to be implemented in two stages: the first would freeze nuclear weapons and rockets and prohibit the establishment of new bases in the area of the zone; and the second would provide for the elimination of nuclear weapons and rockets and the reduction of armed forces and conventional armaments.

The Western powers remained opposed to all of these versions of the Rapacki Plan on the grounds that they were intended to reduce Western nuclear strength in Europe and would give the Soviet Union a military advantage because of its superiority in conventional arms and forces.

In 1964, Poland put forward another proposal, which came to be known as the "Gomulka Plan," proposing a freezing at existing levels in the area of the zone of all nuclear weapons "irrespective of the means of their employment and delivery" under a system of control posts at nuclear plants and at rail, road, sea, and air points of access. Although the Gomulka Plan did not provide for the reduction or elimination of nuclear weapons already in the area but merely banned any increase in their number, the Western powers found it unacceptable for the same reasons that they had rejected the various Rapacki Plans.

None of these plans for freezing or reducing nuclear and conventional arms and forces ever came to anything. Their place was eventually taken by the Vienna Conference on mutual force reductions and associated measures in Central Europe, which is proceeding at the present time.

Africa

The first proposal for a nuclear-free zone in Africa was made in 1960, after the first nuclear test explosion in the Sahara Desert by France. At that time, eight African countries raised the matter but did not press it. The following year, fourteen African states formally proposed in the United Nations General Assembly a resolution preventing the extension of the nuclear arms race to Africa and making Africa a "denuclearized zone." The resolution was approved by the General Assembly. It called on all member states to refrain from conducting nuclear tests in Africa or using the area for testing, storing, or transporting nuclear weapons, and asked them to respect the continent of Africa as a denuclearized zone. The Soviet Union supported the proposal, but the United States and its allies found it unacceptable on the grounds that the prohibition of testing meant an uninspected and uncontrolled moratorium.

In July 1964, at the first Summit Conference of the Organization of African Unity, the heads of state and of the African countries issued a solemn declaration on the denuclearization of Africa and announced their readiness to undertake by treaty not to manufacture or acquire control of nuclear weapons. This declaration was endorsed at a Summit Conference of Non-Aligned Countries held in October of the same year.

In 1965, twenty-eight African states submitted a proposal in the General Assembly endorsing the declaration on the denuclearization of Africa issued at the Summit Conference of the OAU the previous year. The resolution was overwhelmingly approved by the General Assembly in an almost unanimous vote, including all the nuclear powers except France. In addition to endorsing the declaration on the denuclearization of Africa, it (1) reaffirmed the call on all states to respect the continent of Africa as a nuclear-free zone and to abide by the declaration; (2) called on all states not to use or threaten to use nuclear weapons in Africa; and not to test, manufacture, or deploy nuclear weapons in Africa or take "any action which would compel African states to [acquire such weapons]"; (3) urged the nuclear powers not to transfer nuclear weapons, information, or technological assistance to the national control of any state in any form which could assist in the manufacture or use of nuclear weapons in Africa; and (4) expressed the hope that the African states would initiate steps through the OAU with a view to implementing the denuclearization of Africa.

Nothing further was done to implement the declaration or the Assembly's resolution, but nine years later, in December 1974, twenty-six African countries again proposed a resolution in the General Assembly, which was now unanimously adopted by all countries including France, which had some years earlier shifted its nuclear testing from Algeria to the Pacific Ocean island of Mururoa. The resolution reaffirmed the previous resolutions and again called on all states to refrain from testing, manufacturing, deploying, transporting, storing, using, or threatening to use nuclear weapons on the African continent.

One of the problems in connection with the implementation of these declarations and resolutions is that the two African countries most technologically advanced in the field of nuclear energy are in an anomolous position. Because of its policies of apartheid and its refusal to grant independence to Namibia (South West Africa), most of the other African states have instituted a boycott of South Africa and do not wish to deal with or have any traffic with it; although it is a near-nuclear power. At the other end of the continent, Egypt, which is a potential nuclear power although far behind South Africa, does not wish to bind its hands in the nuclear field unless Israel also does so, but it also refuses to deal with or negotiate with Israel. The other African states are much less advanced in the field of nuclear technology; none of them can be considered a near-nuclear power and very few are even potential nuclear powers. While it is quite possible and feasible to establish a nuclear-free zone in Africa without the participation of South Africa and Egypt, there is little sense of urgency about doing so and hence not much impetus in this regard. The matter is therefore likely to proceed slowly and may have to await the achievement of some political accommodations that would alter the situation as regards South Africa and Egypt.

Actually, for practical purposes it might be better to regard Egypt as a Middle Eastern rather than an African state. Egypt would assume all the rights and duties of a member state of a nuclear-free zone whether it joined an African or a Middle Eastern zone, and it would have the option of joining either zone or both. Because of its involvement with Israel, however, it would seem unlikely that Egypt would join an African zone or that it would become a party to a Middle Eastern zone unless Israel also did so.

As was demonstrated at the Organization of African Unity Summit Conference in 1964, and by the unanimous support for the three Assembly resolutions on the part of the African and Arab states, there is a community of interest in Africa supporting the creation of a nuclear-free zone. It would not require a great deal of effort to achieve agreement on such a zone even if it did not at first include all of the countries of the continent. Fourteen African countries are not parties to the NPT, but it is likely that most of them would become parties to a treaty creating a nuclear-free zone in Africa. It would seem to be wise to encourage them to pursue their regional efforts in this regard. Such efforts would have a high chance for success precisely because there is no prospect of any of these countries going nuclear or even acquiring a nuclear option in the immediate future. Once a country acquires a nuclear option, it becomes much more difficult to persuade it to give up that option.

Latin America

The origin and history of the Treaty of Tlatelolco (Treaty for the Prohibition of Nuclear Weapons in Latin America) is outlined in Chapter 4.

The concept of a nuclear-free zone in Latin America originated with a joint declaration of the heads of states of five Latin American countries in 1963 and was approved by the General Assembly in the same year. The Assembly noted with satisfaction the initiative for the denuclearization of Latin America taken in the joint declaration and expressed the hope that the Latin American states would initiate studies and agree upon measures to achieve the aims of the declaration, and it called on all states to cooperate in the realization of any agreement reached.

The Treaty of Tlatelolco, which was signed in 1967, created, for the first time in history, a nuclear-free zone for a populated portion of the earth—here covering some 7.5 million square miles and inhabited by some 200 million people. It was the first treaty in the field of arms control and disarmament that established a system of control and verification under a permanent supervisory organ (OPANAL) and provided for regular inspections to be carried out by the IAEA under the latter's safeguards system as well as special inspections in case of suspicion of violations. (The text of the Treaty is set out in Appendix III.)

The United States supported the treaty and stated that it met the following requirements for the establishment of nuclear-free zones: (1) the initiative originated within the area concerned; (2) the zone was to include all states deemed important; (3) the treaty did not disturb any existing security arrangements; and (4) it provided for verification and follow-up on alleged violations.

After the treaty entered into force in 1969, Secretary-General U Thant hailed the treaty and praised the Latin American states for having "successfully pioneered an important step towards disarmament and the expansion of peaceful uses of nuclear energy," one which gave the world "some novel ideas in the field of control." He was hopeful that the treaty would provide a model for the establishment of other nuclear-free zones and for additional measures of global disarmament.

The Treaty of Tlatelolco in many ways goes further than the NPT. It not only bans the transfer and acquisition of nuclear weapons but provides for the total absence of such weapons from the territory of the zone. It provides that all nuclear materials and facilities are to be used for "exclusively" peaceful purposes and thus totally prohibits the military use of nuclear material or devices. In addition, Protocol II of the treaty contains a specific prohibition on the use or threat of use of nuclear weapons against states in the zone, a commitment which is absent from the NPT. Moreover, in addition to the application of the IAEA safeguards system, the treaty provides for a complete system of control; there is a permanent organ to supervise the implementation of the treaty and to assure compliance with its terms, and a procedure is established whereby any member may challenge a suspected violation. As we indicate in Chapter 4, differences of opinion exist between Argentina and Brazil, on the one hand, who maintain that the treaty permits them to conduct peaceful nuclear explosions, and other signatories of the treaty.

Protocol I provides for the application of the treaty to territories in the zone for which other states have *de jure* or *de facto* responsibility. It has been signed and ratified by the United Kingdom and the Netherlands but not by the United States and France. In 1974, the United Nations General Assembly specifically called on these two countries to sign and ratify Protocol I.

As already mentioned, China, France, the United Kingdom, and the United States have signed and ratified Protocol II, pledging to respect the status of the zone and not to use or threaten to use nuclear weapons against it. Despite more than half a dozen resolutions of the General Assembly urging it to do so, the U.S.S.R. has thus far refused to accede to Protocol II although it has stated that it will respect the nuclear-free status of each state in the area that remains nuclear-free. After India exploded a nuclear device in 1974, the agency established to implement the treaty (OPANAL) also called on India as a nuclear power to accede to Protocol II.

The number of parties to the treaty and of its supporters, including the nuclear signatories of the Protocols, has grown from year to year. As of late 1975, there were 20 full parties to the treaty—all of whom, that is, had deposited a waiver of the conditions for its entry into force. Brazil and Chile have also ratified the treaty, but it has not entered into force for them as they have not deposited a declaration of waiver. It is also not in force in Argentina, which has signed but not ratified the treaty.

Ratification of both Protocols I and II by all the nuclear powers concerned would certainly have some bearing on whether Argentina, Brazil, and Chile decide to become full parties to the treaty.

While there seems little hope for the foreseeable future that either Argentina or Brazil will become full parties to the Tlatelolco Treaty, there would appear to be better prospects for their joining such a regional pact, which ensures equal treatment for all parties on a nondiscriminatory basis, than for their becoming parties to the NPT. They might also find some incentive in the negative security assurance provided by the nuclear powers that they would not use or threaten to use nuclear weapons against members of the zone, an assurance that is not provided to parties to the NPT. Moreover, the possibility is not forever excluded that some compromise formula might be found, or that the advance of technology might facilitate an acceptable solution to the problem of peaceful nuclear explosions. If the nuclear powers would live up to their obligation under the NPT to establish a special international regime for the conduct of peaceful nuclear explosions at a minimum cost to non-nuclear powers, with special concessionary rates for developing countries, there would be less incentive and less need for either Argentina or Brazil to develop their own capability in this respect.

Since Argentina and Brazil each fears or is wary of the other's "going nuclear," it is conceivable that they might both be willing either to remain non-nuclear or to establish a balance of mutual deterrence on the basis of

their becoming peaceful nuclear powers with a ready potential of going
nuclear rather than nuclear-weapons powers engaged in a mutually ruinous nuclear arms race. Certainly there is room for greater nuclear cooperation between them and, perhaps, for the establishment of one or even two
regional fuel cycle centers in which both would participate.

If there is any chance at all of Argentina and Brazil refraining from
going nuclear, it is most likely to be found within the regional context of
the Latin American Nuclear-Free Zone, where they would be conscious
of and receptive to the feelings, desires, and influence of their neighbors,
all of whom are developing countries with problems similar to their own.
At any rate, the Treaty of Tlatelolco holds out more hope in this regard
than does the NPT, which both countries regard as a discriminatory treaty
that the nuclear powers are trying to impose on them.

The Middle East

In 1974, Iran, later joined by Egypt, proposed the establishment of a
nuclear-free zone in the Middle East. In December of that year, the General Assembly commended the idea and called on all parties in the area
to proclaim their intention to refrain, on a reciprocal basis, from producing, testing, obtaining, acquiring, or in any other way possessing nuclear
weapons. It also called on the parties concerned in the area to accede to
the NPT, and requested the Secretary-General to ascertain their views and
report to the Security Council and to the General Assembly.

Unfortunately, there was no prior consultation with important states in
the area and in particular with Israel, the state with the most advanced
nuclear technology in the Middle East, before the issuance of Iran's proposal. Because of the state of belligerency existing between Egypt and
Israel, the fact that Egypt joined with Iran in sponsoring the proposal led
to the suspicion that it was maneuvering to gain, if not some military advantage, then at least some political or propaganda advantage by putting
pressure on Israel not to go nuclear. Any suspicion of this nature would, of
course, have the effect of aborting the entire project and ensuring that no
nuclear-free zone for the area can be expected. Moreover, the Assembly's
approval of the idea did not call on the parties to enter into consultation
with each other but merely requested that the Secretary-General ascertain
their views.

As was to be expected, Israel withheld its support from the Assembly's
resolution. It is interesting to note that all the nuclear powers, including
India, voted for it. Without Israel's support, however, it is unlikely that the
resolution will lead to any productive result. Since Egypt has announced
that it will not ratify the NPT unless Israel does, it is hardly likely that it
would become a party to a nuclear-free zone that did not include Israel.

Some political observers have speculated that Iran probably accepted

Egypt as a cosponsor of its proposal with the understanding that this would almost certainly ensure the failure of the project. Obviously, this supposition casts doubt on the sincerity of Iran's motives.

In any case, if the idea of a nuclear-free zone in the Middle East is to make progress, it will be necessary either to start anew, with prior consultations with Israel, or to envisage a zone of initially more modest scope that would not include Egypt or Israel. It is not clear whether Iran or other Arab states—such as Libya, which has embarked on a program to acquire nuclear reactors—would be attracted by a limited zone. The entire project may have to be postponed until there is some settlement between Israel and the Arab states. On the other hand, Israel's willingness to agree to become a party to such a zone might become a useful bargaining point that could help facilitate an Arab–Israeli political settlement. The Arab states, and in particular Egypt, would certainly be happy to see Israel give up its nuclear option, and they might conceivably consider paying some price therefor. Israel's announced support for the principle of a Middle East nuclear-free zone, and its readiness to participate in a conference convened for that purpose, suggests that the creation of such a zone might be a component part of a Middle East peace settlement.

South Asia

Also in 1974, after India exploded a nuclear device, Pakistan proposed the creation of a nuclear-free zone in South Asia. The General Assembly also endorsed this concept and invited the states of the region and other neighboring non-nuclear states to initiate necessary consultations with a view to establishing a nuclear-free zone. In the interim, it urged them to refrain from any contrary action and requested the Secretary-General to convene a meeting for the purpose of the consultations envisaged.

Here, too, there was no prior consultation among the parties concerned and in particular with India, which had already conducted a nuclear explosion. These circumstances gave rise to the suspicion that the Pakistan initiative was aimed not so much at the actual creation of a nuclear-free zone but in gaining some political or propaganda advantage.

India made its position clear by itself proposing a resolution in which the General Assembly stated that the "initiative" for the creation of a nuclear-free zone in the appropriate region of Asia "should come from the states of the region concerned," taking into account its special features and geographical extent. The Indian resolution was adopted by an overwhelming majority, but with the United States, the United Kingdom, China, France, Israel and Pakistan abstaining. The Soviet Union voted in favor. On the other hand, the Pakistani resolution was supported by the United States and China, with India voting against and the Soviet Union, the

United Kingdom, France, and Israel abstaining. The curious variations in the voting patterns of the nuclear powers and India on the resolutions for nuclear-free zones in the Middle East and South Asia provide an interesting commentary on the extent to which great powers are motivated by political expediency. One can speculate on the degree of their interest in preventing the proliferation of nuclear weapons by means of nuclear-free zones, or on whether they considered the creation of such zones as so unlikely in the near future as to make it more useful for them to gain whatever political benefit they could from their votes.

It is understandable that India might have resented not having been consulted in advance of Pakistan's initiative. But if India is serious in its protestations that its explosion of a nuclear device was solely for peaceful purposes and that it has no intention of developing nuclear weapons, there are sound reasons for India to react positively to Pakistan's proposal and to work for the creation of a nuclear-free zone in South Asia. It would certainly be to India's advantage if Pakistan did not go nuclear and to its disadvantage if Pakistan did, even if it were via the peaceful explosion route. It would also be in India's interest to have a binding pledge from China not to use or threaten to use nuclear weapons against it as a member of a South Asian zone which China undertook to respect.

India may have reacted too hastily in rejecting the Pakistani proposal. If Pakistan should go nuclear, it is difficult to envisage Iran and Indonesia from doing likewise, to the detriment of all four countries as well as others in the area. In fact, one can make a good case, not least in India's interest, for expanding the Pakistani proposal to include both the Middle East and the Far East in the area of the zone. Since, of the four countries mentioned, only Iran is a party to the NPT, the idea of an expanded zone certainly merits further exploration.

Indian Ocean Peace Zone

The concept of a "peace zone" is considerably broader than that of a nuclear-free zone. In 1971, the General Assembly declared that the Indian Ocean was designated for all time as a zone of peace. The declaration called upon the great powers to enter into consultation with the littoral states of the Indian Ocean with a view to halting the further expansion of their military presence in that ocean and eliminating all bases, military installations, nuclear weapons, and other manifestations of great power military presence in the context of great power rivalry. This declaration, if implemented, would amount to the denuclearization of the Indian Ocean, at least by the great powers, and indeed would almost amount to its demilitarization insofar as the great powers are concerned. China and India both voted in favor of the creation of the zone of peace, but the United States, the Soviet Union, the United Kingdom, and France abstained.

In the following year a committee was established, composed of littoral states and other supporters of the zone of peace such as China and Japan, to study the implications of the declaration. In 1973, the General Assembly urged all states to accept the principles and objectives of the declaration, but again the four powers mentioned above withheld their support.

While the actual establishment of a zone of peace is obviously not likely to take place in the near future, it is noteworthy that the concept is supported by practically all of the littoral states of the Indian Ocean, including Australia, and that consultations between them are proceeding and are acquiring increasing support.

It will be noted that the peace zone envisaged does not seek to establish a nuclear-free zone in the territories of the littoral states of the Indian Ocean but rather is aimed at the denuclearization and further demilitarization of the Indian Ocean itself. Thus it differs fundamentally from other nuclear-free-zone proposals in that it is intended to apply to the high seas rather than to bordering states.

Observations and Conclusions

The failure of the Rapacki Plan for a nuclear-free zone in Central Europe, and of other initiatives that were no less persistently pursued, was due to the fact that they were aimed at altering existing security arrangements or the existing military balance in the area. On the other hand, the Latin American initiative succeeded because it was a genuine cooperative effort initiated by the countries of the region in order to keep nuclear weapons out of their area. The initiative was not aimed at any particular country or security arrangement, but was conceived and perceived by the parties concerned as being in their common interest.

Moreover, the Latin American countries went ahead with their project without requiring the participation of every country in the area. They were content to go forward with establishing the zone in the maximum area obtainable. If Cuba was not ready to join, they were prepared to begin on a smaller scale and hoped to achieve their goal of including all states of the region in due course. As previously mentioned, Argentina and Brazil are not full members of the Latin American nuclear-free zone although both have signed the Treaty of Tlatelolco, and Brazil has also ratified the treaty but without waiving the conditions for its entry into force for Brazil.

Since the African nuclear-free zone was also conceived as a genuine cooperative effort in the common interest of the African countries, it, too, has a chance of success. In this case also, however, if the zone is to be created in the foreseeable future, it may be necessary for the countries of

Africa to proceed without the participation of some countries—viz., South Africa and Egypt. While the absence of these two countries, which are the most advanced in nuclear technology, would be a shortcoming that would reduce the effectiveness of the nuclear-free zone, there would always be the possibility of their joining at a later date.

As regards the other proposals for nuclear-free zones that are now actively being considered, namely those for the Middle East and South Asia, the situation is entirely different. Since the proposals in these cases seem to be more of a political gambit than a cooperative effort conceived and worked out in consultation among the main countries of the respective areas, the prognosis for them must be regarded as poor. The situation might, of course, undergo a change if genuine peace were established between Israel and the Arab states or between India and Pakistan. In the absence of such developments, however, it is useless to think that a country can be maneuvered by political gamesmanship into accepting non-nuclear status. No country would agree to become a party to any treaty, let alone one that could affect its security, unless it considered its doing so as being clearly in its interest, or at least not prejudicial to it. In fact, it is axiomatic that even if a country becomes a party to a treaty it will not remain so if it considers that subsequent events have caused the treaty to be against its important interests.

Nevertheless, the idea of nuclear-free zones is undoubtedly a good one. It provides a means whereby non-nuclear countries can, by their own efforts, ensure their greater security. It can be an effective means not only of preventing non-nuclear countries in a given region from going nuclear, but of obtaining pledges from the nuclear powers not to use or threaten to use nuclear weapons against any of the countries in that region. The United States and the United Kingdom, which refused to include such a pledge in either the NPT or the Security Council resolution for security assurances to non-nuclear states, have both agreed to a commitment of this nature by signing and ratifying Protocol II of the Treaty of Tlatelolco. And China and France, which are not parties to the NPT or to the Security Council's security assurances, have likewise become parties to Protocol II. As we indicated earlier, it is also possible that the Soviet Union will become a party, once relations between Cuba and the other Latin American countries are normalized.

Furthermore, nuclear-free zones would also provide a sound reason and logical basis for promoting the peaceful uses of nuclear energy by facilitating the establishment of regional nuclear fuel cycle centers for enriching uranium, reprocessing plutonium, and handling nuclear wastes. In fact, it is not easy to visualize how regional or international fuel cycle centers could be established except within some nuclear-free zone. The economic and security benefits, and the greater effectiveness of safeguards against diversion or theft of nuclear material, that would follow from having a large-scale regional facility rather than a number of smaller, national facilities are themselves powerful arguments in favor of the creation of such zones.

Moreover, such zones could avoid the discriminatory features of the NPT and could provide the mutual security desired by countries who, for one reason or another, do not wish to become parties to the NPT. Thus nuclear-free zones can be a very effective means of promoting and strengthening the non-proliferation regime. Their creation would in no way compete or conflict with the NPT, but would provide a means for extending and reinforcing the objectives of that treaty.

Provided that the idea of a nuclear-free zone is conceived and promoted by the non-nuclear countries of a given area as a genuine effort to increase the security of all of the countries affected and not just of some of them, and is not pursued as a means of political gamesmanship, there is no reason why additional nuclear-free zones should not be established in different areas of the world. Their establishment would be facilitated if the nuclear powers would demonstrate their wholehearted support for the creation of such zones, not solely as a means of preventing the further spread of nuclear weapons but also as a way of furthering the peaceful uses of nuclear energy and providing security assurances to the countries in the zone.

The NPT itself, while not explicity encouraging or facilitating the creation of nuclear-free zones, does nothing to discourage or inhibit their creation. It does, in fact, give them its implied blessing. But the initiative remains with the parties concerned in any region. The nuclear-free zone is one of the easiest and best ways whereby non-nuclear countries can do something by and for themselves. And in a number of important respects it provides a more effective means than the NPT of maintaining and strengthening international peace and security.

At the NPT Review Conference, two proposals were put forward by third-world non-nuclear states calling on the nuclear powers to support the creation of nuclear-free zones and to respect the status of such zones, which would include undertaking not to use or threaten to use nuclear weapons against countries which are members of such zones. Unfortunately, the nuclear powers considered these proposals too sweeping and wished to judge the proposal on its merits with respect to each zone.

A Proposal

While the NPT does not in itself put any specific obligation on the nuclear powers to support or respect nuclear-free zones, the last paragraph of the Preamble, which was added to the treaty on the insistence of Mexico, expressly recalls the United Nations Charter's provisions prohibiting the threat or use of force against any state. This provision is certainly broad enough to include a prohibition on the threat or use of nuclear weapons. Accordingly, despite their reluctance to tie their hands in advance, the nuclear powers should, both as a matter of principle and as a further means of strengthening the NPT, give strong support to the creation of additional nuclear-free zones. In particular, they should take the following actions:

1. Undertake to become a party to Protocol I of the Treaty of Tlatelolco (this would apply only to the United States and France);
2. Undertake to become a party to Protocol II of the Treaty of Tlatelolco (this would apply only to the Soviet Union and possibly India);
3. Issue a joint declaration or separate declarations that they will respect the status of any nuclear free zone and that they will not use or threaten to use nuclear weapons against any such zone;
4. Undertake to actively support and promote the establishment of additional nuclear-free zones.

Chapter 16. The Nth-Country Problem Again: India's Nuclear Explosion

What the Indian Explosion Means

The Indian nuclear explosion of May 18, 1974, has changed all the rules of nuclear non-proliferation and nuclear arms control, as well as the structure of international relations. The test explosion of a nuclear device for peaceful purposes under the Rajasthan desert changed the rules of the game as surely, if not as spectacularly, as did the test explosion of a nuclear device for military purposes above the desert at Alamogordo, New Mexico, on July 16, 1945.

The Alamogordo test proved that a great industrial power could use atomic fission for an explosion that could be used as a devastating bomb in war, but with possible potential for peaceful uses. The Rajasthan test proved that a relatively poor developing country could use atomic fission for an underground explosion (somewhat more complicated than one in the atmosphere) that had definite potential for warlike purposes.

There is no escaping the plain fact: India is now a member of the nuclear club—the world's sixth nuclear power. There is no essential difference between the technology of a nuclear explosion intended for peaceful applications and that of one intended for waging nuclear war. The same explosion that blew a hole in the earth under the Rajasthan desert and left a large crater on the surface could equally well have blown up a city and its inhabitants. The bombs that destroyed Hiroshima and Nagasaki were about the same size as the Indian device—between 15 and 20 kilotons in explosive yield. The main difference was in the intended purpose of the explosion. India has repeatedly declared that its explosion was solely for peaceful purposes and that it has no intention of developing nuclear weapons. But intention is a subjective matter based on a unilateral decision and is subject to change at will, with or without notice. Thus, in the absence of any binding legal commitment, by bilateral or multilateral treaty or agreement, there is nothing to prevent the Indian government—

either the present one or some successor—from changing its mind whenever it wishes and deciding to use its nuclear devices for military purposes,
that is, as nuclear bombs or warheads. Even if we fully accept the Indian
declaration of its intention to use nuclear explosions exclusively for peaceful purposes, the objective fact is that its nuclear devices can also be
used as nuclear weapons whenever India so decides. Unquestionably,
other powers will, and indeed in prudence must, regard India's peaceful
nuclear devices as potential nuclear weapons. Henceforth, irrespective of
repeated and honestly intended declarations and protestations by the
Indian government, India must be regarded by other powers not merely
as a nuclear power but as a nuclear-weapon power. The validity of this
perception was enhanced when a public opinion poll taken in India
soon after the explosion showed that two-thirds of the Indian people
favored India's making nuclear weapons.

The Indian test explosion has also showed the way for other powers
to "go nuclear" under the guise of testing devices for peaceful purposes.
Any one of the potential nuclear powers that has not become a party to
the Non-Proliferation Treaty can emulate India's example. Even countries
that are parties to the NPT retain this option, as the treaty provides that
any party can withdraw on three months' notice.

For several years after the Chinese nuclear explosion in October 1964,
India sought effective guarantees of its security from the nuclear powers,
but its efforts were in vain. Failing to obtain any adequate direct security
assurances, India shifted its emphasis to an indirect approach by insisting
that all the nuclear powers stop testing and manufacturing nuclear weapons and start reducing their nuclear arsenals. When this approach also
seemed likely to fail, India began stressing its right and need to conduct
its own peaceful nuclear explosions for economic development.

It is much easier for a government to assuage both domestic and international opinion by proclaiming its intention to conduct nuclear explosions
solely for peaceful and not for military purposes than to say outright that
it intends to make or acquire the capability of making nuclear weapons.
Nuclear weapons are still, fortunately, looked upon with abhorrence as
weapons of mass destruction that must not be used and that must eventually be eliminated. All five nuclear-weapon states have declared that
they produce nuclear weapons solely for defense and not for aggression
and that they maintain their stockpiles solely for deterrence and not for
attack. We can now look forward to a new chapter in the nuclear story
wherein countries that wish, for whatever reason, to become nuclear-
weapon states, will first go through the stage of exploding and producing
nuclear devices for peaceful purposes. This cosmetic cover will be
sufficient to permit a relatively advanced nation to produce, over a
period of time, a wide range of nuclear warheads for use in tactical
battlefield atomic weapons (mini-nukes) or in strategic intercontinental
hydrogen weapons.

The United States and the Soviet Union have carried out only underground nuclear tests since they signed the Partial Test Ban Treaty in Moscow in 1963; these have ranged from a fraction of a kiloton to five or more megatons in size and have encompassed a large variety of sophisticated weapons. Smaller, poorer countries could not afford, and would have no need, to do likewise. But middle-sized powers and some of the oil-rich smaller countries could, under the pretext of producing a variety of devices for peaceful explosions, build up a capability for producing a broad spectrum of nuclear weapons. And the drives and motivations that fueled the nuclear arms race among the nuclear-weapon states might operate in a similar action–reaction manner among nuclear–peaceful device states and lead to the creation of a second nuclear club of secondary powers. An arsenal of nuclear weapons could be built up under the guise not of a nuclear arms race but of a "peaceful explosion race." Admittedly, any such development is years away and sounds somewhat far-fetched at the present time, but the same could have been said—indeed it *was* said—in the late 1940s of the potential nuclear arms race between the great powers. The logic of both scenarios is parallel and inexorable.

The Legalities of the Case

The Indian government and Indian leaders insist that they broke no law, treaty or agreement in conducting the Rajasthan test. And they are right.

The Non-Proliferation Treaty is the only international instrument that bans the explosion of nuclear devices for peaceful purposes by non-nuclear-weapon states. The transfer to or acquisition of "nuclear weapons or other nuclear explosive devices" is specifically banned for non-nuclear-weapon states by Articles I and II of the treaty. Peaceful nuclear explosions, however, to be carried out only by nuclear-weapon states under an appropriate international regime for the benefit of non-nuclear-weapon states, are expressly envisaged both by the Preamble and by Article V of the treaty. But India is in any case not a party to the NPT and has not signed it. In fact, both during and after the negotiation and conclusion of the NPT, India repeatedly opposed the treaty as discriminatory and unfair, and reserved the right to conduct its own nuclear explosions for peaceful purposes. Thus India cannot be accused of any breach of either the letter or the spirit of the NPT.

On the other hand, India is a member of the International Atomic Energy Agency in Vienna and an active participant in its work. The statute of the agency, which entered into force in 1957, specifically bans the use of atomic energy "in such a way as to further any military purpose," but positively encourages "the development and practical application of atomic energy for peaceful purposes." A number of U.N. and IAEA conferences and meetings of experts from 1958 to 1973 all held out high hopes for the potential benefits that would be obtained from peaceful nuclear explosions. These expectations may, as we discussed in Chapter 13, be largely mythical, but there can be no doubt that over the years nuclear and non-nuclear powers alike were dazzled by the glittering prize that could be theirs when (not "if") peaceful nuclear explosions became feasible. Although the nuclear-weapon-states are apparently becoming increasingly disenchanted by their failure to achieve any important technical or economic objectives after having invested years of effort and hundreds of millions of dollars in testing peaceful nuclear explosions, the poor and developing nations of the world seem to regard such explosions as the key that will help them unlock the door to great industrial and engineering undertakings at little cost. And as recently as July 1974, in the Threshold Test Ban Treaty signed by Nixon and Brezhnev at the Summit Conference in Moscow, specific provision was made for entering into a new Soviet–American agreement for peaceful nuclear explosions at the earliest possible time. Thus, India can hardly be faulted for wanting to achieve what was not prohibited her by any international treaty or agreement and was given the specific blessing of a number of international treaties and studies.

Even the bilateral Canadian–Indian agreements did not ban peaceful nuclear explosions. At most they provided that the nuclear material and equipment furnished by Canada to India for the CIRUS reactor (a 40-megawatt research reactor using natural uranium) should be used exclusively for peaceful purposes. It is true that no specific safeguards or inspections were provided to ensure that there would be no diversion of fissionable material for military purposes. (The agreement for the reactor was entered into in 1956, before there was an IAEA and before the scientists of the Lawrence Livermore Laboratory in California invented the idea of peaceful nuclear explosions and the Plowshare Program in 1957; the reactor began operation in 1960, before there was any effective IAEA safeguards system). But any conceivable IAEA or Canadian safeguards and inspections would have been of no avail. India has not diverted fissionable material from the Canadian reactor clandestinely or otherwise. For years India has publicly stated that it intended to use the plutonium obtained by reprocessing the spent fuel from the reactor (at its own chemical separation plant) for undertaking peaceful nuclear explosions. It can, of course, be argued, and rightly so, that developing and testing peaceful nuclear devices is equivalent to developing and testing nuclear weapons—which is precisely what Prime Minister Pierre Elliott Trudeau argued in 1971, both orally and in writing, to Prime Minister Indira Gandhi when he tried to interpret the Canadian agreements with India as prohibiting peaceful nuclear explosions, although the agreements contained no definition of "peaceful" uses. But his interpretation was an arguable one, and Mrs. Gandhi refused to agree with it. She responded, "It should not be necessary now in our view to interpret these agreements in a particular way, based on the development of a hypothetical contingency."

The weakness of the Canadian case against India is evidenced by the fact that, following the Indian explosion, in all agreements for the sale of nuclear reactors Canada now not only makes provision for their use for exclusively peaceful purposes, but also expressly bans their use for the purpose of peaceful nuclear explosions. In fact, as indicated in Chapter 11, Canada has announced unilateral restrictions on the export of nuclear material, equipment, and technology that provide the strictest safeguards of any nuclear supplier country. However, as explained in that chapter, even these are not sufficient to prevent a country that wishes to do so from acquiring its own nuclear explosive devices.

Irrespective of what one might think of India's tactics and behavior, and convinced as one might be that India will eventually turn her peaceful nuclear devices into nuclear weapons, her declared intention to use these devices exclusively for peaceful purposes and not for developing weapons cannot be disproved. Unless and until India does make a bomb or nuclear warhead from material obligated for exclusively peaceful purposes, and the world finds out about it either because India admits the fact or from independent objective evidence, there is no legal recourse and no way of successfully challenging the Indian contention.

One can only regret that the nation of Gandhi and Nehru (who was the first to propose the cessation of nuclear testing, in 1954) may be responsible for undermining efforts to prevent the proliferation of nuclear weapons. One might also be permitted to doubt the wisdom—in terms of her own ultimate political, economic, and military interests—of India's having decided to go nuclear.

Reactions to the Indian Explosion

Public reactions to the Indian explosion have been few and rather mixed. Among the nuclear-weapon states, not a word of criticism has been heard from the two Asian nuclear powers, China and the U.S.S.R. China has attacked the NPT from its inception as a fraud and a hoax—a device by the two superpowers to maintain their nuclear hegemony and to dominate the non-nuclear states. She has for many years in effect advocated the proliferation of nuclear weapons by supporting the right of the developing countries of the third world to acquire such weapons to protect themselves from threats and blackmail by the nuclear superpowers. In any event, it is unlikely that India could become a threat to China in the foreseeable future, even if it decided to become a nuclear-weapon power. Although India is experimenting with space rockets, it will be a long time before it is in a position to develop sophisticated nuclear delivery systems. Moreover, China has the advantage that her capital, industrial areas, and population centers are a long way from Indian territory, while the reverse is true for India. Nevertheless, in view of India's close relations with the U.S.S.R. and the fact that even before May 18, India was clearly the strongest power in South Asia, China can hardly regard India's growing nuclear-weapon power with equanimity. In the context of Chinese and Indian relations with other Asian countries and the third world, and in particular with Pakistan, with whom China has close and friendly relations, the political implications of the Indian explosion are of greater importance than the military ones. Moreover, if Taiwan, which is a party to the NPT, should be encouraged by the Indian example and decide to withdraw from the NPT and go nuclear, this would pose new and difficult problems for China. It is also difficult to believe that China would be completely unconcerned if South Korea, Indonesia, Australia, or Iran were also to go nuclear. The official silence from Peking, which is itself conducting tests in the atmosphere, may therefore mean only that China has not yet worked out its final position with regard to India's explosion or is biding its time pending the clarification and crystallization of third-world opinion.

On the other hand, the Soviet Union, which together with the United States was the author and chief protagonist of the NPT, can hardly view the Indian action as anything but disquieting. While it, too, has not uttered a single official word of protest or criticism, Soviet diplomats and arms control experts have privately indicated their unhappiness. It could hardly be otherwise. It may be that a nuclear India that continues to be friendly to the Soviet Union provides some benefits or leverage for the U.S.S.R. with respect to China. But any such possible advantages would be far outweighed if India's action should lead to the further erosion of the NPT and the spread of nuclear-weapon capability to other states. The potential nuclear-weapon states would form a nuclear ring, and not necessarily a friendly one, around the U.S.S.R. Countries that now or will in a few years have the capability of going nuclear include Japan, South Korea, and Taiwan to the east; Pakistan, Iran, Israel and Egypt to the south; Yugoslavia, Italy, Switzerland, West Germany, and Sweden to the west; and Canada to the north. If many, or any, of these countries decided to go nuclear, the security of the U.S.S.R. would very clearly not be enhanced. And as one country after another went nuclear, there is no telling where the process might stop. The "nightmare" world that President Kennedy feared in 1963 might be especially nightmarish for the U.S.S.R.

France, which is also conducting tests in the atmosphere, has also made no official statement, but the chairman of the French Atomic Energy Commission sent a congratulatory message to the chairman of the Indian

Atomic Commission. The French position is anomalous. While France is not a party to the NPT, she has announced from the start that she would behave exactly as if she were a party. Nevertheless, France is busy selling nuclear reactors, materials, equipment, and know-how to a number of countries, and while these deals are subject to safeguards (IAEA or bilateral), so far as is known they do not bar peaceful nuclear explosions. Moreover, as has already been mentioned, a French company is also ready and willing to sell complete chemical separation plants for plutonium reprocessing. It is possible that in its zeal to obtain commercial contracts, such as the sale of four or five reactors to Iran and a fast breeder reactor to India, France may be putting short-term economic gains ahead of long-term security considerations.

The United Kingdom, which has also been a strong supporter of the NPT, was at first strongly critical of the Indian explosion. But since its initial criticism little has been heard from the United Kingdom, which has itself been criticized for resuming underground testing in June 1974, when it conducted a test in the United States for the first time since 1965.

The United States was at first rather cautious in its official reaction to the Indian test explosion. It did reiterate to the Indian government its belief that peaceful and military nuclear explosive devices are indistinguishable, but it seems to wish to avoid any public dispute with India. Privately, it has sought a commitment that plutonium produced from nuclear fuel supplied by the United States would not be used for any type of explosion. Failing to receive adequate assurances, the United States delayed the delivery of enriched uranium to fuel India's Tarapur reactor, which was built with American technical and financial assistance. At the time of writing, it appears that India has given the necessary assurances and that the United States will continue supplying uranium to India.

As was to be expected, Pakistan, which signed but never ratified the 1963 Partial Test Ban Treaty and has not signed the NPT, immediately protested in every possible forum against the Indian explosion and called for a halt to further tests. It also announced that it would acquire a similar nuclear capability. Several years ago, before he became Prime Minister of Pakistan, Ali Bhutto announced that, if necessary, Pakistan would "eat grass" in order to keep up with India in the nuclear field. Pakistan has also proposed the creation of a nuclear-free zone in South Asia—which, as anticipated, India rejected. The proposal must be regarded as a tactical political move intended to make clear to the world where the blame lies, if Pakistan decides that it, too, must go nuclear.

Apart from Pakistan, only Canada, Japan, and Sweden, all of whom have the capability of undertaking nuclear explosions, have taken a strong public stand against the Indian test. Canada almost immediately cut off all further nuclear cooperation with India, and all three countries —in statements in their capitals, at the Geneva Disarmament Conference, in messages transmitted to the Indian government, and in the United Nations General Assembly—deplored the Indian explosion and its possible adverse effects on international efforts to prevent the proliferation of nuclear weapons. The Netherlands also has criticized the Indian test.

As for the nonaligned and developing countries, while saying little in public, they have in large part welcomed the Indian test as a technological achievement demonstrating that even a developing country could acquire the know-how to successfully accomplish the sophisticated task of exploding an underground nuclear device, which had for a decade been the exclusive preserve of the five great powers. Yugoslavia, one of the leaders of the nonaligned countries, congratulated India on her technological achievement. Nigeria said that the Indian action was not surprising in view of the lack of progress by the nuclear powers in stopping underground nuclear tests and the nuclear arms race.

The third-world countries were, on the whole, never greatly impressed with the NPT. In fact, Tanzania and Zambia, which have some links with China, voted against the General Assembly resolution which approved the NPT in 1968, while 13 other African states abstained.

Many of those who decided to support and adhere to the treaty did so in the dual expectation that the nuclear-weapon powers would both halt the "vertical" proliferation of nuclear weapons (their further sophistication, development, and deployment), as provided by Article VI of the NPT, and make available to the developing countries the benefits of the peaceful uses of nuclear energy including peaceful nuclear explosions as provided by Articles IV and V. But these countries have become disillusioned by the failure of the nuclear powers to halt the nuclear arms race and by the paucity of the benefits received from the peaceful applications of nuclear energy. They are impressed by the achievements of China and India, and some of the more advanced among them are much more receptive now to the argument that they might better withstand the unspoken threats of the nuclear-weapon states and promote their own security and economic development by going nuclear. In fact, some of the third-world countries that are themselves unlikely to be able to go nuclear for many years to come, and that were originally strong supporters of the NPT, seem to be increasingly inclined to accept the idea that the acquisition of nuclear-weapon capability by some of the near-nuclear powers would place greater restraints on the freedom of action of the nuclear-weapon states, and that the advantages this would bring to the third-world countries would outweigh any potential disadvantages. They seem to have some vaguely defined feeling that if some additional third-world and developing countries went nuclear, it might somehow help to redress the balance between the rich and powerful developed nations and the poor and weak developing ones.

At the United Nations General Assembly in the fall of 1974, apart from the five countries mentioned above and Australia there was practically no criticism of the Indian explosion. It is very clear that, despite some privately held reservations by a few countries, India has succeeded in becoming a nuclear power with astonishingly little adverse comment. India seems to have "pulled it off" at very little, if any, cost in terms of world opinion.

The Nth-Country Problem Again

Talk of the "Nth-country problem" had gone out of fashion in the decade that had passed since China exploded her first nuclear device in 1964. After all, it was argued, France (which went nuclear in 1960) and China were great powers—if not as great as the two superpowers, then at least in the class of the United Kingdom. And in any case, all five—and only these five—were permanent members of the Security Council and, as such, were given a special status under the U.N. Charter. While Japan and West Germany were also great powers, they were special cases, as defeated enemy powers in World War II. Canada, Italy, and Sweden were highly developed near-nuclear countries who could easily go nuclear but had no desire to do so if the nuclear club was restricted to five members, and Canada and Italy had no need to do so since, like Japan and West Germany, they were protected by the U.S. nuclear umbrella. As for the rest of the world, while there were several countries with the potential of going nuclear, in particular India and Israel, it was thought that they were either too poor or too small, and they faced no serious immediate threat from their neighbors such as might impel them to undertake crash programs to become nuclear-weapon states.

In the heady atmosphere of 1968, when, because of the tacit alliance between the nuclear-weapon states and the least developed of the non-nuclear-weapon states, the Non-Proliferation Treaty was commended by the United Nations by the remarkable vote of 95 in favor, 4 against, and 21 abstentions, it was felt that the danger of nuclear proliferation had been put to rest. It was thought that the momentum of a tidal wave of signatures would carry along some of the reluctant non-nuclear-weapon states and that the others would not dare to flout the opinion of the overwhelming majority of the nations of the world. France announced that, although she would not sign the treaty, she would behave exactly as if she had done so, and China was considered relatively unimportant and isolated. (In fact, China, while publicly supporting the idea of proliferation to third-world countries, believes that they must acquire nuclear capability independently through self-help and is the only nuclear power that has not provided any kind of assistance, military or peaceful, to other countries.) The Soviet Union was most pleased that West Germany and all the NATO countries had agreed to sign the treaty.

With the announcement, on the day the treaty was opened for signature (July 1, 1968), that the U.S.S.R. and U.S. had agreed to begin the SALT negotiations, it was felt that the world was finally on the road toward control of the nuclear arms race and that the genie had been pushed back into the bottle.

Within four years of the entry into force of the NPT, the fanfare and the high hopes had all but vanished. And this happened despite the settlement of the Berlin problem, the admission of China and the two Germanys into the United Nations, the withdrawal of American forces from Vietnam, the 1972 SALT agreements at the Moscow Summit Conference, and the beginnings of détente.

The developing non-nuclear-weapon states, on the whole, felt that they had been cheated. They had received very little in the way of assistance with regard to the peaceful uses of nuclear energy (as was pledged under Article IV of the treaty), in particular in the area in which they were most interested—nuclear reactors for the production of power. On the other hand, some more advanced countries such as Italy, Japan, and West Germany that were not parties to the treaty seemed to be treated better by the nuclear powers in this respect and in obtaining supplies of fissionable material than were parties, even though this made a mockery of the NPT. Irrespective of the utility or practicality of peaceful nuclear explosions, no negotiations had been started to set up an international regime to make such explosions available to non-nuclear-weapon states, as was pledged under Article V of the treaty. And, most disappointing of all, the nuclear arms race was going full speed ahead. France and China continued to test in the atmosphere, the U.S. and the U.S.S.R. had not halted underground tests but were conducting them at a greater rate than before the NPT, and the Seabed Treaty and the SALT agreements had the appearance of having been concluded more for cosmetic reasons than as real arms control measures. In fact, as indicated in Chapter 14, the SALT agreements, far from slowing down the nuclear arms race, or even putting any significant limitation on it, seemed merely to institutionalize that race and regulate its continuance: they are in the nature of blueprints for perpetuating the nuclear arms race between the two superpowers. On any showing, despite the pledges made in the NPT, the nuclear arms race was proceeding apace, particularly in its technological and qualitative aspects, and the economic, technological and military gaps between the nuclear and non-nuclear powers were steadily widening.

It is no good telling the non-nuclear powers that their security will be diminished if they go nuclear (which is, no doubt, true), as the same argument also applies to the nuclear powers, yet it neither prevented them from going nuclear nor persuaded them to stop the nuclear arms race in accordance with their promises. In addition, the so-called security assurances to the non-nuclear-weapon states made through the declarations of the nuclear-weapon states in the Security Council in June 1968, after the approval of the NPT by the General Assembly, came to be regarded by the non-nuclear powers as having practically no meaning or significance.

In these circumstances, it is not surprising that even before the Indian nuclear explosion, the NPT had lost a great deal of its credibility and force. The pent-up disappointments and frustrations of a number of non-nuclear-weapon powers may have found a psychological release in India's having breached the walls of the exclusive big-power club.

The Indian explosion also came at a time of a sudden upsurge of interest in nuclear power as a source of energy. The energy crisis and the quadrupling of the price of oil have stimulated the search for alternative sources of energy and have made nuclear power much more economically attractive than it was before. There now appears to be a sort of commercial competition among a number of countries in the Western world to sell reactors, fissionable material, and nuclear equipment. Sales to Argentina, Brazil, Egypt, Israel, India, Indonesia, Iran, and South Korea are merely the most publicized ones.

While it may take a year or two before another country explodes a nuclear device, and several years for some of the other potential nuclear powers to do so, there are more than a dozen countries that can, if they so choose, go nuclear during the next five years, and another one or two dozen that can within the following five years. While very few of these countries have their own chemical separation plants for reprocessing the spent fuel from reactors into fissionable plutonium, such plants can be bought or built without much difficulty. It has been estimated that a reprocessing plant capable of producing enough plutonium for 2 or 3 bombs or explosive devices a year can be built in a year by any reasonably advanced country at a cost of 1 to 3 million dollars. Even if the cost has been underestimated, it is clear that the amount of money involved is not large.

There would appear to be a sort of "domino theory" that seems to have greater applicability to countries going nuclear than to countries falling to a political ideology. Whether it be regarded as the Nth-country problem or as a sort of chain reaction, the fact is that each time a country goes nuclear, it increases the incentives or pressures for its neighbors and other similarly situated countries to do so. Few doubted that, once the Soviet Union joined the United States as a member of the nuclear club, all the great powers would do likewise. So long as there was a sort of "firebreak" separating the great powers, who were permanent members of the Security Council, from all other powers, there was a chance of holding the line against the further horizontal proliferation of nuclear weapons. But once membership in the club is acquired by a middle or smaller power, there is little reason for other middle or smaller powers to refrain from going nuclear. On the contrary, the logic of power would definitely militate in favor of their also going nuclear, whether for security, prestige, or economic reasons.

Now that India has gone nuclear, it is almost inconceivable that Pakistan will refrain from doing so. It won't be necessary for the people of Pakistan to "eat grass" in order for Pakistan to keep up with India in the nuclear field; even without outside assistance, Pakistan can develop its own nuclear explosive device within a few years—around five by most estimates.

If Pakistan goes nuclear, where can a new line be drawn? What new "firebreak" can be postulated or invented to keep Indonesia or Iran from going nuclear?

Even apart from Pakistan, the Indian explosion can provide an excuse for any near-nuclear country in any part of the world to explode a nuclear device for peaceful purposes. And as we discuss in Chapter 17, there are a number of near-nuclear countries which, like India, are not parties to the NPT and which are capable of going nuclear at any time of their own choosing—in a matter of months, not years.

As was indicated earlier, the countries that have not signed the NPT are the most likely candidates to go nuclear. They refrained from signing the treaty precisely because, for one reason or another, they wished to keep their options open. The fact that India has now dared to go nuclear, with overwhelming domestic approval and relatively little international disapproval, may very well encourage other countries to do so, or at the very least weaken those elements in such countries who oppose their going nuclear. The delays in ratification by countries that have signed, but not yet become parties to, the NPT are an indication of a desire on their part to move slowly in this field. Each of these countries has its eyes on the others, and what any one does may depend on what others do.

No country wishes to be left in a position of perceived relative inferiority to others. If one other country should go nuclear, it would be difficult to keep the dam from bursting. As was stated earlier, a chain reaction could easily develop and even some countries that had ratified the treaty might withdraw on three months' notice. As one country after another went nuclear, it would not take long for some parties to give notice of withdrawal and thus mark the inglorious end of the noble attempt to prevent the spread of nuclear weapons.

Unless some very dramatic action is taken by the nuclear powers, in particular by the two superpowers, to demonstrate their renewed dedication to the idea of non-proliferation and to restore the damaged credibility of the NPT, the outook for the non-proliferation regime is bleak.

Chapter 17. The Danger of Proliferation to Additional States

The Near-Nuclear and Potential Nuclear Powers

Previous chapters have dealt with the special concerns of non-nuclear powers who wanted to keep their options open and had therefore not signed the NPT (Chapter 7) and the various motivations that might impel a state to go nuclear (Chapters 14 and 16). In this chapter, we shall discuss the capabilities of various non-nuclear states to go nuclear and the implications of their doing so.

As we indicated previously, the dangers of the further proliferation of nuclear weapons arise, not so much from the inadequacy of the safeguards system, as from the fact that a number of near-nuclear or potential nuclear powers want to keep their options open and have either not signed or not ratified the NPT. The first group includes six countries—Argentina, Brazil, Israel, Pakistan, South Africa, and Spain—all of which have or will soon have the capability of producing nuclear explosive devices and none of which has signed the NPT. In addition to these nonsignatory states, there is a second group of states that can also "go nuclear" which have signed but not yet ratified the NPT. Among these states are the near-nuclear states, Japan and Switzerland, and such potential nuclear countries as Indonesia and Egypt, which are on their way to acquiring nuclear facilities and technology. Finally, there are the near-nuclear powers that are parties to the NPT, such as Canada, Sweden, the Euratom countries, East Germany, Czechoslovakia, and Taiwan, which already have highly developed nuclear facilities and technology and have the capability to go nuclear in the near future if they decide to do so, and countries such as Australia, Norway, Yugoslavia, Iran and South Korea which are well on their way to acquiring a similar capability. If any of these countries should ever regard it as in its vital interests to do so, it could withdraw from the NPT on three months' notice.

A number of other countries will, in the course of the next decade, acquire the nuclear technology and facilities that will give them the trained personnel and the capability of manufacturing nuclear explosive devices. The previous paragraph lists the near and potential nuclear powers on the basis of whether or not they are parties to the NPT. Table 17–1 shows near-nuclear and potential nuclear powers in three categories depending on their capabilities and on the estimated time required for them to go nuclear if they decide to do so.

Categories I and II comprise the "near-nuclear powers." Those listed in category I could go nuclear within a year or two, some of them in a matter of months. Those listed in category II could go nuclear in 2 to 5 years. Category III contains the "potential nuclear powers"—those that could go nuclear in 5 to 10 years. A country could move from a lower to a higher category if it developed its peaceful nuclear capability with sufficient vigor.

Other countries, particularly those that are oil-rich, might also be included in category III, since they will have the wealth and may have the incentive to purchase or otherwise acquire a capability in nuclear technology. Only those are listed, however, that have already acquired some expertise in peaceful nuclear technology or are on the way to doing so.

Countries that are parties to the NPT are marked "P." Those that have signed but not ratified the NPT are marked "S."

TABLE 17–1. Near–Nuclear and Potential Nuclear Powers

I (States able to go nuclear within one or two years)	II (States able to go nuclear within five years)	III (States able to go nuclear within ten years)
1. Argentina	1. Australia (P)	1. Austria (P)
2. Canada (P)	2. Belgium (P)	2. Brazil
3. West Germany (P)	3. Czechoslovakia (P)	3. Bulgaria (P)
4. Israel	4. East Germany (P)	4. Chile
5. Italy (P)	5. Netherlands (P)	5. Cuba
6. Japan (S)	6. Pakistan	6. Denmark (P)
7. South Africa	7. Spain	7. Egypt (S)
8. Sweden (P)	8. Switzerland (S)	8. Finland (P)
9. Taiwan (P)		9. Hungary (P)
		10. Indonesia (S)
		11. Iran (P)
		12. Korea (South) (P)
		13. Libya (P)
		14. Mexico (P)
		15. Norway (P)
		16. Philippines (P)
		17. Poland (P)
		18. Romania (P)
		19. Thailand (P)
		20. Turkey (S)
		21. Venezuela (S)
		22. Yugoslavia (P)

It must be emphasized that merely having the capability of going nuclear is no indication whatsoever that a country has any intention of doing so or is even considering the possibility. In fact, if a country has signed and ratified the NPT, that is the clearest possible indication that it does not intend to go nuclear. As for the non-parties, the most that can be said is that their refusal to adhere to the treaty is not in itself evidence that they have any intention of going nuclear. They may do so, and, again, they may not.

Whether any given country decides to use its capability and to acquire nuclear weapons depends on how that country views its needs and interests in the context of the military, political, economic, and moral climate of the world.

All of the above-named countries have different situations as regards their security, their strategic and political problems, their economic position, and the weight which they attach to matters of status and prestige, and these specific factors will profoundly influence their attitudes towards going nuclear. In general, however, it can be said that, apart from some abnormal or acute circumstance, if the Non-Proliferation Treaty and regime are strengthened and become accepted norms of international behavior and morality, it is likely that most if not all of the above countries will either join the NPT or, at least, continue to abide by its basic objectives and refrain from going nuclear. On the other hand, however, if the treaty and regime are further weakened and eroded, it is likely that a growing number of the above-mentioned states—and not one of them can be excluded—may feel constrained to convert their technological capability into military form, either by the manufacture or acquisition of nuclear weapons or, what is more likely, by exploding a nuclear device for allegedly peaceful purposes.

We cannot exclude the happy possibility that, during the next decade, no country will decide to go nuclear. It is much more likely, however, that a few will do so. It is also possible that many will.

Countries That Have Not Signed the NPT

The most obvious candidate to join the club of nuclear powers is *Pakistan*, which has announced its intention to keep abreast of India. Pakistan also has a nuclear power reactor, fueled by natural uranium, supplied by Canada. Unless Pakistan is helped by China or some other power, however, it may take several years before it acquires a plutonium reprocessing plant and is ready to undertake testing. According to some estimates, it will take Pakistan about five years to go nuclear. It is noteworthy that Pakistan is not a party to either the 1963 Partial Test Ban Treaty or the NPT and thus need have no *legal* inhibitions about testing, even in the atmosphere.

Argentina, like Pakistan, is also not a party to either the PTBT or the

NPT. Nor is it a party to the Treaty of Tlatelolco, which it signed but did not ratify. At the time of its signature it stated that the treaty permitted parties to conduct their own peaceful nuclear explosions. Thus there are no legal restraints against Argentina's conducting any kind of nuclear test. In addition to having several nuclear reactors (under IAEA safeguards), Argentina is negotiating with Canada to buy one or more Canadian reactors which can use Argentine natural uranium. It is also one of the few countries that has a pilot plutonium reprocessing plant as well as a fuel fabricating plant, and it is in the process of acquiring, with French assistance, a larger reprocessing plant. Thus Argentina is in a position to produce its own plutonium and explode a nuclear device whenever it so decides. Argentina has also recently entered into a nuclear cooperation agreement with India. An important restraint on Argentina's going nuclear is that this might tend to speed up Brazil's also doing so. Unless Argentina thinks that it can stay ahead of Brazil indefinitely in any nuclear arms race—a not very likely possibility—there would be little reason for Argentina to initiate such a race. On the other hand, it is extremely difficult to evaluate the nature and importance of domestic factors in Argentina, along with such considerations as status and prestige

Brazil is considerably behind Argentina in nuclear technology but has embarked on a large-scale program that will make it self-sufficient in the entire nuclear fuel cycle. In June 1975, Brazil signed a multibillion-dollar contract with West Germany to acquire a uranium enrichment plant using the Becker jet-nozzle process; a fuel fabrication plant; several large power reactors; and a plutonium reprocessing plant. This program, when completed in the 1980s, will catapult Brazil into a leading position in the field of nuclear technology and enable it to go nuclear at will. (It has plans to build several power reactors in the next two decades.) Brazil regards itself as an emerging great power and expects to achieve that status by the end of the century. It has always upheld its right to conduct peaceful nuclear explosions and claims that they are necessary in order to undertake essential large engineering projects; like Argentina, Brazil maintains that the Treaty of Tlatelolco gives it the right to do so. Although Brazil is a party to the Test Ban Treaty, it is not bound by either the NPT or the Treaty of Tlatelolco. The example of India's nuclear test has, if anything, stimulated Brazil's interest in peaceful nuclear explosions.

If either Argentina or Brazil should go nuclear, it is likely that *Chile* and *Venezuela* might also decide to do so. The latter should be able to acquire all the nuclear technology it requires from its large oil income.

South Africa, in addition to having several nuclear reactors (under IAEA safeguards), is one of the largest producers of uranium. Moreover, South Africa has announced that it has a new, secret process for enriching uranium, in which case it can explode a uranium device without waiting to acquire a plutonium device. The vice-president of the Atomic Energy Board stated after the Indian explosion that South Africa had the capability of making a bomb and was more technologically advanced in the nuclear field than India. He stressed that South Africa would use its available uranium and nuclear know-how only for peaceful purposes (whatever that may now mean). Apart from security considerations, South Africa may have additional incentives to go nuclear. If it has, in fact, invented a new process for enriching uranium, it will wish to find commercial markets for the sale of its enriched uranium; it has recently entered into a nuclear cooperation agreement with France providing for the sale of uranium to that country and is also negotiating with West Germany. It has been suggested that South Africa may also wish to explode a "peaceful" uranium device of its own to demonstrate the effectiveness of its enrichment process, the quality of its product, and its prowess generally in the field of nuclear technology.

Israel has repeatedly stated that it "will not be the first country to introduce nuclear weapons into the Middle East." Most experts believe that all that Israel needs to make an atomic bomb is to turn the last screw. The French-supplied reactor at Dimona, which is not subject to IAEA safeguards, has, since 1964, had the capacity to produce sufficient plutonium to manufacture one bomb a year. It is not known, however, whether Israel has a plutonium reprocessing plant. While Israel does have a very grave security problem, many observers believe that it has a tacit agreement with the United States not to go nuclear, in exchange for an American commitment to provide all the conventional armaments that it may need to defend itself against Arab attack. Nevertheless, Israel certainly has the technological capability, and it is widely believed that Israel may have several unassembled or untested nuclear weapons which it might use in an extreme situation if the survival of its cities and people were in jeopardy. In December 1974, President Katzir of Israel stated in reference to nuclear weapons, "If we need them, we will have them." In the summer of 1975 there were a number of press reports from Boston stating that Israel had 10 or 12 nuclear bombs. At a press conference in Denmark, Prime Minister Rabin denied the reports and stated that Israel did not possess any nuclear weapons, a statement that was repeated in New York by Deputy Prime Minister Yigal Allon in October 1975.

While the present uneasy truce continues, there is no need or reason for Israel to go nuclear, but if the negotiations should break down or an acute threat should suddenly arise, it is possible that Israel might wish to deter an Arab attack by demonstrating her nuclear capability by exploding a nuclear device for peaceful purposes. The Indian test explosion will certainly make it easier for those persons in Israel who support such action to argue in its favor.

Egypt has signed the NPT but has not ratified it and has announced that it will not do so unless Israel does. Egypt is clearly behind Israel in nuclear technology, and stories have circulated in the diplomatic world for years that Egypt has asked India and other countries to help it acquire nuclear weapons or nuclear-weapons capability, but without success. The agreement in June 1974 by President Nixon to provide a 600-megawatt nuclear power reactor to both Egypt and Israel has raised serious questions. Such a reactor could produce enough plutonium to make more than ten 15-to-20–kiloton nuclear bombs or devices each year. No matter what safeguards are written into the agreement, including placing the reactor under IAEA safeguards and returning the spent fuel to the United States for reprocessing, it is always possible for a country wishing to do so to evade its commitments or abrogate an agreement. This has led to various suggestions, such as delaying the implementation of the agreement until there is peace between Israel and Egypt, building one 1,200-megawatt reactor that would be jointly operated by Israelis and Egyptians for the benefit of both countries, and a host of less radical suggestions to ensure that any plutonium produced would not be used for an explosion of any kind. In answer to those who entirely oppose the supply or sale of nuclear reactors to Egypt and Israel, American officials say that if the U.S. does not go ahead, then France or some other country will do so and will probably not insist on as strict safeguards as will the U.S. Because of Israel's opposition to placing all of her fissionable material under international or American safeguards and inspection, the future of the agreement to supply a reactor to Egypt as well as to Israel is unclear. In any case, Egypt is negotiating to obtain a large power reactor from France.

Spain has not signed the NPT and has drawn attention to the treaty's discriminatory character and to its own security situation. It is the only large country in Western Europe that is not a member of NATO, although it does have various defense agreements with the United States and is presumably under the U.S. nuclear umbrella. It is advanced in nuclear technology; it has uranium resources, several nuclear reactors, and a pilot plutonium reprocessing plant, which would enable it to acquire a nuclear explosive capability if it so chooses.

Countries That Have Signed but Not Ratified the NPT

Two countries in this category are near-nuclear powers—Japan and Switzerland. In addition there are several potential nuclear powers, such as Indonesia and Turkey, all of whom have nuclear research reactors in operation and have power reactors either under construction or planned.

Japan not only has a highy developed nuclear technology but also has a reprocessing plant and thus can go nuclear whenever it wishes, if it decides to do so. Public opinion in Japan is overwhelmingly opposed to all forms of nuclear tests and weaponry because of the holocausts of Hiroshima and Nagasaki, and Japanese government officials—the latest being Foreign Minister Toshio Kimura, who announced it in the U.N. General Assembly in September 1974—have repeatedly stated that Japan is preparing to ratify the NPT. Nevertheless, the decision to do so has been repeatedly postponed for one reason or another. There is a considerable division of opinion in the Japanese Diet over the question of NPT ratification, with elements on both the Left and the Right opposed. If Japan follows its traditional practice of making decisions by consensus, it is not likely that the ratification decision will be made soon.

Previously, on March 20, 1973, Prime Minister Kakhai Tanaka had said that the provisions of Japan's constitution, which limited it to forces only for self-defense, did not prohibit Japan from having nuclear weapons for self-defense, but that Japan had no intention of acquiring any. Rather surprisingly, there have been occasions recently at which some Chinese nuclear experts have privately urged that Japan go nuclear. There appear to be growing tendencies in Japan to delay ratification until the future of the NPT is clarified, and these tendencies seem to have been strengthened by the Indian explosion. Whether Japan ratifies the NPT or not, however, it is unlikely that it will exercise the option to go nuclear at any time within the foreseeable future. As the country with the third highest gross national product, Japan aspires to become a permanent member of the U.N. Security Council and to play a political role in international affairs more commensurate with its economic role. Some observers believe that Japan's decision to adhere to the NPT may be linked in some degree to its aspirations in that regard.

Switzerland also has a highly developed nuclear technology. A great debate took place in Switzerland before it signed the NPT as to whether it should do so or not. Both because of its policy of neutrality and because of the nature of its industrialized economy, Switzerland appears to be reluctant to foreclose its nuclear options. Even after the Euratom countries ratified the NPT, Switzerland continued to maintain its independent attitude. At the NPT Review Conference, it registered its strong discontent at the failure of the nuclear powers to live up to their obligations under the treaty.

Indonesia has a research reactor and appears to be in the process of acquiring some power reactors, which should not be difficult in light of its rapidly growing oil revenues. Following the Indian explosion, there were public statements in Indonesia calling on it to go nuclear. Any such possibility, however, is not likely to occur for some years.

Turkey, too, has a research reactor and also has considerable uranium resources. Following the cutoff of U.S. aid after the Cyprus hostilities, government officials announced that Turkey intended to acquire a nuclear weapons capability.

Potential Nuclear Powers That Are Parties to the NPT

Canada and *Sweden* are examples of countries that have had the capability for a number of years to go nuclear, but have unilaterally decided that it is not in their interest to do so. Other countries with highly developed nuclear technologies are *Australia, Norway,* and *Taiwan.* Taiwan also has a pilot reprocessing plant and thus can quite easily exercise the nuclear option if it chooses. After some press reports in the summer of 1975 that Taiwan was capable of going nuclear and might be planning to do so, several government officials publicly denied that Taiwan planned to go nuclear and stressed that all of its technology was for peaceful purposes only and was under IAEA safeguards. Taiwan was, however, expelled from the IAEA, and it does have a grave security problem with respect to China.

Iran, which now has only a research reactor, is somewhat further down the line, but after the oil price increase and the Indian explosion it embarked on a program to acquire more than a dozen large power reactors. It has entered into agreements with the United States, France, and West Germany to purchase several power reactors and in 1974 was also contemplating the purchase of a Canadian reactor. In addition, it has an agreement with the United States whereby the latter will undertake enrichment services for Iranian uranium and it has agreed to participate in building a large enrichment plant in France. It is also negotiating to acquire plutonium reprocessing facilities. With its rapidly increasing wealth from oil, Iran can readily acquire a potential nuclear capability, and there are some elements in the country that are urging it to do so. Iran also envisages itself as a great power by the end of the century. It has always had special security problems because of its geographical position, and now it has three nuclear powers—the Soviet Union, China, and India—as bordering states or near neighbors. At various times in the last few years there have been reports that Iran intended to go nuclear when it acquired the capability to do so, but this has been officially denied. However, the Shah of Iran stated in September 1975 in a press interview with the *New York Times:* "I am not really thinking of nuclear arms. But if 20 or 30 ridiculous little countries are going to develop nuclear weapons, then I may have to revise my policies. Even Libya is talking about trying to manufacture atomic weapons."

Yugoslavia has both research and power reactors and is rapidly acquiring considerable expertise in nuclear technology. It also has a continuing security problem, both internally and externally. It is one of the leaders of the nonaligned powers, and it is a Communist country trying to follow an independent line in foreign affairs. Although it was, at first, one of the strongest supporters of the NPT, it has become disillusioned by the failure of the superpowers to live up to their NPT obligations. At the NPT Review Conference, it announced that it would "reexamine" its attitude toward the treaty.

South Korea also has research reactors and is building power reactors. It is in the process of purchasing a natural uranium reactor from Canada and a plutonium reprocessing plant from France. South Korea has a special security problem because of its relations with North Korea and thus has some inducements to acquire at least the option to go nuclear.

Middle East Countries

Apart from Israel, Egypt, and Iran, no other Middle East country has any potential nuclear capability at the present time. Nevertheless, the combination of the unstable political situation in that part of the world, the Arab–Israeli conflict, and the vast wealth that is being accumulated by the oil-rich countries of the area would seem to make the Middle East an area of particular concern. There have already been diplomatic and press reports of countries in the region (Egypt and Libya, for example) being interested in buying or otherwise acquiring nuclear weapons or nuclear-weapons capability. The Indian explosion will certainly not dampen any such ideas and might even tend to encourage them. In May 1975 it was announced that the Soviet Union had agreed to sell Libya a small nuclear reactor.

In addition to action by governments in the region, there is always the growing danger that dissidents, terrorists, or criminal elements might try to hijack or steal a nuclear weapon or fissionable material either for blackmail or for ransom. This danger will, of course, increase over the years as nuclear power reactors and fissionable materials proliferate in the area and in the world at large. The world has not been conspicuously successful up to now in dealing with Arab hijacking and blackmail involving infinitely less dangerous weapons (see Chapter 19).

Warsaw Pact Countries

All of the Warsaw Pact allies of the Soviet Union have been assisted by the U.S.S.R. to build research reactors, and nearly all of them have power reactors in operation or under construction. *East Germany* and *Czechoslovakia* are the most technologically advanced of these countries. All of them are parties to the NPT. It is clearly in the interest of the Soviet Union that none of them should acquire any nuclear explosive capability, and they are not likely to do so as long as they remain members of the Warsaw Pact and the NPT remains an effective treaty with any legal or moral force.

The Increased Danger Posed by Smaller Nuclear Powers

About the time that France exploded its first atomic bomb in 1960, the French General Pierre Gallois propounded a theory, which came to be known as "the Gallois approach," to the effect that the spread of nuclear weapons to additional countries might not necessarily be a bad thing and might have some advantages. He argued that just as the nuclear super-powers were deterred from waging war, both nuclear and conventional, by the awful destructiveness of nuclear weapons, so, too, would smaller nuclear countries be deterred from attacking each other by a balance of mutual terror. Consequently, the possession of nuclear weapons even by smaller hostile powers might have a mutually deterrent and stabilizing effect.

The Gallois approach, while it still has some supporters, is at variance with that of the overwhelming majority of nuclear strategists and experts. President John F. Kennedy expressed the majority view when he warned in 1963 about the nightmare we would face in the 1970s if there were then not just four but perhaps ten or fifteen nuclear powers. He feared that the genie would be out of the bottle.

The number of countries that have gone nuclear is, as of this writing, less than that feared by President Kennedy, for two reasons: first, the growth of the peaceful nuclear industry and the proliferation of power reactors proceeded at a much slower rate than expected; and second, the idea of non-proliferation was widely accepted in the 1960s. But the risks of proliferation have increased with the sudden surge of interest in nuclear power.

As we pointed out in Chapter 7, in 1966 and '67, when the former Secretary of Defense, James Schlesinger, was a fellow at the Rand Corporation, he took a somewhat different position from Gallois. Although he did not favor the idea of nuclear proliferation, he did not consider that it posed any particular threat to the United States in either the military or political fields. He considered that nuclear weapons were not at all "equalizers," and that any new nuclear powers would be so weak as compared with the truly overwhelming nuclear power of the United States as to pose no unmanageable problems for the United States (or for the U.S.S.R.). He stated in 1967: "While admittedly little good can be expected from acquisition (of nuclear forces), happily such acquisition need not lead to disaster. The consequences of further proliferation remain controllable."

The problem is not, however, as simple as General Gallois or Mr. Schlesinger would have us believe. If nuclear weapons do spread to a number of smaller countries, the outlook for world survival becomes much more gloomy. It is not, as some of the nuclear-weapon states have sometimes said or hinted, that the middle-sized or smaller powers are less responsible than the two superpowers or the other great powers, or that they would represent a direct threat to the present nuclear powers. The problem arises from the fact that some, at least, of the new nuclear powers may not have the resources or the time to build sophisticated second-strike deterrent forces. They may opt for a small nuclear striking force, not to compete with the great nuclear powers on any scale, but to give them a decisive advantage in their own local region or to increase their security by providing them with a deterrent against attack by a neighbor. (In my opinion, the ultimate result may be to reduce rather than increase their security—as may very well turn out to be the case with India if Pakistan, Indonesia, or Iran should go nuclear.)

The danger is that a small or middle-sized nuclear power that was involved in an acute crisis and that did not have an invulnerable retaliatory capacity might fear that a nuclear neighbor would launch a first strike against it and, in order to prevent that possibility, might decide to launch a preemptive strike first. Since the advantage would lie with whichever country struck first, this would create almost intolerable pressures to be first to use nuclear arms and could set off a completely unnecessary and unwanted nuclear war.

Apart from the danger of the outbreak of such a nuclear war by intention or design, there is the more likely possibility of its occurring as the result of accident, miscalculation, misinterpretation of orders, blackmail, or sheer madness.

There are real dangers of such an "accidental" war even between the great nuclear powers, but the dangers are becoming less because of the "Hot Line" communication links, better command and control, and the development of détente. In a world of nuclear first-strike powers the dangers become infinitely greater. If one were to try to work out all the possible permutations and combinations of the possibilities for such a war, the probability of its happening sooner or later would become almost a certainty.

Whether a local or regional war could occur without involving the great nuclear powers is highly speculative. No one can, of course, foresee how events might develop, and here too an almost infinite number of scenarios are possible. But the important thing is that the risks of an "accidental" nuclear war would become greatly multiplied and the developing situation would become, if not unmanageable, then at least incalculable— that is, incapable of accurate assessment and control. This would result in a form of either Russian or American "nuclear roulette" that would pose almost unimaginable perils of a nuclear holocaust.

Chapter 18. Failure at the NPT Review Conference

Convening the Conference

When the provisions of the Non-Proliferation Treaty were negotiated in 1967 and 1968, the non-nuclear states felt that they were being asked to give up important elements of their sovereignty by signing away their option to go nuclear and by accepting international safeguards to deter any violation of this commitment. These specific and concrete obligations took effect immediately upon the treaty entering into force for these states. On the other hand, the commitments undertaken by the nuclear powers as the *quid pro quo* were merely promises by them to take action in the future—to promote the peaceful uses of nuclear energy, to make the benefits of peaceful nuclear explosions available under a special international regime, to halt nuclear weapons testing and reverse the nuclear arms race, and, by Security Council Resolution 255, to provide security assurances to the nuclear parties to the treaty.

No provision was included in the treaty for creating any organ or body to supervise or report on its implementation. The IAEA safeguards were a means of verifying that the non-nuclear parties were living up to their pledges not to go nuclear, but the treaty contained no means of verifying that the nuclear parties were abiding by *their* pledges.

In order to provide some means of checking up on how the nuclear states were living up to their promises, and in order to give them some leverage in this respect, the non-nuclear states insisted, and the nuclear states reluctantly agreed, that a Review Conference should be held five years after the treaty entered into force. The conference was "to review the operation of this Treaty with a view to assuring that the purposes of the Preamble and the Provisions of the Treaty are being realized." While the text was drafted in diplomatic language, its intent was clear—viz., to ensure that the nuclear powers were fulfilling their commitments.

Since the NPT entered into force on March 5, 1970, the Review Conference was due to take place in 1975. A Preparatory Committee was set up, and it was agreed that the conference would take place in Geneva for four weeks from May 5 to May 30, 1975. The nuclear states and some of their allies used the fact that the conference was to be a gathering only of the parties to the treaty and not a conference of all states or of U.N. members as an additional argument as to why some of the important signatory states should ratify the treaty and become full participants; and the treaty was in fact ratified late in April, on the eve of the conference, by five Euratom countries—West Germany, Italy, the Netherlands, Belgium, and Luxembourg—and by South Korea. During the conference, several other countries, including Libya, became parties either by ratification or by accession. No doubt some of these adherences were hastened in order to facilitate some pending deals; for example, Canada was in the process of negotiating the sale of a nuclear reactor to South Korea, and the Soviet Union was engaged in selling a nuclear reactor and some conventional arms to Libya. All told, during the Review Conference the number of parties to the NPT rose to 96.

The Review Conference was at first hailed as the most important arms control conference since World War II. The participants hoped that the conference would help strengthen the NPT, whose credibility had been shaken by India's nuclear explosion. They also hoped it would help persuade some of the near-nuclear countries that had never joined the treaty to sign up and some of the reluctant signatories to ratify. Despite the renewed impetus given by the accession of some 10 new countries, however, only 57 of the 96 parties to the treaty considered the conference important enough to merit their participation. In addition, one of the parties to the treaty (Iraq) sent an observer. Only one foreign minister (Canada's) put in an appearance, when he came to one meeting to deliver a general statement of Canadian views. Of the 15 countries that had signed but not ratified the treaty, 7—Egypt, Japan, Panama, Switzerland, Trinidad and Tobago, Turkey, and Venezuela—were present, but not Indonesia, a potential nuclear power. Of the 40 countries of the world that had not signed the treaty, 7—Algeria, Argentina, Brazil, Cuba, Israel, South Africa, and Spain—attended as observers, but not Pakistan, which is also a potential nuclear power. All of the seven nonsignatory nations that did attend are near-nuclear or potential nuclear powers. Taiwan, which is a party to the treaty and also a near-nuclear power, but which had been expelled from the United Nations and the International Atomic Energy Agency, was not invited to the conference. China, France, and India, which are nonsignatory nuclear powers, also did not attend, but nobody saw fit to mention their absence.

Some hopes were at first entertained that the presence as observers of the 7 near- and potential nuclear countries that had not signed the NPT indicated the possibility of their awakening interest in it. But as the conference degenerated into a struggle by the non-nuclear parties to extract concrete commitments from the nuclear powers to implement their treaty obligations, and a refusal by the latter to budge, whatever interest the observers might have had in the NPT quickly vanished.

The conference largely repeated the pattern of recent international conferences on such global problems as development, environment, population, food, the law of the sea, energy, and raw materials—that of a confrontation between the "have" and the "have-not" countries. But unlike those other conferences, where the parties were trying to grapple with new problems or new aspects of old problems, at the NPT Review Conference the non-nuclear powers were asking only that the nuclear powers live up to treaty commitments already undertaken by them.

The Approach of the Nuclear Powers

The three nuclear parties—the United States, the Soviet Union and the United Kingdom—held a private meeting in London just before the opening of the Review Conference in order to concert their positions. They had developed no new non-proliferation strategy and agreed only on a minimalist or "stonewalling" approach—to make as few concessions as possible to the anticipated demands of the non-nuclear powers. In their general statements at the beginning of the conference, they reaffirmed their support for the NPT as the best way to prevent the spread of nuclear weapons and called for further ratifications and accessions, but they put forward no new ideas that might provide any incentive for reluctant countries to join.

The basic policy of the nuclear powers was to avoid the so-called "political" issues and concentrate on the "technical" ones, such as more effective safeguards, the export policies of the supplier countries, the physical security of nuclear materials and facilities, the possibility of establishing regional or multinational nuclear fuel cycle centers, and the feasibility of and problems connected with peaceful nuclear explosions. While the solution of all these technical problems is important and would help to guard against the diversion of nuclear material to the manufacture of nuclear explosives, it is clearly far from sufficient by itself to prevent the spread of nuclear weapons. Technical progress alone, without simultaneous progress toward the solution of the essential political problems, cannot achieve the basic goals of non-proliferation.

Even as regards these technical problems, the nuclear powers were not prepared to go sufficiently far.

In the field of safeguards, while they were interested in tightening international controls and improving the IAEA's safeguards system, the three nuclear powers and the other supplier states, such as Canada and West Germany, would not undertake to supply nuclear material and equipment only to non-nuclear states that agreed to place *all* of their nuclear material and activities under IAEA safeguards. By refusing to go that far, they preserved the absurd situation whereby nonparties to the treaty are in a more advantageous position than are parties, since Article III, paragraph 1, of the treaty contains such a requirement for non-nuclear parties. In fact, although the text is ambiguous, some experts maintain that the intention of Article III, paragraph 2, is to extend the same obligation to non-parties. In any case, non-parties, by being given preferential treatment in this regard, are provided with an additional reason for not becoming parties to the NPT. Unless safeguards apply to the entire fuel cycle they leave a loophole large enough to drive a nuclear bomb through. This extraordinarily shortsighted position is due almost entirely to commercial rivalry and the competition for markets. It is likely to facilitate rather than curb the proliferation of nuclear weapons to additional countries.

As regards the improvement of international safeguards and of national measures to ensure the physical security of nuclear materials and facilities, the nuclear powers had no very clear ideas and were content to leave it to the IAEA to work out concrete recommendations.

In connection with the promotion of the peaceful uses of nuclear energy, the nuclear powers supported the idea of regional or multinational nuclear fuel cycle centers. The establishment of such centers, with uranium enrichment and fuel fabrication facilities, plutonium reprocessing plants, and waste management and storage facilities, would provide many advantages. It would remove or at least lessen the temptation of non-nuclear powers to produce or divert enriched uranium and plutonium for military purposes, and thus provide some reassurance to their neighbors; it would be more economical to carry out such operations in a few large-scale regional or multinational centers than in a number of smaller national facilities; and it would reduce the number of plant sites and the amount of nuclear materials in storage and in transit, and thus reduce the problems of safeguarding the nuclear materials and the dangers of theft, hijacking, and sabotage.

Unfortunately, however, the nuclear powers had only the vaguest ideas as to how the non-nuclear countries, particularly those that already had pilot facilities or wanted their own large-scale plants, might be persuaded to agree to regional instead of national fuel fabrication and reprocessing centers. They also had no plans or proposals as to who would pay for the heavy costs of financing and constructing such centers. They were willing to have the IAEA study the matter, but they made no commitments for the practical implementation of such projects. Thus, although the idea has merit and was broadly acceptable, it did not generate much enthusiasm.

On the subject of peaceful nuclear explosions, the views of the two superpowers were somewhat divergent. The United States had doubts about the feasibility and wisdom of conducting such explosions, while the Soviet Union maintained that their feasibility for industrial applications had already been established. The nuclear powers and their allies were agreed, however, that the matter required further study and development, and that the IAEA should play the central role in this whole field and should set up machinery for intergovernmental discussions. They were not prepared, however, as required by Article V of the NPT, to commence immediate negotiations to prepare a special international agreement on this subject.

On all of these technical matters, while there were of course differences of detail between the nuclear powers and their respective non-nuclear allies, the latter, on the whole, supported the approach of the nuclear powers. Only Romania, among all of the NATO and Warsaw Pact powers, refused to go along with its allies and, as we explain later, joined the third world or "Group of 77" developing countries.

The third-world countries were not opposed in principle to dealing more effectively with the technical aspects of non-proliferation or to improving international safeguards. What they were opposed to was the imposition of stronger safeguards on their peaceful nuclear activities and of stricter controls and limitations on their nuclear imports, while the nuclear powers refused to accept such controls and restraints for themselves. They regarded this not merely as perpetuating the discriminatory features of the NPT but as constituting a form of nuclear neocolonialism.

The Approach of the Third-World Non-Nuclear Powers

The developing countries of the third world, who are almost all non-aligned states from Africa, Asia, and Latin America, are also known as the "Group of 77" countries. This group first came together at the United Nations Conference on Trade and Development in the 1960s. Although their number has since risen to over 100, they still retain the appellation "Group of 77." Just as the NATO and Warsaw Pact countries tended to meet together in their respective caucuses in order to exchange views and endeavor to concert their policies, so, too, did the Group of 77 countries. The main difference between this group and the other two is that all the members of the Group of 77 are non-nuclear and none of them is directly under the nuclear umbrella of either superpower; moreover, almost all of them are also developing or "have-not" nations, jealous of their independent sovereignty and nonaligned status and desperately anxious to improve their economic and social conditions.

It is not surprising, therefore, that these non-nuclear powers evinced little interest in the technical aspects of non-proliferation and concentrated instead on the large political issues. Since they felt that they had lived up to their commitments under the NPT and that the nuclear powers had not done so, they put forward a number of specific demands for action by the nuclear powers. The most important were for: (1) an end to underground nuclear tests; (2) a substantial reduction in nuclear arsenals; (3) a pledge not to use or threaten to use nuclear weapons against non-nuclear parties to the NPT; (4) concrete measures of substantial aid to the developing countries in the peaceful uses of nuclear energy; (5) creation of a special international regime for conducting peaceful nuclear explosions; and (6) an undertaking to respect all nuclear-free zones.

The leaders of the Group of 77 countries were Mexico, Nigeria, Romania, and Yugoslavia. They were joined by the Philippines, which was most active in regard to assistance in the peaceful uses of nuclear energy. Ambassador Alfonso Garcia Robles of Mexico, the "father" of the Treaty of Tlatelolco, led the revolt against the hegemony of the superpowers, and was the dominant figure at the conference.

Since the resolutions of the General Assembly calling for an end to nuclear testing by a fixed date and for the establishment of a comprehensive program for disarmament with a fixed timetable had been ignored by the nuclear powers, Garcia Robles tried a novel approach, which linked progress towards an underground test ban and towards substantial reductions of strategic nuclear arsenals with progress in strengthening international security. He proposed two draft Protocols: the first, dealing with underground nuclear weapons tests, was cosponsored by twenty non-nuclear third-world states, and the second, dealing with strategic nuclear arms, was cosponsored by nineteen states. Under Protocol I, the nuclear parties would suspend all underground tests for ten years as soon as the number of NPT parties reached 100, and would extend the moratorium by three years each time 5 more states became parties; the moratorium would become permanent as soon as the other nuclear states agreed to become parties to the NPT. Under Protocol II, the superpowers would reduce the Vladivostok ceilings of 2,400 delivery vehicles and 1,320 MIRVed missiles by 50 percent as soon as the number of NPT parties reached 100, and would carry out further reductions of 10 percent from the respective ceilings of 1,200 and 660 each time 10 more states became parties. The withdrawal clause of the NPT would also apply to these Protocols. Garcia Robles explained that what was important was the new approach to halting and reversing the nuclear arms race and that the number of new accessions in each case and their "quality" (i.e., the specific countries, taking into account their nuclear capabilities) could be negotiated.

The nuclear powers explicitly rejected this new approach, as they did the idea of fixed timetables, as being artificial and because they did not want to tie their hands in advance. They put forward no new ideas or counter-proposals but contended themselves with extolling the virtues of the SALT agreements, the Threshold Test Ban Treaty, and the Vladivostok agreement, although most of the non-nuclear states regard these agreements merely as providing programs and timetables for the continued vertical proliferation of nuclear weapons under agreed-upon terms and conditions. The two superpowers considered the SALT negotiations as their exclusive preserve, and the Soviet Union even warned the non-nuclear powers not to meddle in those negotiations.

The problem of security assurances affects almost all non-nuclear countries and not merely those of the third world. Concern about their security is the overriding reason why some of the near-nuclear and potential nuclear powers have not become parties to the NPT. Yet no nuclear state and none of the NATO or Warsaw Pact allies of the nuclear powers (except Romania and such American allies as Australia, Iran, Japan, and New Zealand) supported more effective security assurances for non-nuclear parties. The nuclear powers even praised Security Council Resolution 255, which is intended to provide security assurances to the non-nuclear powers, even though the latter consider it worthless.

Romania took the lead on the question of security assurances and, together with ten third-world states, proposed Protocol III. This draft Protocol provided for an undertaking by the nuclear powers (a) not to use or threaten to use nuclear weapons against non-nuclear parties to the NPT whose territories were free from nuclear weapons, (b) to refrain from the first use of nuclear weapons against any other non-nuclear parties, (c) to encourage negotiations to establish nuclear-free zones and to respect any zones established, and (d) to provide immediate assistance, without prejudice to their obligations under the U.N. Charter, to any non-nuclear party threatened or attacked with nuclear weapons, at the request of the victim of such threat or attack. This Protocol, like the other two, was to be subject to the withdrawal clause of the NPT.

The nuclear powers completely rejected Protocol III, as they had Protocols I and II. It was not very surprising that the United States rejected this negative form of security assurance, as it had always opposed any pledge of nonuse or non-first-use of nuclear weapons. What was astonishing was that the Soviet Union which had always supported such pledges, no longer did so. In fact, it appeared to have abandoned the Kosygin Formula, which it had proposed during the negotiation of the NPT, which called precisely for an undertaking not to use nuclear weapons against non-nuclear countries that had no nuclear weapons in their territory.

Many of the non-nuclear powers, especially those that were not under the nuclear umbrella of either superpower, felt particularly bitter about the unwillingness of the nuclear powers to give even such a negative form of security assurance. They felt that only a combination of arrogance and immorality could lead the nuclear powers to insist that the non-nuclear powers forswear the acquisition of nuclear weapons, while they themselves continued to add to their fearful nuclear overkill capacity and at the same time refused to undertake not to use or threaten to use these weapons against non-nuclear parties to the treaty. Ironically, only China and France, which are not parties to the NPT, or to the Security Council resolution on security assurances, are prepared to give such negative security assurances to all non-nuclear states.

On the subject of the peaceful uses of nuclear energy, the Philippine delegate pointed to the paltry sums (a few million dollars a year) devoted to nuclear technical assistance and noted that, if only one percent of the astronomical amounts spent on armaments each year by the developed countries were devoted to providing nuclear grants and loans to the developing countries for power reactors and training, it would amount to more than two billion dollars a year.

The Philippines, together with Mexico, Nigeria, and South Korea, proposed a resolution calling for (a) preferential treatment and concessional terms to be provided to the developing non-nuclear parties in the supply of nuclear material, equipment, and technology, (b) the creation of a Special Fund financed by the nuclear powers (60%) and the developed non-nuclear powers (40%) to provide the developing non-nuclear NPT parties with assistance in the peaceful uses of nuclear energy, including research reactors and fuel, and (c) the creation of a Special Nuclear Fund, financed in the same manner, to provide financing under concessional terms for nuclear projects in the territories of the developing non-nuclear parties.

Neither the nuclear powers nor the developed non-nuclear powers were prepared to lend their support to any of these proposals. The furthest they would go was to agree that in the provision of assistance in the peaceful uses of nuclear energy they would "give weight" to adherence to the NPT by recipient states, and that they would be willing to consider supporting "technically sound" requests for technical assistance submitted to the IAEA by developing parties to the treaty. Needless to say, in light of their previous experience since the conclusion of the NPT in 1968, the refusal of the nuclear powers to give any firm pledges or to consider specific figures for greater aid left the developing countries cold.

As regards peaceful nuclear explosions, Mexico and seven other third-world states proposed a resolution urging the three nuclear powers to initiate immediate consultations with all treaty parties to reach agreement on the date and place for holding a meeting to conclude the basic special international agreement to provide peaceful explosive services, as required by Article V of the NPT. The nuclear powers and their allies were opposed to this approach and wanted the entire matter left to the IAEA. Apart from the fact that this is contrary to both the provisions of the NPT and the undertakings given by the two superpowers in May 1968, before the NPT was approved by the General Assembly, the third-world countries are not as enamored of the IAEA as are the nuclear powers and their allies. The developing countries fear that the IAEA, because of its constitutional structure and the authority and role of its Board of Governors, is dominated by the nuclear powers and that as a result they (the developing countries) have a much weaker voice in the IAEA than they have in the United Nations.

Although the NPT does not itself encourage or facilitate the creation of nuclear-free zones or require powers to support or respect them, the non-nuclear countries now attach more importance to them than they have in the past. Interest in the subject of nuclear-free zones has revived during the last few years, and several new proposals have been presented involving third-world regions. Moreover, these zones are envisioned as a way of obtaining negative security assurances from the nuclear powers.

In addition to the support for such zones expressed in draft Protocol III, Iran proposed a resolution inviting the nuclear powers to cooperate with those states which decide to establish such zones and urging the nuclear powers to undertake never to use or threaten to use nuclear weapons against countries comprising such zones. Even these rather mild and not unreasonable proposals failed to gain the support of the nuclear powers. While the latter indicated their support in principle and in general terms for the concept, as a way to complement the NPT in preventing the spread of nuclear weapons, they hedged their support with reservations and refused to give any specific commitments.

Other proposals met with similar opposition by the nuclear powers. One such was that of Romania for the retrieval, distribution, and analysis of information on armaments and disarmament by the United Nations. A proposal by Yugoslavia to halt the further deployment of nuclear-weapon systems, especially tactical nuclear weapons, on the territories of non-nuclear parties, and for the withdrawal of these weapons, likewise fell on deaf ears.

In fact, there was not a single formal proposal put forward by any third-world country that was accepted by the nuclear powers, or even regarded by them as negotiable.

Deadlock at the Conference

It was agreed by the participants that all decisions of the Review Conference should be taken by consensus and that, if a consensus was impossible, decisions would be made by a two-thirds majority vote. One of the main purposes of the Conference was to try to prevent the emergence of the seventh, eighth, or ninth nuclear powers. Thus, the consensus approach was eminently sound, because, in a conference such as this, any decision arrived at only by a simple majority, even a large one, or indeed by anything short of unanimity or a genuine consensus, would have been an indication of failure.

In any case, no group could command a two-thirds majority. The two superpowers and their allies could muster only some 20 votes and the Group of 77 some 30 votes. Hence any decision would have to be arrived at by consensus or not at all. This meant that the two groups would have to work with, and not against, each other in order to arrive at a real accommodation and achieve an acceptable compromise.

But that was not the way it happened. The nuclear powers were adamant and rejected out of hand and in almost brutal fashion all of the proposals of the Group of 77. They made no counter-proposals and no attempts at compromise. They showed no flexibility whatsoever on the political issues and accused the third-world countries of a "revisionist" or "unrealistic" approach to the NPT.

The Group of 77 countries were willing to negotiate on the political issues. They would also have been willing to accept the additional restraints and controls worked out by the nuclear powers with the developed non-nuclear powers if the nuclear powers had been willing to accept any concrete or binding limitations on their own freedom of action in the nuclear field. But they were determined not to accept compromises on the technical questions unless similar compromise agreements were achieved on the political questions. The nuclear powers, however, were prepared to agree only to a cosmetic and tranquilizing declaration on these issues in which they would merely reaffirm their unfulfilled treaty pledges and promise to try a little harder. This was unacceptable to the developing countries, who felt that they had been deceived by the nuclear powers ever since the NPT was signed in 1968. Thus the conference became deadlocked.

It is almost incredible that the nuclear powers, whose interest in the survival and strengthening of the NPT is at least as great as, and indeed probably far greater than, that of the non-nuclear powers, could have been so insensitive to the legitimate demands of the third-world countries that they live up to their treaty obligations. They were much more rigid and less willing to compromise at this Review Conference than they had been with respect to the demands formulated at the Conference of Non-Nuclear-Weapon States in September 1968. They had at least showed some interest in the outcome of that conference or paid some lip service to the decisions taken there.

Although it can hardly have been their intention, the actions of the two superpowers seemed almost deliberately calculated to anger the third-world countries without heed as to whether this might do damage to the NPT. The actions of the superpowers outside of the conference, in addition to their behavior at the conference, demonstrated that they did not regard the conference as a matter of major interest. The Soviet Union conducted an underground nuclear test on the eve of the conference, and the United States conducted one in the middle of the conference. Also, during the conference American generals and officials publicly reaffirmed their intention to initiate the first use of nucelar weapons if it were necessary to repel an attack launched with conventional arms.

In the end, in an attempt to break the deadlock and save the conference from complete failure, the president of the conference, Inga Thorsson of Sweden, proposed her own draft declaration. It was a bland compromise incorporating the broadly acceptable technical proposals and urging greater efforts by the nuclear powers to carry out all their treaty commitments. It was far too little for the developing non-nuclear powers and somewhat too much for the nuclear powers, but it provided the basis for an artificial consensus. Some of the dissenting third-world countries felt that it would have been better not to agree to the adoption of any declaration and that the publicly acknowledged failure of the conference might serve to shock the nuclear powers into a reassessment of their positions. Others felt that the nuclear powers had no reasons to be complacent over the outcome of the conference and that failure to adopt some form of declaration might be more harmful to the NPT than the adoption of a largely meaningless one.

Actually, the so-called consensus was nonexistent. The Group of 77 countries explicitly stated, in an "interpretative statement" that they insisted be incorporated in the final document of the conference, that they had agreed not to oppose the declaration for two reasons: first, because of their high regard for Mrs. Thorsson; and second, on the basis of the express understanding that they interpreted the relevant provisions of the declaration, in particular those concerning the ending of nuclear testing, the drastic reduction of nuclear arsenals, and security assurances to non-nuclear parties to the NPT, in light of the three Protocols and the other proposals submitted by the third-world countries. By reaffirming that they not only stood by their political proposals but also interpreted the declaration in the light of those proposals, the Group 77 completely negated the consensus agreement on the declaration.

Apart from the fundamental objections to the provisions of the declaration by the Group of 77 countries, a number of other countries, including the two superpowers, expressed formal reservations to it. Yugoslavia stated that the conference had failed to reach a consensus on any substantive issue and that the fault lay with the nuclear powers; it therefore announced that it would "reexamine its attitude" toward the NPT.

Assessment of the Conference

What, if anything, did the conference achieve?

While it is clear that it served to focus attention on both the political and the technical problems of non-proliferation, it did not solve any of them. It did make possible a thorough discussion of the loopholes and shortcomings of the international and national systems of safeguards and control measures and pointed the way to dealing more effectively with them.

In this connection, if the nuclear powers and other supplier states are really serious about improving safeguards and controls on nuclear materials, they can proceed by agreement among themselves either through the IAEA or outside of it, without the backing or support of the NPT Review Conference. This will require the cooperation of all supplier states, including France and South Africa, and the potential supplier states that are not parties to the NPT. But it seems that the supplier states are more interested in sales and profits and are unwilling or unable to make the necessary decisions.

The ineffectiveness of the "suppliers club" and the difficulties facing proposals for regional or multinational nuclear fuel cycle centers were demonstrated by the West German agreement to sell to Brazil a complete nuclear fuel cycle, including uranium enrichment, fuel fabrication, and plutonium reprocessing facilities as well as several nuclear reactors. While representatives of West Germany at the Review Conference were supporting more effective controls and restrictions on sales and exports, other West German officials were busy negotiating the reported $4 billion sale to Brazil, which was signed on June 27, 1975. Although all the facilities are to be placed under the IAEA safeguards and Brazil has agreed not to produce any nuclear explosives for either military or peaceful purposes, Brazil will acquire the technology for building its own unsafeguarded facilities and using its own uranium, if it should wish to make nuclear explosives. If it should decide to do so, there will be no more recourse against Brazil than there was against India.

Perhaps the worst result of the conference is that it developed into a political confrontation between the nuclear powers and the third-world countries that portends serious trouble ahead. The superpowers do not yet seem to understand that they cannot impose their will on the non-nuclear powers and that they need them to make the NPT work. Nor do they seem to recognize that they have the chief responsibility for as well as the major interest in preventing the erosion of the NPT. It is unlikely that the conference will have shocked the nuclear powers sufficiently to make them reassess their position and adopt the policies necessary to save the Non-Proliferation Treaty from oblivion.

It is true that no party has announced its intention to withdraw from the NPT and that nearly all participants in the Review Conference reaffirmed the importance they attach to the treaty. But it is extremely doubtful whether the conference did anything to help the NPT survive. It did nothing that could provide any incentive to the near-nuclear holdouts to give up their option to go nuclear. On the contrary, it could provide arguments and pretexts *for* them to go nuclear. Many of the non-nuclear parties are angry, and it must be remembered that they can withdraw from the NPT on three months' notice. In this connection, the Yugoslav warning is a cause for concern.

Unfortunately, the conference turned out to be merely another in the long series of lost opportunities in the field of arms control.

There may still be time over the next two or three years to save the NPT. If the nuclear powers act quickly and sensibly to live up to all their treaty obligations and to provide credible security assurances to the non-nuclear powers, they might be able to create the incentives necessary to attract new parties to the NPT and to avoid withdrawals by some of the present parties. Unless they do so, there will be little likelihood of another review conference in 1980 and no point in holding one.

Proposals for the Future

A new impetus is necessary to provide credibility and renewed viability to the concept of nuclear non-proliferation, either within or outside the context of the NPT. Such an impetus can be achieved only if a combination of both political and technical measures is put into effect.

The most important, and probably the minimum, political measures are the following:

1. an immediate moratorium by the U.S. and the U.S.S.R. suspending all underground nuclear tests for five years, and the commencement of negotiations to achieve agreement on a permanent ban of such tests;
2. an immediate qualitative "freeze" by the U.S. and the U.S.S.R. on the production of any new nuclear weapons systems or any other new weapons of mass destruction for a period of five years, and the commencement of negotiations for the progressive reduction of the number of existing nuclear weapons on the basis of the now accepted principle of equal security;
3. an immediate joint declaration by the U.S. and the U.S.S.R. not to use or threaten to use nuclear weapons against any non-nuclear state that does not have any nuclear weapons in its territories.

The most important technical measures are the following:

1. a joint declaration by the U.S. and the U.S.S.R. together with as many members of the "suppliers club" as possible, not to provide any nuclear material, equipment, or technology to any non-nuclear country unless the latter undertakes
   (a) to accept IAEA safeguards over *all* its nuclear material and facilities;

    (b) not to conduct any nuclear explosion of any kind, whether for peaceful or military purposes; and

    (c) not to build or operate any uranium enrichment or plutonium reprocessing plant under its national control;

2. a joint declaration by the U.S. and the U.S.S.R. that they would undertake to finance and build regional, multinational, or international plants for uranium enrichment and plutonium reprocessing that would be under U.N. or IAEA supervision and control;

3. a joint declaration by the U.S. and the U.S.S.R. that they would undertake to conduct underground nuclear explosions for peaceful purposes, either *for themselves* or for non-nuclear states, only when authorized to do so by some competent international authority to be established for that purpose, and that they would begin immediate consultations to convene a conference for the creation of a non-discriminatory and equitable special international regime for the conduct of peaceful nuclear explosions;

4. the strengthening of all international and national measures for safeguarding nuclear materials and equipment to prevent their loss, diversion, theft, or hijacking.

The implementation of either list of political or technical measures alone would not be sufficient to attain the desired objective; only the implementation of *both* lists of measures would ensure the success of the non-proliferation regime. There is already a broad basis of general agreement on the technical measures. But agreement on the political measures, which is more difficult to obtain, is needed to create the right political and psychological climate to make the technical measures fully acceptable in practice.

The above lists of political and technical measures do not exhaust the possibilities of what could and should be done to strengthen the non-proliferation regime. They are all related to, but not as numerous or extensive as, the various proposals and suggestions contained in preceding chapters dealing with the various articles of the NPT. For example, Chapter 10 on international safeguards lists nine specific proposals and Chapter 14 lists twelve disarmament proposals. The two above lists are based on the major subjects stressed at the NPT Review Conference, either by the nuclear powers and their allies or by the third-world countries, on which immediate action is essential. They do not conflict with the longer lists of proposed measures contained in other chapters; in fact, they can be regarded as immediate steps that should be taken towards the implementation of longer-range objectives. In a sense they represent a sort of emergency program to save the NPT.

The present proposals, which may seem rather radical and far-reaching, are not unreasonable and *are* possible of achievement. Nothing short of them is likely to be adequate. Either the nuclear powers are serious about trying to prevent the further proliferation of nuclear weapons and are willing to undertake the necessary measures to do so, or they—and the rest of the world—will be condemned to live in a world of many nuclear powers.

One thing is certain. Unless the nuclear powers take effective steps to stop the vertical as well as horizontal proliferation of nuclear weapons, the world will inevitably be faced with the much more fearsome and much less manageable threat of nongovernmental proliferation—the acquisition of nuclear weapons by terrorist and other politically or criminally motivated groups. That could mean the establishment of police states and the disintegration of society as we know it, even without the actual use of nuclear weapons.

Chapter 19. The Danger of Proliferation to Terrorists and Criminals

A Nuclear Black Market

There is nothing in the Non-Proliferation Treaty to prohibit a party to the treaty from making all preparations down to the last step but one for completing or "perfecting" a nuclear weapon or device. The activities of the state in question might or might not attract the attention of the IAEA's inspectors, depending on which of the country's nuclear activities were under IAEA safeguards and on whether the country in question had developed and produced its own supply of unsafeguarded fissionable materials. Even if the safeguarded activities of a country aroused the suspicions or alerted the interest of the IAEA, or of other countries' intelligence services, it would be difficult to prove that the country in question was not merely developing and improving its capability in the various stages of the fuel cycle. A country could, therefore, accumulate a small stock of nearly completed nuclear weapons and then give three months' notice of withdrawal from the treaty. Furthermore, non-parties to the treaty, whether signatories or not, have no legal restraints on them whatsoever, and can go ahead with the manufacture or acquisition of nuclear weapons or other nuclear explosive devices, subject only to whatever political, economic, or moral restraints they operate under or which they fear might be imposed on them by other states.

In order to manufacture its own bomb or peaceful nuclear explosive device, a country must have enriched uranium of weapons grade, plutonium or U233. The more advanced a country is as regards its nuclear power industry and nuclear technology, the easier it is for such a country to make a bomb or explosive device. It must be able either to manufacture or reprocess its own fissionable material or to purchase it from non-parties to the NPT or else to obtain it on a black market, if such should develop in the course of the rapid expansion of nuclear power plants and technology in the world. Even a country that does not yet have a highly de-

259

veloped nuclear technology might arrange to purchase both the requisite nuclear materials and the services of experts in order to fabricate an explosive device.

In the case of the less advanced potential nuclear powers, it is conceivable, given the mushrooming spread of nuclear reactors, nuclear materials, and nuclear technology, that they could arrange to buy a bomb or nuclear explosive device either from some other state that is in possession of such, or from some criminal or terrorist group that has stolen or hijacked a complete bomb or the ingredients for making one. They might even acquire a bomb or its ingredients on a black market such as one can envisage developing over the next decade. There have already been a number of reports of Middle East countries, in particular Egypt and Libya, making efforts to acquire or buy a bomb. Whether these stories are true or not, and there is some substantial evidence indicating that they may be true, it is certainly within the bounds of possibility that some oil-rich state could arrange, either by purchase or otherwise, to acquire a bomb or nuclear explosive device before such a state was in a position to manufacture its own.

At the present time, it is difficult to conceive of any of the six nuclear powers selling a nuclear explosive device to any other country. It is not difficult, however, to visualize various scenarios in which such an eventuality could take place within the next decade, particularly if there are more than six nuclear powers. It is even easier to visualize the emergence of a black market in plutonium in view of the vast quantities of that element that will be available in the future. Several studies have been made on the subject, and a former U.S. AEC commissioner has stated that

> once special nuclear material is successfully stolen in small and possibly economically acceptable quantities, a supply-stimulated market for such illicit material is bound to develop. And such a market can surely be expected to grow once the source of supply has been identified. As the market grows, the number and size of thefts can be expected to grow with it, and I fear such growth would be extremely rapid once it begins. . . . Such theft would quickly lead to serious economic burdens to the industry, and a threat to the national security.

The author has been informed by two persons, nationals of different countries, that within the last few years they have been offered black market plutonium in a European country. The offers were not accepted. The author has no way of proving or disproving the information, but he is well acquainted with both informants and has confidence in their reliability and integrity.

Since both parties and non-parties to the NPT (the former by withdrawing) can, if they choose, arrange to acquire nuclear weapons or devices legally, they would have little need or reason to engage in the clandestine diversion or theft of nuclear materials. The existence of a black market in fissionable material, however, would multiply the chance that a country might be tempted to develop a bomb in secret. It would certainly create a most dangerous new category of risks by making it possible for nongovernmental groups to acquire a nuclear bomb—what we might call "nongovernmental proliferation."

The Danger of Nuclear Theft by Criminals

When the present nuclear powers exploded their first nuclear weapons and began their nuclear activities, their civilian programs were an insignificant or minuscule by-product of their military programs. As a result of the tight military controls imposed over nuclear energy, there was little possibility of diversion of either weapons or nuclear materials. Originally all special material in the United States was owned by the government, but since the mid-1960s it may be owned by private persons and companies. The government has recently proposed that private companies also be able to own and operate uranium enrichment as well as fuel reprocessing plants. Moreover, in the future, civilian nuclear programs will by far exceed the military ones, and it is quite clear that the controls over such civilian programs will be much less strict than in the case of the military ones. This raises the entire question of the physical security of plants and of nuclear materials.

There are a number of ways in which nuclear materials could be stolen. Petty thieves or disgruntled employees could smuggle out small amounts of fissionable material over a period of time for purposes of sale or sabotage. But it would seem highly unlikely that this could be a serious threat for the foreseeable future, since it is not easy for isolated individuals to steal or hide dangerous radioactive material. A much greater threat could arise from organized criminal groups working for financial gain, who could burglarize a plant or hijack a vehicle in transit for the purpose of selling either a complete bomb or the requisite fissionable material to some terrorist group or foreign government, or perhaps even to sell the bomb or material on a black market. While at the present time it would seem that the narcotics trade is an easier and less dangerous area of operations for organized criminal groups, it must be realized that they have in the past engaged in such large-scale and dangerous ventures as international gun running, train and bank robberies, and large-scale smuggling. In any case, when nuclear materials become plentiful, it is not difficult to envisage the development of an active black market such as would attract the attention and interest of such groups.

Politically Motivated Groups and Terrorism

Great as is the threat posed by the spread of nuclear weapons to additional countries by open or secret decision of their governments, there is now growing recognition that the greatest danger of all is that arising from the acquisition of nuclear weapons by fanatical nongovernmental groups or subnational organizations. Extremists, dissidents, and disaffected groups are not limited to Palestinian Arabs, Irish nationalists, "Red Army" groups, African liberation movements, or Asian and Latin American revolutionaries. They are present in practically all countries, whether they are called terrorists, freedom fighters, revolutionaries, or urban guerillas. The U.S. press is full of reports of assassinations, hi-jackings, and kidnappings by disaffected elements. West Germany and Japan have their share of violence-oriented groups, as do France and India. Great Britain has Scottish and Welsh nationalists in addition to Irish ones. Even a stable society such as Canada's has its Quebec nationalists and native Indians, and Switzerland has its Jurassiens. While there are fewer reports of violence by terrorists or dissidents in the Soviet Union or China, there have been such reports from the Communist countries of Eastern Europe. It would be a rash man who would say that the relative absence of violent protest movements in any country is likely to continue indefinitely. In fact, violence and terrorism seem to be increasingly frequent phenomena in modern times.

In 1973, the London-based Institute for the Study of Conflict reported that there were 78 extremist terrorist organizations based in 41 countries. A 1974 study by the United States Atomic Energy Commission identified more than 400 incidents of terrorism by more than 50 well-armed and well-financed international terrorist groups in the preceding six years. The number of acts of national terrorism and violence by small groups is very much greater, but many national groups appear to have international links and to rely on foreign groups and governments for assistance and asylum.

In 1972, a Soviet spokesman at the United Nations remarked:

> Modern terrorists prefer to have rifles and bombs, and tomorrow it's quite possible they will have death-carrying germs or maybe stolen atomic bombs. And with the help of these bombs they can blackmail any government.

In 1974, a report prepared for the AEC about the possibility of theft of nuclear material by a terrorist or criminal group concluded that United States safeguards against such possible theft were "entirely inadequate to meet the threat." The study added:

> These groups are likely to have available to them the sort of technical knowledge needed to use the now widely disseminated instructions for processing fissile materials and for building a nuclear weapon. They are also liable to be able to carry out reasonably sophisticated attacks on installations and transportation.

A highly motivated and determined terrorist group might be willing to incur great risks in order to obtain a bomb or fissionable material which could be used for political blackmail or ransom. Such groups very often act out of desperation and have little or nothing to lose by resorting to violence in order to gain their ends. If they fail, they have nothing to lose but their lives or their freedom, which they tend to regard as worth little in their existing circumstances and therefore as expendable; if they succeed, however, they stand to gain, in their view, the whole world. Hence almost any risks are considered worthwhile. Thus terrorism becomes a form of total warfare, subject to no rules or restraints, that considers its aims to be promoted by acts of terror inflicted indiscriminately on all and sundry, including children and innocent bystanders. In fact, the more shocking the act of terrorism, the more likely it is to gain its objective.

Any form of political blackmail based on violence is a form of aggression, and nuclear blackmail is the worst form. If terrorists with a known record of violence were to announce that they have planted a nuclear bomb in a city and will explode it unless their demands are met, there would be a strong and practically irresistible likelihood, indeed a practical certainty, of their blackmail succeeding. Even if there were a great deal of skepticism about the truth of their claim, the risk of not giving in to them would be too great. Who would dare to call their bluff and risk the tremendous devastation that would result from even a small portable bomb of 15-kiloton size, the size of the Hiroshima bomb? Such a bomb need contain less than 10 kilograms of plutonium and could be easily transported in a small truck. Whole cities and even countries could become hostages to the threat of nuclear destruction unless they paid the political or financial ransom demanded.

Governments have had very little success thus far in coping with blackmail threats of hijackers of planes, kidnappers of individuals, and even bombers using ordinary chemical explosives. It is not difficult to imagine the infinitely greater danger that would arise in the case of nuclear blackmail. Since blackmail always feeds on its successes and raises its demands, it could bring modern society to the very brink of total disintegration if not destruction. It would certainly lead to the establishment of police states and the most drastic control over civilian activities and freedom.

Even a hoax might be successful. There is a well-known case of a 14-year-old high school student in the city of Orlando, Florida, who made an extortion attempt in 1970 by threatening to blow up the town unless one million dollars in cash was paid. The student included with his demand a not very convincing diagram of a nuclear device and said that he had fissionable material stolen from AEC shipments. The ransom money was assembled; but the culprit was caught before it was paid. Fortunately the Orlando case proved to be a hoax. What was most disturbing about the attempt, however, was that the AEC could not assure the city that no nuclear material was missing. The former director of the AEC's Division of Nuclear Materials Safeguards could only say that there was no known displacement or missing shipment, and he added: "There's no way of knowing if a portion of any shipment has been smuggled out."

A similar danger could arise not only from a terrorist group but also from a political faction within a national government. Such a faction might attempt to seize power by persuading the owners or managers of a nuclear facility to transfer or divert some of the material under their control to them. Or the armed forces of a country (or part of them) might be persuaded to participate in a rebellion or plot to either seize nuclear material or perhaps steal or capture one or more complete nuclear weapons. A terrorist group or political faction could steal or hijack some small tactical nuclear weapon from a storage bunker or in transit.

In 1973, a United States Senate report criticized the deficiencies and lax practices involved in the storage of U. S. tactical nuclear weapons in Europe. In 1975, the General Accounting Office reported that the Army and the Navy were transporting nuclear warheads between missile sites in motor convoys that were unsafe and vulnerable to potential terrorist activity. Although steps were taken to remedy the shortcomings in both cases, it is simply not possible to foresee and provide for all contingencies or prevent all human oversight or error. Protection and control of inventories cannot be made perfect, and the risks can be reduced but not entirely eliminated. Neither detection nor protection are perfectable, and yet perfection is the only acceptable standard of control to ensure that terrorists cannot destroy many hundreds of thousands of lives, or renegade governments or factions trigger a nuclear war.

A terrorist group might also seize fissionable material at fuel enrichment and fabrication plants, at reprocessing plants, or from facilities now used for storing large accumulations of plutonium. It would not be beyond the capacity and ingenuity of such groups, judging from some of their past exploits, to hire expert engineers or physicists to help them fashion a crude nuclear weapon. Some students of the problem have noted that plutonium and highly enriched uranium are *less* effectively protected by physical barriers, alarm systems, and armed guards than are large quantities of money or bullion stored in banks or shipped by armored cars—that have themselvs been subject to burglary and hijacking. The most vulnerable area of all is that of transport—that is, when weapons or fissionable material are in the course of transit either within a country or between countries. Fissionable material in transit creates special problems of security that have not been satisfactorily solved.

There are some who assert that the danger of the theft or seizure of nuclear materials or nuclear weapons by rebels or terrorist groups has been highly overstated and is somewhat remote. Nevertheless, there have been several incidents in which such seizures were regarded as distinct possibilities. On April 22, 1961, there began what came to be known as the "Revolt of the Generals" in Algeria; because of fears that these French generals might attempt to seize a nuclear device from the test site in Algeria, the scientists at the site were authorized to explode it so as to remove it from the possibility of seizure, and it was exploded on April 25, earlier than had been planned. In early 1967, during the Cultural

Revolution in China, there were reports that the military commander of Sinkiang Province had threatened to seize the nuclear base there if the Maoists attempted to take over the provincial government. In March 1973, an armed terrorist group attacked and briefly occupied the Atucha nuclear power plant in Argentina.

Hannes Alfven, Swedish Nobel laureate in physics who was president of the Pugwash Conferences on Science and World Affairs, has highlighted the problems and the need for virtually foolproof precautions and security measures:

> Fission energy is safe only if a number of critical devices work as they should, if a number of people in key positions follow all their instructions, if there is no sabotage, no hijacking of the transports, if no reactor fuel processing plant or reprocessing plant or repository anywhere in the world is situated in a region of riots or guerrilla activity, and no revolution or war—even a "conventional one"—takes place in these regions. The enormous quantities of extremely dangerous material must not get into the hands of ignorant people or desperados. No acts of God can be permitted.

The problem is not merely a national or subnational one or one that affects merely international transfers of nuclear material. Rather, it goes to the root of the entire safeguards system, both national and international, and affects its efficacy and credibility. Every country is vulnerable to nuclear terrorism wherever it might take place, and the weakest national link in any safeguards system could affect all other countries. For example, no matter how effective safeguards may be in the United States or Canada, if they are not totally effective in Argentina or France or in one of the Arab countries, for example, then the American and Canadian governments and peoples may find themselves threatened by nuclear materials stolen or hijacked in some other part of the world.

One would have thought that this was one area in which all governments could agree that the problem was a threat to each of them and that they should and would cooperate to prevent the theft of nuclear weapons and materials by terrorists or other politically motivated groups. But this may not necessarily be the case. The Hague Convention, co-sponsored by the U.S. and U.S.S.R. in 1971 to deal with the problem of airplane hijacking, was opposed by Cuba, Algeria, and other Arab states. For several years it has therefore not been possible for the United Nations to take any action to halt or prevent terrorism in the international field. Some governments, in fact, connive at helping terrorists in other countries. The examples that come most readily to mind are the countries of the Middle East and Africa, but these are not by any means the only ones.

Unfortunately, most African and Arab states oppose laws and controls against terrorists as they feel that these may be aimed at, or in any case used against, national liberation groups and movements. But a fundamental distinction must be made between ordinary, conventional terrorism, which is bad enough even if intended for political ends, and nuclear terrorism, which can lead to the most appalling, indeed unthinkable, catastrophes.

Fortunately, the question of aiding politically motivated groups has not yet arisen in connection with nuclear terrorism and blackmail, but it is far from clear that the outcome would be any different from what it has been in the case of conventional terrorism and blackmail.

Making a "Homemade" Bomb

There is some disagreement about just how simple or difficult it is to make an atomic bomb. Many experts regard it as a comparatively simple matter. Mason Willrich and Theodore B. Taylor are two leading experts in the field who state that an atomic bomb can be constructed quite easily. In their book *Nuclear Theft: Risks and Safeguards* (Cambridge, Mass.: Ballinger Publishing Co., 1974) they state that "the design and manufacture of a crude nuclear explosive is no longer a difficult task technically." They go on to say that "if the essential nuclear materials are at hand, it is possible to make an atomic bomb using information that is available in the open literature." They then go on to cite an article in the *Encyclopedia Americana* outlining in detail how to make a fission bomb. And they add,

> Unlike most national governments, a clandestine nuclear bomb maker may care little whether his bombs are heavy, inefficient, and unpredictable. They may serve his purposes so long as they are transportable by automobile and are very likely to explode with a yield equivalent to at least 100 tons of chemical explosive.

The views of Willrich and Taylor seem to be confirmed by a 1974 report to the AEC, which stated that

> Because of the wide-spread dissemination of instructions for processing special nuclear materials and for making simple nuclear weapons, acquisition of special nuclear materials remains the only substantial problem facing groups desiring to have such weapons.

As we indicated earlier, it would not seem to be too difficult for a determined group to obtain the required fissionable material by stealing or hijacking it or perhaps by purchasing it on a black market.

Many people were startled in March 1975 when a television program called "Nova" told how a 20-year-old undergraduate student in chemistry at the Massachusetts Institute of Technology was asked to design a nuclear bomb in his spare time without talking to any experts and using only available, public reference works. In a few weeks the student designed a bomb about the size of a large desk, requiring between 5 and 10 kilograms of plutonium, that would weigh between 500 and 1,000 pounds. This meant that it could easily fit into a small truck. The design was studied by experts who were convinced that it would create a workable bomb of low yield, less than 1 kiloton. The student said that "I have come to feel that designing and building a bomb—assuming you had the plutonium—would not be much harder than building a motorcycle." He thought that starting from scratch and with the assistance of three or four persons, he could build the device in a couple of months.

It is clear that if an undergraduate student could design a workable atomic bomb, then engineers and physicists with more expertise could certainly do so. As Theodore Taylor has stated, the undertaking would not be particularly difficult and the people who could do it number in the many tens of thousands.

Dispersal of Radioactivity and Sabotage of Nuclear Facilities

It is not even necessary to make a homemade atomic bomb, as a plutonium dispersal device is simpler to make than an explosive and could also be effective for blackmail purposes. A plutonium dispersal device would constitute a radiological weapon that could be very effective. Plutonium is amongst the most poisonous substances known. It is about 20,000 times more toxic than cobra venom or potassium cyanide and 1,000 times more toxic than modern nerve gases. An airborne plutonium particle the size of a speck of dust and weighing a total of some 10 millionths of a gram, if inhaled, is likely to cause lung cancer. A few thousandths of a gram of small particles can cause death within a time period of a few weeks to years. One hundred grams (3½ ozs.) could be a deadly risk to everyone working in a large office building or factory if it were effectively dispersed through the ventilating system by an aerosol can or some other dispersing device. A dispersal device could also be made with a delayed timing device. Thus plutonium can be used not only for a nuclear bomb but also as a deadly radiological weapon, although it would probably affect a smaller number of persons than a bomb and its effects would be delayed.

The whole idea sounds like science fiction, but so have some other successful terrorist ventures. It is hardly necessary to point out that in addition to terrorists and other politically motivated groups, there is also the problem of individual and organized criminals, not to speak of madmen. In the 1950s the City of New York was the scene of a number of explosions of homemade conventional bombs by a "mad bomber."

There is also the possibility of sabotaging or threatening to sabotage nuclear power plants or nuclear waste storage facilities to release radioactive material as a threat to populated areas. For example, the inventory of radioactive material in the core of nuclear power stations using enriched uranium or plutonium, if dispersed in the atmosphere upwind of a heavily populated area, could cause many human casualties and widespread land contamination. If a terrorist group seized control of a nuclear power station and blew up the plant with conventional explosives, causing the core to melt, a substantial amount of radioactivity would be released. In similar fashion, waste material in storage could be blown up and radio-activity dispersed. The dangers from such acts of sabotage, however, would be much less than from the effective dispersal of a kilogram or so of plutonium throughout a very large office building, and very much less than from the explosion of a nuclear device in a highly populated area. A crude, low-yield nuclear bomb could immediately kill tens of thousands of people in the business section of a large city, and a megaton nuclear weapon could kill as many as a million or more, not counting the slower deaths from radioactivity.

Possibilities of Theft and Hijacking

As we indicate above, it seems that the greatest threat is posed by terrorists stealing or hijacking a nuclear weapon. Since these weapons are widely dispersed throughout the world, terrorists would aim at the weakest spot and try to seize such a weapon from a place where physical security measures would pose the least risk for them. Because military information on security measures is classified, ordinary laymen and the author can not accurately assess the effectiveness of safeguards for nuclear weapons; presumably, organized terrorist groups might be in a better position to do so. The 1973 U.S. Senate report and the 1975 report of the General Accounting Office revealed a number of shortcomings in the handling of nuclear weapons. No matter what measures were taken to remedy them, the physical protection of such weapons can never attain "zero-risk" proportions.

More likely than a terrorist group's stealing one or more nuclear weapons is the possibility of their stealing weapons-grade fissionable material that can be used to make a bomb. As we have explained, it is not difficult to make a bomb; the problem is to obtain the plutonium or other material necessary to make it explode.

With the rapid proliferation of nuclear power reactors throughout the world, the amount of explosive nuclear material in existence is also growing rapidly—both the amount present in nuclear plants and in transit. It is generally recognized that the material being transported from one place to another is most vulnerable to seizure. A terrorist group might find it relatively easier to steal or hijack the nuclear material for making a bomb from civilian rather than military sources. No matter how difficult the operation may be, it seems obvious that at least some of the well-organized and determined terrorist groups will succeed in seizing the necessary quantities of nuclear explosive material. It is a matter for speculation as to whether improvements in safeguarding techniques and physical protection measures will keep pace with the growing availability of nuclear materials that can be used for making bombs.

Finally, if a black market should develop in plutonium or other weapons-grade fissionable material, the problem of obtaining such material will be reduced largely to a question of monetary cost.

What Can Be Done To Cope with the Problem

It is obvious that drastically improved national and international safety measures to detect, deter and prevent thefts, and to pursue and recover stolen material, must be enacted and enforced in order to begin to cope with the problem of nongovernmental proliferation. It is also obvious that no system can give 100-percent assurance against theft or hijacking of nuclear materials, any more than good police protection and safety regulations can prevent all crime or burglary. The difficulties of the problem are compounded because of the large and constantly increasing quantities of fissionable material that will become available. A greatly improved security system, however, may have an inhibiting or deterrent effect on those who might contemplate the possibility of diversion, theft, or hijacking. In any case, it is generally agreed that nuclear materials should be made as safe and secure as human ingenuity can devise.

As we indicated in Chapter 11, the IAEA, which has no statutory authority in this respect, has assumed an advisory role and has drawn up "Guidelines for the Physical Protection of Nuclear Material against Loss, Theft, etc.," and it has made its recommendations available to interested states. These are being studied and further strengthened. They should be made the subject of a binding international treaty with sanctions against states that violate the treaty, or that give assistance or asylum to nuclear terrorists.

The initial and primary responsibility for the safety of nuclear materials, however, rests with national governments. A government, moreover, has police and regulatory powers which go far beyond any safeguarding authority that has been or is likely to be granted to the IAEA. As a result of the growing concern over the danger of theft and hijacking of nuclear material, a number of useful and practical national studies have been made on how to improve the physical security of the material.

As regards material in a nuclear plant or other facility, there are a number of fairly obvious steps which can be taken to increase its physical security. These include the erection of barriers such as fences and walls, the introduction of electronic alarm systems and closed-circuit television monitoring, the permanent stationing of armed guards, and the establishment of a strict system of clearance and passes for employees and of inspection of vehicles and packages entering or leaving the plant. As regards material in transit, different measures may have to be taken for transport by road, by rail, by sea, and by air, but there are some common measures that could apply to any form of transit. These could include the provision of armed guards and regular two-way radio telecommunication, with reporting to some central point. Arrangements could be made for the material to be transported in heavy containers (for example, over 500 pounds each), so that they could not be moved by one or two men alone. The containers and the vehicles transporting them or the storage areas within such vehicles could be secured by special locks and seals; it could also be arranged that the vehicle make no stops or have a minimum of stops en route. It has been suggested by some students of the problem that trucks might be equipped with special devices that could blow off their tires or axles or disable their engines in order to prevent hijackings.

The United States Atomic Energy Commission was sufficiently impressed with the risks involved that in 1974 it amended its previous regulations in a number of important respects in order to strengthen the requirements for the physical protection of nuclear materials. New provisions included many of the measures mentioned above, so that at the present time, the national security system in effect in the United States is greatly improved and is regarded by some experts as the best in the non-Communist world. Other experts, however, regard the American safety regulations as still inadequate and believe that much more is required to make them fully effective. Some implied recognition of this is contained in an AEC statement at the beginning of January 1975 which said:

> In recognition of the increase in acts of sabotage and terrorism in society today—and the fact that the uses of nuclear materials are growing—the AEC has had a major effort underway to strengthen future procedures for protecting nuclear material in the fuel cycle nuclear power program and transportation.

Unfortunately, little is known about the efforts of other governments to develop and enforce national safety systems to protect nuclear materials in their countries against theft. Very little consideration has been given to this problem on the international level, and there has been an almost total absence of serious discussion about it. Only within the last year or so is the problem beginning to receive the attention it requires.

Early in 1975, Fred Ikle, director of the U.S. Arms Control and Disarmament Agency, publicly proposed the establishment of an international police force to prevent thefts of nuclear materials—a sort of nuclear super-Interpol. Others have suggested the establishment of secret intelligence and counterintelligence systems of a high order as a way to forestall or or cope with potential terrorist activities in this field.

The NPT Review Conference did focus attention on this question; it

(1) urged that the IAEA elaborate further concrete recommendations for the protection of nuclear material in use, storage, and transit; and (2) called on states to enter into international agreements to ensure such protection and to apply the IAEA's recommendations to improve their own protection systems.

A drastic method of lessening the likelihood of violent seizure of plutonium would be to store the spent fuel rods without separating out or reprocessing the plutonium, as is now done in Canada with the spent fuel from their natural uranium reactors. This poses a double problem for any potential hijackers—first, the danger of intense radioactivity from the gamma rays in the various radioactive materials contained in the spent fuel, which makes it too "hot" to handle, and second, the need to undertake the somewhat complicated process of separating out the plutonium at a chemical separation plant. However, given the expected shortage of uranium and the savings in cost from plutonium recycling or the use of fast breeder reactors, it is likely that in the future more, rather than less, plutonium will be reprocessed for reactor fuel.

It would, of course, reduce the danger of theft and hijacking of nuclear material if all of the nationally owned uranium enrichment and plutonium reprocessing plants were replaced by a few large regional nuclear fuel cycle centers. This would reduce the amount of fissionable material in transit and would improve the possibilities for protection both of the plant and of the shipments.

Another possible means that has been suggested for reducing the likelihood of theft or hijacking of nuclear material is to mix or add some radioactive material with a high percentage of gamma rays (e.g., cobalt 60) to the enriched uranium or plutonium used in reactors. Although plutonium, as previously indicated, is one of the most toxic substances known, it is dangerous only when particles are inhaled into the lungs or come into contact with the skin. Its radiation, like that of uranium 235, is not very dangerous as it comes mainly from alpha rays, which have a weak power of penetration and can be stopped by ordinary clothing; it has very weak gamma rays, which are the penetrating and dangerous ones that require thick shielding for protection. Hence, adding other radioactive material high in gamma rays to fuel rods or stocks of enriched uranium fuel and plutonium would have the effect of making them much more dangerous to handle, and would therefore act as some deterrent to violent seizure. This method of preventing or reducing the risk of seizure is still controversial. It has been criticized as being too expensive because of the shielding and other safety measures that would be required to protect the working personnel at the plants and storage facilities.

Other suggestions for improving the security of fissionable material are set out at the end of Chapter 11 on international safeguards. The improvement of the entire system of international safeguards would also help to improve national security systems intended to ensure the safety of fissionable material within states.

Nongovernmental proliferation of nuclear explosive capability by theft, hijacking, or black market purchase, to nongovernmental groups or organizations, which include a broad spectrum of dissidents, extremists, disaffected persons, revolutionaries, and other politically motivated and criminal groups, is the most dangerous form of proliferation. The problem of preventing it or making it improbable is clearly the most intractable problem in the whole field of safeguarding nuclear materials. Yet it is only one facet, albeit the most dangerous one, of coping with the entire problem of terrorism. It is possible that the best approach to a solution to the problem of nuclear theft and attempted blackmail by terrorists lies in treating it as part of the larger, worldwide problem of terrorism. The almost unimaginable dangers posed by the threat of nuclear terrorism and blackmail may be so grave a threat to all governments as to lead them to cooperate in joint or coordinated efforts to stamp out terrorism in general, at least on the international level. Unless that happens, however, the threat of the acquisition of nuclear explosives by terrorists and other nongovernmental groups will remain the least controllable and the most dangerous aspect of the proliferation of nuclear weapons.

Just as terrorist proliferation can perhaps best be dealt with as one aspect of the larger problem of terrorism, so, too, the problem of nongovernmental proliferation in general can most usefully be approached as part of the larger problem of nuclear proliferation.

Fortunately for the world, there has as yet been no proliferation to terrorist groups. But with the increasing proliferation and availability of nuclear weapons, nuclear reactors, and fissionable material around the world, it seems almost inevitable that nuclear explosive capability will spread to nongovernmental groups, including terrorists. Vertical and horizontal nuclear proliferation pose tremendous dangers to the human race, but their risks are to a considerable extent calculable and perhaps even, though to a lesser extent, manageable. But the risk of nongovernmental proliferation to a black market and to terrorists appears to be almost completely incalculable and certainly unmanageable in any meaningful sense of the word.

We might even develop a table of comprehensive degrees of danger: vertical proliferation is bad; horizontal proliferation is worse; nongovernmental proliferation s worst.

Each category of proliferation makes the next one more possible, indeed probable. There is a natural, almost inevitable progression from one to the other. The most effective way to prevent the third and worst category from developing would be to halt the other two and then to begin to reverse both of them. If this were to happen, it might help to reduce the present tendency to magnify and even glorify nuclear weaponry and serve instead to create a political and moral climate wherein nuclear explosives played a much smaller part in the affairs of nations and in human consciousness.

What we must aim at is denuclearization in the case of the nuclear powers, non-proliferation in the case of the non-nuclear powers, and what we might call the "psychological denuclearization" of both.

A planned and concerted effort must be undertaken in order to de-emphasize the importance of nuclear weapons. It may be impossible to prevent nongovernmental proliferation in any case, but the best chance of doing so is by concentrating on building a world society wherein nuclear weapons are relegated to a minor role in human and national conscious-ness as has been done with biological weapons and germ warfare. There are, in fact, a number of similarities between biological weapons and nuclear weapons. Both are horror weapons of mass destruction that dare not to be used because they can present as big a danger to the user as to the victim. There have been very few, if any, attempts to use biological weapons by terrorists. The United States unilaterally decided to foreswear all biological weapons and destroy its stockpiles, and it persuaded the Soviet Union and other countries to conclude an international convention for their complete elimination. I am not proposing that the United States unilaterally give up its nuclear weapons, but it could agree to their non–first use (which it now opposes) and work much harder for balanced, drastic reductions of the present insane nuclear overkill capacity, which is, for all practical purposes, approaching infinity. The United States and the Soviet Union cannot maintain the mad momentum of the nuclear arms race without madmen and martyrs getting into the act.

For several years, in the 1950s and 1960s, efforts were made by a number of people in Great Britain—including influential members of the Labour Party and not merely pacifist and disarmament groups—to per-suade the British government to give up nuclear weapons altogether. At times it seemed that these anti-nuclear forces were making some headway, but their efforts have, unfortunately, almost ceased. Perhaps the terrible dangers of nongovernmental proliferation might help to revive the idea or produce some contemporary pressure groups to succeed the former Committee for Nuclear Disarmament. If one nuclear power would agree to give up its nuclear weapons, that could have a dramatic effect in down-grading and deemphasizing the overpreoccupation with these unusable weapons.

Admittedly, the hopes of finding some way of coping with the risks of nongovernmental proliferation by dealing with the larger problems of both terrorism and proliferation are rather weak reeds to rely on. But there are no strong reeds, and no easy or effective solutions to the problem. Any approaches or measures that might help to postpone the evil day of nongovernmental proliferation or that might help, if only in part, to con-tain it, should not be left untried. A combination of technical, disarmament, political and social measures would provide the best means for dealing with nongovernmental proliferation.

Chapter 20.   Man Is an Endangered Species

The Future Looks Gloomy

The outlook for the future of the NPT, which is the main pillar of the non-proliferation regime, is not promising. And if non-proliferation fails, the prospect for humanity is not promising. The trend of events in the world today is in the direction of further militarization and of vertical, horizontal, and nongovernmental nuclear proliferation. Despite the erosion of the cold war and the beginning of détente; despite the withdrawal of American troops from Vietnam and some softening of the rigid Soviet position on some aspects of human rights, such as the emigration of Jews and other Soviet nationals; despite the Berlin settlement, the admission of the two Germanies to the United Nations, and the seating of the People's Republic of China; despite the achievement of more than a dozen arms control agreements in the last twelve years and the signing of the Helsinki Declaration on security and cooperation in Europe, the arms race is proceeding at full speed in both the nuclear and conventional fields. Global military expenditures continue to escalate, economic rivalry is rife, hunger and poverty are increasing, the population explosion seems beyond control, and tension and insecurity hold sway among nations. A feeling of pessimism and fear, almost of hopelessness, is abroad in the world.

Notwithstanding the increasing evidence and recognition that all nations and all global problems are interdependent, nations, instead of moving toward greater international cooperation, are moving in the direction of promoting their own national self-interest at the expense of other nations and the world community. With these tendencies rampant in the world, the likelihood is not for less but for more militarization. A fearful, selfish, competitive spirit that fosters economic and political nationalism, rather than internationalism and a sense of world community, will also facilitate military nationalism. As a result, instead of non-proliferation and progress towards disarmament, we can look forward to further nuclear proliferation and widespread armament.

There are four "time bombs" threatening human survival and welfare, each linked in some degree to the other. The first, and most dangerous, is the nuclear bomb, with its continuing vertical and horizontal proliferation and the increasing likelihood of its nongovernmental proliferation. The second is the population bomb, with its associated problems of dwindling natural resources, food shortages, and hunger. The third is the poverty bomb, which is evidenced by the widening gap between the rich and the poor nations on the international level and by unemployment, economic dislocation, and human decay on the national level. The fourth is the pollution bomb, which is aggravated both by population growth and by increasing industrialization, and which itself adversely affects the food supply from both land and water. Each one these bombs has many manifestations that lead to growing competition and violence in the world. Science, technology, and economic growth, which were to have provided the solution to most of mankind's problems, seem instead to have compounded and added to them.

The threat posed by each one of these bombs makes man an endangered species. The explosion of any one of them could bring an end to civilization as we know it. Although they are all on the verge of exploding, there *are* possibilities for dealing with each of them, and there is still time to do so.

There is room for differences of opinion on what priority should be given to each problem and what is the point of no return with respect to each. The nuclear threat, however, is clearly the most urgent and nearest to the point of no return. It is the number-one peril facing humanity because it is an immediate threat—now. Nuclear weapons ready for instantaneous launching can destroy the entire world—and, as they spread to additional nations and to terrorist groups, there is an increasing likelihood that they will do so. The three "P" bombs—population, poverty, and pollution—can perhaps be defused, given time and the application of the necessary resources and determination. But in order to gain time to work out solutions to these problems, it is necessary, as the first-priority problem, to contain the "N" bomb—the nuclear threat.

The threat of the nuclear bomb is greatly aggravated by the existence and growing threat posed by the other three bombs. The development gap between the rich and the poor countries continues to widen and the situation of the poor countries to worsen because of the population explosion, to which have recently been added, as sources of upheaval, the energy and food crises. What Adlai Stevenson termed the "revolution of rising expectations" is now an accepted fact in the world. Because information media are now worldwide, the peoples of the world are better informed than ever before. They are not likely to be willing to continue to suffer hunger, disease, and the prospect of death by starvation in a world in which they see a few rich nations waste more food and resources than many of the poorer countries consume.

Because of the existence of various international organizations and institutions, such as the United Nations, the various regional organizations, and the periodic conferences of the nonaligned countries, the developing countries are now in a much better position to exchange views on their problems and to concert their policies and actions. If any evidence of this were necessary, it has been amply provided by the operation and activities of the Organization of Petroleum Exporting Countries (OPEC) and by the deliberations of the sixth and seventh Special Sessions of the General Assembly in April 1974 and September 1975, which were called to discuss the problems of raw materials and development. The poor countries have voting control in the United Nations and other world forums and can adopt any resolution or decision they wish, but they cannot implement these decisions. Only the great powers and the developed countries control the wealth and resources required to do so. The repeated adoption by the poor countries of programs that remain dead letters serves only to feed the frustration of the poor countries and nourish their anger against the rich countries.

Any solution to the problem of the developing countries can be found only in achieving a more equitable sharing of the world's wealth, which is a euphemistic way of describing a lowering of the standard of living in the rich countries in order to help raise the standard of living in the poor countries. A redistribution of the world's wealth is something that will have to be undertaken by the rich countries, either voluntarily in their own long-range self-interest, or involuntarily, as a result of the growing power of the poor countries.

Confrontation between the Rich and the Poor Nations

The rich, white, industrialized nations (with the exception of Australia, New Zealand, and South Africa) are nearly all concentrated in the northern part of the world, with the poor, colored, developing nations on their southern borders or further south. Sometimes the "rich north" is taken to mean Europe and North America and the "poor south" to mean the countries of Asia, Africa, and Latin America. The latter group, comprising more than 100 countries, is frequently described as the "third world" to distinguish it from the two "worlds" of some 20 developed capitalist and some 10 not quite so fully developed communist countries. More recently, since the emergence of the oil-rich nations of the third world, it is becoming common to refer to the very poorest countries of the third world as the "fourth world." Those latter countries, numbering around 50, are at the bottom of the scale of development, and their outlook seems bleak for a long time to come.

During the last few years, despite the efforts made within and outside of the United Nations, including the declaration by the United Nations of the 1960s as the Development Decade and of the 1970s both as the Second Development Decade and as the Disarmament Decade, the world has been affected by three phenomena. The first is that the economic and social gap between the rich and the poor countries is not being closed or even narrowed but is in fact widening. The second is that military expenditures are continuing to increase, not only in absolute figures but also in terms of constant dollars—that is, at a greater rate than inflation or the cost of living. The third is the growing confrontation between the rich and the poor countries.

According to the unanimous report on Disarmament and Development submitted to the U.N. Secretary-General in 1972 by an international group of experts, at the end of the First Development Decade in 1970 the flow of official developmental assistance to the poor countries amounted to ony $7.7 billion, or about 0.35 percent of the gross national product of the rich donor countries. In order to achieve the target set for the Second Development Decade of 6 percent annual growth in the poor countries, official developmental assistance would have to be doubled to about 0.7 percent of the gross national product of the developed countries, a goal which, it seems, at the halfway mark of the decade, is unlikely to be achieved. (The amount of such assistance has in fact fallen to 0.3 percent of the donors' gross national product.) Even if it is achieved, the improvement in the standard of living of the poor countries would be painfully slow and unsatisfactory.

On the other hand, the global figure of world military expenditures at the halfway mark of the decade is approaching the astronomical sum of $300 billion per year, of which some $20 billion represents the sale and export of arms by the major producers to other countries. The military expenditures of the developed countries, which are the main military spenders (more than 90 percent of the total) as well as the main suppliers of developmental aid (nearly 80 percent of the latter), was more than 25 times greater than the official developmental assistance they provided.

It has sometimes been argued that the percentage of the world's gross national product devoted to military purposes has remained fairly constant, at between 6 and 7 percent, or has even declined slightly in the case of some of the rich developing countries. But there is nothing sacrosanct about continuing to increase military expenditures or keeping them at a more or less constant proportion of a country's increasing gross national product. Military expenditures are usually regarded as a wasteful rather than productive way of investing a country's wealth and resources. In fact, the report of the United Nation group of experts mentioned above drew attention to the "blatant contrast between this waste of resources and the unfilled needs of development."

The growing gap between the rich and poor countries has led to a growing confrontation between them. In the last few years this has been evident in almost every international conference and at the annual sessions of the U.N. General Assembly, where the developing countries are calling with increasing insistence for the establishment of a new international economic order. As we mentioned in Chapter 18, the NPT Review Conference was only the latest but perhaps one of the most dangerous manifestations of the confrontation. It repeated and confirmed the pattern that has developed in international conferences that have dealt with the problems of development, environment, population, food, the law of the sea, energy and raw materials, and the status of women. As time goes by, the developing countries are becoming increasingly impatient and angry over the relative worsening of their situation, and increasingly determined to obtain satisfaction of their demands.

At the present time the poor, southern countries outnumber the rich, northern countries in population by about 2½ to 1. The rich countries are beginning to approach zero population growth, while the poor countries continue to increase in population at the fairly constant rate of about 2.5 percent. If these rates are maintained, the poor people of the world will outnumber the rich by about 5 to 1 in twenty-five years and by about 10 to 1 in fifty years. If this should in fact transpire, then the rich countries will soon find themselves beleaguered. In their efforts to hold the poor countries at bay, they may find themselves forced to using the nuclear threat if not nuclear weapons themselves. In order to prevent or deter such nuclear threats or attacks, the poor countries, many of whom will have the capability of going nuclear, may acquire nuclear weapons and resort to threats of nuclear attack themselves, either in an attempt to achieve their goals or as a counter to the threats of the rich nuclear powers. Such mutual nuclear blackmail can lead only to a nuclear disaster.

It appears to be becoming generally accepted that the raising of the standard of living of the poor countries is the best way—indeed, perhaps the only effective way—of lowering their rate of population growth. The rich nations have thus far failed to raise that standard of living in any significant way, and it seems unlikely that they will succeed in doing so without a drastic reordering of priorities. Unless they can manage to effect a major reduction in the huge sums now wasted on military expenditures and rechannel them to effectively relieve international poverty, there is probably little hope. Disarmament and a drastic decrease in military spending would seem to be necessary in order to obtain the funds necessary to cope with the problems posed by the three "P's." And disarmament itself can be achieved only by first halting the nuclear arms race as well as the further proliferation of nuclear weapons.

Up until now the rich nuclear powers have shown little disposition either for disarmament or for massive developmental aid. But both are essential if the world is to avoid a north–south or, what is worse, a racial confrontation and the possibility of a nuclear holocaust.

President Kennedy once said: "Those who make peaceful revolution impossible make violent revolution inevitable." The widening development gap and the population explosion could by themselves be sufficient to tilt the scales toward violence and provoke convulsive changes. Growing international tensions between the developing and the developed countries, and perhaps also among either the developing or developed countries themselves, coupled with the widespread availability of mass destruction weapons and material, could lead to an extraordinarily dangerous conjunction of forces.

There could be a dozen or more new nuclear powers within five years and a second dozen in the following five years, at least ten of them being developing countries. Poor countries and not only rich ones may acquire nuclear weapons and be in a position, if they chose, to hold the developed countries up to economic and political ransom. There is no reason to assume that they will not support what they regard as their just demands with implicit or even explicit nuclear threats. And they will be able to justify their threats on the basis of the moral authority of decisions of the international community as expressions of the judgment of the nations of the world. Less stable governments led by less responsible leaders might take unilateral action without waiting for the slower processes of development and the sanction of international law.

Even worse is the prospect of utter anarchy resulting from nongovernmental proliferation. Terrorists and other politically motivated groups that have obtained nuclear weapons or plutonium by illegal means could of their own accord decide to use them, or be hired to do so, for economic and political blackmail not merely against wealthy multinational corporations but against the governments of their own and other countries, rich or poor.

Members of government, diplomatic representatives, and wealthy corporations are already subject to kidnapping, bombings, blackmail, and ransom demands by such groups, using only conventional weapons and traditional threats. The danger of such groups' using nuclear weapons against whole cities or countries is appalling in its implications.

Some Radical Suggestions

It is clear that there is no simple solution to the uncommonly complicated problem of preventing the proliferation of nuclear weapons in the world. Some observers have urged that what they regard as the aspirins and tranquilizers thus far prescribed to control the nuclear infection have served only to disguise the condition and delay the treatment. They say that the disease is not merely an infection but a cancer and that radical surgery is needed. Various proposals have been made for a restructuring of society in ways not dealt with by the existing non-proliferation regime and the NPT.

One suggestion that has been put forward from time to time, and that is still being urged by groups that are concerned about the environmental and safety problems associated with using nuclear energy for power, is to begin to phase out nuclear power reactors entirely and to replace them with other sources of energy. In September 1973, the twenty-third Pugwash Conference on Science and World Affairs concluded:

1. Owing to potentially grave and as yet unresolved problems related to waste management, diversion of fissionable material, and major radioactivity releases arising from accidents, natural disasters, sabotage, or acts of war, the wisdom of a commitment to nuclear fission as a principal energy source for mankind must be seriously questioned at the present time.

2. Accordingly, research and development on alternative energy sources—particularly solar, geothermal and fusion energy, and cleaner technologies for fossil fuels—should be greatly accelerated.

These comments and suggestions were made not with the intention of reducing the risk of proliferation of nuclear weapons, but rather from the point of view of health and safety. Nevertheless, if they were implemented, they would certainly help to make the problem of nuclear proliferation much more manageable. Unfortunately, however, it is probable that, even without the energy crisis, the utilization of nuclear energy for the production of power has passed the point of no return. With the vast amounts of plutonium already available and the enormous investment in nuclear reactors already in operation and contracted for, the possibility of reversing the proliferation of reactors and gradually eliminating them seems almost nil. At this stage, it even seems doubtful if the fast breeder reactor or the use of plutonium recycling to fuel commerical reactors can be prohibited or otherwise somehow eliminated. If other, safer sources of energy prove to be practical and cheaper than nuclear energy, then there are real hopes that they will, in time, replace nuclear energy. But it seems clear that, at least for the coming decade, there is no alternative to nuclear energy in order to keep up with the constantly increasing demands for electric power. Even if massive efforts were undertaken to speed up the development of alternative energy sources, it would take at least a decade before they were fully operating and even longer for them to replace nuclear energy. While they could make a great contribution to the improvement of human health and safety, it seems clear that they would come too late to prevent the escape from the bottle within the next decade of the genie of nuclear weapons proliferation.

Another suggestion that has been discussed by some students of the problem, but not yet put forward by any government, is to revive some features of the old Baruch Plan. Proponents of this idea suggest that what is needed is some supranational authority that could manage, operate, and control all nuclear materials and facilities even if it did not actually own them—in other words, a sort of mini-Baruch plan updated to present circumstances. However, the mere mention of the Baruch Plan immediately summons to mind all of the problems that led to the failure of that plan. Is it any more likely that the Soviet Union would be willing, under present circumstances, to agree to the creation of such a supranational authority, even one that did not own the nuclear materials and facilities? Would not the creation of such a supranational authority run counter to basic Marxist–Leninist doctrine and philosophy? And assuming, even for purposes of argument, that the Soviet Union and the United States could agree on the creation of such an authority, would China, France, India, and South Africa, to mention a few countries, be willing to extend their cooperation? And in any case, in a world of six nuclear powers wherein more than forty countries have already acquired facilities, materials, and technology, is it not too late? It would take several years to put such a plan into operation, and the world would never know for certain that all facilities and materials were brought under the control of the supranational authority.

A third suggestion that has been made is that, if the nuclear powers would provide sufficient or adequate assurances of security to the non-nuclear powers, they could remove at least one of the main incentives that presently impel countries toward considering going nuclear or at least obtaining or retaining a nuclear option. Such security guarantees or assurances would have to be far-reaching and would have to encompass not merely the threat of nuclear attack but also the threat of con.entional attack. Is it conceivable that the Soviet Union and the United States would be willing to enter into such worldwide commitments, covering all the areas of tension in the world? It hardly seems likely that the proponents of free enterprise in the United States and the apostles of Marxism–Leninism in the Soviet Union would agree to become the joint guarantors of the peace of the world. Even if by some stretch of the imagination one could conceive of their agreeing to do so, it is simply not conceivable that China would agree. Any such course of action, with its implications of the preservation of the status quo and the maintenance of the so-called hegemony of the superpowers, runs contrary to all Chinese views of the structure of international society. Chinese policies and propaganda are rooted in the concept of the struggle of the third-world nonaligned and developing countries against the domination of the superpowers and include the concept of "just wars" as both necessary and desirable to redress ancient wrongs and injustice. Moreover, China officially favors third-world and developing countries going nuclear as a result of their own independent efforts in order to defend themselves against nuclear "enslavement" by the superpowers, although, in fact, it is becoming more ambiguous and less categorical in expressing these views as time passes.

But again, assuming for purposes of argument that the United States and the Soviet Union would be prepared to enter into such sweeping security guarantees, it is far from certain that countries with special security problems would regard them as adequate. Would such countries, as India, Israel, South Africa, Taiwan, or South Korea, for example, find such security guarantees credible, or would they give greater heed to the fears expressed by de Gaulle concerning the possible unreliability of similar American assurances to France?

A fourth suggestion is that the United Nations should be strengthened and the enforcement powers originally envisaged for the organization (which were written into its Charter) implemented. In other words, the Security Council should have at its disposal the armed forces and facilities required for U.N. enforcement action, and the Military Staff Committee, composed of the five nuclear-weapon powers, should be reactivated. In a world of nuclear powers, with a number of states having the capability of going nuclear, any such U.N. military force would have to be a nuclear force; or, alternatively, all other powers would have to give up their nuclear weapons so that only the U.N. force would possess any. In either case, the problems would immediately arise of where such weapons and forces would be kept, what other armed forces would be needed to protect them and what nationality they would have, who would pay for them, and many other such.

Apart from even these administrative and technical problems, there are the overriding and, for the present at least, insuperable political problems of obtaining the agreement necessary to the creation of any such U.N. Police Force. All of the basic political problems which have until now prevented the creation of even a conventional army for the U.N. would be greatly multiplied in the case of a nuclear force and would suffice to block its creation. It was difficult enough for the Security Council to organize and maintain the peace forces that are deployed in the Middle East and in Cyprus. It would, of course, help to increase confidence in the U.N. and promote international peace and security if such peacekeeping activities were strengthened and expanded. But at the present stage of the U.N.'s development, and given the almost certain opposition of China, many middle-sized powers, and the developing countries, who would regard the idea as a plot to perserve the status quo, it is simply not possible to envisage the establishment of even a U.N. military force of the great powers, let alone a U.N. nuclear force.

A fifth suggestion has been made by those who are supporters of a new world order or of global reform. They regard the cessation of the arms race and nuclear disarmament as unattainable under the existing world system of nation-states, and believe that only radical modifications in the nature and structure of society would make possible the conditions necessary for such disarmament. They consider that first steps and partial disarmament measures are likely to be deceptive and to repeat the inadequate arms control arrangements of the past fifteen years unless they are put within the context of political, economic, and social changes that are conducive to real disarmament. In sum, they regard what's attainable in the arms control field as not important, and what is important as not attainable—owing, internationally, to the dynamics of the nation-state system, to conflict and distrust between the superpowers, and to the glaring disparities of economic development and state power in the world; and nationally, to the entrenched national military, industrial, scientific, and bureaucratic interests seeking to continue the arms race and perpetuate the status quo.

Proponents of this school of thought believe that the alleviation of the other global problems such as the three "P's," above all that of poverty on both the international and national levels, is essential in order to make possible the achievement of disarmament. To bring about the alleviation of these other problems, it is argued, it is necessary to form a consensus about objectives and the means of achieving them, to mobilize public opinion, and to transform institutions and behavioral patterns.

The author has no quarrel with the objectives of those who support global reform and a new world order. But he believes that we dare not give up, postpone, or slacken the struggle for non-proliferation, for a halt to the nuclear arms race, and for general disarmament while we work towards longer-range goals. He fears that if we put global reform ahead of disarmament, we shall probably achieve neither, and that the risks of nuclear proliferation are so great that first priority must be given to avoiding those risks.

Finally, it has been suggested by some scholars that the only thing that could shock the nations of the world, and in particular the superpowers, into taking any really effective action would be the occurrence of a nuclear disaster or catastrophe. This counsel of despair is based on the belief that it is only in times of great crisis or calamity that the nations and peoples of the world are roused out of their apathy and inertia and galvanized into taking action. The hope of such persons is that the anticipated nuclear catastrophe would be sufficient to stimulate necessary action, but not so great as to cause an unmanageable holocaust or an uncontrollable chain reaction. The trouble with this approach, however, is that its risks and consequences are unknown and incalculable. It is a form of "nuclear roulette" that constitutes an abdication of responsibility and involves too great a gamble with human lives. It may lead to the very evil that we are trying to prevent or avoid. Nevertheless, unless effective measures are taken as a result of rational decisions to prevent the proliferation of nuclear weapons, such a calamity may indeed occur. Whether it will produce the right reactions and lead to the desired and beneficial actions, nobody knows.

It would seem, therefore, that none of these radical suggestions is likely to extricate the world from the predicament of the nuclear peril. If there is a way out, it can be found, in our view, only along two paths:

first, by improving and strengthening the NPT, and second, by creating a moral and political climate in the world that would eliminate or minimize the need for nuclear weapons.

Suggestions To Strengthen the NPT

In order to be able to cope with the problem of nuclear proliferation, time is essential. To gain time, it is of utmost importance that the nuclear non-proliferation regime and the NPT be preserved for as long as possible. Any time gained is important for two reasons. First, as was pointed out earlier, anything which can postpone the decision of any country to go nuclear is clearly beneficial, because problems that seem acute and intractable now will often disappear or be settled, or become less important, with the mere passage of time. Second, time will permit more careful study of the problem and provide opportunities to deal with it, as well as more time to cope with the other perils facing the world and to reduce the exacerbating effect they have on the instant problem.

There is a large number of things that can be done to help strengthen the Non-Proliferation Treaty and give it a new lease on life. Even within the context of the treaty a number of measures can be taken that are sufficiently far-reaching as to ensure the continued survival of the treaty and make it a powerful instrument of non-proliferation.

The first and most important requirement, of course, is that the provisions of the treaty be fully implemented and strictly observed. Up to the present, Article III on safeguards, Article IV on promoting the peaceful uses of nuclear energy, Article V on peaceful nuclear explosions, and, above all, Article VI on halting the nuclear arms race and nuclear disarmament have been ignored or violated. It is not a very radical suggestion to say that the parties to the treaty, in particular the nuclear powers who have the most to gain from it, should carry out their legal obligations under it. An ancient and honorable rule of international law, *pacta sunt servanda*, requires that treaties must be observed.

Had the provisions of the treaty been carried out faithfully since its entry into force on March 5, 1970, the world might not be in its present nuclear predicament. Even now, if the nuclear powers were to convince the non-nuclear powers, who feel that they have been deceived and misled, that they would henceforth live up to all their obligations under the treaty, there is a good chance that the treaty could be saved and the non-proliferation regime preserved.

There are a number of other important steps, beyond the strict and full implementation of the NPT, that could and should be taken. Throughout this book, various suggestions have been made of ways to strengthen the Non-Proliferation Treaty that would help to increase the effectiveness of the non-proliferation regime. They concern almost every article of the NPT, and some, such as those concerning security assurances, are outside of the treaty framework. They are summarized in Appendix VI, "List of Proposed Measures to Strengthen the Non-Proliferation Treaty." If the measures listed were implemented, in whole or even in large part, the author feels confident that the Non-Proliferation Treaty and the non-proliferation regime would not only survive but be greatly strengthened. But the author is *not* very confident that enough of them will be carried out in order to achieve that result.

In order to take advantage of the existing last chance to prevent the uncontrolled proliferation of nuclear weapons, small incremental steps of secondary importance will not suffice. Only dramatic and drastic action is likely to turn the tide.

The Indian nuclear explosion of May 18, 1974, was an event of truly transcendental importance. It breached the walls of the "nuclear club" and once again raised the spectre of the *n*-th country problem. So long as the nuclear club was restricted to the five permanent members of the Security Council, there was a very good chance that those walls would hold. At this point, it is extremely difficult to see how the walls can be rebuilt. If one more country goes nuclear, it will probably be impossible to rebuild them at all. There are a number of measures that can be taken to increase the security of such countries as Pakistan, Israel, Argentina, and South Africa and reduce the likelihood of their going nuclear. But more is needed than just security guarantees to these countries, who have not signed the NPT, in order to save the treaty.

One would have thought that, given the rather discouraging prospect of the likely further proliferation of nuclear weapons, the nuclear powers, who have the most to lose, would be spurred into some sort of action in an attempt to prevent the emergence of a world of nuclear powers. But such has not been the case. There is no evidence of any understanding on their part of the seriousness of the situation or, if there is such understanding, of any real sense of urgency in attempting to cope with the problem. Perhaps it is a case of their knowing what must be done to salvage the situation, but of their being unable or unwilling to do what is necessary.

If the NPT and the non-proliferation regime are to be saved, however, the nuclear powers must meet the requirements of the new situation in the world today. That situation is that more and more countries will go nuclear unless it can be clearly demonstrated to them that they have no need to do so and that it is not in their interest to do so. Sanctions in the way of withholding nuclear assistance are hardly likely to be effective against countries already in possession of nuclear technology or against the newly rich oil- and other raw material–exporting countries in a situation in which the nuclear powers and other supplier states are competing with each other to sell nuclear reactors, equipment, and materials to them. Nor are they likely to be much more effective against the poor countries, who are determined to close the gap between themselves and the rich countries and who see nuclear technology or possibly nuclear terrorism as ways of doing so. Countries that are determined to evade controls will find ways to do so. With China encouraging the poor countries to be more activist, and with the example of India as evidence that the wishes of the big powers may be flouted with impunity, these countries may be willing to exploit their sheer numerical majority to engage in confrontations with the rich countries in order to extract concessions from them.

If the superpowers were to take adequate and timely emergency action to meet the urgent concerns of those near-nuclear powers under the greatest pressure to go nuclear, they might be able to persuade them to postpone doing so. They could, for example, give joint or separate guarantees of security to Israel, the Arab states, and Pakistan that would be adequate and sufficiently credible to remove the need of those countries to acquire a nuclear deterrent. If, in addition, the nuclear powers were to agree to implement a substantial part of the suggestions contained in Appendix VI, they could buy time to take other measures necessary to ensure the continued existence of the treaty and the non-proliferation regime for a number of years to come. That would certainly serve, at least, to slow down the trend toward going nuclear.

Creating the Right Climate in the World

In order to maximize the possibility of continuing the non-proliferation regime, much more will have to be done than merely to strengthen the Non-Proliferation Treaty. If the regime is to be preserved for the indefinite future, and indeed if the world is to survive, it will be necessary to bring about some basic improvements in the human condition and in modern society.

It has often been said in the past that mankind was at a critical crossroads and was faced with the choice of taking either the road to a better world or the road to destruction. But never before in history could it be said that mankind possessed the means for bringing about the complete destruction of life on this planet. In 1946, Bernard Baruch said that we must make a choice between the quick and the dead, that we must elect world peace or world destruction. That choice is still before us, with the essential difference that the odds have tilted towards death and destruction. There are no guarantees that the world can avoid the further proliferation of nuclear weapons, with all its attendant dangers. Having eaten of the fruit of the tree of nuclear knowledge, mankind may be condemned to earn its survival in the future by undertaking the very difficult and complicated task of effecting fundamental changes in human society.

Efforts to achieve this goal must be directed towards disarmament and a peaceful world. Substantial and concrete progress must be made on three fronts.

The first is in the field of arms control and disarmament. The nuclear powers must demonstrate that they are, in fact, as indeed they are committed in law to do by the NPT, taking vigorous action to achieve a cessation of the nuclear arms race and nuclear disarmament. The two superpowers must, of course, lead the way.

The second field is that of development. Here, too, the two superpowers, with the cooperation of the other developed countries and of the oil-rich countries, must take practical measures to reduce the development gap, even if these measures mean a temporary lowering of the standard of living of the developed countries. The problem of the developing countries cannot be solved unless there is a more equitable distribution of the world's wealth. In order to achieve this, disarmament and a major reduction in military expenditures may be necessary.

The third area in which definite progress must be made is that of international organization. There is no feasible alternative to the United Nations. As the authors of the Three-Power Declaration of November 15, 1945, recognized, maintaining the rule of law and banishing the scourge of war can be brought about only by "giving wholehearted support to the United Nations Organization and by consolidating and extending its authority." The world organization, whose prestige and authority have eroded in recent years, must be strengthened and its operations improved so that it becomes a credible and effective instrument for achieving peace, progress, and justice. This will require that all powers, the great and the small but particularly the great, make full use of the organization as well as use it more effectively. The great powers, who have the right of veto in the Security Council, and the smaller, third-world countries, who have an automatic voting majority in the General Assembly, must both exercise restraint as well as demonstrate their active commitment to the ideals of the charter. They must find a way to move in the direction of taking decisions by a genuine consensus rather than by voting in order to make them broadly acceptable and capable of producing concrete results.

It may be argued that these goals are too idealistic and utopian to be achieved in practice. Idealistic they certainly are, but in the increasingly dangerous world that confronts us it may well be that idealism is the only sensible form of realism. Even substantial progress towards these idealistic objectives may not suffice to avoid a nuclear holocaust and to ensure the survival of the human race. There are no absolute assurances in any field of human endeavor, least of all in a world that is permanently poised on the edge of the nuclear abyss. But sustained, serious efforts and concrete programs to achieve these goals might at least provide the possibility of creating the conditions necessary for the continued survival of the human race.

The elaboration of action programs intended to achieve definitive progress towards all three goals is outside the scope of this book, which is limited to dealing with the problems of the nuclear arms race and of nuclear proliferation. A program for immediate action in this field, however, may be found in Chapter 14, Chapter 18, and Appendix VI. The two nuclear superpowers must demonstrate that, at least in the field of mass destruction weapons, they are really serious in their stated desires and intentions to control and reverse the nuclear arms race. Tangible progress in this field will help to facilitate progress in the other two fields.

The Last Chance

Whether the countries possessing or soon to possess a nuclear option decide to exercise it within the next few years will depend mainly on domestic considerations in each country and on its perception of its security requirements, its role and status in the world, and its hopes (whether rightly or wrongly held) for future economic development through the application of nuclear energy. But the decision in each country will be influenced in large part by the international climate of opinion in the world. A most important factor in creating the right moral and political climate will be the actions of the great powers, in particular the two superpowers. The standard of international behavior they set, in all of the three fields mentioned above but especially in the field of nuclear arms control, is bound to have a great and, perhaps, decisive influence on the actions of the non-nuclear powers. Only the superpowers, by their leadership and example, can succeed in having the non-proliferation regime accepted as a norm of international life. They are the ones that must take the lead in replacing the ethic of the arms race with an ethic of arms control.

The U.S. and the U.S.S.R. must accept the burden of changing the world's attitude toward nuclear weapons. Only they can halt and reverse the vertical proliferation of nuclear weapons, which may well be a necessary condition for preventing horizontal proliferation and nongovernmental proliferation. If they continue to militarize the world with both nuclear and conventional weapons, they can hardly expect that other countries, and eventually terrorist and other nongovernmental organizations, will refrain from acquiring such weapons. They have the great responsibility of establishing the illegitimacy of the nuclear arms race and the legitimacy of nuclear restraint and arms control.

If it becomes clear that the nuclear-weapons states are prepared—as a first step towards a saner and better world—to live up to the obligations and commitments they undertook in the NPT, then there is a chance that the treaty can be strengthened and revived. This is probably the last chance for the NPT and for the prevention of an uncontrolled, and perhaps uncontrollable, nuclear arms race. There is no guarantee, even if the nuclear-weapon states avail themselves of this last chance, that they will finally succeed in halting the trend toward proliferation. But if they do not now make an all-out and credible attempt to do so, then it would seem to be inevitable that other non-nuclear countries will follow the lead of India. We shall then all have to learn to live as best we can in a world of many nuclear powers, with the truly terrible prospect of nuclear threats and blackmail by terrorist groups.

Appendix I. Chronology of the Development of Nuclear Weapons and of Arms Control Measures

1945 July 16   –   First atomic bomb exploded at Alamogordo, New Mexico.

      Aug. 6   –   United States drops atomic bomb on Hiroshima and three days later drops another atomic bomb on Nagasaki.

      Nov. 15   –   The United States, the United Kingdom, and Canada propose a United Nations atomic energy commission to ensure the use of atomic energy for exclusively peaceful purposes and to eliminate atomic weapons.

1946 Jan. 24   –   The United Nations Atomic Energy Commission, composed of members of the Security Council plus Canada, is established.

      June 14   –   The United States presents the Baruch Plan for an international authority to own and manage all atomic materials.

      June 19   –   The U.S.S.R. proposes a draft convention banning the use and production of atomic weapons and providing for the destruction of all stockpiles.

      Dec. 14   –   The U.N. General Assembly adopts a resolution on the principles for the general regulation and reduction of armaments.

1947 Feb. 13   –   The U.N. Security Council sets up a Commission for Conventional Armaments, to deal with the general regulation and reduction of armaments and armed forces.

1948 May 17   – The United Nations Atomic Energy Commission
                      suspends work because of the Soviet–Amercian
                      deadlock over the Baruch Plan.

      Nov. 4   – The U.N. General Assembly adopts a resolution
                      approving the Baruch Plan.

1949 Sept. 23   – The Soviet Union explodes its first atomic bomb.

      Dec. 5   – The U.N. General Assembly adopts a French pro-
                      posal for the submission by member states of full
                      information on conventional armaments and armed
                      forces and verification thereof.

1952 Jan. 11   – The U.N. sets up the Disarmament Commission to
                      deal with both atomic and conventional weapons.

      Oct. 3   – The United Kingdom explodes its first atomic
                      bomb.

      Nov. 1   – The United States explodes its first hydrogen bomb.

1953 Aug. 12   – The Soviet Union explodes its first hydrogen bomb.

      Dec. 8   – President Eisenhower makes his "Atoms for Peace"
                      proposal to the U.N. General Assembly.

1954 April 2   – Prime Minister Nehru of India proposes the sus-
                      pension of all nuclear tests by the nuclear powers.

1955 July 18–23 – The Summit Conference of France, the U.S.S.R.,
                      the United Kingdom, and the United States is held
                      in Geneva.

1957 May 15   – The United Kingdom explodes its first hydrogen
                      bomb.

      July 29   – Statute of the International Atomic Energy Agency
                      enters into force.

1958 March 31   – The Soviet Union announces a unilateral suspen-
                      sion of nuclear tests.

      Aug. 21   – An East-West Conference of Experts unanimously
                      agrees that it is feasible to establish a control sys-
                      tem to supervise the suspension of nuclear tests.

      Aug. 22   – The United States and the United Kingdom an-
                      nounce their suspension of nuclear tests for one-
                      year periods depending on agreement with
                      Moscow on a control system.

      Oct. 31   – The Conference on the Discontinuance of Nuclear
                      Weapon Tests begins in Geneva.

      Nov. 10 to   East–West Conference of Experts on Surprise At-
      Dec. 18   – tack meets in Geneva.

1959	Nov. 20	–	U.N. General Assembly unanimously adopts a resolution approving the idea of general and complete disarmament.
	Dec. 1	–	The nuclear powers and other countries sign the Antarctic Treaty banning nuclear tests and military bases in that area.
1960	Feb. 13	–	France explodes its first atomic bomb.
	March 15 to June 27	–	Ten-Nation Disarmament Committee meets in Geneva until Soviet walkout on June 27.
	Aug. 18	–	The U.N. Disarmament Commission urges the resumption of East–West negotiations
1961	Aug. 30	–	The Soviet Union announces the resumption of nuclear tests.
	Sept. 15	–	The United States resumes underground tests.
	Dec. 13	–	The U.N. General Assembly approves the American–Soviet Agreed Principles for Disarmament Negotiations and the creation of an Eighteen-Nation Disarmament Committee consisting of five Eastern countries, five Western countries, and eight nonaligned countries.
1962	March 14	–	The Eighteen-Nation Disarmament Committee holds its first session in Geneva. France is not represented. In 1969, it is enlarged to twenty-six members and its name is changed to Conference of the Committee on Disarmament (CCD). In 1974 it is enlarged to thirty-one members.
	March 15	–	The Soviet Union proposes a draft treaty for general and complete disarmament.
	April 18	–	The United States submits an outline of a treaty on general and complete disarmament in a peaceful world.
1963	June 20	–	The Soviet Union and United States sign the "Hot Line" agreement.
	Aug. 5	–	The United States, the Soviet Union, and the United Kingdom sign the Partial Test Ban Treaty. Subsequently 106 countries become parties to it.
1964	Oct. 16	–	China explodes its first atomic bomb.
1967	Jan. 27	–	The Outer Space Treaty, governing the exploration of outer space and banning nuclear weapons there, is signed.

Feb. 14 – The Treaty of Tlatelolco, banning nuclear weapons in Latin America, is signed.

June 17 – China explodes its first hydrogen bomb.

1968 June 12 – The U.N. General Assembly "commends" the Treaty on the Non-Proliferation of Nuclear Weapons by a vote of 95 to 4, with 21 abstentions.

June 19 – The U.N. Security Council adopts Resolution 255 on security assurances to non-nuclear-weapon states by a vote of 10 to 0, with 5 abstentions.

July 1 – The Treaty on the Non-Proliferation of Nuclear Weapons (NPT) is signed.

Aug. 24 – France explodes its first hydrogen bomb.

Aug. 29 to Sept. 28 – The Conference of Non-Nuclear-Weapon states meets in Geneva.

1969 Nov. 17 – Strategic Arms Limitation Talks (SALT) begin.

Dec. 16 – U.N. General Assembly declares the decade of the 1970s a Disarmament Decade.

1970 March 5 – The Non-Proliferation Treaty enters into force.

1971 Feb. 11 – The Seabed arms control treaty, which bans the emplacement of nuclear weapons on the seabed or ocean floor, is signed.

Sept. 30 – The U.S.S.R. and the United States sign an agreement to reduce the risk of accidental nuclear war.

– The U.S.S.R. and the United States sign an agreement to improve the "Hot Line."

Oct. 25 – The U.N. decides to give the seat of China to the People's Republic of China and to expel the Republic of China (Taiwan); a few days later the People's Republic of China takes the China seat; calls superpowers' arms control efforts and agreements a "hoax."

1972 April 10 – The Convention for the elimination of biological and toxin weapons is signed.

May 26 – The U.S.S.R. and the United States sign a treaty limiting ABM systems to two sites in each country with 100 ABMs at each.

– The U.S.S.R. and the United States sign a five-year agreement and protocol limiting strategic offensive arms to 710 SLBMs in 44 submarines and 1,000 ICBMs for the United States and 950 SLBMs in 62 submarines and 1,410 ICBMs for the Soviet Union.

1973   June 21   – The U.S.S.R. and the United States sign an agreement on principles for negotiating further limitations of strategic offensive weapons.

June 22   – The U.S.S.R. and the United States sign an agreement on the prevention of nuclear war.

July 3   – Conference on security and cooperation in Europe begins in Helsinki.

Oct. 30   – Conference on mutual force reductions in Central Europe begins in Vienna.

1974   May 18   – India explodes its first nuclear device for peaceful purposes.

July 3   – The U.S.S.R. and the United States sign protocol to 1972 ABM treaty limiting ABM systems to one site with 100 ABMs in each country.

– The U.S.S.R. and the United States sign Threshold Test Ban Treaty, limiting underground nuclear weapons tests to a yield of 150 kilotons each after March 31, 1976. No limitation on underground nuclear tests for peaceful purposes.

– The U.S.S.R. and the United States sign a joint statement agreeing to discuss and advocate measures to overcome the danger of environmental warfare.

Nov. 24   – U.S.S.R. and United States agree at Vladivostok to limit strategic offensive arms until 1985 to 2,400 for each, of which 1,320 ICBMs and SLBMs can be MIRVed.

1975   May 5–30   – The NPT Review Conference meets in Geneva.

Aug. 1   – The Declaration on Security and Cooperation in Europe is signed at Helsinki.

Appendix II. Treaty Banning Nuclear Weapon Tests in the Atmosphere, in Outer Space and Under Water*

The Governments of the United States of America, the United Kingdom of Great Britain and Northern Ireland, and the Union of Soviet Socialist Republics, hereinafter referred to as the "Original Parties",

Proclaiming as their principal aim the speediest achievement of an agreement on general and complete disarmament under strict international control in accordance with the objectives of the United Nations which would put an end to the armaments race and eliminate the incentive to the production and testing of all kinds of weapons, including nuclear weapons,

Seeking to achieve the discontinuance of all test explosions of nuclear weapons for all time, determined to continue negotiations to this end, and desiring to put an end to the contamination of man's environment by radioactive substances,

Have agreed as follows:

ARTICLE I

1. Each of the Parties to this Treaty undertakes to prohibit, to prevent, and not to carry out any nuclear weapon test explosion, or any other nuclear explosion, at any place under its jurisdiction or control:

(a) in the atmosphere; beyond its limits, including outer space; or under water, including territorial waters or high seas; or

(b) in any other environment if such explosion causes radioactive debris to be present outside the territorial limits of the State under whose jurisdiction or control such explosion is conducted. It is understood in this connection that the provisions of this subparagraph are without prejudice to the conclusion of a treaty resulting in the permanent banning of all nuclear test explosions, including all such explosions underground, the

---

* Signed at Moscow by the Union of Soviet Socialist Republics, the United Kingdom and the United States of America on 5 August 1963.

conclusion of which, as the Parties have stated in the Preamble to this Treaty they seek to achieve.

2. Each of the Parties to this Treaty undertakes furthermore to refrain from causing, encouraging, or in any way participating in, the carrying out of any nuclear weapon test explosion, or any other nuclear explosion, anywhere which would take place in any of the environments described, or have the effect referred to, in paragraph 1 of this Article.

ARTICLE II

1. Any Party may propose amendments to this Treaty. The text of any proposed amendment shall be submitted to the Depositary Governments which shall circulate it to all Parties to this Treaty. Thereafter, if requested to do so by one-third or more of the Parties, the Depositary Governments shall convene a conference, to which they shall invite all the Parties, to consider such amendment.

2. Any amendment to this Treaty must be approved by a majority of the votes of all the Parties to this Treaty, including the votes of all the Original Parties. The amendment shall enter into force for all Parties upon the deposit of instruments of ratification by a majortiy of all the Parties, including the instruments of ratifications of all of the Original Parties.

ARTICLE III

1. This Treaty shall be open to all States for signature. Any State which does not sign this Treaty before its entry into force in accordance with paragraph 3 of this Article may accede to it at any time.

2. This Treaty shall be subject to ratification by signatory States. Instruments of ratification and instruments of accession shall be deposited with the Governments of the Original Parties—the United States of America, the United Kingdom of Great Britain and Northern Ireland, and the Union of Soviet Socialist Republics—which are hereby designated the Depositary Governments.

3. This Treaty shall enter into force after its ratification by all the Original Parties and the deposit of their instruments of ratification.

4. For States whose instruments of ratification or accession are deposited subsequent to the entry into force of this Treaty, it shall enter into force on the date of the deposit of their instruments of ratification or accession.

5. The Depositary Governments shall promptly inform all signatory and acceding States of the date of each signature, the date of deposit of each instrument of ratification of and accession to this Treaty, the date of its entry into force, and the date of receipt of any requests for conferences or other notices.

6. This Treaty shall be registered by the Depositary Governments pursuant to Article 102 of the Charter of the United Nations.

ARTICLE IV

This Treaty shall be of unlimited duration.

Each Party shall in exercising its national sovereignty have the right to withdraw from the Treaty if it decides that extraordinary events, related to the subject matter of this Treaty, have jeopardized the supreme interests of its country. It shall give notice of such withdrawal to all other Parties to the Treaty three months in advance.

ARTICLE V

This Treaty, of which the English and Russian texts are equally authentic, shall be deposited in the archives of the Depositary Governments. Duly certified copies of this Treaty shall be transmitted by Depositary Governments to the Governments of the signatory and acceding States.

IN WITNESS WHEREOF the undersigned, duly authorized, have signed this Treaty.

DONE in triplicate at the city of Moscow the fifth day of August, one thousand nine hundred and sixty-three.

Appendix III. Treaty for the Prohibition of Nuclear Weapons in Latin America*

Preamble

In the name of their peoples and faithfully interpreting their desires and aspirations, the Governments of the States which sign the Treaty for the Prohibition of Nuclear Weapons in Latin America,

Desiring to contribute, so far as lies in their power, towards ending the armaments race, especially in the field of nuclear weapons, and towards strengthening a world at peace, based on the sovereign equality of States, mutual respect and good neighbourliness,

Recalling that the United Nations General Assembly, in its Resolution 808 (IX), adopted unanimously as one of the three points of a coordinated programme of disarmament "the total prohibition of the use and manufacture of nuclear weapons and weapons of mass destruction of every type",

Recalling that militarily denuclearized zones are not an end in themselves but rather a means for achieving general and complete disarmament at a later stage,

Recalling United Nations General Assembly Resolution 1911 (XVIII), which established the measures that should be agreed upon for the denuclearization of Latin America should be taken "in the light of the principles of the Charter of the United Nations and of regional agreements",

Recalling United Nations General Assembly Resolution 2028 (XX), which established the principle of an acceptable balance of mutual responsibilities and duties for the nuclear and non-nuclear powers, and

Recalling that the Charter of the Organization of American States proclaims that it is an essential purpose of the Organization to strengthen the peace and security of the hemisphere,

* Signed at Mexico City on 14 February 1967.

CONVINCED:

That the incalculable destructive power of nuclear weapons has made it imperative that the legal prohibition of war should be strictly observed in practice if the survival of civilization and of mankind itself is to be assured,

That nuclear weapons, whose terrible effects are suffered, indiscriminately and inexorably, by military forces and civilian population alike, constitute, through the persistence of the radioactivity they release, an attack on the integrity of the human species and ultimately may even render the whole earth uninhabitable,

That general and complete disarmament under effective international control is a vital matter which all the peoples of the world equally demand,

That the proliferation of nuclear weapons, which seems inevitable unless States, in the exercise of their sovereign rights, impose restrictions on themselves in order to prevent it, would make any agreement on disarmament enormously difficult and would increase the danger of the outbreak of a nuclear conflagration,

That the establishment of militarily denuclearized zones is closely linked with the maintenance of peace and security in the respective regions,

That the military denuclearization of vast geographical zones, adopted by the sovereign decision of the States comprised therein, will exercise a beneficial influence on other regions where similar conditions exist,

That the privileged situation of the signatory States, whose territories are wholly free from nuclear weapons, imposes upon them the inescapable duty of preserving that situation both in their own interests and for the good of mankind,

That the existence of nuclear weapons in any country of Latin America would make it a target for possible nuclear attacks and would inevitably set off, throughout the region, a ruinous race in nuclear weapons which would involve the unjustifiable diversion, for warlike purposes, of the limited resources required for economic and social development,

That the foregoing reasons, together with the traditional peace-loving outlook of Latin America, give rise to an inescapable necessity that nuclear energy should be used in that region for peaceful purposes, and that the Latin American countries should use their right to the greatest and most equitable possible access to this new source of energy in order to expedite the economic and social development of their peoples.

CONVINCED FINALLY:

That the military denuclearization of Latin America—being understood to mean the undertaking entered into internationally in this Treaty to keep their territories forever free from nuclear weapons—will constitute a measure which will spare their peoples from the squandering of their limited resources on nuclear armaments and will protect them against possible nuclear attacks on their territories, and will also constitute a significant contribution towards preventing the proliferation of nuclear weapons and a powerful factor for general and complete disarmament, and

That Latin America, faithful to its tradition of universality, must not only endeavor to banish from its homelands the scourge of a nuclear war, but must also strive to promote the well-being and advancement of its peoples, at the same time co-operating in the fulfilment of the ideals of mankind, that is to say, in the consolidation of a permanent peace based on equal rights, economic fairness and social justice for all, in accordance with the principles and purposes set forth in the Charter of the United Nations and in the Charter of the Organization of American States,

Have agreed as follows:
Obligations

Article 1

1. The Contracting Parties hereby undertake to use exclusively for peaceful purposes the nuclear material and facilities which are under their jurisdiction, and to prohibit and prevent in their respective territories:

(a) The testing, use, manufacture, production or acquisition by any means whatsoever of any nuclear weapons, by the Parties themselves, directly or indirectly, on behalf of anyone else or in any other way, and

(b) The receipt, storage, installation, deployment and any form of possession of any nuclear weapons, directly or indirectly, by the Parties themselves, by anyone on their behalf or in any other way.

2. The Contracting Parties also undertake to refrain from engaging in, encouraging or authorizing, directly or indirectly, or in any way participating in the testing, use, manufacture, production, possession or control of any nucelar weapon.

DEFINITION OF THE CONTRACTING PARTIES

Article 2

For the purposes of this Treaty, the Contracting Parties are those for whom the Treaty is in force.

DEFINITION OF TERRITORY

Article 3

For the purposes of this Treaty, the term "territory" shall include the territorial sea, air space and any other space over which the State exercises sovereignty in accordance with its own legislation.

ZONE OF APPLICATION

Article 4

1. The zone of application of this Treaty is the whole of the territories for which the Treaty is in force.

2. Upon fulfilment of the requirements of article 28, paragraph 1, the zone of application of this Treaty shall also be that which is situated in the western hemisphere within the following limits (except the continental part of the territory of the United States of America and its territorial waters): starting at a point located at 35° north latitude, 75° west longitude; from this point directly southward to a point at 30° north latitude, 75° west longitude; from there, directly eastward to a point at 30° north latitude, 50° west longitude; from there, along a loxodromic line to a point at 5° north latitude, 20° west longitude; from there, directly southward to a point at 60° south latitude, 20° west longitude; from there, directly westward to a point at 60° south latitude, 115° west longitude; from there, directly northward to a point at 0 latitude, 115° west longitude; from there, along a loxodromic line to a point at 35° north latitude, 150° west longitude; from there, directly eastward to a point at 35° north latitude, 75° west longitude.

DEFINITION OF NUCLEAR WEAPONS

Article 5

For the purpose of this Treaty, a nuclear weapon is any device which is capable of releasing nuclear energy in an uncontrolled manner and which has a group of characteristics that are appropriate for use for war-like purposes. An instrument that may be used for the transport or propulsion of the device is not included in this definition if it is separable from the device and not an indivisible part thereof.

MEETING OF SIGNATORIES

Article 6

At the request of any of the Signatory States or if the Agency established by article 7 should so decide, a meeting of all the signatories may be convoked to consider in common questions which may affect the very essence of this instrument, including possible amendments to it. In either case, the meeting will be convoked by the General Secretary.

ORGANIZATION

Article 7

1. In order to ensure compliance with the obligations of this Treaty, the Contracting Parties hereby establish an international organization to

be known as the "Agency for the Prohibition of Nuclear Weapons in Latin America", hereinafter referred to as "the Agency". Only the Contracting Parties shall be affected by its decisions.

2. The Agency shall be responsible for the holding of periodic or extraordinary consultations among Member States on matters relating to the purposes, measures and procedures set forth in this Treaty and to the supervision of compliance with the obligations arising therefrom.

3. The Contracting Parties agree to extend to the Agency full and prompt co-operation in accordance with the provisions of this Treaty, of any agreements they may conclude with the Agency and of any agreements the Agency may conclude with any other international organization or body.

4. The headquarters of the Agency shall be in Mexico City.

ORGANS

Article 8

1. There are hereby established as principal organs of the Agency a General Conference, a Council and a Secretariat.

2. Such subsidiary organs as are considered necessary by the General Conference may be established within the purview of this Treaty.

THE GENERAL CONFERENCE

Article 9

1. The General Conference, the supreme organ of the Agency, shall be composed of all the Contracting Parties; it shall hold regular sessions every two years, and may also hold special sessions whenever this Treaty so provides or, in the opinion of the Council, the circumstances so require.

2. The General Conference:

(*a*) May consider and decide on any matters or questions covered by this Treaty, within the limits thereof, including those referring to powers and functions of any organ provided for in this Treaty.

(*b*) Shall establish procedures for the control system to ensure observance of this Treaty in accordance with its provisions.

(*c*) Shall elect the Members of the Council and the General Secretary.

(*d*) May remove the General Secretary from office if the proper functioning of the Agency so requires.

(*e*) Shall receive and consider the biennial and special reports submitted by the Council and the General Secretary.

(*f*) Shall initiate and consider studies designed to facilitate the optimum fulfilment of the aims of this Treaty, without prejudice to the power of the General Secretary independently to carry out similar studies for submission to and consideration by the Conference.

(g) Shall be the organ competent to authorize the conclusion of agreements with Governments and other international organizations and bodies.

3. The General Conference shall adopt the Agency's budget and fix the scale of financial contributions to be paid by Member States, taking into account the systems and criteria used for the same purpose by the United Nations.

4. The General Conference shall elect its officers for each session and may establish such subsidiary organs as it deems necessary for the performance of its functions.

5. Each Member of the Agency shall have one vote. The decisions of the General Conference shall be taken by a two-thirds majority of the Members present and voting in the case of matters relating to the control system and measures referred to in Article 20, the admission of new Members, the election or removal of the General Secretary, adoption of the budget and matters related thereto. Decisions on other matters, as well as procedural questions and also determination of which questions must be decided by a two-thirds majority, shall be taken by a simple majority of the Members present and voting.

6. The General Conference shall adopt its own rules of procedure.

THE COUNCIL

Article 10

1. The Council shall be composed of five Members of the Agency elected by the General Conference from among the Contracting Parties, due account being taken of equitable geographic distribution.

2. The Members of the Council shall be elected for a term of four years. However, in the first election three will be elected for two years. Outgoing Members may not be re-elected for the following period unless the limited number of States for which the Treaty is in force so requires.

3. Each Member of the Council shall have one representative.

4. The Council shall be so organized as to be able to function continuously.

5. In addition to the functions conferred upon it by this Treaty and to those which may be assigned to it by the General Conference, the Council shall, through the General Secretary, ensure the proper operation of the control system in accordance with the provisions of this Treaty and with the decisions adopted by the General Conference.

6. The Council shall submit an annual report on its work to the General Conference as well as such special reports as it deems necessary or which the General Conference requests of it.

7. The Council shall elect its officers for each session.

8. The decisions of the Council shall be taken by a simple majority of its Members present and voting.

9. The Council shall adopt its own rules of procedure.

THE SECRETARIAT

Article 11

1. The Secretariat shall consist of a General Secretary, who shall be the chief administrative officer of the Agency, and of such staff as the Agency may require. The term of office of the General Secretary shall be four years and he may be re-elected for a single additional term. The General Secretary may not be a national of the country in which the Agency has its headquarters. In case the office of the General Secretary becomes vacant, a new election shall be held to fill the office for the remainder of the term.

2. The staff of the Secretariat shall be appointed by the General Secretary, in accordance with rules laid down by the General Conference.

3. In addition to the functions conferred upon him by this Treaty and to those which may be assigned to him by the General Conference,—the General Secretary shall ensure, as provided by article 10, paragraph 5, the proper operation of the control system established by this Treaty, in accordance with the provisions of the Treaty and the decisions taken by the General Conference.

4. The General Secretary shall act in that capacity in all meetings of the General Conference and of the Council and shall make an annual report to both bodies on the work of the Agency and any special reports requested by the General Conference or the Council or which the General Secretary may deem desirable.

5. The General Secretary shall establish the procedures for distributing to all Contracting Parties information received by the Agency from governmental sources and such information from non-governmental sources as may be of interest to the Agency.

6. In the performance of their duties the General Secretary and the staff shall not seek or receive instructions from any Government or from any other authority external to the Agency and shall refrain from any action which might reflect on their position as international officials responsible only to the Agency; subject to their responsibility to the Agency, they shall not disclose any industrial secrets or other confidential information coming to their knowledge by reason of their official duties in the Agency.

7. Each of the Contracting Parties undertakes to respect the exclusively international character of the responsibilities of the General Secretary and the staff and not ask to influence them in the discharge of their responsibilities.

CONTROL SYSTEM

Article 12

1. For the purpose of verifying compliance with the obligations entered into by the Contracting Parties in accordance with article 1, a con-

trol system shall be established which shall be put into effect in accordance with the provisions of articles 13–18 of this Treaty.

2. The control system shall be used in particular for the purpose of verifying:

(*a*) That devices, services and facilities intended for peaceful uses of nuclear energy are not used in the testing or manufacture of nuclear weapons,

(*b*) That none of the activities prohibited in article I of this Treaty are carried out in the territory of the Contracting Parties with nuclear materials or weapons introduced from abroad, and

(*c*) That explosions for peaceful purposes are compatible with article 18 of this Treaty.

IAEA SAFEGUARDS

Article 13

Each Contracting Party shall negotiate multilateral or bilateral agreements with the International Atomic Energy Agency for the application of its safeguards to its nuclear activities. Each Contracting Party shall initiate negotiations within a period of 180 days after the date of the deposit of its instrument of ratification of this Treaty. These agreements shall enter into force, for each Party, not later than eighteen months after the date of the initiation of such negotiations except in case of unforeseen circumstances or *force majeure*.

REPORTS OF THE PARTIES

Article 14

1. The Contracting Parties shall submit to the Agency and to the International Atomic Energy Agency, for their information, semi-annual reports stating that no activity prohibited under this Treaty has occurred in their respective territories.

2. The Contracting Parties shall simultaneously transmit to the Agency a copy of any report that they may submit to the International Atomic Energy Agency which relates to matters that are the subject of this Treaty and to the application of safeguards.

3. The Contracting Parties shall also transmit to the Organization of American States, for its information, any reports that may be of interest to it, in accordance with the obligations established by the Inter-American System.

SPECIAL REPORTS REQUESTED BY THE GENERAL SECRETARY

Article 15

1. With the authorization of the Council, the General Secretary may request any of the Contracting Parties to provide the Agency with com-

plementary or supplementary information regarding any event or circumstance connected with compliance with this Treaty, explaining his reasons. The Contracting Parties undertake to co-operate promptly and fully with the General Secretary.

2. The General Secretary shall inform the Council and the Contracting Parties forthwith of such requests and of the respective replies.

SPECIAL INSPECTIONS

Article 16

1. The International Atomic Energy Agency and the Council established by this Treaty have the power of carrying out special inspections in the following cases:

(*a*) In the case of the International Atomic Energy Agency, in accordance with the agreements referred to in article 13 of this Treaty;

(*b*) In the case of the Council:

(i) When so requested, the reasons for the request being stated, by any Party which suspects that some activity prohibited by this Treaty has been carried out or is about to be carried out, either in the territory of any other Party or in any other place on such Party's behalf, the Council shall immediately arrange for such an inspection in accordance with article 10, paragraph 5.

(ii) When requested by any Party which has been suspected of or charged with having violated this Treaty, the Council shall immediately arrange for the special inspection requested in accordance with article 10, paragraph 5.

The above requests will be made to the Council through the General Secretary.

2. The costs and expenses of any special inspection carried out under paragraph 1, sub-paragraph (*b*), sections (i) and (ii) of this article shall be borne by the requesting Party or Parties, except where the Council concludes on the basis of the report on the special inspection that, in view of the circumstances existing in the case, such costs and expenses should be borne by the Agency.

3. The General Conference shall formulate the procedures for the organization and execution of the special inspections carried out in accordance with paragraph 1, sub-paragraph (*b*), sections (i) and (ii) of this article.

4. The Contracting Parties undertake to grant the inspectors carrying out the special inspections full and free access to all places and all information which may be necessary for the performance of their duties and which are directly and intimately connected with the suspicion of violation of this Treaty. If so requested by the authorities of the Contracting Party in whose territory the inspection is carried out, the inspectors designated by the General Conference shall be accompanied by representatives

of said authorities, provided that this does not in any way delay or hinder the work of the inspectors.

5. The Council shall immediately transmit to all the Parties, through the General Secretary, a copy of any report resulting from special inspections.

6. Similarly, the Council shall send through the General Secretary to the Secretary-General of the United Nations, for transmission to the United Nations Security Council and General Assembly, and to the Council of the Organization of American States, for its information, a copy of any report resulting from any special inspection carried out in accordance with paragraph 1, sub-paragraph (*b*), sections (i) and (ii) of this article.

7. The Council may decide, or any Contracting Party may request, the convening of a special session of the General Conference for the purpose of considering the reports resulting from any special inspection. In such a case, the General Secretary shall take immediate steps to convene the special session requested.

8. The General Conference, convened in special session under this article, may make recommendations to the Contracting Parties and submit reports to the Secretary-General of the United Nations to be transmitted to the United Nations Security Council and the General Assembly.

USE OF NUCLEAR ENERGY FOR PEACEFUL PURPOSES

Article 17

Nothing in the provisions of this Treaty shall prejudice the rights of the Contracting Parties, in conformity with this Treaty, to use nuclear energy for peaceful purposes, in particular for their economic development and social progress.

EXPLOSIONS FOR PEACEFUL PURPOSES

Article 18

1. The Contracting Parties may carry out explosions of nuclear devices for peaceful purposes—including explosions which involve devices similar to those used in nuclear weapons—or collaborate with third parties for the same purpose, provided that they do so in accordance with the provisions of this article and the other articles of the Treaty, particularly articles 1 and 5.

2. Contracting Parties intending to carry out, or to co-operate in carrying out, such an explosion shall notify the Agency and the International Atomic Energy Agency, as far in advance as the circumstances require, of the date of the explosion and shall at the same time provide the following information:

(*a*) The nature of the nuclear device and the source from which it was obtained,

(*b*) The place and purpose of the planned explosion,

(*c*) The procedures which will be followed in order to comply with paragraph 3 of this article,

(*d*) The expected force of the device, and

(*e*) The fullest possible information on any possible radioactive fall-out that may result from the explosion or explosions, and measures which will be taken to avoid danger to the population, flora, fauna, and territories of any other Party or Parties.

3. The General Secretary and the technical personnel designated by the Council and the International Atomic Energy Agency may observe all the preparations, including the explosion of the device, and shall have unrestricted access to any area in the vicinity of the site of the explosion in order to ascertain whether the device and the procedures followed during the explosion are in conformity with the information supplied under paragraph 2 of this article and the other provisions of this Treaty.

4. The Contracting Parties may accept the collaboration of third parties for the purpose set forth in paragraph 1 of the present article, in accordance with paragraphs 2 and 3 thereof.

RELATIONS WITH OTHER INTERNATIONAL ORGANIZATIONS

Article 19

1. The Agency may conclude such agreements with the International Atomic Energy Agency as are authorized by the General Conference and as it considers likely to facilitate the efficient operation of the control system established by this Treaty.

2. The Agency may also enter into relations with any international organization or body, especially any which may be established in the future to supervise disarmament or measures for the control of armaments in any part of the world.

3. The Contracting Parties may, if they see fit, request the advice of the Inter-American Nuclear Energy Commission on all technical matters connected with the application of this Treaty with which the Commission is competent to deal under its Statute.

MEASURES IN THE EVENT OF VIOLATION OF THE TREATY

Article 20

1. The General Conference shall take note of all cases in which, in its opinion, any Contracting Party is not complying fully with its obligations under this Treaty and shall draw the matter to the attention of the Party concerned, making such recommendations as it deems appropriate.

2. If, in its opinion, such non-compliance constitutes a violation of this Treaty which might endanger peace and security, the General Conference shall report thereon simultaneously to the United Nations Security Council and the General Assembly through the Secretary-General of the United Nations, and to the Council of the Organization of American States. The General Conference shall likewise report to the International Atomic Energy Agency for such purposes as are relevant in accordance with its Statute.

UNITED NATIONS AND ORGANIZATION OF AMERICAN STATES

Article 21

None of the provisions of this Treaty shall be construed as impairing the rights and obligations of the Parties under the Charter of the United Nations or, in the case of States Members of the Organization of American States, under existing regional treaties.

PRIVILEGES AND IMMUNITIES

Article 22

1. The Agency shall enjoy in the territory of each of the Contracting Parties such legal capacity and such privileges and immunities as may be necessary for the exercise of its functions and the fulfillment of its purposes.

2. Representatives of the Contracting Parties accredited to the Agency and officials of the Agency shall similarly enjoy such privileges and immunities as are necessary for the performance of their functions.

3. The Agency may conclude agreements with the Contracting Parties with a view to determining the details of the application of paragraphs 1 and 2 of this article.

NOTIFICATION OF OTHER AGREEMENTS

Article 23

Once this Treaty has entered into force, the Secretariat shall be notified immediately of any international agreement concluded by any of the Contracting Parties on matters with which this Treaty is concerned; the Secretariat shall register it and notify the other Contracting Parties.

SETTLEMENT OF DISPUTES

Article 24

Unless the Parties concerned agree on another mode of peaceful settlement, any question or dispute concerning the interpretation or application of this Treaty which is not settled shall be referred to the International Court of Justice with the prior consent of the Parties to the controversy.

SIGNATURE

Article 25

1. This Treaty shall be open indefinitely for signature by:

(a) All the Latin American Republics, and

(b) All other Sovereign States situated in their entirety south of latitude 35° north in the western hemisphere; and, except as provided in paragraph 2 of this article, all such States which become sovereign, when they have been admitted by the General Conference.

2. The General Conference shall not take any decision regarding the admission of a political entity part or all of whose territory is the subject, prior to the date when this Treaty is opened for signature, of a dispute or claim between an extra-continental country and one or more Latin American States, so long as the dispute has not been settled by peaceful means.

RATIFICATION AND DEPOSIT

Article 26

1. This Treaty shall be subject to ratification by signatory States in accordance with their respective constitutional procedures.

2. This Treaty and the instruments of ratification shall be deposited with the Government of the United Mexican States, which is hereby designated the Depositary Government.

3. The Depositary Government shall send certified copies of this Treaty to the Governments of signatory States and shall notify them of the deposit of each instrument of ratification.

RESERVATIONS

Article 27

This Treaty shall not be subject to reservations.

ENTRY INTO FORCE

Article 28

1. Subject to the provisions of paragraph 2 of this article, this Treaty shall enter into force among the States that have ratified it as soon as the following requirements have been met:

(a) Deposit of the instruments of ratification of this Treaty with the Depositary Government by the Governments of the States mentioned in article 25 which are in existence on the date when this Treaty is opened for signature and which are not affected by the provisions of article 25, paragraph 2;

(*b*) Signature and ratification of Additional Protocol I annexed to this Treaty by all extra-continental or continental States having *de jure* or *de facto* international responsibility for territories situated in the zone of application of the Treaty;

(*c*) Signature and ratification of the Additional Protocol II annexed to this Treaty by all powers possessing nuclear weapons.

(*d*) Conclusion of bilateral or multilateral agreements on the application of the Safeguards System of the International Atomic Energy Agency in accordance with article 13 of this Treaty.

2. All signatory States shall have the imprescriptible right to waive, wholly or in part, the requirements laid down in the preceding paragraph. They may do so by means of a declaration which shall be annexed to their respective instrument of ratification and which may be formulated at the time of deposit of the instrument or subsequently. For those States which exercise this right, this Treaty shall enter into force upon deposit of the declaration, or as soon as those requirements have been met which have not been expressly waived.

3. As soon as this Treaty has entered into force in accordance with the provisions of paragraph 2 for eleven States, the Depositary Government shall convene a preliminary meeting of those States in order that the Agency may be set up and commence its work.

4. After the entry into force of this Treaty for all the countries of the zone, the rise of a new power possessing nuclear weapons shall have the effect of suspending the execution of this Treaty for those countries which have ratified it without waiving requirements of paragraph 1, sub-paragraph (*c*) of this article, and which request such suspension; the Treaty shall remain suspended until the new power, on its own initiative or upon request of the General Conference, ratifies the annexed Additional Protocol II.

AMENDMENTS

Article 29

1. Any Contracting Party may propose amendments to this Treaty and shall submit its proposals to the Council through the General Secretary, who shall transmit them to all the other Contracting Parties and, in addition, to all other signatories in accordance with article 6. The Council, through the General Secretary, shall immediately following the meeting of signatories convene a special session of the General Conference to examine the proposals made, for the adoption of which a two-thirds majority of the Contracting Parties present and voting shall be required.

2. Amendments adopted shall enter into force as soon as the requirements set forth in article 28 of this Treaty have been complied with.

DURATION AND DENUNCIATION

Article 30

1. This Treaty shall be of a permanent nature and shall remain in force indefinitly, but any Party may denounce it by notifying the General Secretary of the Agency if, in the opinion of the denouncing State, there have arisen or may arise circumstances connected with the content of this Treaty or of the annexed Additional Protocols I and II which affect its supreme interests or the peace and security of one or more Contracting Parties.

2. The denunciation shall take effect three months after the delivery to the General Secretary of the Agency of the notification by the Government of the signatory State concerned. The General Secretary shall immediately communicate such notification to the other Contracting Parties and to the Secretary-General of the United Nations for the information of the United Nations Security Council and the General Assembly. He shall also communicate it to the Secretary-General of the Organization of American States.

AUTHENTIC TEXTS AND REGISTRATION

Article 31

This Treaty, of which the Spanish, Chinese, English, French, Portuguese and Russian texts are equally authentic, shall be registered by the Depositary Government in accordance with article 102 of the United Nations Charter. The Depositary Government shall notify the Secretary-General of the United Nations of the signatures, ratifications and amendments relating to this Treaty and shall communicate them to the Secretary-General of the Organization of American States for its information.

Transitional Article

Denunciation of the declaration referred to in article 28, paragraph 2, shall be subject to the same procedures as the denunciation of this Treaty, except that it will take effect on the date of delivery of the respective notification.

IN WITNESS WHEREOF the undersigned Plenipotentiaries, having deposited their full powers, found in good and due form, sign this Treaty on behalf of their respective Governments.

DONE at Mexico, Distrito Federal, on the Fourteenth day of February, one thousand nine hundred and sixty-seven.

Additional Protocol I

The undersigned Plenipotentiaries, furnished with full powers by their respective Governments,

Convinced that the Treaty for the Prohibition of Nuclear Weapons in Latin America, negotiated and signed in accordance with the recommendations of the General Assembly of the United Nations in Resolution 1911 (XVIII) of 27 November 1963, represents an important step towards ensuring the nonproliferation of nuclear weapons.

Aware that the non-proliferation of nuclear weapons is not an end in itself but, rather, a means of achieving general and complete disarmament at a later stage, and

Desiring to contribute, so far as lies in their power, towards ending the armaments race, especially in the field of nuclear weapons, and towards strengthening a world at peace, based on mutual respect and sovereign equality of States.

Have agreed as follows:

Article 1. To undertake to apply the statute of denuclearization in respect of warlike purposes as defined in articles 1, 3, 5 and 13 of the Treaty for the Prohibition of Nuclear Weapons in Latin America in territories for which, *de jure* or *de facto,* they are internationally responsible and which lie within the limits of the geographical zone established in that Treaty.

Article 2. The duration of this Protocol shall be the same as that of the Treaty for the Prohibition of Nuclear Weapons in Latin America of which this Protocol is an annex, and the provisions regarding ratification and denunciation contained in the Treaty shall be applicable to it.

Article 3. This Protocol shall enter into force, for the States which have ratified it, on the date of the deposit of their respective instruments of ratification.

IN WITNESS WHEREOF the undersigned Plenipotentiaries, having deposited their full powers, found in good and due form, sign this Protocol on behalf of their respective Governments.

Additional Protocol II

The undersigned Plenipotentiaries, furnished with full powers by their respective Governments,

Convinced that the Treaty for the Prohibition of Nuclear Weapons in Latin America, negotiated and signed in accordance with the recommendations of the General Assembly of the United Nations in Resolution 1911 (XVIII) of 27 November 1963, represents an important step towards ensuring the non-proliferation of nuclear weapons,

Aware that the non-proliferation of nuclear weapons is not an end in itself but, rather, a means of achieving general and complete disarmament at a later stage, and

Desiring to contribute, so far as lies in their power, towards ending the armaments race, especially in the field of nuclear weapons, and towards promoting and strengthening a world at peace, based on mutual respect and sovereign equality of States,

Have agreed as follows:

Article 1. The statute of denuclearization of Latin America in respect of warlike purposes, as defined, delimited and set forth in the Treaty for the Prohibition of Nuclear Weapons in Latin America of which this instrument is an annex, shall be fully respected by the Parties to this Protocol in all its express aims and provisions.

Article 2. The Governments represented by the undersigned Plenipotentiaries undertake, therefore, not to contribute in any way to the performance of acts involving a violation of the obligations of article 1 of the Treaty in the territories to which the Treaty applies in accordance with article 4 thereof.

Article 3. The Governments represented by the undersigned Plenipotentiaries also undertake not to use or threaten to use nuclear weapons against the Contracting Parties of the Treaty for the Prohibition of Nuclear Weapons in Latin America.

Article 4. The duration of this Protocol shall be the same as that of the Treaty for the Prohibition of Nuclear Weapons in Latin America of which this Protocol is an annex, and the definitions of territory and nuclear weapons set forth in articles 3 and 5 of the Treaty shall be applicable to this Protocol, as well as the provisions regarding ratification, reservations, denunciation, authentic texts and registration contained in articles 26, 27, 30 and 31 of the Treaty.

Article 5. This Protocol shall enter into force, for the States which have ratified it, on the date of the deposit of their respective instruments of ratification.

IN WITNESS WHEREOF, the undersigned Plenipotentiaries, having deposited their full powers, found to be in good and due form, hereby sign this Additional Protocol on behalf of their respective Governments.

Appendix IV. Treaty on the Non-Proliferation of Nuclear Weapons*

The States concluding this Treaty, hereinafter referred to as the "Parties to the Treaty",

Considering the devastation that would be visited upon all mankind by a nuclear war and the consequent need to make every effort to avert the danger of such a war and to take measures to safeguard the security of peoples,

Believing that the proliferation of nuclear weapons would seriously enhance the danger of nuclear war,

In conformity with resolutions of the United Nations General Assembly calling for the conclusion of an agreement on the prevention of wider dissemination of nuclear weapons,

Undertaking to co-operate in facilitating the application of International Atomic Energy Agency safeguards on peaceful nuclear activities,

Expressing their support for research, development and other efforts to further the application, within the framework of the International Atomic Energy Agency safeguards system, of the principle of safeguarding effectively the flow of source and special fissionable materials by use of instruments and other techniques at certain strategic points,

Affirming the principle that the benefits of peaceful applications of nuclear technology, including any technological by-products which may be derived by nuclear-weapon States from the development of nuclear explosive devices, should be available for peaceful purposes to all Parties to the Treaty, whether nuclear-weapon or non-nuclear-weapon States.

Convinced that, in furtherance of this principle, all Parties to the Treaty are entitled to participate in the fullest possible exchange of scientific information for, and to contribute alone or in co-operation with other States to, the further development of the applications of atomic energy for peaceful purposes

Declaring their intention to achieve at the earliest possible date the

ned at London, Moscow, and Washington on 1 July 1968.

cessation of the nuclear arms race and to undertake effective measures in the direction of nuclear disarmament.

Urging the co-operation of all States in the attainment of this objective,

Recalling the determination expressed by the Parties to the 1963 Treaty banning nuclear weapon tests in the atmosphere, in outer space and under water in its Preamble to seek to achieve the discontinuance of all test explosions of nuclear weapons for all time and to continue negotiations to this end,

Desiring to further the easing of international tension and the strengthening of trust between States in order to facilitate the cessation of the manufacture of nuclear weapons, the liquidation of all their existing stockpiles, and the elimination from national arsenals of nuclear weapons and the means of their delivery pursuant to a treaty on general and complete disarmament under strict and effective international control,

Recalling that, in accordance with the Charter of the United Nations, States must refrain in their international relations from the threat or use of force against the territorial integrity or political independence of any State, or in any other manner inconsistent with the Purposes of the United Nations, and that the establishment and maintenance of international peace and security are to be promoted with the least diversion for armaments of the world's human and economic resources,

HAVE AGREED AS FOLLOWS:

Article I

Each nuclear-weapon State Party to the Treaty undertakes not to transfer to any recipient whatsoever nuclear weapons or other nuclear explosive devices or control over such weapons or explosive devices directly, or indirectly; and not in any way to assist, encourage, or induce any non-nuclear-weapon State to manufacture or otherwise acquire nuclear weapons or other nuclear explosive devices, or control over such weapons or explosive devices.

Article II

Each non-nuclear-weapon State Party to the Treaty undertakes not to receive the transfer from any transferor whatsoever of nuclear weapons or other nuclear explosive devices or of control over such weapons or explosive devices directly, or indirectly; not to manufacture or otherwise acquire nuclear weapons or other nuclear explosive devices; and not to seek or receive any assistance in the manufacture of nuclear weapons or other nuclear explosive devices.

Article III

1. Each non-nuclear-weapon State Party to the Treaty undertakes to accept safeguards, as set forth in an agreement to be negotiated and co

cluded with the International Atomic Energy Agency in accordance with the Statute of the International Atomic Energy Agency and the Agency's safeguards system, for the exclusive purpose of verification of the fulfilment of its obligations assumed under this Treaty with a view to preventing diversion of nuclear energy from peaceful uses to nuclear weapons or other nuclear explosive devices. Procedures for the safeguards required by this article shall be followed with respect to source or special fissionable material whether it is being produced, processed or used in any principal nuclear facility or is outside any such facility. The safeguards required by this article shall be applied on all source or special fissionable material in all peaceful nuclear activities within the territory of such State, under its jurisdiction, or carried out under its control anywhere.

2. Each State Party to the Treaty undertakes not to provide: (*a*) source or special fissionable material, or (*b*) equipment or material especially designed or prepared for the processing, use or production of special fissionable material, to any non-nuclear-weapon State for peaceful purposes, unless the source of special fissionable material shall be subject to the safeguards required by this article.

3. The safeguards required by this article shall be implemented in a manner designed to comply with article IV of this Treaty, and to avoid hampering the economic or technological development of the Parties or international co-operation in the field of peaceful nuclear activities, including the international exchange of nuclear material and equipment for the processing, use or production of nuclear material for peaceful purposes in accordance with the provisions of this article and the principle of safeguarding set forth in the Preamble of the Treaty.

4. Non-nuclear-weapon States Party to the Treaty shall conclude agreements with the International Atomic Energy Agency to meet the requirements of this article either individually or together with other States in accordance with the Statute of the International Atomic Energy Agency. Negotiation of such agreements shall commence within 180 days from the original entry into force of this Treaty. For States depositing their instruments of ratification or accession after the 180-day period, negotiations of such agreements shall commence not later than the day of such deposit. Such agreements shall enter into force not later than eighteen months after the date of initiation of negotiations.

Article IV

1. Nothing in this Treaty shall be interpreted as affecting the inalienable right of all the parties to the Treaty to develop research, production and use of nuclear energy for peaceful purposes without discrimination and in conformity with articles I and II of this Treaty.

2. All the Parties to the Treaty undertake to facilitate, and have the right to participate in, the fullest possible exchange of equipment, materials and scientific and technological information for the peaceful uses of

nuclear energy. Parties to the Treaty in a position to do so shall also co-operate in contributing alone or together with other States or international organizations to the further development of the applications of nuclear energy for peaceful purposes, especially in the territories of non-nuclear-weapon States Party to the Treaty, with due consideration for the needs of the developing areas of the world.

Article V

Each Party to the Treaty undertakes to take appropriate measures to ensure that, in accordance with this Treaty, under appropriate international observation and through appropriate international procedures, potential benefits from any peaceful applications of nuclear explosions will be made available to non-nuclear-weapon States Party to the Treaty on a non-discriminatory basis and that the charge to such Parties for the explosive devices used will be as low as possible and exclude any charge for research and development. Non-nuclear-weapon States Party to the Treaty shall be able to obtain such benefits, pursuant to a special international agreement or agreements, through an appropriate international body with adequate representation of non-nuclear-weapon States. Negotiations on this subject shall commence as soon as possible after the Treaty enters into force. Non-nuclear-weapon States Party to the Treaty so desiring may also obtain such benefits pursuant to bilateral agreements.

Article VI

Each of the Parties to the Treaty undertakes to pursue negotiations in good faith on effective measures relating to cessation of the nuclear arms race at an early date and to nuclear disarmament, and on a treaty on general and complete disarmament under strict and effective international control.

Article VII

Nothing in this Treaty affects the right of any group of States to conclude regional treaties in order to assure the total absence of nuclear weapons in their respective territories.

Article VIII

1. Any Party to the Treaty may propose amendments to this Treaty. The text of any proposed amendments shall be submitted to the Depositary Governments which shall circulate it to all Parties to the Treaty. Thereupon, if requested to do so by one third or more of the Parties to the Treaty, the Depositary Governments shall convene a conference, to which they shall invite all the Parties to the Treaty, to consider such an amendment.

2. Any amendment to this Treaty must be approved by a major' the votes of all the Parties to the Treaty, including the votes of all n

weapon States Party to the Treaty and all other Parties which, on the date the amendment is circulated, are members of the Board of Governors of the International Atomic Energy Agency. The amendment shall enter into force for each Party that deposits its instrument of ratification of the amendment upon the deposit of such instruments of ratification by a majority of all the Parties, including the instruments of ratification of all nuclear-weapon States Party to the Treaty and all other Parties which, on the date the amendment is circulated, are members of the Board of Governors of the International Atomic Energy Agency. Thereafter, it shall enter into force for any other Party upon the deposit of its instrument of ratification of the amendment.

3. Five years after the entry into force of this Treaty, a conference of Parties to the Treaty shall be held in Geneva, Switzerland, in order to review the operation of this Treaty with a view to assuring that the purposes of the Preamble and the Provisions of the Treaty are being realized. At intervals of five years thereafter, a majority of the Parties to the Treaty may obtain, by submitting a proposal to this effect to the Depositary Governments, the convening of further conferences with the same objective of reviewing the operation of the Treaty.

Article IX

1. This Treaty shall be open to all States for signature. Any State which does not sign the Treaty before its entry into force in accordance with paragraph 3 of this article may accede to it at any time.

2. This Treaty shall be subject to ratification by signatory States. Instruments of ratification and instruments of accession shall be deposited with the Governments of the Union of Soviet Socialist Republics, the United Kingdom of Great Britain and Northern Ireland and the United States of America, which are hereby designated the Depositary Governments.

3. This Treaty shall enter into force after its ratification by the States, the Governments of which are designated Depositaries of the Treaty, and forty other States signatory to this Treaty and the deposit of their instruments of ratification. For the purposes of this Treaty, a nuclear-weapon State is one which has manufactured and exploded a nuclear weapon or other nuclear explosive device prior to 1 January 1967.

4. For States whose instruments of ratification or accession are deposited subsequent to the entry into force of this Treaty, it shall enter into force on the date of the deposit of their instruments of ratification or accession.

5. The Depositary Governments shall promptly inform all signatory and acceding States of the date of each signature, the date of deposit of each instrument of ratification or of accession, the date of the entry into force of this Treaty, and the date of receipt of any requests for convening a conference or other notices.

6. This Treaty shall be registered by the Depositary Governments pursuant to Article 102 of the Charter of the United Nations.

Article X

1. Each Party shall in exercising its national sovereignty have the right to withdraw from the Treaty if it decides that extraordinary events, related to the subject-matter of this Treaty, have jeopardized the supreme interests of its country. It shall give notice of such withdrawal to all other Parties to the Treaty and to the United Nations Security Council three months in advance. Such notice shall include a statement of the extraordinary events it regards as having jeopardized its supreme interests.

2. Twenty-five years after the entry into force of the Treaty, a conference shall be convened to decide whether the Treaty shall continue in force indefinitely, or shall be extended for an additional fixed period or periods. This decision shall be taken by a majority of the Parties to the Treaty.

Article XI

This Treaty, the Chinese, English, French, Russian and Spanish texts of which are equally authentic, shall be deposited in the archives of the Depositary Governments. Duly certified copies of this Treaty shall be transmitted by the Depositary Governments to the Governments of the signatory and acceding States.

IN WITNESS WHEREOF the undersigned, duly authorized, have signed this Treaty.

DONE in triplicate at the cities of Washington, London and Moscow, this first day of July, one thousand nine hundred and sixty-eight.

Appendix V. Status of the Non-Proliferation Treaty, January 1, 1976

A. Parties (96)

Afghanistan
Australia
Austria
Bahamas
Belgium
Bolivia
Botswana
Bulgaria
Burundi
Cameroon
Canada
Central African
  Republic
Chad
Costa Rica
Cyprus
Czechoslovakia
Dahomey
Denmark
Dominican Republic
Ecuador
El Salvador
Ethiopia
Fiji
Finland

Gabon
Gambia
German Democratic
  Republic (East
  Germany)
Germany, Federal
  Republic of (West
  Germany)
Ghana
Greece
Grenada
Guatemala
Haiti
Holy See
Honduras
Hungary
Iceland
Iran
Iraq
Ireland
Italy
Ivory Coast
Jamaica
Jordan
Kenya

Khmer Republic
Korea (South)
Laos
Lebanon
Lesotho
Liberia
Libya
Luxembourg
Malagasy Republic
Malaysia
Maldive Islands
Mali
Malta
Mauritius
Mexico
Mongolia
Morocco
Nepal
Netherlands
New Zealand
Nicaragua
Nigeria
Norway
Paraguay
Peru

Philippines
Poland
Romania
Rwanda
San Marino
Senegal
Sierra Leone
Somalia
Sudan
Swaziland

Sweden
Syrian Arab Republic
Taiwan
Thailand
Togo
Tonga
Tunisia
Union of Soviet Socialist
    Republics
United Kingdom

United States of
    America
Upper Volta
Uruguay
Vietnam (South)
Western Samoa
Yugoslavia
Zaire

B. Signatories (15)

(have signed the treaty, but have not completed the process of ratification)

Barbados
Colombia
Indonesia
Japan
Kuwait
Panama

Singapore
Sri Lanka
Switzerland
    Trinidad and Tobago
Turkey

United Arab Republic
    (Egypt)
Venezuela
Yemen, Arab Republic of
Yemen, Democratic
    Republic of

C. Nonsignatories (44)

Albania
Algeria
Angola
Argentina
Bahrain
Bangladesh
Bhutan
Brazil
Cape Verde
Chile
China
Congo
Cuba
Equatorial Guinea
France

Guinea
Guinea-Bissau
Guyana
India
Israel
Liechtenstein
Korea (North)
Malawi
Mauritania
Monaco
Mozambique
Nauru
Niger
Oman
Pakistan

Papua New Guinea
Portugal
Qatar
Rwanda
Sao Tome and Principe
Saudi Arabia
South Africa
Spain
Tanzania
Uganda
United Arab Emirates
Vietnam (North)
Zambia

Appendix VI.   List of Proposed Measures To Strengthen the Non-Proliferation Treaty

This list of proposed measures to strengthen the Non-Proliferation Treaty is compiled from the various suggestions made throughout the book. For purposes of convenience the proposals are grouped under the respective articles of the treaty. Each of them can be adopted and implemented by the parties affected, however, without going through the cumbersome process of formal amendment of the treaty.

The proposed undertaking not to use or threaten to use nuclear weapons against non-nuclear states is listed as a separate security assurance; it could be adopted as an independent security measure or as a Protocol to the NPT.

In view of the nonparticipation in the NPT of China, France, and India and of a number of non-nuclear states, all of the proposed measures could be adopted and implemented outside of the framework of the NPT as separate treaties, agreements, or undertakings.

. . .

Security Assurances – The nuclear powers should undertake in legal instruments either

(a) not to use or threaten to use nuclear weapons against any non-nuclear state that has no nuclear weapons in its territory, or

(b) not to use or threaten to use nuclear weapons against any non-nuclear state unless that state is engaged in an armed attack on another state with the assistance of a nuclear power.

Article I   – The nuclear-weapon states should undertake not to render assistance to any recipient whatsoever in the manufacture or acquisition of any nuclear weapon or nuclear explosive device.

Article II — The non-nuclear weapon states should undertake not to transfer technology or assistance in regard to nuclear weapons or nuclear explosive devices to any other non-nuclear-weapon state.

Article III — (1) The nuclear-weapon states should undertake to accept IAEA safeguards over all their peaceful nuclear activities.

(2) The nuclear states and other nuclear supplier states should undertake not to transfer nuclear information or technology and not to supply nuclear material or equipment to any state, whether nuclear or not, unless that state undertakes either to become a party to the NPT or to accept equivalent restraints and to place *all* of its peaceful nuclear material in *all* of its peaceful nuclear activities under IAEA safeguards.

(3) Measures to strengthen the IAEA/NPT safeguards system should be adopted. In particular, procedures which enable a state to delay, hamper, or circumvent inspections or other applications of safeguards should be removed.

(4) All spent fuel should either be returned to the supplier state for reprocessing, or for storing if reprocessing is not necessary, or be sent to some internationally operated and safeguarded plant.

(5) The nuclear states and other nuclear supplier states should agree not to export any chemical separation plant for plutonium reprocessing that might come under national control.

(6) Regional, multinational, or international fuel cycle centers should be established for uranium enrichment, fuel fabrication, reprocessing, spent fuel storage, and waste management.

(7) The nuclear states and other nuclear supplier states should agree not to export any nuclear material or equipment to any non-nuclear state that owns or acquires any plutonium reprocessing plant under national control.

(8) An international treaty should be adopted establishing physical security systems, both national and international (a) to prevent the theft or hijacking of nuclear material by individuals or nongovernmental groups, either at nuclear facilities or during transport; (b) to provide for an international intelligence and police system to prevent thefts and hijackings; (c) to provide a system of sanctions against states that violate the treaty or that give assistance

or asylum to individuals or groups that commit thefts or hijackings or make nuclear threats against others.

(9) The nuclear states and other nuclear supplier states should adopt sanctions in case of violation by any state of any established safeguards, providing for the immediate withholding of *all* nuclear assistance until the violation is remedied.

Article IV — (1) See also, under Article III above, items (2), (4), (5), and (6).

(2) The nuclear powers, other supplier states, and the oilrich countries should agree to establish a "suppliers club" for furnishing nuclear assistance, including loans and grants for nuclear power reactors, to non-nuclear states, in particular the developing ones.

(3) The U.S. and the U.S.S.R. should issue a joint declaration undertaking to finance and build regional, multinational, or international nuclear fuel cycle centers.

Article V — (1) The General Assembly of the U.N., the Board of Governors and the General Conference of the IAEA, parties to the NPT, and other supplier states should issue a public declaration that peaceful nuclear explosions under national control are incompatible with the peaceful utilization of nuclear energy and should be carried out only under an agreed-upon system of *international control*.

(2) As an interim measure, a moratorium on all underground tests of nuclear devices for peaceful purposes should be declared, pending the establishment of an international regime to conduct such explosions.

(3) As a permanent measure a special international regime should be established to conduct peaceful nuclear explosions, whereby,

(a) The carrying out of all such explosions would be banned except as provided for under the new regime.

(b) All projects for such explosions would be first examined and approved by some international committee or body.

Article VI — (1) All underground nuclear-weapons tests should be prohibited. As indicated above under Article V, peaceful nuclear explosions could be carried out only when authorized under a special international regime. Pending agreement on a permanent ban on weapons tests, the U.S. and the U.S.S.R. should agree to a five-year moratorium.

(2) The nuclear powers should agree to the cessation of production of fissionable material for weapons purposes and the transfer of all future production and of progressive portions of existing stocks to peaceful purposes.

(3) The superpowers should begin immediate negotiations to reduce and phase out all land-based ICBMs with a view to their elimination within six to ten years.

(4) The superpowers should begin immediate negotiations to reduce SLBMs to 10 percent of the levels authorized by the SALT I Interim Agreement of May 1972.

(5) The superpowers should begin immediate negotiations to reduce their long-range bombers with a view to their elimination.

(6) The superpowers should begin immediate negotiations to ban the testing, manufacture, and deployment of new nuclear weapons and delivery systems, and should declare a qualitative "freeze" for five years pending agreement on a permanent ban and on reductions of existing systems.

(7) The superpowers should begin unilaterally to pull back and reduce tactical nuclear weapons in Central Europe, and the NATO and Warsaw Pact powers should begin immediate negotiations to limit their deployment.

(8) The superpowers should undertake to present within one or two years new draft treaties for negotiation on general and complete disarmament.

(9) The superpowers should agree to freeze their military expenditures at existing levels and to begin negotiations for their progressive reduction.

(10) The superpowers should agree to reduce their armed forces and conventional armaments and to drastically reduce their sales and transfers of arms to third-world countries.

(11) The superpowers should actively promote the convening of a World Disarmament Conference of all countries within one or two years. It would deal with all aspects of disarmament, including nuclear, conventional, chemical, environmental, and all other forms of warfare.

Scientists and engineers should stop all further research and development of military weapons and delivery systems.

Article VII – All nuclear powers should declare that they will respect, and accept binding legal obligations to do so, all regional treaties creating nuclear-free zones or peace zones.

Article VIII – (1) The parties to the NPT should undertake to hold review conferences every five years to assure that the purposes of the Preamble and the provisions of the Treaty are being realized.

(2) The parties to the NPT should agree to create committee of Consultation, consisting of the nuclear powers plus ten members (two each from Africa, Asia

America, Eastern Europe, and Western Europe and associated states) to be elected at each review conference, to consult on the implementation and operation of the treaty, to hear complaints, to make recommendations, and to submit an annual report to the parties and to the General Assembly of the United Nations.

Index